THE
ENTREPRENEURIAL
AGE

Awakening the Spirit of Enterprise
in People, Companies, and Countries

LARRY C. FARRELL

ALLWORTH PRESS
NEW YORK

TO MY WONDERFUL FAMILY

"Staying alive is the key to the benefit program."

05   04   03   02   01   00   5   4   3   2   1

Published by Allworth Press
An imprint of Allworth Communications
10 East 23rd Street, New York, NY 10010

Cover design by Douglas Design Associates, New York, NY

Page composition/typography by SR Desktop Services, Ridge, NY

ISBN: 1-58115-077-6

Library of Congress Cataloging-in-Publication Data

Farrell, Larry C.
    The entrepreneurial age : awakening the spirit of enterprise in people, companies, and countries / Larry C. Farrell.
        p. cm.
    Includes index.
    ISBN 1-58115-077-6
    1. Entrepreneurship. 2. New business enterprises. 3. Industrial promotion. I. Title.

HB615 .F315 2000
658.4'21-dc21

                                                                    00-052556

Printed in Canada

Contents

ACKNOWLEDGMENTS   vii

PREFACE   ix
   Oops! Who's Excellent Now?
   The Entrepreneurial Premise: Confirmed
   The Enterprise of People, Companies, and Countries

INTRODUCTION: *Great Myths and Simple Truths*   xix
   Learning the Hard Way
   Great Myths: The Rise of the Expert Class
   Reviving the Entrepreneurial Spirit
   The Life Cycle of All Organizations
   Simple Tuths: The Four Fundamental Practices of the World's
      Great Entrepreneurs
   Welcome to the Entrepreneurial Age

PART I: ENTREPRENEURIAL PEOPLE
*Entrepreneurship—The Best Weapon You'll Ever Have
to Survive a Downsized and Uncertain World*

1   THE NEW ENTREPRENEURS: *They Are Us!*   3
   More Myths and Truths
   Start-Up: *The* Moment of Truth

2   SENSE OF MISSION: *Leaving Footprints in the Sand*   11
   The *What* and the *How* of the Mission
   Creating Entrepreneurial Business Plans
   Picking Market/Product Winners
   Creating Entrepreneurial Business Values
   Keeping It Alive
   The Mission of Buel Messer

3   CUSTOMER/PRODUCT VISION: *My Customer, My Product,*
     My Self-Respect   31
     The Real Magic of Disney
     The All-American Internet Entrepreneur
     Loving Customers and Products
     "Loving" the Customer
     "Loving" the Product
     The Sights and Sounds of Taylor & Boody

4   HIGH-SPEED INNOVATION: *When Your Life Depends on It*   57
     The Two Golden Rules
     The Necessity to Invent
     The Freedom to Act
     Reinventing PR for the New Economy

5   SELF-INSPIRED BEHAVIOR: *Love What You Do and Get Very*
     Good at Doing It   79
     High Commitment and High Performance
     Entrepreneurial Commitment: "I Love What I Do"
     Entrepreneurial Performance: "I'm Good at Doing It"
     Entrepreneurial Behavior and the Almighty Power of Consequences
     It's All in the Family
     Good for the Business, Good for the Soul

6   *What's Really Required to Become an Entrepreneur*   95
     Corporate Charlie Finally Gets the Message
     The Three Requirements

PART II: ENTREPRENEURIAL COMPANIES
Reviving the Spirit of Enterprise in Your Business

7   *The New Corporate Entrepreneurs*   121
     The Most Entrepreneurial Big Company in the World

8   *Keeping the Sense of Mission Alive As You Grow*   127
     Corporate Strategy à la Matsushita
     What's in *What?*
     Creating an Entrepreneurial Strategy
     The Criteria that Count
     Corporate Culture à la Watson
     Creating an Entrepreneurial Culture
     Keeping It Alive

9 *Reinstilling Customer/Product Vision in Every Employee* **147**
The Functional Organization: Death of the Craftsman
Creating an Obsession for Customers and Products
Loving the Customer
Loving the Product
A Final Thought: Growing the Old-Fashioned Way

10 *Fostering High-Speed Innovation* **167**
The Seven Deadly Sins Against High-Speed Innovation
The Golden Rules of High-Speed Innovation
The Necessity to Invent
The Freedom to Act

11 *Making Self-Inspired Behavior the Organization Standard* **189**
Creating High Comment and High Performance
High Commitment: Getting Employees to Love What They Do
High Performance: Getting Employees to Be Good at What They Do
Inspiring Others: Creating Mini-Entrepreneurs
The Power of Consequences
Three Proven Ways to Instill Consequences
Creating an Entrepreneurial Performance System (EPS)
God Help You and Your Employees

12 *What's Really Required to Create the Entrepreneurial Organization* **211**
The Three Requirements
The Three Requirements: A Summary
A Final Thought from Lincoln Electric

PART III: ENTREPRENEURIAL COUNTRIES
Creating an Entrepreneurial Economy to Win the Twenty-first Century Global Economic War!

13 *The Great Unanswered Mystery of Economics* **231**
The Twentieth Century's Greatest Minister of Economics
The Prosperity Cycle of Nations
Countries: Here Come the Vikings!

14 *The Entrepreneurial Economy* **251**
The Entrepreneurial Basics: Applied to the Economy
Creating a National Sense of Mission
We're Going to Hell, But We're Going First Class
States: Kentucky's Entrepreneurial Conscience

15 *What's Really Required to Create an Entrepreneurial Economy* **269**

The Three Requirements: The *New York Times* Gets It!

Entrepreneur-Friendly Countries, States, and Cities

Cities: The Godfather of Silicon Alley

CONCLUSION: *Getting Entrepreneurial!* **299**

Do Something Great!

Doing It Just for the Money: A Recipe for Disaster

Starting Over with the Basics

Welcome to the Entrepreneurial Age: One Last Time

INDEX **307**

ACKNOWLEDGMENTS

The smartest thing I did in planning this book was to ask my literary agent, Bob Diforio, to find a small- to mid-sized publisher to work with. The publisher of my first book happened to be the American subsidiary of the largest publishing company in the world. It was a nightmare working with them. It wasn't because they were bad people. It was because of everything I have ever written about what happens when a company becomes a giant—bumbling bureaucracy seems doubly true in the publishing industry. My book was one of thousands they published that year, I never once had a serious discussion with my editor about the content of the book, and their publicity department was a revolving door of uninspired kids who started every conversation with: "Now, what's the name of your book again?" It finally dawned on me that I was writing about the power of the entrepreneurial spirit—and I had signed on with one of the world's great bureaucracies to publish it.

Working with Allworth Press has been like night and day compared to that experience. Tad Crawford, the founder and publisher of Allworth Press, was the first publishing executive I had ever met who was actually interested in the content and purpose of what I was writing. My editor, Nicole Potter, has always made time to talk to me and actually seems to *like* my book—a radical departure from the earlier experience. And the rest of the people at Allworth Press, whether in editorial or marketing or publicity, all actually know my name, the name of my book, and most importantly seem truly enthusiastic about the publishing of *The Entrepreneurial Age*.

It's a new world from the Vice President who signed me up at the "bigger-is-better" publishing conglomerate. As it was my first book, I asked him for any suggestions he could give me on how to write a successful book. His immediate answer: "Make it 300 pages so we can charge at least $20 and get on Oprah Winfrey." I said: "Is that it?" The reply: "That's it."

So thank you God that smaller, entrepreneurial companies can and do still exist in the book publishing business. And thank you all at Allworth Press!

PREFACE

As identifiers of companies sure to score on Wall Street, Peters and Waterman ought to find another line of work.
—Graef Crystal
The Crystal Report

To this day I carry the November 5, 1984 issue of *Business Week* in my briefcase. I carry it to keep me humble and to remind me to never believe anything management consultants say, even if it's written down in the most famous business book in history. My fledgling company had actually been founded on the strength of having the contract to introduce Tom Peters's Excellence seminars internationally. We were making steady progress, having set up joint ventures in some fifteen countries, when the famous "Oops!" cover of *Business Week* appeared. The feature story rolled out the awful truth that in less than two years since *In Search of Excellence* had been published, fully one-third of the list of "America's best-run companies" were on their knees financially.

OOPS! WHO'S EXCELLENT NOW?

Today, that list of forty-three Excellent companies looks truly crazy. An up-to-the-minute analysis shows that only thirty-one of the forty-three companies are even still around—in name at least. Graef Crystal, the United States' most famous compensation consultant, who is usually berating CEOs for raking in fat paychecks while their companies implode, turned his eagle eye on how well the remaining *In Search of Excellence* companies have performed for their shareholders. The results are not encouraging. Crystal reports: "Faithful adherence to the Peters-Waterman thesis would have earned much less than by simply tossing the money into a fund tied to the Standard & Poor's 500." Over the period being calculated, Crystal found $100 invested in the Excellent companies would be worth $863 today—while putting on a blindfold and tossing a dart at S&P indexed funds would have produced $1,046—a 21 percent better result. If the Excellent companies can't even beat the average of all big companies, what's the point? Good question. Crystal was then asked for his own ideas on what management criteria Peters and Waterman should have used in selecting the best-run American companies. In a final kick in the shin to all blue-chip consultants, his answer: "I don't know anything about how to manage a company. I've been a consultant all my life." Ouch!

Clearly something had gone wrong with the conclusions of this famous book. But I had a more immediate problem. I needed a new product, fast. It had been tough enough to get the Germans, Japanese, and others in my global territory to buy anything based on American management prowess in the early eighties. Now, thanks to *Business Week* and the sorry facts they reported, Excellence was beginning to look like just another American management fad that didn't work. My first entrepreneurial effort was in dire need of "Plan B."

As often happens, necessity became the mother of invention. I hit upon two simple ideas, directly related to my predicament. First, I thought, if even *In Search of Excellence* didn't get to the bottom-line truth about what creates growth and prosperity in business, where in the world could we find those answers? It struck me that maybe Peters and Waterman and the whole crazy industry of management gurus were asking the wrong questions—or at least looking in the wrong places for the answers. Maybe the place to look wasn't the world's famous, giant companies. Maybe by the time they became famous giants, it was already too late. What if they were already past their prime and their current management practices were the reason for their approaching decline, not the cause of their earlier years of growth? Bingo! To find the true basics of successful enterprise, I had to look no further than the entrepreneurs who actually created and propelled all those famous companies during their start-up and high-growth years.

The second idea—and one clearly related to the first—was the notion that companies *do* change over time. And the real key may be to understand the phases of a company's life, as opposed to taking a snapshot and assuming that today's hot management idea is the source of all business success. Understanding the dynamic of the life cycle of organizations turned out to be the single most important discovery we made. Admittedly, these insights came a lot easier because I had just started my own company. I could see that, as an entrepreneur, the priorities I felt, and what I had to do every day to get the business up and running, were completely different from what I did as a president and senior manager of the larger, more mature organizations where I had formerly worked. I was getting more and more excited by all this. So for the first time in my business life, I began to do some serious, hands-on research to flush these ideas out. By late 1985 (one year after the *Oops!* revelations), I believed I was onto something very interesting and possibly very important. Additionally motivated by the ongoing need to meet payrolls in my London, Hong Kong, and U.S. offices, my associates and I began giving lectures and seminars on the power of entrepreneurial practices to anyone who would listen. The standard pitch was part-confession and part-promise:

> We've all gotten it wrong for fifty years. Here, finally, is the simple, old-fashioned truth about growing your business. Growing and managing a business are separate universes. Entrepreneurs grow businesses and managers manage businesses. So more manage-ment theories, another restructuring, and sending everyone off to business school won't get you a penny of growth. To get growth, you've got to have high purpose, absolute focus on customer and product, a lot of action, and self-inspired people. It's called getting entrepreneurial.

Of course, we were talking about the four entrepreneurial basics we still teach today; these form the core "technology" of this book. Unfortunately, we were a few years ahead of the market—which is the entrepreneurial way of saying we had a very hard time getting anyone to lis-ten. I still recall, with some pain, those tough days of the mid-1980s when I was trying to convince corporate executives that they should be training their managers to behave more like entrepreneurs on the job. The very first sales presentation I ever made on entrepreneurship was to IBM Asia in October 1985. The division president's eyes seemed to roll back in his head as I spoke, sending a clear message: "We're IBM. Why the hell would we want our managers to behave like entrepreneurs?" What a difference a decade or so can make.

THE ENTREPRENEURIAL PREMISE: CONFIRMED

We may have been a few years ahead of the market back in 1985, but fifteen years later the idea of instilling entrepreneurial practices in orga-nizations to achieve high growth has captured the imagination of people worldwide. My first book on the subject, *Searching for the Spirit of Enterprise,* was published in 1993. Our premise was (and still is) this: It's the entrepreneurial spirit, not the managerial technique, that drives successful, high-growth companies everywhere. In *Spirit of Enterprise* I argued that big business was being smothered under an avalanche of management fads, people theories, financial wizardry, and bureaucratic rules, none of which had anything to do with growing a business. The prescription was detailed and blunt: It was high time to dismantle the twentieth-century corporation and start over with the entrepreneurial basics.

In the seven years since that book was published, I've met a lot of people around the world who like this prescription. Whether clients, colleagues, or journalists, their support and real-world application of our entrepreneurial premise has been the best confirmation we could ask for. Most of them have been company executives, anxious to find completely new ways to grow their business in today's super-competitive global economy. Many, to my surprise, were government officials. They ranged from administrators wanting to make the bureaucracy more customer focused and innovative, to policy makers already using the power of entrepreneurship in job creation and economic development. And of course there were always the "closet entrepreneurs"—individuals from all walks of life looking for the right moment to take the entrepreneurial plunge with their own start-up business. The common ground shared by all these remarkable people from every corner of the world is that they are all eager to participate in the biggest shift in the pursuit of prosperity since the Industrial Revolution. Here's a sampling:

Lincoln Electric, in Cleveland, Ohio, may be the most entrepreneurial big company in the world. With sales pushing $1.5 billion a year, it's also the world's largest maker of welding equipment. The company's most amazing feat, however, is that Lincoln employees are the highest-paid factory workers in the world. I wanted to learn all I could about this unique company, so I went to see Fred Mackenbach, the president and the epitome of Midwestern common sense. He started with a question: "Why is it that large organizations tend to be entrenched in attitudes—and platitudes—that are so at odds with the entrepreneurial spirit?" Without skipping a beat, he answered his own question: "We think it's pretty simple really. When workers are treated like entrepreneurs, they behave like entrepreneurs. People are amazed when I tell them that Lincoln factory workers can and do earn in excess of $100,000 a year. Well, why shouldn't they? They are, in fact, dedicated entrepreneurs who constantly seek a better way to produce a lower-cost product for sale to an ever-increasing number of customers." Mackenbach concluded with the kind of enlightened passion I found in so many believers in corporate entrepreneurship: "What our employees do is much more important than just improving the bottom line of the Lincoln Electric Company. Think about it: They are the true foundation of our free enterprise system."

Jannie Tay founded The Hour Glass, a $300 million watch and jewelry business in Asia, based in Singapore. I first met her when we were both speakers at a Singapore conference on entrepreneurship in 1995. I knew from the moment she started speaking that I had to have a full interview with her in my next book. She agreed, and I think you will enjoy it. You will see that her mission in life is passing on the entrepreneurial spirit to her employees. Just one comment from that interview will show why she is one of Asia's best spokespersons for entrepreneurship: "You know, just a few years ago, entrepreneurship was not recognized as something to be proud of. Entrepreneurs were wheelers-dealers. They were people who did not succeed in a job in a company. And they all had to be a little crooked. That was the image in Singapore. After all these years, I now know that being an entrepreneur is about integrity, honesty, truth, and credibility."

Then there was Robert Storey, the CEO of a modest-sized Credit Union in Wisconsin, who proved that entrepreneurial principles can be equally important and exciting to small organizations. He wrote me saying how much he enjoyed reading "this truly great business book." His title on the letterhead was "CEEO." I called him to thank him for his very kind words and asked what CEEO stood for: "I used to be Chief Executive Officer of the Credit Union, but after reading your book I just had to change it to Chief Entrepreneurial & Executive Officer. I had the entire staff also read the book and now we're all very caught up in becoming more entrepreneurial." Bob Storey was the world's first CEEO and he became our most passionate believer in Wisconsin.

Speaking of passionate believers, it would be hard to top Franco Calandra, who was the president of Rockwell International of Brazil. Of course, Brazilians don't take a back seat to anyone in the passion category. Franco was a very competitive guy in the cutthroat business of manufacturing auto parts. He was also completely taken with the idea of turning all his people into mini-entrepreneurs. He told us, "The *Spirit of Enterprise* program (our seminar) not only changed the way we do business; it changed our lives." We receive the same passionate response from clients all over Brazil, and from the thousand-plus Brazilian managers who have attended our seminars in conjunction with Disney University in Orlando. And in return I have to rate Brazilians as just about the most enthusiastic students of entrepreneurship in the world. They may have a financial crisis every few years, but never count them out. The entrepreneurial spirit, especially the passionate variety, is alive and well in Brazil.

Dr. Douglas Notman is director of Endocrinology at St. Mary's Hospital in Grand Rapids, Michigan. I was in town to give a lecture and Dr. Notman took the time and trouble to come by the hotel for a chat. He did all the talking. He had a hundred new ideas for improving the hospital, starting with the breakthrough medical concept that patients are actually customers. Once hospital executives recognize this, he reasoned, patients might even be asked for their opinion about the hospital's product and service, and their suggestions for improvement. He added that if I thought he was making any of this up, I hadn't been in a big, busy, bureaucratic hospital lately. I had to admit, I'd never seen a patient suggestion box in a hospital—or a doctor's office for that matter. He capped it off by saying *Searching for the Spirit of Enterprise* "has changed my concept of the way a hospital should be run. This is revolutionary stuff for doctors and administrators." And so it seems. Check any poll on which industries give the worst service to customers. Admittedly, the box marked "Absolutely Awful" is a very crowded place, but health care usually manages to squeeze itself in there somehow. We all wish the good doctor great success in his revolutionary efforts.

Dr. Bernie Villegas is a leading economist in Asia and was an economic advisor to former President Corazon Aquino. He is also the founder and dean of the University of Asia and the Pacific, which has been the Farrell Company's affiliate in the Philippines for several years. Bernie is especially knowledgeable and articulate on the economic power of entrepreneurship in developing economies: "My theory of economic development is that it has to be entrepreneurship-based. The focus has to be on small- to medium-sized businesses. They're more labor intensive and more adaptive to changing environments. These two characteristics make them extremely valuable to any developing economy."

It's fair to say that Bernie's comments can apply to any economy, even the U.S. economy. Kris Kimel, president of the Kentucky Science & Technology Council, is a strong advocate of creating entrepreneurial economies. While working on his project, "Creating an Entrepreneurial Economy in Kentucky," I got to hear his take-no-prisoners point of view a lot: "The last thing we should be spending time and money on is getting another Toyota plant in Kentucky. They're wonderful while they're here, but when they leave, as they often do, you're left with an economic catastrophe. We need 'homegrown' prosperity. We need a Kentucky 'Microsoft' and that's why this project is so important."

Of course, I can't forget Kim Gantz, the irrepressible editorial director for *Business Week*'s CEO and President Conferences. Kim speaks in "*Business Week*–ese," which means she knows how to get your attention. She called out of the blue one day to tell me: "You may not know it yet, Larry, but you've got the hottest topic of the year so we've decided to build our entire CEO conference around it." This was big news given that ten years earlier you could hardly find a paragraph on entrepreneurship in *Business*

Week or *Fortune* or the *Wall Street Journal.* The message has now gone way beyond a Kim Gantz–style "what's hot this year" conference. In the blue-chip business press today, special sections on small business and cover features on entrepreneurs abound. John Naisbitt, of *Megatrends* fame, told me he tracks the future of entrepreneurship the same way he tracks everything else—by the increase in lines of press coverage on the subject. On that score, you can quadruple everything I've said so far about the significance of the fast-approaching Entrepreneurial Age!

To find the most dramatic evidence of corporate entrepreneurship in the world today, you'll have to—are you ready for this?—go to Paris. In this city, more famous for culture than commerce, you can see a truly challenging transformation from bureaucracy to enterprise. And Hervé Hannebicque is one Frenchman who loves a challenge. He's charged with creating 53,000 company entrepreneurs over five years—the largest such project by any company, anywhere in the world. He's certainly got the title for it. Hervé is the first senior vice president of entrepreneurship I've ever met. He's doing all this entrepreneuring at Thomson Multimedia S.A., the giant ($8 billion U.S. in sales) French electronics company, which operates globally as Thomson Consumer Electronics/RCA. I first met Hervé on a Saturday in Washington, D.C. We talked while I drove him around the capital city which he had not visited before. The meeting turned into an all-day, wide-ranging discussion of what makes American managers tick to why France is fast becoming the entrepreneurial incubator of Europe.

Hervé explained that how he got to his current challenge was no accident: "President [Jacques] Chirac of France asked our CEO Thierry Breton to take over Thomson which was owned by the French government. The idea was to make it profitable and privatize it. Of course, Breton and his team, which included me, had just accomplished the privatizing of Bull S.A. (France's big computer company). I was VP of human resources at Bull, but I pleaded with Thierry to just let me focus on this one thing at Thomson. I figured we could do the same thing we did at Bull but in half the time. What I learned at Bull was that developing better managers was not the answer to turning around a company. You have to get beyond managing. Every employee has to learn to behave as if the company were his own—like a true entrepreneur. Having that focus from day one, on the people side, is what will cut the time to privatization in half. This is why we are calling this worldwide project 'Managing to Entrepreneuring' and why the project has to hit all 53,000 employees very quickly." I'm pleased to say that since that first get-together a couple of years ago, we've been able to give Hervé and Thomson Multimedia some assistance in their efforts to move from "managing to entrepreneuring."

I have also been surprised and honored over the years to meet many government officials eager to learn about the job-creating and economic development power of entrepreneurship. At the top of the list would have to be thirty-two-year-old Tomas Sildmae, Estonia's first minister of economy after the country gained its independence from the Soviet Union. He was trying to foster an entrepreneurial economy in the country but was receiving hopelessly complicated advice from Western economic experts. While thanking me for making entrepreneurship so simple "that even former communists can understand it," he added this comment that gives one food for thought: "I was amazed that the IMF advisors actually made capitalism sound more complicated than the Five Year Plans we used to receive from Moscow." One can only wonder if these are the same people advising Russia today.

In Malaysia, the Honorable Mustapa Mohamed was the mild-mannered minister of the world's only Ministry of Entrepreneurial Development. After hearing my talk on what entrepreneurs actually do, he hired our firm on the spot to train the entire senior staff of his Ministry. He later offered this brutally honest reason: "Neither I nor my senior staff had any idea what entrepreneurship was." I would hope that the economic development leaders of your government were as honest about what they don't know as he was.

Closer to home, Nora Chang Wang had the challenging task of implementing New York City's massive Welfare-to-Work program. As Mayor Rudolph Giuliani's commissioner of employment, her agency was responsible for finding jobs for the 470,000 people scheduled to come off welfare. Since, according to the best estimates, it would take over twenty years for New York City's general economy to create this many new jobs, Commissioner Wang was looking for ways to jump-start the process. She attended a talk I gave on the job-creating, economic power of entrepreneurship. It was a special presentation for city officials sponsored by the Private Industry Council of New York. She became extremely interested and after the talk approached me, saying: "This concept has hit me like a steamroller. I've just called my staff to cancel other meetings today so we can develop an immediate plan to bring entrepreneurship into the city's program. Are you ready to help us do this?" Of course we were—and we did. I learned one thing: Government agencies can move with the speed of light when the top executive really wants to.

And, finally, there was the truly amazing scene of the president of Uruguay, Luis Alberto Lacalle, staring out his office window toward the Parliament building, waving a copy of my book and angrily proclaiming: "They stand in the way—they're ripping up the Magna Carta before my eyes." I was stunned into silence by this wonderful display of a presidential temper tantrum. I later learned from my host (the president's commissioner of economic reform) that President Lacalle had been very frustrated with Parliament over their refusal to support his top economic priority: the privatization of all government-owned businesses. He believed this was Parliament's way of keeping the nation's wealth under government control and out of the hands of the citizens of Uruguay. Thus his memorable Magna Carta outburst. Clearly our discussion on "the enterprise of nations" had triggered a very raw entrepreneurial nerve in the reform-minded president. I must admit, I liked it.

Perhaps the man who summarized it best was Nigel Bruce, for many years the erudite—and brave—editor of the *Financial Mail,* South Africa's top business magazine. Nigel introduced me to a *Financial Mail* conference in Johannesburg, with his own explanation of why the entrepreneurial message was so critical to the future of the new South Africa. His opening remarks, while squarely directed at the new power structure of South Africa, stood as a warning to us all: "For the past thirty-six years my publication has been trying to persuade the government of this country that wealth is created not by legislation or by theft, but by ordinary people who apply a rare blend of enterprise, courage, and skill to satisfy the requirements of their fellow men. It is my great privilege this morning to introduce to you a man of extraordinary insight. For he has learned what we all want to know: Who shall inherit the earth? But more important than that, he has what Wordsworth called 'intimations of immortality.' For if you listen to him carefully, you may find an answer to an even more difficult question: Having inherited the earth, how do you get to keep it?"

The people whose words and ideas grace these pages,[1] and millions more like them, are clearly "eager to participate in the biggest shift in the pursuit of prosperity since the Industrial Revolution." If you are eager, ready, and willing as well, you will be in good company. You will be among those twenty-first-century enterprisers who indeed "shall inherit the earth" and maybe even "get to keep it!"

THE ENTERPRISE OF PEOPLE, COMPANIES, AND COUNTRIES

The message of *The Entrepreneurial Age* is that the entrepreneurial spirit can and should be applied to three broad economic areas: individual

---

[1]In our files, there are literally hundreds of other inspiring testimonies on learning and applying the power of the entrepreneurial spirit. I have tried here to use an interesting, wide-ranging sample for illustrative purposes. I apologize in advance to all other friends and clients, whose equally inspiring stories are not included due to space limitations.

achievement, organizational success, and national economic development. The question is: How exactly do we do that? Are there common principles underlying success in the Entrepreneurial Age? The good news is that the entrepreneurial basics probably haven't changed for the past thousand years. They certainly haven't changed since 1985 when we began our research—and distilled them into a set of common-sense practices. The same basics of enterprise that were described in my first book make up the "technology" presented in this book. Of course, we have made minor, common-sense adaptations in applying the practices to individual people, companies, and countries. But the essential character of the entrepreneurial basics remains the same across the board. Those four fundamental practices, that we believe underpin the success of all entrepreneurs, high-growth companies, and prosperous countries alike, are:

THE ENTREPRENEURIAL BASICS

Sense of Mission

Customer/Product Vision

High-speed Innovation

Self-inspired Behavior

INTRODUCTION:
Great Myths and Simple Truths

Bigger is better *turned out to be another twentieth-century myth.*
                                                    —PETER DRUCKER

I had just addressed *Business Week*'s Asian CEO Conference in Taipei, and was waiting nervously for the grand old man of management to follow me to the podium. I had delivered my standard pitch that big business management theory was mostly nonsense and would never be a match for old-fashioned entrepreneurship—with Peter Drucker, the father of modern management, sitting in the first row staring at me. Drucker was not known for subtlety. After all, this was the same man who had called *In Search of Excellence* "a book for juveniles." So I was preparing myself for public humiliation and probable early retirement as a *Business Week* speaker after he got through with me. However, to my everlasting gratitude, Dr. Drucker's opening comment was: "*Bigger is better* turned out to be another twentieth-century myth, and Larry Farrell has eloquently explained why." Many people at the conference, including the *Business Week* brass, would later shake my hand, give that knowing nod, and congratulate me for "getting it right" according to Drucker.

LEARNING THE HARD WAY

Drucker later explained to me, in private, that only recently had it become clear to him that size, mass, and economy of scale—at some critical point—begin to make companies less competitive, not more. He noted that, in almost all industries, the best company—certainly the most profitable one—is rarely the biggest. He even confided that he no longer accepted consulting requests from giant companies: "You can give them the best advice in the world, and they just can't implement it. It's so frustrating; I've stopped trying to tell them anything."

Most management gurus of last century kept telling us in no uncertain terms that *bigger is always better.* We all bought into that notion and, as with most big myths in life, we've learned the hard way that it just isn't so. In fact, much of modern management "science" has been based on myths and half-truths. Of course, the same can be said for other "enlightened" fields like economics, psychology, and certainly public policy development. For business, the high-water mark came with America's invention of that be-all-end-all of managerial prowess, the MBA. After World War II, this became the holy grail of business, and we embraced it with a frenzy. By 1980 America was producing an astonishing 75,000 MBAs a year—never stopping to wonder how Japan and Germany, with no business schools at all, were busily stealing a full 33 percent of our worldwide market. Some management science diehards will still say: "What about all those Asians and Europeans piling into Harvard, Stanford, and Wharton in record numbers today? Doesn't that prove the value of an American MBA?" I really doubt it. What I'm *hoping* it proves is that America has finally come to its senses and has come up with a new, secret strategy: Give enough Germans and Japanese an MBA, and we'll get our markets back.

GREAT MYTHS: THE RISE OF THE EXPERT CLASS

The serious point is that, for much of the twentieth century, most of us believed that big business was the economic hand that fed us and big government was the benevolent overseer that maintained the system. And we, the people, were the necessary cogs in the system. Or at least that was the way it was supposed to work. But along the way to economic prosperity and social nirvana, something went terribly wrong.

One thing that went wrong was that about halfway through the century, we got too smart for our own good. Before the 1950s, America was kept busy dealing with two World Wars and the Great Depression. We didn't have the time to indulge ourselves in too many theoretical possibilities. But after World War II all that changed. Times were good. Everyone was studying something at a university and, before long, everywhere you turned you bumped into a recent grad eager to shove the latest socioeconomic theory down your throat. A new class of American was definitely on the rise: the know-it-all "expert." Quite predictably, theories, fads, and myths began to explode on every front.

Industry led the charge in the burgeoning business of fad creation, but it certainly wasn't alone in substituting myth and theory for common sense. Along with the MBAs, professionally trained bureaucrats, economists, and psychologists multiplied like rabbits. These well-paid experts, with their armies of planners, counselors, and bean counters, reigned supreme. It was as if the entire country had been invited to check common sense at the door and take all this nonsense on blind faith. From sensitivity training in business to never-ending welfare systems by government, to prefrontal lobotomies being prescribed like aspirin by psychiatrists, every nutty idea was offered up as another breakthrough. It was truly the era of the new expert class.

By the nineties we had accumulated a world full of evidence that the laws of diminishing returns were setting in on all the expert advice we had gotten, particularly with regard to improving our economic life. In fact, the best-laid plans for creating prosperity were going haywire.

The simultaneous near-collapse of three great icons of big business in the mid-eighties had startled even the most cynical critics of American management methods. It was hard to believe that General Motors, IBM, and Sears could all be in financial free fall and, despite all their market power and financial clout, seemed helpless to stop the bleeding. For the first time in the history of the three wounded giants, getting smaller looked better than getting bigger. When it was all over, IBM did what its founder, Thomas J. Watson, Sr., said would never be done and ravaged its workforce by downsizing 180,000 employees. GM followed suit and cut 200,000 jobs, while Sears laid off 50,000 people and closed hundreds of stores. Seeing some of the twentieth century's greatest companies on their knees was symbolic evidence that an era was over.

For anyone who took the trouble to notice, the problem had been building for years. The *Fortune 500*'s revenue growth rate had been in decline for three decades. It peaked in the sixties at 9.2 percent, slipped to 5.5 percent in the seventies, was a paltry 0.7 percent in the 1980s, and actually turned negative in the recession of the early nineties. The rest of the world was not immune from this terrible trend. Global giants were reluctantly joining the race to get smaller. The first layoffs ever in giant Japanese firms were in full swing. Many large European companies simply gave up on growth and embraced downsizing with a passion, helping produce painful 10–20 percent unemployment rates across the EU. Back in the United States, after years of wringing out every possible cost and laying off millions of employees, profits did tick upward in the mid-nineties. Acquisitions produced some one-time revenue growth, but this would be a short-lived rebound. Sure enough, the 1999 *Fortune 500* report (the most current as of this writing) showed anemic revenue growth of 4 percent and an embarrassing 1.8 percent decline in profits. It's a pretty dismal result considering the American economy overall is booming. But the *Fortune Global 500* did even worse: revenue up a tiny 0.1 percent and profits plummeting 6.1 percent. The reality is, there's no fat left to cut in these big companies and they need to learn how to produce real growth, real fast.

At the same time that GM headquarters on Michigan Avenue was reporting billion-dollar losses, the Kremlin in Red Square was announcing even more shocking economic news from the noncapitalist world. The Soviet Union was throwing in the towel on its own version of *bigger is better*—the centrally controlled economy. When Mikhail Gorbachev visited the United States for the first time in 1985, he introduced us to *perestroika* (economic restructuring) and declared: "We must find the spirit of enterprise in our people." The cover of *Newsweek* proclaimed, in very uncommunist fashion, "Gorbachev's Big Surprise!" But it was no surprise to Gorbachev's new team of bean counters in the Kremlin. They knew the empire was bankrupt and they had the numbers to back it up. They showed Gorbachev case after case of economic horror stories, such as factories in which the value of the finished products was less than the value of the raw materials used to make them. Impossible? Not in the socialist paradise. And at the Ministry of Agriculture, they determined that the 4 percent of the farmland tilled privately as "family plots" was actually producing a whopping 35 percent of the food in the Soviet Union. Who could blame Gorbachev for turning to the "spirit of enterprise in the people"? He may have been a communist, but he wasn't an idiot.

While perhaps an extreme case, the Soviet Union was not alone in discovering that its political and economic baggage was making people poorer, not richer. To billions of poor people around the world, political platitudes and economic theories were wearing thin. The worst-performing economies of the world were in dire need of new, real-world solutions for eliminating poverty and raising prosperity. Certainly, getting lousy advice from experts doesn't only happen to communists and third world countries. It could, and did, happen everywhere—even in New York City. Politicians and public policy experts designed a welfare system for New York that produced an explosion of welfare cases—from 250,000 in 1960 to 1.1 million by 1990—and was literally bankrupting the city. Mayor Rudy Giuliani, who vowed to eliminate welfare entirely by the end of the twentieth century, loves to show a large graph of that dramatic increase and tell anyone who will listen: "This wasn't an accident, it wasn't an atmospheric thing, it wasn't supernatural. This is the result of policies and programs designed to have the maximum number of people on welfare."

Master economic development plans, bigger-is-always-better business strategies, and massive "I-feel-your-pain" government programs were not delivering economic prosperity or social tranquility. Average workers and average citizens everywhere were getting fed up and began asking tough questions like: "Where's all this gobbledygook coming from?"

FROM THOSE WONDERFUL FOLKS AT HARVARD AND MCKINSEY

It's a good question. Where *have* all these experts come from? And how did big business and big government get into such a mess? In the case of big business, the companies have no one to blame but themselves—and the strange worldwide network of management gurus from Harvard, McKinsey, and a thousand other places that all feed at the trough of the world's giant corporations. For much of the twentieth century, the professors and consultants of management have offered up theory after theory. Most of them have been colossal and expensive failures. Look at the track record. What happened to all the theories about economy of scale, learning curve theory, and strategic planning? What has become of the almighty promise of conglomerates, matrix management, and sensitivity training? And it continues to this day. We now learn that reengineering, the rage of the 1990s, wasn't such a good idea after all. As one middle manager at a *Fortune 500* company put it: "We're simply drowning in theories that don't work. More help like this from Harvard and McKinsey and we'll all be working out of a garage in our backyard."

Of course, business is always an easy target in the myth-creating game. But make no mistake: Crazy fads and foolish ideas have come and gone on everything from people development to local government regulation to global economic theory. To illustrate just how whacky the gurus in all these areas can be, we offer a believe-it-or-not example from each. We call these "great myths in action" or, more colloquially, "daily doses of nonsense from the expert class."

- The first thing to say about people development ideas is—watch out! They represent, without a doubt, the outer fringe of the expert class. The programs range from mildly useful to crazy to downright dangerous. One of the most famous was *sensitivity training*. It came roaring on the scene in the sixties. Aramco, the old Arabian-American Oil Company in Saudi Arabia, was making a fortune producing oil. Everyone was happy, including the workers who were mostly Saudis and Americans with a few British thrown in for good measure. The only thing the workers did was pump and refine oil. After work, they all went home to their own separate enclaves and did whatever Saudis or Americans or British do for fun. The U.S. partners—Texaco, Mobil, and Standard Oil—had set up a stateside headquarters in Houston to supply the operating company in the oil fields of the desert kingdom. Being an American operation, the people in Houston figured they had to have a state-of-the-art Personnel Department. In those days Personnel was the province of psychologists and educators with various axes to grind and agendas to promote—all of which had little to do with growing a business. Predictably, the personnel people in Houston wanted to "help" the guys (and they were only guys) pumping oil in Saudi Arabia. They got the bright idea that it would be very progressive to have the multicultured workforce in the oilfields and the refineries "level" with each other and become more of an open and sensitive team.

So sensitivity training instructors were sent to Saudi Arabia and the first wave of participants signed up for the workshops. When the instructors told the participants they should honestly and openly tell the rest of the group how they felt about them, the participants did exactly what they were told. It turned out the Americans didn't like the Saudis much, the Brits weren't crazy about the Yanks, and the Saudis could care less about both groups of foreigners and would be quite happy if they would just all leave and go home. None of this went over too well and the exchanges became more and more heated. To make a long, miserable story mercifully short, sensitivity training caused enormous ill will among the workers and practically brought Aramco to its knees. The chairman finally had to step in and close down the operation. He then banned sensitivity training at Aramco forever. Eventually, everyone went back to work pumping and refining oil—and kept their personal thoughts to themselves—and tranquility reigned once again. The moral of the story? Beats me, but I wouldn't suggest you try any nineties "new age" seminars in your foreign operations any time soon—or even in Houston for that matter.

- Even when governments try to help, they often end up shooting themselves and everyone else in the foot. Consider this recent catch-22 story of the government trying to protect workers. It took place in the normally probusiness state of Virginia. The state enforces a well-intentioned law that employers pay their workers time and a half after forty hours a week. Nobody I know would disagree with this section of the Fair Labor Standards Act. Unless, of course, you find yourself in the Kafkaesque dilemma that faced Dr. Daniel Woodworth and his Woodworth Animal Hospital. It seems that his fifteen employees requested a flexible schedule so they could all have some three-day weekends over the summer. They offered to make up the hours on alternate weeks to get the coveted long weekend. Dr. Woodworth readily agreed, and everyone was happy. That is, until the Department of Labor auditors showed up one day and informed the good veterinarian-entrepreneur that he owed $7,315 in back overtime pay for all those weeks his staff put in more than forty hours. He paid up, reluctantly cancelled the flex-time program, and everyone lost. Final score: Bureaucracy, 1–Enterprise, 0.

- For economic theory run amuck, you need look no further than the 1998 collapse of Long-Term Capital Management, the brainchild of Nobel Prize–winning economists, Robert Merton and Myron Scholes. They won the 1997 Nobel Prize in economics for their work on risk management. They then decided to put their theories to work in the real world, and promptly created the biggest Wall Street risk of the decade. Federal Reserve Board Chairman Alan Greenspan had to construct an unprecedented bailout to prevent the $4 billion fiasco from crippling the entire market. The *New York Times* got it right: "[The] doctorate-toting, computer crazy strategists had the rococo world of 90's global finance all figured out. Then, last August, it got bad, fast. None of the young professors at Long-Term Capital, it turns out, had ever considered how weird, how irratrional—how human!—even their elegant, highly esoteric financial markets can be." One is only left to wonder what this says about the "experts" in Oslo who hand out the Nobel Prize in economics.

At the end of the day, we are all searching for individual, organizational, and national economic well-being. The huge question is: How do we move beyond the myths and reach some simple truths about creating prosperity in the twenty-first century? Here are a couple of thought starters to consider. Instead of churning out those 75,000 MBAs a year, or even more Ph.Ds. in theoretical economics, or another generation of social psychologists, maybe it's time to look to the true masters of enterprise for our prosperity-building lessons. Surely the time-honored lessons of world-class entrepreneurs, such as Lever, Honda, Disney, and Estée Lauder, would be closer to the mark than the next hot theory from management professors, economists, or psychologists.

REVIVING THE ENTREPRENEURIAL SPIRIT

Business and economic thinking have come full circle over the past hundred years. The nineteenth century was shaped by the industrial age and produced world-famous captains of industry. Daimler, Carnegie, Rockefeller, and a thousand others reinvented the world and became fabulously wealthy in the process. The twentieth century brought us the managerial age, with professionally trained managers and bureaucrats poised to offer the answer to everything. As personalities, they were, by and large, rather forgettable characters on the world scene. But as the quintessential "organization men," they vowed to run big business and big government with precision planning and ever-increasing efficiency. In their world of *big is beautiful,* small business was relegated to second-class status. It was something you did if you couldn't land an upwardly mobile position at a giant, blue-chip multinational corporation. Being an entrepreneur was almost a dirty word in polite society—an avenue reserved for shysters and get-rich-quick types.

During the last two decades of the twentieth century, however, another "age" was beginning. At first, it was just a byline here and there. Then a few economic studies on new business start-ups. And then we began to see some startling reports on the power of entrepreneurship, like these:

- A Wall Street study showed that, since 1920, small company stocks on the New York Stock Exchange have outperformed the largest companies by a staggering 300 percent.

- U.S. Department of Labor statistics on new job creation showed entrepreneurs and small businesses were creating all the jobs in America—an astounding 21 million during the decade of the eighties and 15 million more in the nineties.

- Arthur Young & Company published research on the cost of innovation at large and small companies. The startling conclusion: Small business produces twenty-four times more "innovations" (new patents obtained and new products introduced) than large companies per R&D dollar. This is the kind of competitive disadvantage that can keep a *Fortune 500* CEO awake at night. It can also get people thinking that maybe all those stories about inventing products in garages are true.

- And finally there was the well-publicized Hay Associates, Inc. magazine survey on Employee Satisfaction. On every question they asked, researchers found that the employees of small companies had a much higher level of job satisfaction than their counterparts at large companies. The real shocker, of course, was that employment costs at small companies run only about 55 percent of those at the blue-chip giants. So we end up with an astonishing result—small-company employees have a higher level of job satisfaction with a lower level of pay. There's a lesson in there somewhere.

So it's not surprising, with so much evidence pouring in, that most of the world now knows that big business isn't the world's engine of prosperity that we once thought it was. And it's certainly not the preferred place of employment for most young workers entering the job market. These are landmark changes in national attitude. Millions of people today are looking to small firms and self-employment as a respected, even preferred, alternative to working for the IBMs of the world. There is clearly a lot of reinforcement in the culture for this shift. The press now proclaims that the "new" backbone of the economy is entrepreneurship and small business. The new "heroes" of the business world are colorful entrepreneurs like Steve Jobs, Richard Branson, and Jannie Tay—in marked contrast to the pinstriped executives of yesteryear. And perhaps the ultimate recognition that times are changing comes from the Harvard Business School which, after a century of avoiding the subject, now offers courses on entrepreneurship. Today, becoming an entrepreneur is definitely "in."

What *has* been surprising is how quickly governments around the world have also embraced the entrepreneurial idea. Even welfare recipients can't avoid the rush to entrepreneurism and self-employment. City governments in the United States, desperate to create jobs for people forced off the dole by the Welfare Reform Act of 1997, are pushing self-employment as an alternative to entry-level jobs at large companies. New York City, for example, is banking heavily on entrepreneurial micro-enterprises as an alternative to the increasingly difficult task of finding openings at existing companies for their welfare-to-work graduates. As Mayor Giuliani says, it may very well come down to this: "If you can't get a job, start a small business. Start a little candy store. Start a little newspaper stand. Start a lemonade stand." The social critics howled but, in reality, this may be the best advice in the world for anyone hoping to prosper in the coming entrepreneurial economy.

Today, for the first time in history, the entire world is moving in the same economic direction. Both of the twentieth century's great experiments—big business and big government—seem to have run their course, at least in the hearts and minds of the public. In their place has come a mighty, global push for searching out and reviving the entrepreneurial spirit in people, companies, and entire countries. The available evidence does point to one simple truth: The entrepreneurial spirit is the best model ever invented for creating growth and prosperity. And in a rare display of agreement, business and government leaders, economists, the press, and even much of academia have bought into this notion. So for countries and companies and ordinary people everywhere, the operative question becomes: What exactly is the entrepreneurial spirit, and how can we harness it in our work and life?

We start with two important observations that are fundamental to understanding the process of entrepreneurship. First, all companies (as well as people and countries, of course) have a life cycle. And within that cycle, it's natural that small entrepreneurial companies will get bigger and bigger over time, which ultimately makes them less competitive, not more. This is the point that Drucker, and most other management "experts," have belatedly conceded. Second, growing a business and managing a bureaucracy are fundamentally different arts. This dichotomy is compounded by the related observation that entrepreneurs never replace themselves with entrepreneurs, but with professional managers. So all companies, even good ones, will eventually face the double whammy of being a huge bureaucracy, managed by a band of MBAs. Understanding the tough-to-break life cycle of companies, and recognizing that more MBA management know-how is the last thing you'll need to overcome it, are the essential first steps in learning the process of entrepreneurship.

THE LIFE CYCLE OF ALL ORGANIZATIONS

> *Now I see the problem with lifetime employment. People live longer than their companies.*
>
> —JAPANESE MANAGER
> TEXAS INSTRUMENTS, JAPAN

At a lecture in Tokyo several years ago, I was showing a slide with this rather startling statistic: Of the hundred largest U.S. companies in 1900, only sixteen are still in business. The Japanese manager from Texas Instruments, quoted above, was attempting humor, but his joke actually lays bare a sobering fact of life about organizations. Companies, like people and countries and everything else on the planet, exist in a life cycle. Over time, all organizations will pass through the different phases of that life cycle, as shown in the diagram.

THE LIFE CYCLE OF ALL ORGANIZATIONS

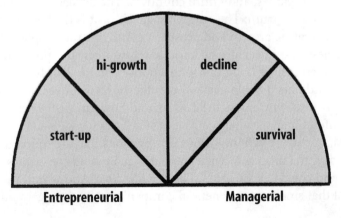

It's a pretty simple concept actually. There's creation followed by growth. Growth peaks and decline sets in, leading ultimately to death. And, of course, there's always the possibility of untimely death along the way.

All companies begin with an abundance of the entrepreneurial spirit, inspiring workers as well as owners. Basic entrepreneurial practices fuel the start-up and drive the company well into a phase of high growth. During the start-up and high-growth eras, everyone is fixated on a few fundamental notions, such as getting customers, because it's the only way to get paid.

The resultant high growth gets you size. And the passage of time gets you new leaders. The new leaders are almost always professional managers. These subtle shifts in size and leadership produce a new set of objectives. Presto! Planning, streamlining, and controlling the enterprise become the new order. Managing this and that become more important than making this and selling that. The highest-paid jobs become managing other managers. Meetings, reports, and bureaucracy proliferate on every front. And, slowly but surely, lost in the shuffle are the simple, entrepreneurial basics that got you going in the first place.

The dominant style of companies on the right-hand side of the cycle—the larger and more mature organizations—is "managerial." These companies are typically past their prime and on the downside of the cycle. Even so, it is the study of these companies, by the business schools and management consultants that serve them, that has produced most of the management theories and fads over the past fifty years.

Conversely, the growth phases on the left-hand side of the cycle are highly "entrepreneurial." The behaviors and practices of the entrepreneurs and their employees during the start-up and high-growth phases of the life cycle have historically been of little interest to the Harvards and McKinseys of the world. This is precisely where we part company with such blue-chip management experts. It seems pretty obvious that it's a lot more valuable to learn how to create and maintain a high-growth enterprise than it is to learn how to manage a declining bureaucracy.

The important questions are why do companies almost always make the shift from high growth to decline and what can be done about it? Indeed, what really caused 84 percent of America's biggest, richest, most powerful companies to bite the dust in less than a century? It's clear that beating the natural life cycle is tough indeed. It is incredible, even paradoxical, that the high growth that all managers want to achieve produces the mass and weight, which in turn, produces a growing bureaucracy. To add to the burgeoning problems, the new leaders know next to nothing about the entrepreneurial approach to running a business. This is a deadly combination. As the company reaches "mid-life," it's big and bureaucratic and the entrepreneurial spirit becomes buried under an avalanche of bureaucracy and management theory—a classic example of throwing out the baby with the bath water.

The logical solution is to reverse the organization life cycle, and move back to the high growth phase. To do this, high-growth entrepreneurial practices have to be reinstilled in the company. This, of course, assumes that managers and employees know what these practices are and how to use them. But that shouldn't be a problem. They're pretty simple actually. After all, this isn't brain surgery or flying to the moon. It's just business.

SIMPLE TRUTHS: THE FOUR FUNDAMENTAL PRACTICES OF THE WORLD'S GREAT ENTREPRENEURS

The conduct of successful business merely consists in doing things in a very simple way, doing them regularly, and never neglecting to do them.

—WILLIAM HESKETH LEVER
FOUNDER, LEVER BROTHERS (UNILEVER)

What are those *things* we must do simply, regularly, and never forget to do? You won't find them on the managerial side of the cycle. They're not the things that business schools teach or management consultants preach. If you want to find the bedrock fundamentals of enterprise, those simple things practiced obsessively, you've got to look at the entrepreneurial phase of business. Here you will find the lessons of the world's greatest enterprisers, from past masters such as Lever, Matsushita, and Disney, to more recent icons like Honda, Walton, Roddick, Branson, and Jobs. When you think about it, if you're searching for the basics of enterprise, why would you look anywhere else?

1. SENSE OF MISSION

A decrease in profit . . . or a loss of revenue is proof that we have not fulfilled our obligations to society.

—KONOSUKE MATSUSHITA
FOUNDER, MATSUSHITA ELECTRIC

High-minded? You bet. The fact is entrepreneurs believe they are doing something important in the world. They believe they're creating value for customers, employees, and, of course, themselves. We call it having a *sense of mission* about their work. Such high purpose, however, gets quickly translated into two very practical questions: *What* do you do? (essentially what products for what customers) and *How* do you go about doing it? To legendary entrepreneurs like Matsushita, Lever, and Watson, these simple questions are the two most important in business. In modern management lingo, the entrepreneurial *what* and *how* amount to a no-frills version of corporate strategy and corporate culture. Unfortunately, in many big companies, strategy and culture live in separate universes—one the domain of number-crunching planners, the other the province of touchy-feely culture gurus. In too many big companies, neither have much to do with the real running of the business. In stark contrast, entrepreneurs live and die on their answers to *what* and *how*—and these two facets of business are inextricably connected.

Strategy isn't a week in Bermuda with the consultants; it's a matter of survival. What products you're going to make and in what markets you're going to sell them is the whole ball game. And when you get right down to it, it doesn't matter if you do strategy on the back of a napkin, or use ten-pound planning books. The part you absolutely have to get right is this: what products and what markets. On the other hand, the purpose of creating a company culture is not to make more wall plaques or hold more meetings to bounce around soft, side issues of the business. The only purpose is to get everyone focused on those few values that will give you the competitive advantage to make the business strategy come true. When the values directly support the product/market strategy, watch out! It's the most powerful way known to energize a group of individuals to achieve a common purpose.

Consider a company like 3M, where growth from new products is the corporate strategy—and innovation has been the central value since six Minnesota miners ended up owning a worthless gravel pit and invented sandpaper. Today with $15 billion in sales and 58,000 products, this value permeates the entire company. Inventing products *is* the culture. Every employee knows it. The result? 3M has the highest ratio of new product revenue (30 percent plus) of any large company in the world. Would 3M achieve this remarkable strategic result without a powerful and pervasive culture of innovative action? Never, in a hundred years.

2. CUSTOMER/PRODUCT VISION

"The computer is the most remarkable tool we've ever built . . . but the most important thing is to get them in the hands of as many people as possible."

—STEVE JOBS
FOUNDER, APPLE COMPUTER, NeXT INC., PIXAR

Steve Jobs wasn't talking about how to manage, or the latest marketing technique, or even how to grow Apple Computer. He was, and still is, obsessed with the two most fundamental ideas in enterprise—customer and product. He said the only thing more important than making computers was having satisfied customers actually use them. Of course, along the way, Apple reached the *Fortune 500* roster faster than any company in history.

What was the big secret? Jobs had a big vision. A vision of "the most remarkable tool we've ever built." But then he continues: "the most important thing" is to get them used in every office, in every home, and by every child in every classroom. Like no other computer maker, Jobs understood the needs of naïve users. That's why Apple made them inexpensive, easy to learn, and fun to use. Jobs was an expert on both products and customers. The classic vision of an entrepreneur.

The really important lesson to draw from Jobs and from most great entrepreneurs is that, at heart, they are craftsmen. They have a single, integrated vision of customers and products. They know they need both to survive. They are, in fact, obsessed with making products that customers will buy. But along came the modern functional organization, with its all-out quest for efficiency, and in one fell swoop the craftsman was killed. The functional separation of customer and product is the single most devastating blow to the entrepreneurial spirit ever concocted by management science.

This is not a theoretical problem. Losing the entrepreneur's integrated vision of customer and product can cost you dearly. The classic example is Xerox, which has lost billions over the years by inventing products in California that the Marketing Department, 3,000 miles away in Connecticut, simply never got around to selling. The first personal computer, the first fax machine, the first laser printer—the list of Xerox innovations goes on and on. Today companies all over the world are trying to put their functionalized organizations back together. They could have saved themselves a lot of trouble by watching Eiji Toyoda at Toyota. In 1947, on his only trip to America, he became fascinated with the supermarkets' daily delivery of milk from the cow to the customer. He saw this as the ultimate customer-driven organization. He decided to make cars this way. He organized horizontally, called it *kanban,* and the rest is history.

To regain customer/product vision, you can start by tossing out those convoluted five-page job descriptions and replace them with three simple questions: Who are my customers? What are my products? And what must I do to satisfy my customers? The message is simple: *Everyone* has a small business to run. This sounds simple but the number of employees who can't answer these basic questions is shocking. And a final thought—it's not a one-year program. It has to be a lifetime obsession, as it's been for Charles Forte. From one sweet shop on Oxford Street to the 800 hotels in the Trusthouse Forte empire, he's been absolutely consistent on product quality and customer service—and he's been at it for sixty-five years. It may sound monotonous but it has one redeeming virtue: If you do it long enough and hard enough, you get very, very good at it.

3. HIGH-SPEED INNOVATION

We Japanese are obsessed with survival.

—AKIO MORITA
FOUNDER, SONY CORPORATION

High-speed innovation is the entrepreneur's ultimate weapon—and it's virtually free. Entrepreneurial Davids like nothing better than competing against muscle-bound Goliaths. So where does high-speed innovation come from? For starters you can be sure it's not a genetic trait. And the current fads of setting up innovation departments or hiring consultants to teach creativity miss the point by a mile. It's a natural, human response we all possess, and the bottom line is, anyone can be innovative and move with the speed of light if his life depends on it. We all know that more gets done in a day of crisis than a month of complacency. The trick, then, is to keep this sense of urgency alive in the business—so that innovation becomes a necessity and everyone has the freedom to act, and act quickly.

While the rest of the world were convincing themselves that the Japanese weren't innovators, Akio Morita was crawling around on his hands and knees in a bombed-out building in Tokyo, cutting long strips of newsprint and coating it with ferrous oxide to make recording tape. Like everyone else in postwar Japan, the young founder of Sony was "obsessed with survival." With no jobs, money, or raw materials, creating something that someone might buy was an absolute necessity to putting rice on the table. This goes to the heart of the matter, proving once again that necessity is the mother of invention. It also helps explain why a too big, too comfortable bureaucracy is the last place you'll find high-speed innovation. But you don't have to wait for disaster to strike to get your innovative juices flowing. You can start today. A daily dose of urgency and an occasional injection of crisis is guaranteed to conquer anyone's complacency.

Just moving quickly could be the greatest innovation of all for big business. But what it takes is the freedom to act, not exactly an abundant resource in procedure-driven companies. Take the race against time to dominate the world's newest super-industry, biotech. Here's an industry promising more change in medicine and agriculture in the next ten years than in the last hundred—and a huge $100 billion market. Actually the race is over and the entrepreneurs have won hands down. While the giant pharmaceutical companies researched it to death through layers of management, a thousand scientist-turned-entrepreneur start-ups have exploded on the scene since 1980. As Ed Penhoet, Ph.D. and founder of industry star Chiron, says: "Everyone's smart in the field, but smart doesn't make it. Biotech is a horse race. Getting to the finish line first is what counts." High-speed innovation could be anyone's or any organization's ultimate weapon. Why not? All it takes is feeling the necessity to do it better—and the freedom to do it faster.

4. SELF-INSPIRED BEHAVIOR

I'm looking for people who love to win. If I run out of those, I want people who hate to lose.

—ROSS PEROT
FOUNDER, EDS, PEROT SYSTEMS

Self-inspired behavior—perhaps the sharpest difference of all between entrepreneurs and bureaucrats. But what does this phrase actually mean? What are entrepreneurs self-inspired to do? When I think of legends like Perot, or William Lever, or Soichiro Honda, a couple of images always come to mind. First, they love what they do—they're highly committed to their work. And second, they constantly try to get better at what they do—their performance is high. These two ideas, high commitment and high performance, are the backbone of an entrepreneurial approach to work. When you think about it, it's pretty tough to beat people who love what they do and are damn good at doing it.

The much tougher question is how do we create self-inspired employees? Alongside Lever and Honda, no company leader ever did a better job at this than Ross Perot, the quintessential American entrepreneur. Of course, it's also Perot who loves to fire off Texas-sized sound bites like "people who love to win and hate to lose." This one, however, is based on a very solid idea. It's the idea that drives almost all human behavior. Since the beginning of time, people have tended to behave in their own self-interest: They do things that bring them positive consequences and they avoid doing things that bring negative consequences. What this really means at work is that everybody wants an answer to that eternal question: What's in it for me if I do, and what happens to me if I don't?

Entrepreneurs are mightily self-inspired to win and not lose because they face the consequences, positive or negative, of their behavior every day. This almost never happens in a bureaucracy. In some companies, nothing much good happens to people even when they and the company perform well. In other companies, everyone gets a pat on the back and an annual increase even if the enterprise is headed for the trash heap. The most common situation, however, is the complete absence of either positives or negatives. Managers and workers just float in perpetual limbo, oblivious to the fortunes or misfortunes of the company and their part in it all. If you boil it down to one thing, the single biggest difference between entrepreneurial and bureaucratic behavior is answering the "what's in it for me" question. Entrepreneurs get their answers powerfully and frequently. Companies must do the same if they're really looking for high performance and high commitment from workers. You're never going to revive the enterprise if you can't revive the enterprisers.

STARTING OVER WITH THE BASICS

The inclination of my life has been to do things and make things which will give pleasure to people in new and amazing ways. By doing that I please and satisfy myself.
—WALT DISNEY
FOUNDER, THE WALT DISNEY COMPANY

Walt Disney said it best. He described the four fundamental practices of entrepreneurs perfectly: "Inclination" as *mission;* "making things and giving pleasure to people" is all about *customer/product vision;* "new and exciting ways" is a perfect description of *innovation;* and, finally, "by doing that I please myself" speaks to the *self-inspired nature of his work.*

These are the simple things you need to address regularly, and never neglect. If you're not doing them now, it's time to learn these very old lessons, very fast. It's time to forget the great myths and start over with the simple truths of enterprise: sense of mission, absolute focus on customer and product, a lot of innovative action, and self-inspired people. They may just be your last, best hope for creating prosperity for yourself, your company, and your country in the entrepreneurial age.

WELCOME TO THE ENTREPRENEURIAL AGE

If the nineteenth century gave us the industrial age, and the twentieth century produced the managerial age, all the current signs say the twenty-first century is shaping up as the Entrepreneurial Age. The coming age, like the earlier eras, will carry implications for the world beyond business. In many ways, the impact promises to be much broader and deeper than the earlier changes in the world of work. The growing popularity of entrepreneurship has not only captured the imagination of individuals everywhere, who are determined to start their own business, but also managers of giant organizations fighting for survival in a supercompetitive global economy, and even economic planners who believe a more entrepreneurial economy is the key to raising national prosperity.

The Entrepreneurial Age describes in practical terms, how those "fundamental practices of great entrepreneurs" can be applied to each of these three critical areas of economic life in the twenty-first century. The three areas, forming the core chapters of the book, are defined as follows:

➤ *Entrepreneurial People*

Getting entrepreneurial could very well be the best weapon you'll ever have to survive and prosper in the future world economy. It's no longer an alternative lifestyle for a few go-getters. Being prepared to survive by your own wits is an absolute necessity for everyone who has to work for a living. Like it or not, we're all part of it. From entrepreneurial education for school children, to "commercialization" training for scientists, to start-up financing available on an unprecedented scale, it seems everyone in the world is thinking about entrepreneurship. And well they should. It is truly everyone's last line of defense in a downsized and uncertain world.

➤ *Entrepreneurial Companies*

The need is great in all organizations, from *Global 1000* giants fighting for survival, to fast growing start-ups fending off bureaucracy, to smart government agencies that know they can be privatized in a New York minute. In a world where 70 percent of the original 1955 *Fortune 500* is gone, and 50 percent of all economic growth now comes from industries that didn't exist fifteen years ago, becoming an "entrepreneurial organization" is the only way to keep up. And with forward-thinking organizations such as Intel openly warning their employees to "get entrepreneurial," becoming a "corporate entrepreneur" is exactly what it's going to take to keep both you and your company in the game.

➤ *Entrepreneurial Countries*

The idea that entrepreneurship is the driving force of national prosperity has become a central theme of politicians and economists all around the world. There is unprecedented interest by governments in fostering "entrepreneurial economies" to create jobs and spur economic growth. From South Africa, Brazil, and Northern Ireland, to Singapore, New York City, and the State of Kentucky, governments are rethinking basic economic development policy of the past hundred years. The end result could be nothing less than unlocking the greatest unsolved mystery in economics: why some countries are rich and others are poor.

As you read and think about the great power of the entrepreneurial spirit—in creating success and prosperity for people, companies, and entire countries—I hope you will find *The Entrepreneurial Age* of great and practical value in your career and in your life.

—LARRY FARRELL, June 2000

part i
entrepreneurial people

Entrepreneurship—The Best Weapon You'll Ever Have to Survive a Downsized and Uncertain World

THE NEW ENTREPRENEURS:
They Are Us!

*As I said, everybody here has the ability absolutely to do any-
thing I do and much beyond. Some of you will, and some of
you won't. For the ones who won't, it will be because you get
in your own way, not because the world doesn't allow you.*
—WARREN BUFFETT
FOUNDER, BERKSHIRE HATHAWAY

Look around you. Seventy out of the next one hundred people you see are thinking about becoming an entrepreneur. Fifteen of the hundred will actually give it a go in the next twelve months. At least five will be successful on their first try. All of them, the dreamers, the doers, and the dazzling few, are part of the greatest explosion of entrepreneurship the world has ever seen. They all know the rules of survival have changed in a downsized and uncertain world. And more and more they believe the best weapon for winning the economic wars of the twenty-first century will be themselves—their labor, their knowledge, and their own entrepreneurial spirit. Of course, they're right. Whether you work for a giant company, someone else's mid-sized enterprise, or for yourself, getting entrepreneurial has become the name of this game. Like it or not, we're all working and living in the Entrepreneurial Age.

In modern industrial history, there have actually been two prior waves of important, but narrow, individual entrepreneurial activity. The first coincided with the rise of the industrial age in the 1860s to 1880s. It produced a few captains of industry and more than a few robber barons. The second, fueled by the promise of unlimited capital, occurred between 1910 and 1929, and was cut short by the Great Depression. In fact, these early eras produced few entrepreneurs, relative to the size of the workforce.

Even more striking, the entrepreneurial activity that did occur was severely limited in geographic scope. The United States and northwestern Europe accounted for an overwhelming share of the entrepreneurs. Certainly, in terms of historical significance, these earlier entrepreneurial bursts were swamped by much bigger socioeconomic waves. In the nineteenth century, the boom in entrepreneurial activity was just a necessary piece of the industrial age, along with mass production, organized labor, and the emergence of the first truly big businesses. All this fed into the twentieth century, whose early entrepreneurs became buried in the modern managerial age, and were quietly replaced by the organization man. The entrepreneur was effectively driven into second-class status for much of the century.

While these two earlier entrepreneurial eras produced some famous companies, and an impressive array of new technologies and products, nothing in our history has prepared us for what is occurring today. The current entrepreneurial revolution is simply unprecedented in size and scope. With over 2.5 million start-ups a year (1.3 million in the United States alone), the numbers are staggering. Even more dramatic is the truly global reach of this revolution. India, Brazil, and China are as chock full of entrepreneurial fervor as the United States. Even Japan has joined the trend, proving once again there's nothing like a good recession with a lot of American-style downsizing to get the entrepreneurial juices flowing. And money is no problem for the rising entrepreneur class. With $25 billion available from 300 venture capital firms and 250,000 private investors (as in "Silicon Valley angels"), and government "Enterprise Funds" springing up in every country, there's more start-up capital around than entrepreneurs of the past dared dream about. The fact is, the average cost of a business start-up in America is only around $14,000, and the two biggest sources of "entrepreneurial funding" are available to anyone: personal savings and credit cards. And take my word for it: The list of great companies started for less than $10,000 is very, very long.

All this leads to the most unique characteristic of our twenty-first–century entrepreneurial revolution: Very ordinary people are the main players. This is not a revolution being played out by or for the rich and powerful. It is a new page in economic history that welcomes the participation of everyone, from welfare-to-work graduates starting private day-care centers, to university scientists becoming biotech CEOs, to anyone reading this book who will make a product or deliver a service that someone, somewhere, needs.

Of course, the questions that may be on your mind are: What exactly would I do? If I quit my job, or, God forbid, get fired, or just want to do something when I retire, what would it be? And how would I go about it?

What should I really concentrate on, day in and day out, to ensure success? Well, read on. We've got the answers for you—the proven lessons of entrepreneurial enterprise. Learning these lessons may not turn you into the next Warren Buffett, but they are the guaranteed first step toward making sure you don't "get in your own way."

MORE MYTHS AND TRUTHS

When I started Microsoft, I was so excited that I didn't think of it as being all that risky. . . . The thing that was scary to me was when I started hiring my friends, and they expected to be paid.

—BILL GATES
COFOUNDER, MICROSOFT

In spite of the occasional high-profile oddball—Ross Perot comes to mind—entrepreneurs are not much different from you and me. The really good news is that no one, no matter what his station in life, is disqualified from playing this game. Evidence the fact that a whopping 15 percent of Americans now work at least part-time from home in a self-employed capacity. The reality is that millions of new businesses each year are fueling economies all around the world. The people behind these start-ups come from every walk of life. All the statistics show they're a pretty average lot. Most never planned to be entrepreneurs. It happens because of circumstance. It's usually a circumstance of crisis—like being dirt poor or feeling full of frustration or getting fired—the last of these being the number-one reason that people go into business for themselves. Yes, these are ordinary people who simply find themselves in extraordinary situations.

This point is important to remember as both business and the popular media bombard us with entrepreneurial myths. It's absolutely essential to keep this in mind if you're thinking about becoming an entrepreneur yourself. Here are some of the more damaging myths about people who create and build businesses.

MYTH NUMBER 1
Entrepreneurs are born, not made. It's in their genes. This is the most common myth of entrepreneurship.

The Truth
If you really believe it's genetic, you never visited communist East Germany. Listen to Claus Schröder, the founder of a container-shipping

business in Hamburg, describe what forty-five years of goose-stepping communism gets you. Claus says Germany's big gift at the end of the cold war was getting 20 million East Germans who wouldn't know a hard day's work if it were injected into their socialist veins. His parents were originally from the East and in the early nineties he eagerly expanded his business to the former communist region. Motivated by both family sentiment and business possibilities, his decision turned into a nightmare: "It's just unbelievable. I can't believe they're Germans. They have no concept of work. If the container ship isn't sitting at the dock when they arrive in the morning, they just go home for the day. The ship docks thirty minutes later for unloading and there it sits until tomorrow. Nobody thinks, nobody acts, nobody cares. I'm afraid the whole generation is lost. Maybe their children and grandchildren will be different." Entrepreneurs are born, not made? Baloney! In western Germany, you had hard-working, self-motivated people who transformed their land from total ruin to the world's third-richest economy. In eastern Germany, you had lazy, uninspired louts, looking for a government handout—and they all came from the same grandparents! The difference has nothing to do with genes. It has everything to do with their political, social, and economic environment. It really all boils down to one word, which we'll talk about a lot in this book—consequences.

Myth Number 2

Entrepreneurs all invented something in a garage when they were twelve, wear strange clothes to work, and speak in technobabble. We may have the same grandparents, but they are kind of weird and just different from you and me. I call this the "nerd" theory of entrepreneurship.

The Truth

The mundane facts are, the average entrepreneur is thirty-five to forty-five years old, has ten years plus experience in a large company, has an average education and IQ, and, contrary to popular myth, has a surprisingly normal psychological profile. Entrepreneurs dress, talk, and look a lot like you and me—a fairly average bunch.

Myth Number 3

The overriding goal is to be a millionaire. They do it for the money, pure and simple.

The Truth

Every shred of research belies this myth. Relatively few entrepreneurs ever earn the kind of bucks paid to CEOs these days. The entrepreneur's real obsession is to pursue his own personal sense of mission. Money is the necessary fuel to do this. Venture capitalists, shrewd evaluators of the entrepreneurial quotient in people, can spot the "get rich quick" types in a minute and avoid them like the plague.

MYTH NUMBER 4

Entrepreneurs are unscrupulous characters, ready to take legal shortcuts, and are generally on the prowl for suckers to screw. Reading between the lines, this myth really says that big, well-known corporations and their executives are more trustworthy than entrepreneurs.

The Truth

This nasty myth gets harder to believe every time another blue-chip corporate executive marches off to jail. And, compared to some well known CEOs, raking in their $10 million a year salary even as their employees and shareholders are bleeding, entrepreneurs don't seem so greedy after all. With the Sumitomo Bank scandal in Japan, the colossal fraud of Nick Leeson in bringing down Britain's oldest merchant bank, and Michael Ovitz's $92 million paycheck for fourteen months as president of Disney, the Hondas, Bransons, and Waltons of the world look more and more like saintly protectors of old-fashioned virtue. The unhappy fact is that low ethics and illegal tactics seem pretty well distributed throughout the population.

MYTH NUMBER 5

They're high risk takers. Real dart throwers.

The Truth

The subtitle of this chapter is: "Entrepreneurship is the best weapon you'll ever have to survive a downsized and uncertain world." That sentiment comes on good authority—every entrepreneur I've ever met believes the greatest risk today is to leave your future in the hands of a series of corporate bosses, all of whom have their own agendas to push. Betting on the corporate lottery for the next thirty years is a risk entrepreneurs weren't willing to take. So the "risk" of leaving a corporate job and starting out on your own has become, as they say, relative.

And once they get started, a lot of entrepreneurs turn downright conservative. They're still innovators but that doesn't make them fools. Remember: It's their money they're risking. The reality is big company executives regularly take greater risks with shareholders' money than entrepreneurs are willing to take with their own.

MYTH NUMBER 6

Getting an MBA is the way to go. Business school will now teach you how to be an entrepreneur.

The Truth

Save your $50,000 and go learn something useful that can help you create a product the world needs—just as 99.9 percent of the world's entrepreneurs still do. This myth is just the latest "big lie" propagated by the business education establishment to boost enrollments. Back in the eighties, the MBA factories saw that button-down, IBM-style management was out and entrepreneurial chaos, à la Apple Computer, was in. So they jammed a course on entrepreneurship in between financial management and long-range planning and called themselves the new breeding ground for the next Steve Jobs. Of course, they forgot how Steve Jobs himself complained about MBA managers after he hired some at Apple: "The managers we hired knew how to *manage* but they couldn't *do* anything." The moral? Until you learn how to *do* something, don't even think about becoming an entrepreneur.

START-UP: *THE* MOMENT OF TRUTH

Avoiding these common myths leads us back to the big question: What do you actually do when you start your own business? What will your priorities be on your first day as an entrepreneur? Here's a glimpse into how it usually works.

About fifteen minutes into the first morning of your new little business, it hits you like a ton of bricks. Who's going to pay your salary for the week? You certainly don't have a payroll department to cut a check. In fact, you don't even have the cash to cover a check. The sweat begins to break out on your forehead. Then, the moment of truth flashes before you: The only way you're going to get paid this week, and every week for the rest of your life, is to make something or do something that someone in the world will pay you cold, hard cash for. You need a product and a customer—this week—or your kids won't eat. Welcome to the world of true believers who know exactly why a clear customer/product vision is the most fundamental of all entrepreneurial practices.

Next, as you contemplate creating the product and finding a customer, two more insights hit home. First, you realize you have to do this very fast. So you start working at high speed—not because it's your natural bent, but because you have to get this done before you run out of cash. The second insight is this: The very best chance you will have of getting someone to buy your product is to make sure they see that it's different and better than other products they could buy. So you know you'll have to be a bit creative and innovative to come up with something that is better, or cheaper, or faster, or easier to use, or *something* to give you the competitive edge. You've now learned, early in the game, why high-speed innovation is so important to entrepreneurs.

Jump forward a few days or even months. You've been able to create and produce a product or a service. And you've also been able to find, sell, and service a few customers. Now your thoughts turn to growing a bit. It's clear that you alone can handle the current product and customer load, but you can't do much more. There just aren't enough hours in the week. You're going to have to take on a partner or an employee to help you grow. So you search around for relatives, friends, or former colleagues who are willing to take a chance and sign on with your fledgling business. After you hire one of them, get him trained, pay him a couple of times, a brand new thought begins to sink in. If this first employee does bring in a few more customers over the next six months, the company will grow and everyone will be happy. If, on the other hand, this first employee doesn't bring in any customers for six months, you're probably facing bankruptcy. You see this as a matter of survival. Your employee sees it as something to cover in his first-year performance review. You've just tripped over the single greatest difference between entrepreneurial and employee behavior—having to face the real-life consequences, positive and negative, of your job performance. It's what fuels the next fundamental practice of entrepreneurship, which we call *self-inspired behavior.*

Somehow you survive all these challenges, and complete your first year as an entrepreneur with a nice little business and a bright future. You've become rightfully proud of what you and your small team have accomplished. You think that what you're doing is important, and it has the potential to create a lot of value. You even allow yourself to think you may be creating a bit of a legacy for future generations—or at least leaving a few footprints in the sand. You are now deep into that overarching entrepreneurial practice we've labeled *sense of mission.* An entrepreneurial sense of mission usually doesn't form until you begin to believe you're going to survive the start-up phase. You'll know you're getting it when, for the first time, you take a few quiet moments to contemplate what marvelous and profound things the company could achieve over the next several years. In other words, when you actually begin to sense the future mission of your creation.

So, yes, despite all the myths, the truth is the new entrepreneurs *are* us, and our coworkers, our friends, and even our families. And the things they, and you, will have to do as new entrepreneurs are not so strange or complicated after all. In fact, creating and building a company is sounding more and more like—well—a lot of common sense. For a complete look at each of the four fundamental practices of successful entrepreneurs, read on.

SENSE OF MISSION:
Leaving Footprints in the Sand

Tremendously important to me was the feeling that we were doing something that had a significance far beyond building a company or what the financial rewards could be. I was convinced we were doing something that had tremendous importance in the world.

—BENJAMIN B. TREGOE, PH.D.
COFOUNDER, KEPNER-TREGOE

Have you ever noticed that entrepreneurs talk a lot about their company or their product? My experience has been (and I should know after interviewing hundreds of them) that if you ask an entrepreneur, "How are you?" you get several hours of monologue about what a great product he invented or what a terrific company he started. It's gotten so bad that when I'm on a long flight and I think the person sitting next to me may be an entrepreneur, I put on the headset and try to avoid all conversation. A couple of years ago I took a flight from San Francisco to Singapore. It takes about twenty hours, so you have to be careful who you sit next to. On this particular flight, my seatmate was a friendly-looking fellow from Seattle. I know Seattle is full of entrepreneurs but this guy looked more like an athlete than a business type, so I made the huge mistake of saying those fatal words: "How are you?" Sure enough, he was an entrepreneur—and I got twenty hours on how his fantastic product was going to change the world. And what was this earth-shattering product? Well, hang on to your seat. He and his company had come up with a machine that made perfect sand for golf courses. And since Asians love golf, they were falling all over themselves to get their hands on his wonderful machine—thus his travels across the Pacific. Now I don't play golf or even watch it on TV, but I heard more about sand and sand traps than I thought anyone could possibly know. Boring? You bet! But the point is this: The young entrepreneur from

Seattle really believed that he had created something of importance and value for the world. Value for his customers, for his employees back in Seattle, and, undoubtedly, for himself.

This is the built-in advantage of all entrepreneurs. They really believe they're doing something important, creating a lot of value, and in some small way, at least, leaving a footprint in the sand. They're on a mission—and that sense of mission gives them incredible energy, desire, and pride. When is the last time you met a government or corporate bureaucrat with a true sense of mission about his work? Or one who talked your ear off for hours about what a fabulously important thing he was doing for the world? Not lately? That's the point. We call it having a *sense of mission* and it's the first, fundamental practice of entrepreneurship.

THE *WHAT* AND THE *HOW* OF THE MISSION

If you ask an entrepreneur, "What's your sense of mission?" he may look at you like you're crazy—or at least suspect you're a management consultant. Entrepreneurs aren't typically up on such fancy-sounding phrases. But what they are up on, and can articulate with unbelievable clarity, is *what* they're doing and *how* they go about doing it. When you think about it, to succeed at any mission—whether it be a business mission, a military mission, or a political mission—you absolutely have to know these two things: what the mission is, and how you're going to accomplish it. We've labeled these two critical aspects of the sense of mission the *strategy* (the *what*) of the business and the *culture* (the *how*) of the business. If the words strategy and culture sound a bit grandiose to describe your first time entrepreneurial start-up, just call them your *business plan* and your *business values.* Whatever we call them, being very good at both—setting a smart strategy and creating a strong, supportive culture—is a characteristic all great entrepreneurs share. It is also absolutely necessary to the creation of a successful, high-growth enterprise.

One of the most articulate entrepreneurs I've ever come across on this point is a man named Ben Tregoe[1] in Princeton, New Jersey. Tregoe, a Harvard Ph.D., left the Rand Corporation (the famous think tank) and founded a company to do one thing: to teach business people around the

---

[1]Our description of the entrepreneurial approach to strategy is influenced by and in part modified from the original work of my friend and former boss, Dr. Benjamin B. Tregoe. These descriptions and modifications appear in Part One and more significantly in Part Two of the book. We have applied his description of strategy to the entrepreneurial approach for one reason only—it so clearly illustrates why entrepreneurs do what they do. I highly recommend Ben Tregoe's (or Kepner-Tregoe, Inc.'s) own books and advisory services on the broader subject of corporate strategy.

world how to improve their analytical decision-making skills. In 1958 that was kind of a nutty idea. Nobody even thought about how to do that. Forty years later, the firm he cofounded, Kepner-Tregoe, Inc., has taught some 5 million people around the world, in over twenty languages, exactly how to do that. Ben Tregoe is truly a man with a mission.

Just listen to him. You can feel it in his words:

"We had this strong sense that we were onto something here that was terribly important. Something that could help improve the quality of the world. We had this feeling, and it sounds very presumptuous to say, but we felt that we could really improve the rationality of the world and it was terribly important to get this out to companies everywhere. We believed we could help improve the communication between organizations and between people. This sense of purpose, this sense of mission, is tremendously important. I mean, I know if we had started the business and just said, 'It looks like we can make some money doing this, so let's try it and so on,' we never could have gotten this thing up and running. It was too damn difficult."

Tregoe's sense of mission, however, wasn't based on hyperbole or theoretical pie in the sky: "When you talk about the strategy of a company, when you talk about the direction that any company is going, it all boils down to your values, your beliefs, and your basic purpose, and then to a real understanding of the product and market. I mean all this stuff about strategy and so on, if it doesn't get down to product/market and your product/market priorities, you really don't have anything. The way you describe any organization, a company or a nonprofit, is basically what products and services does it offer and to whom does it offer them."

Tregoe also knows what it takes to stay true to your sense of mission over time: "A statement of purpose, the beliefs or values of a company, the product/market statement or strategy statement of a company is essential. But it's only useful if it's guiding what the organization does. If it's guiding the decision making on a day-to-day basis. And the only way it's going to guide the behavior of a company on a day-to-day basis, is if it's filed up here in the heads of the people in the business. And that means it's got to be pretty specific and pretty simple."

The bottom line is this: Entrepreneurs are highly focused on both *what* they are doing (the strategy or plan) and *how* they go about doing it (the culture or values). Whether you're General Motors or a one person start-up, the challenge is to be great at both. It's not good enough to have a smart business plan, but a weak, disconnected set of operating values. Conversely, strong values will never overcome a stupid plan. And, of course, you won't be around long if you know neither what to do *nor* how to do it.

SENSE OF MISSION

	−	+
+	stupid plan strong values	smart plan strong values	**+**
"HOW" **Business** **Values**	stupid plan weak values	smart plan weak values	
−			**−**
	−	+

"WHAT" Business Plans

New entrepreneurs quickly learn that while both the *what* and the *how* are essential, the plan of the business comes first. You have to know what you're doing before you can determine how to do it. This relationship between your company plan and your company values is often lost as the organization grows big and all manner of management practices are adopted. The reality is, until you set the *what* of the business—what markets to approach, what products to offer, and so on—you have no idea what kind of operating values and priorities you need. Indeed, the only purpose of developing a set of company values is to get absolutely focused and operationally superb on those few things that will ensure that your business plan succeeds. And the operating factors that are essential for company A, may not be important at all for company B. For example, if you're starting a commuter airline, safety had better be at the top of your values list. There's no faster way to bankrupt an airline than having a few headline-grabbing crashes. On the other hand, if your entrepreneurial start-up is in the software business, where the life cycle of each product is less than six months, product innovation and speed are the values you will need to focus on.

One of the great mistakes young companies make is to read about and then try to copy the culture and values of some big company they admire. The values of Daimler-Benz or Sony or Wal-Mart may have worked wonders for them, but that doesn't mean the same values will make your company plans come true. To keep on track with this fundamentally important point, simply go back to the basic purpose and relationship of the *what* and the *how:* First determine what you are going to do, and then get very good at those few things that are crucial to doing it.

CREATING ENTREPRENEURIAL BUSINESS PLANS

There is no more overhyped and overused business activity than corporate strategy and planning. For some never-explained reason, this rather passive aspect of enterprise has generated more books, techniques, diagrams, and consultant engagements than anything else. And, almost without exception, would-be entrepreneurs at business schools are advised that the most important step in starting up a company is to write a great business plan. Three hundred pages with lots of charts and financial projections is strongly recommended. Of course, no one bothers to remind the eager-beaver MBA students or, for that matter, the millions of cubicle-bound bureaucrats dreaming about striking out on their own, that no great enterpriser from Lorenzo de Medici to Bill Gates ever started a business this way.

Fortunately, there is a simpler way to make up a business plan. It's the old-fashioned, entrepreneurial way. First, ask yourself what you really like to do and what you are really good at doing. Make as complete an inventory as possible. Then examine what needs are going unmet, or are being poorly met, in markets you're familiar with, for which you could possibly produce a superior product or service. And, finally, for each possible product/market idea you've come up with, rate your likely competitive position against the very best providers you know of for that particular product or service. By making these assessments, you will find the product/market business(es) that carry the highest chance of success for you as an entrepreneur.

Does this sound too simple? Would you feel better with something more sophisticated? Do you want to conduct a full market study, bring in focus groups, and produce reams of financial analysis? Certainly, you can do all that and more—if you've got all the time in the world and buckets full of money. Just put this book down and get ready to spend the next year of your life doing research and writing a business plan. But remember—that's not the way great entrepreneurs have ever done it since the beginning of time. If you want to try their way first, read on.

Here are the questions you need to ask. Knowing the answers won't *guarantee* your entrepreneurial success. But it will guarantee that you have asked yourself the rock-bottom questions every entrepreneur in the world must ultimately answer:

➤ *What Do I Have a Passion For?*
What do I really like to do?

➤ *What Product or Services Could I Provide?*
What am I really good at doing?

➤ *What Customers/Markets Might I Pursue?*
What is the market need for products or services based on the things I
like to do or am good at doing?

➤ *What Competitive Position Would I Have?*
For each possibility, what would my competitive position be, compared
to the best providers of similar products and services to my projected
markets?

That's right, the questions are all about products and markets.
There may be other things to examine, but I will *guarantee* you this: These
questions have to be answered. Disregard them at your peril. Which is
another way of saying that, if you can't answer them, do yourself (and your
family) a huge favor and don't quit your day job just yet!

As Ben Tregoe says: "If it [your business plan] doesn't get down
to product/market and your product/market priorities, you really don't
have anything." To the entrepreneur, the *what* of the enterprise always
revolves around this question: What customers and what products will
we pursue? After all, customer and product are not functions or departments of the business: They *are* the business. Being wrong about either
of these two questions puts you on the road to bankruptcy. In this environment, strategy and planning have to be all about choosing the right
products and markets. So the business plan, however it is done, takes on
specific meaning and awesome importance. Being close to customers
and products is not just a good idea; it's the most valuable weapon the
entrepreneur has in making the most critical decisions in business. The
more we see, the more an entrepreneurial plan looks like a blueprint for
survival. It sure doesn't look anything like strategic planning à la
Harvard Business School. The entrepreneurial approach may not be so
elegant or sophisticated, but it has one redeeming quality: It works wonders for getting new businesses up and running.

PICKING MARKET/PRODUCT WINNERS
Whether your planning process is formal or informal, six months
out or ten years, uses discounted cash flows or numbers on a napkin—the
part you have to get right is what customers you are targeting and what
products you are offering. So how do you do this? First of all, where do
you even come up with market and product ideas? Then how do you
choose among them? What criteria should be guiding your choices? Are
there any rules to follow in picking customers/markets and products or

services? You are now face to face with the number one question in enterprise. As Tregoe so simply put it: "What products and services will you offer and to whom will you offer them?" You can read a ton of research and hire a thousand consultants to help you figure this out, but at the end of the day, there are just three things you absolutely, positively, have to do. Here they are:

➤ Stay Focused on Customers
Think of every market you know anything about, either as a customer or just an observer. What needs do you see that are going unmet or are not being met satisfactorily? Carefully thinking this through can be a rich source of business ideas for entrepreneurs. Thomas Watson, the founder of IBM, used to say that the ideas for 95 percent of all IBM products came from customers. This is why staying focused on potential markets and customers is so important.

➤ Stay Focused on Products
What do you like to do? What are you good at doing? Answering these two questions happens to be the number-one way successful entrepreneurs identify the kind of business they start. So if you don't want to miss the greatest source of entrepreneurial ideas you'll ever have, you had better stay focused on possible products and services.

➤ Know the Criteria That Count
There are only two make-or-break criteria in choosing markets and products. They are *market need* and *competitive position*. Entrepreneurs always want to know the specific needs of the markets they enter and every possible way they can raise the competitive position of the products they offer.

So in choosing the products and markets for your start-up venture, you have to know the answers to these simple questions: "How good is my market?" and "How good is my product?" The market need you may pursue can range from great in every way to downright lousy. And the competitive position of your product can be anywhere from the best in the world to absolutely awful. To keep it simple, we'll just use "big" and "small" to rate market need, and "high" and "low" for competitive position.

The best story to illustrate the power of these two criteria actually occurred, believe it or not, on one of those dreaded, long flights sitting next to an entrepreneur. It was the Stockholm to New York run, and the Swedish scientist in the next seat was already giving me his life story: "So I now live in Florida. . . . I used to be an R&D director for Squibb Pharmaceutical. . . . I worked at their headquarters in Lawrenceville, New Jersey. . . . After years of seeing Squibb reject so many good products because the market need was not big enough for them, I left to start my own small medical products business. . . ." Whoa! This was getting interesting. I turned ever so slightly toward him, airplane etiquette for "OK, you've got my attention, so please make it good." He not only made it good, he provided a terrific entrepreneurial application of the market need/competitive position idea.

As he told it, everyone in the industry knows there are hundreds of small, unmet needs in the medical and pharmaceutical markets. Giant companies, like his former employer, can't afford to even think about them. A "tiny" $25 million market doesn't get a second look—according to my seatmate. His first product, diapers for elderly people, was a no-brainer. There was a small but real need in the market, and no one was producing diapers specially for aging adults. He leased time at one of the numerous medical research facilities available today, perfected his design, contracted for production and distribution, and had his first successful product. He agreed that it fit squarely in the upper left-hand corner of the Market Need/Competitive Position matrix: small market need/high competitive position.

This led to a full discussion of his broad perspective on inventing products for different types of markets, first as a small cog in a giant wheel and now as the "big wheel" in his own business. As he described the rich array of market and product possibilities in the industry, he verbally categorized each one. So we can, courtesy of my Swedish seatmate, complete the explanation of the Market Need/Competitive Position matrix with examples from the world of medicine.

I can't bring myself to label the upper left-hand quadrant the "elderly diaper business." But never mind; there are plenty of limited medical needs in the world for which there are no products or only inferior products. Take elephantiasis, for example. A form of leprosy, it's a horrible disease with a relatively small number of cases—and no cure. And why is there no cure? Mostly because it's a small market and the Squibbs of the world aren't working on a cure for it. Suppose you and your team make a breakthrough and discover the cure. You would have a classic example of a small market need/high competitive position product. The "elephantiasis business" category is a common place for entrepreneurs. They can do extremely well in these niche-type businesses.

How about the flip side of the "elephantiasis business"? Think of the biggest display section in every drugstore in America. That's right; it's the "painkiller" section. It seems that all 280 million Americans are suffering from headaches, the flu, and allergies. There are dozens of brands and hundreds of variations. They all make the same claims and have similar-sounding ingredients, allowing, of course, for the big medical innovation of nonaspirin "aspirin." I recently noticed that the ingredients are exactly the same for two separate products from the same company. Check it out. Extra Strength Excedrin and Migraine Excedrin are identical, right down to the 65 milligrams of caffeine in each. Why all this marketing madness? Because the market is so damn big. We call it the "headache business" and it perfectly fits the big market need/low competitive position quadrant of the matrix. Entrepreneurs can prosper here as well, if they're ready to compete on price at the low end of the market.

The place no entrepreneur wants to be is in the small market need/ low competitive position quadrant. There are plenty of recognizable medical needs here—mostly diseases that have been virtually wiped out years ago like polio, smallpox, and scarlet fever. These are markets that are dead or dying, and even if they weren't, the old product patents have expired and everyone could be in the market tomorrow with a me-too, low-cost cure. Anyway, the "polio business" arena is no place for fast-moving, entrepreneurial start-ups. There's little money to be made here by entrepreneurs, pure and simple. Interestingly, some old, big companies, not necessarily pharmaceutical manufacturers, do seem to keep plugging away in this quadrant. Instead of hanging on with commodity products in dying markets, they should probably kill these businesses and move on to something with a future.

And finally we come to the place where most big companies and entrepreneurs dream about—the big market need/high competitive position quadrant. Think about this. The number-one killer in the world, for both men and women, has always been and still is heart disease. There have been advances in treating all types of heart problems, but there's still no cure in sight. What if—and here comes the dream—what if you and your band of entrepreneur-scientists come up with the absolutely perfect, rejection-free, artificial heart. You could give a lifetime guarantee to your customers, which is a lot better than they get when they're born. So your "heart disease business," would rank right up there with the wheel, electricity, cars, computers, and penicillin, as one of history's true blockbuster products. Can entrepreneurs be successful in this arena? Absolutely. Success is virtually guaranteed—with one caveat. You may become too successful. Getting too successful here will practically guarantee hordes of envious competitors, and open the door to government busybodies, all of whom will do almost anything to take you down several pegs. Ask AT&T, IBM, and Microsoft how it works. So go for it by all means—and get ready to take the heat of intense competition and the weight of maddening government regulation.

To summarize, here's how the four medical examples would be positioned using the criteria of market need and competitive position:

PICKING WINNERS

high ↑	**"elephantiasis business"** Small Market Need High Comp. Position	**"heart disease business"** Big Market Need High Comp. Position
Competitive **Position**	**"polio business"** Small Market Need Low Comp. Position	**"headache business"** Big Market Need Low Comp. Position
low		

small ————————————→ **big**
Market Need

Beyond helping you pick market/product winners and getting your entrepreneurial venture off the ground, the two criteria—market need and competitive position—will continue to be important as you grow. They will always tell you what kind of actions you need to take to improve each of your market/product businesses. For example, if you're in the small market need/high competitive position quadrant, you need to find more customers for your great product. So a focus on marketing, distribution, exporting, and the like would be essential to growing your business. Conversely, if you're in the big market need/low competitive position quadrant, you need to raise the competitiveness of your product. This means that improving product innovation, quality, and costs would be key to generating more growth. The bottom line is this: These criteria will help you grow your business—which is what all entrepreneurs are after.

CREATING ENTREPRENEURIAL BUSINESS VALUES

If planning is the most overused management practice in business, creating and maintaining values is surely the most misused. A couple of decades ago, the whole subject of corporate culture and values burst on the scene. It was quickly co-opted by industrial psychologists, organizational development gurus, and various other corporate do-gooders. They hoisted values up as the new-age redefinition of the purpose of enterprise. Every big corporation worth its salt had to have a mission statement, and framed editions of company values began popping up on office and factory walls everywhere. It quickly became the new, lucrative area in the field of management consulting. Being good to customers, employees, shareholders, communities, and anyone else the "values task force" could think of, passed as evidence that you were an enlightened and presumably successful company. This was clearly the route to take to get on one of those annual lists of "best companies." A lot of otherwise good managers actually began to believe that business values were things you dreamed up in a staff committee, plastered on every available wall, and then forgot about when you went back to your real job. All this was, and is, downright ridiculous.

While such shenanigans may sound silly in hindsight, they were actually quite damaging. Creating cleverly worded value statements became a goal unto itself. Wall plaques displaying the corporate mission statement and core values evolved into an official statement of *how* to operate, with virtually no regard to *what* the business was all about. As discussed a few pages earlier, the purpose—the *only* purpose—of creating and maintaining business values is to make sure you focus on and get very good at those few operating factors critical to the accomplishment of your business plan. Exhorting everyone to pursue a company culture that is unrelated to the company strategy is a fundamental disconnect for any business.

Entrepreneurs clearly have to get this right. Concentrating your energies on becoming the best in the world at one or two key things produces powerful, competitive advantages. This is why focusing on a few performance-defining values that directly support your market/product plan is so important. Nowhere is this more true than with the young start-up venture. In the not-so-complex world of the entrepreneur, it sometimes seems to naturally come with the territory. But be forewarned: Your entrepreneurial values probably won't sound anything like the beautifully crafted platitudes of the *Global 1000*. For example, if you're a small player in a very competitive, low-margin business, you quickly learn that letting up on cost control, from salaries to paper clips, is a one-way ticket to bankruptcy. But cost control rarely makes it onto a big company's list of values. The reasons are clear: The value statement has nothing to do with the product/market plan, and, anyway, cost control doesn't have that warm fuzzy ring big business PR departments like to promote. Fortunately, the start-up entrepreneur doesn't carry any of that big business baggage, and the question of "What should our business values be?" can be answered directly and simply.

First, the question has to be answered by you, the entrepreneur of the business. It can't be delegated. It's essentially your answer to "How am I going to go about my business?" The answers will determine what's important to do and not to do in the enterprise and, ultimately, how all employees should behave toward customers and products. The answers also specify the company's mission overall. The values you choose should be based on two no-nonsense criteria: "What behavior will give us competitive advantage and what behavior must we be personally committed to without compromise?" So here are the two criteria you have to use in creating your entrepreneurial business values:

➤ ### How Can I Raise my Competitive Advantage?
What values, behaviors, or practices will most powerfully raise your competitive position? Which of those practices are absolutely critical to the successful accomplishment of your market/product plan? Product quality? Innovation? Employee relations? Customer service? Cost efficiency? Fast action? Whatever those few items are, they must become the operating values of your business.

➤ ### How Can I Get Everyone Committed?
Becoming the very best in the world at those few practices most critical to your competitiveness requires an uncompromising, emotional commitment from you as the leader. Ultimately, it will also require the personal commitment of at least a critical mass of your entire workforce. This means your own day-in-and-day-out behavior, the organization rituals and practices you instill, and most certainly the reward/punishment system you put in place for your employees, must all support and reinforce your business values. This process is the entrepreneurial way to bring business values to life in an organization—and the best way in the world to get groups of disparate people to focus on and achieve a common goal.

So fostering an entrepreneurial business culture, underpinned by the specific values that will give you the most competitive advantage, has little to do with those feel-good platitudes you've seen decorating the walls of big business and big government. Instead, entrepreneurial business values are the most powerful weapons ever invented to beat your competitors and ensure the accomplishment of your market/product business plan.

KEEPING IT ALIVE

Sure, you have to get the business going before you start worrying about keeping it alive. But in the spirit of "an ounce of prevention," a final thought on business values may be worth its weight in gold. Obviously, the core values of your business have to be reinforced day in and day out to do you any good. If your values are indeed: "those few operating factors critical to the accomplishment of your business plan," letting them die is exactly what you can't afford to do. So for your future reference, at least, the three greatest influences on keeping values alive are: the daily behavior of your senior management; the organization rituals and practices you develop; and, of course, the reward and penalty systems you install to manage your people. If these all-important "cultural influencers" support your company values, you can be sure the values you put in place will stay alive. If they don't support your values, or even worse, subvert them, your values will be quickly lost—and with them, the best insurance you could ever have for achieving your entrepreneurial dreams.

Going right to the central point of this book, you might decide that you can gain a lot of competitive advantage by making "entrepreneurial behavior on the job" a core business value. But what if, after five years, there's still no employee stock ownership program, and the pay-for-performance plan is a joke. Plus, the "promote from within" policy doesn't seem to apply to any opening above that of clerk, and everyone has learned that the surest way to get in trouble is to try something new without getting prior approval. Finally, even worse than not seeing rewards for "being entrepreneurial," it's become clear that there's no penalty for the bureaucrats in the company who don't even try. You don't have to be a rocket scientist to answer the "what if" question. Anyone could figure out that the "being entrepreneurial" value never got off the ground in this company.

And speaking of rocket scientists, it should be clear by now that it doesn't take one to have an entrepreneurial sense of mission. It's all simple stuff: creating simple plans, picking market/product winners, determining a few values, and keeping them alive. But it's also powerful stuff. If you want to see just how simple and powerful it can really be, the closing story of this chapter will do it. Welcome to the Mission of Buel Messer—and one of the truly unforgettable characters I've ever known.

THE MISSION OF BUEL MESSER

How can a blind man rustle cattle? Not very well. That's why I got caught.

—BUEL MESSER
FOUNDER, MESSER LANDSCAPE, INC.

On a snowy Friday in 1980, Buel Messer was home. He didn't have work. There weren't a lot of career possibilities for a convicted felon, a cattle rustler. Out of boredom and frustration, he grabbed his two young sons and a shovel: "Let's go shovel some snow for the neighbors." He needed the boys to be his "eyes." Buel Messer is blind.

Hardly the stuff of a great story of enterprise? Think again. It's just a little more earthy than you'll find in the *Harvard Business Review*. From shoveling snow and mowing lawns, always with his boys, Messer has created a multimillion dollar landscaping empire. Today, Messer Landscape has thriving retail operations and a booming wholesale tree business, and large commercial projects are taken in stride. Not bad for a blind ex-con turned entrepreneur. Buel Messer's story has a lot of lessons. The one we're interested in here is all about building a business—to feed your family and regain your name—and doing it without resources, without theories, with absolutely nothing but a driving sense of mission.

Messer was born dirt poor in the impoverished hills of eastern Kentucky. He was also born with optic atrophy, leaving him with only a tiny sliver of sight, about 5 percent, in one eye. He struggled through grammar school and was finally admitted to a state-supported high school for the blind in Ohio. School didn't interest him, but competitive athletics did. On a sports scholarship, he went off to college. To see if he could do it, he made the Dean's List his first and last semesters in college. In between, he was an intercollegiate wrestling champion, and set the state record for the mile in Ohio. In a moment of glory, he ran in Madison Square Garden on national TV, against the world record holder, Jim Ryan. Ryan blew the field off with one of the first "under four minute" miles on an indoor track. Still, a pretty good day's work for a poor, blind kid from Kentucky.

Because of his boundless energy and his triumph over his own handicap, Messer was a natural as a role model for handicapped students. He threw himself into his first job at the School for the Visually

Handicapped in Wisconsin. There he became interested in helping the multiple-handicapped and started graduate study at night. In Wisconsin, he met and married his wife of thirty-five years, also a sightless person. From there, Messer transferred to the Virginia School for the Deaf and Blind. He completed his master's degree in education at the University of Virginia and enrolled in the doctoral program.

Being an academic in the challenging but specialized world of teaching the handicapped wasn't the only thing Messer thought he could do. Along the way, he dabbled in other things that he knew, like farming. He started a small cattle and hog operation. For several years he taught by day and worked the farm all night. Being a farmer-entrepreneur became more and more the passion of his life. He expanded the business. In the early days, financing was relatively easy to come by. His reputation was excellent. He expanded again and again. But he was getting deeper and deeper into debt. With the first hint of trouble, the lenders cut off his credit. Now everything was at risk. He didn't know where to turn—until one black night, when he signed on with a group of desperadoes to make a few "easy" bucks and his world fell apart. In a single act of desperate dishonesty, Buel Messer's hard-earned accomplishments and his family's modest but honorable way of life, came crashing down around him.

When I first learned about his earlier criminal activity, like most people, I was overcome by curiosity. So I asked Messer, How could it be? In his always upbeat and honest manner, he gave his classic answer: "How can a blind man rustle cattle? Not very well. That's why I got caught." Despite the novelty, judges and peers weren't amused. In rural Virginia, stealing livestock is as much a sin as a crime. Not only do first offenders do hard time in prison, they can do hard time forever back in their community. This was the bleak outlook on that snowy Friday in 1980. The family was wiped out financially. Messer was *persona non grata* in the academic world. And decent jobs didn't go to ex-cons. An eventual full pardon by the governor restored his voting rights, but not his dignity.

Never one to feel sorry for himself or blame others, Messer says of that period: "I didn't hold it against anybody. I was the one who created it, and I recognized that. I think the fact that I had, through my own bad judgment, committed the criminal acts way back then, has forced me to do things honestly and forthrightly ever since. I vowed that if I did anything the rest of my life, I was going to prove—not to everybody, I know that I'll never convince everybody—that I'm honest at what I do. It's been a challenge and a driving force for me."

Let's take Buel Messer at his word. The overarching mission of his life became the redemption of his honor. He had few options but to reach for it through his own enterprise. How has he done it? What exactly is his sense of mission? To get in sync with Messer's approach to business, it's necessary to relearn plain, blunt English. You'll find no "corporate-ese" here. Instead of *backward integration,* Messer says: "We had to have our own trees to sell"; and *market segmentation* gets translated into "little old lady types versus fussy lawyer and doctor types." Once you get the language down, you begin to understand that Messer speaks with a passion and focus rare in business. He knows his markets, he knows his products, and he knows exactly what it takes to beat his competitors. This is the "no frills" version of a sense of mission. It's creating business plans and business values—entrepreneurial style.

Starting with the snow shovel back in 1980, Buel's description of the start-up is pure passion: "I had to completely liquidate . . . while I was in prison, which was real depressing and demoralizing. . . . It really was rock bottom for me. I'm thinking all the time that there's got to be some way back to something. I've always had a lot of plans and thoughts, but my mind is fatigued. . . . So my two young sons, who were about nine and eleven years old at that point, and I went around the neighborhood shoveling snow for people. It began to look pretty lucrative. That gave me the idea that snow shoveling was really needed and was almost a public service–oriented type thing. So that week I stuck an ad in the paper, hoping to get something for the two kids and me that we could do together in the summer. We ran the ad: 'Wanted, in the North-End, Lawns to Mow for the Season.' This was in the first week of March. So we get about twenty-five or thirty responses to an ad that ran two or three weeks. We selected fifteen—well, between selecting and people deciding whether they wanted us—about fifteen lawns in our neighborhood. They had to be where we could ride a small riding lawn mower to and pull a small cart behind since I didn't drive and the boys weren't old enough. So that's the way Messer Landscape began. And that was twenty years ago this past season.

"I thought it'd be just a little something really to keep the boys occupied and out of trouble. That's what I thought. But I got tired of cooking and cleaning house pretty quickly. And I didn't know there were so many related things to doing those lawns that summer—that one we did just led to another. And I had more time now to think about things. You know, to really let some creative imagination take place. At any rate, we began to do some sidelines. A lot of them were retired people or little old ladies that we were working for. Those were the types we thought would be best, rather than work for doctors and lawyers and people who had lots of money. We felt they might be a problem for us. They'd be too fussy, and we didn't know what we were doing anyway. We thought that little old ladies would better put up with what we had. I should really say, only *I* thought that, because the boys didn't have any input at that point. It was hard enough keeping them working at it. Mainly they were my eyesight of course, early on, since I didn't see well enough to do what we were doing. With them I was able to actually mow the lawns myself and so forth. So, anyway, there was the thing of: 'Would you prune my shrubbery?' And I would say sure, we'll try it. We'd never pruned a bush of our own before but got to doing it and got to reading articles and things about how to do it. It just seemed pretty natural, after that. That first year we had a gross income of $5,400.

"I guess the next major step was a realtor/builder–type person I knew, who had two spec houses that he'd built. . . . He wanted to know if we'd be interested in taking some rakes and trying to rake that rough ground out and put in some grass for him. This was our second year. We'd expanded to the point where we had this one part-time guy with his own truck. Think he might have had his own wheelbarrow, too. Anyway, that's how we got back and forth to the job to do those houses. We did rake those out and put in seven or eight shrubs in front of them, mulched them, and miraculously the grass grew and everything did well. So right away, we're landscapers! My mind starts going kind of wild at that point."

Enterprise doesn't get any more basic. What's behind it? Doing something of value, something worthwhile, pursuing an honorable mission. This is what drives people to create miracles in all walks of life. It's what enables groups of people to do the impossible. Value-driven missions are personal. They don't come out of the mouths of consultants. Yours will be uniquely yours. Buel Messer's meant overcoming incredible odds to redeem his dignity: "It gave me an opportunity to prove that I was not altogether dishonest. Probably I've bent over backwards trying to prove my honesty all along the line. I will say this quite frankly: I've not knowingly or intentionally done one other dishonest thing since. I think I was trying to prove something. I was trying to prove that despite the terrible reputation that I had developed, I still could be a success and a viable entity in the business world and this community . . . which I feel like I have."

I asked Messer to describe how he goes about designing his company plans and whether or not he tries to create company values. As you might guess, his description of company plans and values is unadulterated common sense. It has none of the management consultant's conceptual elegance. It's not "big picture" stuff. Buel Messer's business plan comes straight from the marketplace. Where he's headed with customers and products underscores his knowledge of and respect for the market. He turns almost reverential when talking about it: "The plan is not from me . . . it's from the need in the marketplace. There's a strong need out there. I've been able to see areas where there's a strong need, or will be in the future, that I can capitalize on." His sense of gratitude toward customers borders on the Japanese approach: "I just feel really fortunate that we were able to convince the public that we would give them their money's worth and if something went wrong we'd make it right."

The key Messer Landscape value is a direct reflection of Buel Messer's eternally optimistic view of human potential. He sees his employees as great contributors to a great cause. His greatest responsibility is to make it all happen: "I love taking people, who maybe have not had a good opportunity or something of that sort, and motivating them, seeing them grow. And through their growth, the business is going to grow. I've always had the theory that you don't necessarily need to hire all the highly trained personnel that some people might see a need for. I feel like I'm a good teacher. I thrive on being able to develop people to help them to be better than they were. You've got to make people feel strong about themselves and be motivated. I would say being able to motivate and inspire people might be the secret to everything."

Our story wouldn't be complete without one real-life example of how Buel Messer keeps his mission alive. Clearly, personal integrity, honesty, and rising above your circumstances are important values to Messer. But how does he instill these values in his company—stuck in an industry notorious for high turnover, low wages, and temporary help? By chance, I came across a small but telling illustration of the extent to which Messer Landscape tries to communicate its values.

A Dartmouth College student needed a summer job. This Ivy Leaguer found himself interviewing for a lowly pick and shovel job at Messer Landscape. It turns out that even part-time laborers are hired primarily on the basis of their character. The interview was full of questions about honesty and integrity. Here's a sampling: "If the essence of law were defined as protection against insult and slander, would you consider yourself to be a law breaker? When was the last time you cheated on something? How do you feel about cheating? What do you feel to be your most important personal right? Talk about the last time your personal rights were violated." Messer's personnel manager went on to explain the purpose of these questions to the startled Dartmouth man: "The thing you can add to Messer Landscape, aside from doing the necessary work—the real thing, is going to come from your character. So we want to see what kind of character is inside of you. This helps us figure out whether or not you and Messer Landscape can work and grow together."

Such questions might not raise eyebrows at the Philosophy Department at Dartmouth, but they're a little surprising coming from a landscaping company in rural Virginia. What's not surprising is that they got the Ivy Leaguer's attention. And that's the point. If your sense of mission isn't getting your employees' attention, you're headed down the wrong track. Your entrepreneurial mission has to have high purpose and set high standards—like Buel Messer's. It has to be profound and simple at the same time—like Buel Messer's. And, the good news is, do it right and your results will be great—like Buel Messer's. The incredible start-up and astonishing growth of Messer Landscape has truly come from its founder's profound need to survive and redeem himself—backed up by his simple, Tennessee common sense.

There's a lot of Buel Messer in all of us. Everyone is missionary about *something*. The trick is to direct it into your entrepreneurial start-up. This really isn't so difficult—especially if you're doing something you love as most entrepreneurs do. It's probably easier than spending two years of your life getting an MBA. It may even be easier than slogging through another dozen books on how to manage. All you have to do is get your entrepreneurial juices flowing about—*what* you want to do and *how* you're going to do it. If it can work miracles for a blind landscaper in Virginia, just imagine what it could do for you!

3 CUSTOMER/PRODUCT VISION: *My Customer, My Product, My Self-Respect*

When you buy an organ from us . . . you can be sure we've never built that same organ before.

—JOHN BOODY
COFOUNDER, TAYLOR & BOODY ORGANBUILDERS

You'll find a Taylor & Boody pipe organ in the chapel at the Harvard Business School. You'll also find one at majestic St. Paul's Cathedral on Fifth Avenue in New York City. You'll even find five of them installed in Japan. And at their wood mill and workshop in Virginia, you'll find young apprentices from Germany, the center of the universe for handcrafted organs for hundreds of years, learning their trade from two Americans, George Taylor and John Boody. This is an industry enjoying a global renaissance, and Taylor & Boody is leading the revival in the United States. There are about thirty-five Taylor & Boody pipe organs around the world, each one custom designed, handmade, and lovingly installed over the past twenty-three years. That works out to about one and a half a year—and the current backlog of orders stretches out five years into the twenty-first century.

When I saw their client list, my first thought was about the missed opportunity at Harvard. What a shame that the powers that be at Harvard Business School didn't have the good sense to invite Messrs. Taylor and Boody over to a classroom to give their students a lesson on the art of "loving" customers and products. It's a safe bet that young MBA candidates—at any business school in the world—will never hear anything even close to the passion that Taylor and Boody bring to their business.

Listen to John Boody on what it takes to become one of the top companies in the world making and selling large, traditional pipe organs. First, the Taylor & Boody relationship with customers: "A big organ is the only musical instrument that's tied to its room. It's not like a harp or a piano that you tote in there and take what you get and then tote it away. So it's very critical that we get good spaces. We can't work with a lot of new churches and music buildings because they're so flimsy, thin walled, and just bad acoustically. So we have to work hand in glove with our customers, going out and hammering these projects into line and then servicing the instrument over the years. We always say that when you buy an organ from us, we're going to join your church or join your family. Our customers become our friends. They call us up all the time and we're in constant communication with them. Every year we go around and visit our customers, including those in Japan—and "lay our hands" on the instruments and keep them in good condition. We oversee the constant maintenance and tuning of all our own organs. As the years go by, this is getting to be a bigger and bigger activity for us as we have thirty-five out there now. In any event, we are exceptionally close to our customers. There's no other way to do this work.

"We've developed a motto here of 'Just say no.' This is because our reputation rides on the success of each instrument. If we don't see any possibility for success for the customer, then we shouldn't build the instrument. The first organ we built in Japan was for a university in Yokohama. We were thrilled with this opportunity. They were designing a music auditorium and we went there to consult about the building of the organ. Their building design was so bad that we came back here, and with some acoustical designer friends, conceived of a building, made a cardboard model, and sent it to them. We told them: 'The building you're designing is all wrong. It's not going to be a success at all unless you do it our way—and we won't build the organ unless you do it our way.' There was a very long silence and we were sure we had lost the business. Then, they came back to us and said OK. They changed the whole design of the building, making it very tall and open in the interior, with galleries around three sides, and so on. All things that had never been done in Japan. We built and installed a big, three-manual organ for them, and today this auditorium is a very influential music room in Japan. The university is delighted and, of course, this was our entree into the Japanese market. I suppose if we were starving, maybe we'd have to say yes, but we've been really fortunate up to now in that we can say *no*. The bottom line is people don't just buy our product, they buy Taylor & Boody. Of course, the product has to be good, but all that aside, when people are looking to purchase a very high-dollar item, they have to be able to look you straight in the eye and know you can get along. They have to like you and they have to trust you."

Boody could talk for days about the Taylor & Boody approach to their product. Here's a sample: "We're a craft business. We're not a manufacturer in the sense of someone who makes toasters, honing their product and turning it out one after another. George and I, and everyone in our company, are essentially handcraftsmen which is a very unusual thing in this day and age. We know the music that we have to play on these instruments. And we know what it takes to make the pipes work really well. And we've become very well known for our architectural ability to do the designs, the moldings, the carvings, the very look of the instruments. You have to couple the musical training with the craftsmanship to build a great musical instrument. Of course, this is all very labor intensive. Ninety-five percent of our costs are directly in labor—handwork. There's no production line. Every organ is handmade and custom made. When you buy an organ from us, like the big one you see out on the shop floor now, you can be sure we've never built that same organ before."

The process of organ building is both time-consuming and incredibly demanding. To illustrate, here's Boody's description of just one of the important steps—the preparation of the wood: "We cut all our own timber and saw our own lumber. Because a pipe organ is a big wooden machine, we found early on that if we didn't have strict control of our materials we couldn't get the quality we wanted. So now we control the preparation of the wood from start to finish. The drying is very critical and we have a dry kiln so we can dry our wood to specification. We have our own wood storage warehouse at our mill so we can keep wood over a long period of time, which gives us very good stability and very good quality. We're known now worldwide for the quality of our wood and we actually supply about ten different organ builders around the country with our surplus, so the wood business has become sort of a subroutine of our organ-building business."

After all this tender loving care, it's not surprising that Taylor & Boody's end products are simply awe-inspiring to look at and listen to. As I was leaving the interview with Boody, he handed me a CD titled *Great Organs of America: Modern Landmarks*. This was obviously something pretty special. He explained: "This is a recording of the largest organ we've built. It's at Holy Cross College in Massachusetts. Listen to it. I think you'll like it." I did listen. Several times. Even to my untrained ear, it was glorious and powerful. I can only imagine what it must sound like in person. There was a printed message on the CD's inside cover from George Taylor and John Boody: "The Holy Cross Organ represented a pioneering effort to construct a large contemporary organ conceived in the high Renaissance tradition of Dutch organ-building. The organ's main case is thirty-two feet high and sixteen feet wide. Together with its 3,822 pipes, twelve wind-chests, bellows and Rückpositiv case of solid American white oak, it weighs some nine tons. Building the Holy Cross Organ was a daring adventure. From the outset it has been a challenge to builder and player alike in understanding a great tradition. From a builder's perspective this organ presented, above all, an opportunity to enter a world of rarely heard sounds and practice our craft on an unprecedented scale. The rewards have been great."

And indeed they have. Taylor & Boody is living proof that a small company can do great things in the world. Business writers might even call George Taylor and John Boody *visionaries*. Of course, everyone these days says entrepreneurs have *vision*. It's about the most commonly used word to describe them. But it's also about the most vague. The question is: vision of what? This is an incredibly important question if you're aspiring to be one of those entrepreneurial visionaries yourself. The good news is we may have just gotten the answer. The Taylor & Boody story, and a thousand more like it, makes it pretty obvious what the two most important words in business are.

Think about it. Imagine that you're starting your own small business tomorrow morning. What will you be thinking about? What do you absolutely, positively have to be racking your brain over? If you're going to get to day two of the enterprise, you'd better be thinking about: "What can I make or do that someone will pay me hard money for?" In the mundane world of day-to-day entrepreneurship, the vague notion of vision can only mean one thing. The single, critical vision all entrepreneurs must have is a clear picture of a specific set of customers who need and will pay for a specific set of products and services. The vision is precise. It is intense. All else revolves around it. Entrepreneurs are blessed and obsessed with this integrated vision of customers and products. It's not really so surprising when you think about it. Business can take many forms, but there's never been a business, or at least a business that survived, without a product or service of some sort and a customer somewhere willing to pay for it. If you really want to get down to the basics of enterprise, this is where you start.

Now here's the point that's gotten lost in the shuffle. Great entrepreneurs are not product inventors alone. Nor are they just great promoters. Was Walt Disney a "product person" or a "marketing person"? Did Ray Kroc at McDonald's have a great product concept or a great customer concept? Is Steve Jobs a scientist or a salesman? The truth is, entrepreneurs are both. By necessity, they have an inseparable vision of customer and product. Like the craftsman of old, they have to make *and* sell. And like and George Taylor and John Boody, old-world organ builders in a new global market, their vision generates focus, expertise, and respect for both customers and products. It also produces great competitive advantage against those who don't have it.

THE REAL MAGIC OF DISNEY

Go down any list of famous entrepreneurs. Think of old-timers like Thomas Watson, Karl Benz, and Konosuke Matsushita. Or newer faces such as Richard Branson of Virgin Atlantic and Internet entrepreneurs like Meg Whitman at eBay or Amazon.com's Jeff Bezos. They all share a finely tuned passion for producing things exactly the way customers want them. It's a rare skill when you think of the hundreds of businesses you deal with that just don't seem to get this simple concept.

There's never been a better example of 20/20 customer/product vision than Walt Disney. Some call him the greatest product creator of the twentieth century. Anyone who can create the second most recognized product in the world out of a mouse called Mickey (Coca-Cola is first) must be a great "product person." The list of Disney's technology and product achievements is long: the first "talking" cartoon; the first animated color feature (*Snow White* in 1937); 3D movies; 360-degree screens; stereophonic sound; the longest-running TV series in history (*True-Life Adventure*'s twenty-nine years); and numerous film classics like *Pinocchio, Cinderella, Peter Pan, Sleeping Beauty,* and *Alice in Wonderland.* He invented and created so many things that he sounds almost like a scientist.

Others, however, call Disney the greatest customer-focused marketeer ever. Certainly, the Disney theme parks, pushing a hundred million customers a year, are far and away the top entertainment show in history. Four generations of "guests" have now been dazzled by Disney's "picture perfect" quality and service. Disney World in Florida is the biggest tourist attraction in the world, drawing more tourists than entire countries. Disney was the first person in the service industry to understand that service is everyone's responsibility. And that it has to permeate every aspect of the business. His attention to detail is legendary. Every inch of the theme park had to be perfect. Not just the streets and the attractions, but the details of every cast member's appearance. And the money just pours in from Anaheim, Orlando, Tokyo, and now Paris. This man must have been some salesman.

Yet the real magic of Disney was simple. He was a product expert and a customer expert at the same time. A scientist and a salesman. An unbeatable combination. The perfect entrepreneur. It's the beautiful balance between these two basics of business that make the world of Disney what it is. Focus on both is the answer. How could it be otherwise? Well, unfortunately it can, and often is, *otherwise.* There are at least three other possibilities. You'll recognize them all. I call them the Scientist, the Salesman, and the Bureaucrat.

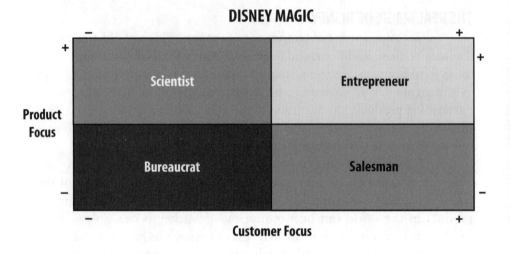

THE SCIENTIST

Ever come across people, or even whole companies, who are so into their technology or product, they forget they're creating it for someone else to use? I call it the *scientist syndrome*—or loving the product and hating the customer. This is more common than you may think. It ranges from user-unfriendly products to simply unusable products, to the adding of so many bells and whistles to a product that no one can afford it. Scientists often have a peculiar disdain for the need to sell and satisfy customers. They tend to look down a bit on their own sales people and even their customers. Of course, there's nothing wrong with being a scientist for science's sake—if everyone agrees that's the mission. In business, the trouble occurs when you end up with exotic products that nobody needs or wants. This is always a vulnerability for the product-driven entrepreneur, and can be best avoided by spending a lot of time with unconvinced prospects and disgruntled customers.

THE SALESMAN

These are the people who know more about how to sell than they do about how their product works. It's the *salesman syndrome,* more graphically defined as loving the customer and hating the product. You know the type—the professional salesman who loves to sell but doesn't give a damn about what he's selling. Cars last year, computers this year, Mexican real estate next. Substituting courtesy for competence is a common tactic. It's the ever-courteous voice on the phone who never solves your billing problem. Or the smiling baggage clerk who announces that your luggage just went to Karachi. The bottom line is this: Customers don't want or need more selling and smiling. The harsh fact is, nobody even wants to see a salesperson. They want to see real product and service experts—the ones who really care about the product and really know how to make it work! For the entrepreneur about to fall into the salesman trap, forget about more marketing and sales training, and start spending a lot more time making yourself into a product expert.

THE BUREAUCRAT

If you hate both your product and your customer, consider going to work for the government or at least a really huge company. You'll never make it as an entrepreneur, but you'll be a perfect bureaucrat. The *bureaucrat syndrome* is painfully commonplace. Just think of the last few times you had to contact the federal government about anything—or American Express customer service from Istanbul, when you found out they cleverly put only 800 numbers on their cards that don't work outside the United States—or the United Airlines supervisor in San Francisco to get a straight answer about why it was going to cost you an extra $400 to terminate your $8,000 round-the-world ticket in Washington D.C., and *not* continue on with the twenty-five minute commute to Charlottesville. Enough of these experiences and you could get the idea that bureaucracy is the true driving force behind most of the places you deal with! Bureaucrats demonstrate zero excitement about customers or products. They sometimes even show disdain for the people who make the products and sell the customers. This is a crazy state of affairs—but it may not be entirely their fault. Many employees have never seen a customer or touched the company's product. It's hard to be excited about things you never see. While the new entrepreneur shouldn't encounter the bureaucrat syndrome for at least five years into the business, I'm reminded that my friend Tom Peters always claimed that any company with three or more employees could turn into a raging bureaucracy. It's probably best to stay vigilant about this, and make sure all your employees, from the very first one, are intimately involved with both customers and products.

THE ENTREPRENEUR: DISNEY MAGIC

How about "loving" the customer *and* "loving" the product? Of all the characteristics of entrepreneurial behavior, this dual focus on customer and product best illuminates the difference between entrepreneurs and professional managers. Like the craftsperson of old, entrepreneurs are intimately involved in both making products *and* selling to customers.

Naturally, entrepreneurs are close to their products. They're intensely interested in the design, manufacture, and use of their product or service. They take it personally. They're ashamed when the quality is bad and they're proud when they get it right. They're thrilled when customers "love" their product. They are clearly product experts.

Entrepreneurs are also very close to their customers. They have to be. They know their paycheck depends on it. They never forget that they need the customers a lot more than the customers need them. They push their organization to its limits to meet the special requests of customers. They listen carefully to customers, not because someone told them to, but to pick up any new idea to improve their product or service. If a customer is unhappy, it's a major crisis. They are clearly customer experts.

Does all this still apply in the cyberspace world of the twenty-first century? Are these basics a little too basic for our high-tech businesses? Well, you're not going to find anything more high tech than the booming industry of business-to-business (B2B) online exchanges. Called Internet-based transaction marketplaces, the companies here are leading the B2B revolution that is sweeping the entire world of e-commerce. I interviewed the CEO of the leading company in this revolution. See for yourself if knowing your product and knowing your customer still matters, if having a powerful customer/product vision is old hat or is still the key to entrepreneurial success!

THE ALL-AMERICAN INTERNET ENTREPRENEUR

I will tell you . . . it was very hard selling out there, because people just didn't get it.

—MARK HOFFMAN
CHAIRMAN & CEO, COMMERCE ONE
FOUNDER, INTRAWARE
COFOUNDER, SYBASE

"At Commerce One, we were very early into the marketplace. My vice president of marketing says that when he'd go out and talk to customers about online exchanges, 'It was like dogs watching TV.' They were looking at the screen, but they weren't seeing anything."

This is Mark Hoffman, Internet entrepreneur, describing his early entry into the B2B online transaction industry. What a difference a couple of years can make in the Internet world! Today everyone is "seeing" Mark Hoffman and his company, Commerce One. And it couldn't have happened to a nicer guy. Hoffman's is an all-American story in an industry often dominated by—how shall I put it?—socially challenged eccentrics. For starters,

Hoffman has been married to the same woman for twenty-eight years and they have two grown children—a son and a daughter, naturally. He grew up in Windom, a small town in the southwestern corner of Minnesota, where his family owned and ran the local dry cleaners. You can't be much more Main Street America than this. He was nominated to, and graduated from, the U.S. Military Academy at West Point—where the government foots the bill for educating America's future officer corps. After serving his time in the U.S. Army, he got an MBA from the University of Arizona, about as far removed as you can get from the consultant and banker incubators at the Harvards of the world. Take my word for this one—I grew up in Arizona *and* attended the Harvard Business School. But, of course, as nice as all that is, being the all-American family man doesn't get you into a book about great entrepreneurs. And it certainly doesn't get you into feature stories at *Fortune,* the *New York Times, USA Today,* and London's *Financial Times*— all in the span of a few months.

Let's go back to Hoffman's story to find out how this nice guy from Windom, Minnesota did it:

"We recognized very early on that this was going to be a big business. And a business that would change other businesses. I mean, when I came here in 1996,[1] I didn't want to go to a business that was just another application. I didn't want to go to the next generation of database companies. I had zero interest in doing that. But in this business I recognized that you could build a whole marketplace. You would be defining and building a market, not just a product that you were bringing to market. So early on we recognized that, and began to go after that vision.

"You know, we didn't have everything right up front. We were listening to a lot of sources and adapting to the marketplace. The big thing that we did early on was we built this portal in trying to solve this B2B problem. And back at that time there was nobody talking about an exchange-driven solution. So we were the first ones to do it and to see what the power of that exchange could be. Anyway, this is why we have the best product today. And I will tell you that in 1998 and the first half of 1999, it was very hard selling out there, because people just didn't get it. And it wasn't until

---

[1]I'm violating my own rule of never writing about entrepreneurs and companies who have been in business less than ten years. This rule has stood me well since my *Excellence* days, when Tom Peters was going gaga over companies that fell apart before the ink was dry. However, can one really write a book today on *The Entrepreneurial Age* and not mention Internet entrepreneurs? But, since the entire industry isn't ten years old, this poses a dilemma. I've hedged my bets by highlighting entrepreneurs with great track records beyond their current Internet activity, such as Mark Hoffman. I hope (for them and me) they will still be around when you read this.

about September of 1999 that people really began to get it and jump on the bandwagon. We already had our IPO in July—the business was building enough to do the IPO and we felt confident—but it was very hard work, I'll tell you that! Then it was very hard work finding the customers and getting them to sign on. Now it's still very hard work, its always hard work. But now we've got so much opportunity sitting there, and we're chasing so many deals and bringing those deals in and getting people up and running, that it's a different kind of hard work. It's still hard work but it's different than it was a year ago.

That hard work has made Commerce One, along with Oracle and Ariba, one of the big three makers of software for the booming B2B online exchange industry. Commerce One appears to be ahead of the pack, having already established up-and-running Web portals or exchanges—such as the landmark GM TradeXchange for the auto industry.

As Mark Hoffman states in the interview, people don't get what the B2B exchange world is all about. I was definitely in that camp but made an effort to play catch-up before and after my interview with Hoffman. One of my source documents, a *New York Times* article from May 7, 2000, put it this way: "No category has done more to push business to business e-commerce to the front of investors' minds in recent months than the debut of online marketplaces, often referred to as exchanges. These are one-stop shops for various industries that give commercial buyers and sellers a place to display their goods, sell them at auction, put out requests for proposals, and perform other business functions that used to be the domain of the telephone and fax machine. The sector has two parts. First, are those companies that build or run the exchanges, like VerticalNet, Ventro, and Internet Capital Group. Second are the companies that want to sell software to the exchanges, like Oracle, Ariba, and Commercial One." This is clearly a moving feast. Mark Hoffman says that Commerce One is in both parts of the online exchange business—actually conceiving and running portal exchanges, and not just developing software for them.

The customer/product vision at Commerce One also seems to be heavily focused on international markets: Certainly more so than its competitors. I asked Hoffman if that was actually true, and why: "It's very true. I just believed from day one that there's going to be an international market. And that the international market is going to grow very quickly. I also believed that if we didn't get into those markets very quickly, somebody else would and we'd begin to fall behind. I learned a lot about the international markets at Sybase where I pretty much had the same philosophy, by the way. So I knew how to go after those marketplaces and how to get started in all of these different areas. We have, from day one, aggressively gone after the international markets. If you look at the B2B business as a global trading Web, and you look at the competition, there is nobody else today that has even announced or said anything about their vision of a global trading Web. They've not put it together yet. So I think our competition is a long way from being able to achieve that kind of a vision."

Yes, Commerce One is very hot. Unlike the zillion e-commerce companies that had gone public and then disappeared in the great NAS-DAQ slide of early 2000, Commerce One just keeps getting more and more attention. The reason is, Mark Hoffman and his people are out there building real products and selling real customers, and supporting it all with a real business infrastructure. Commerce One is not still fiddling around in a "virtual reality" business. It's already playing in the major leagues, with some very heavy hitters in its corner.

The same week this is being written, the *Financial Times* reported a major alliance between Commerce One and SAP in Germany: "SAP, Europe's largest software group, is to link up with U.S. rival Commerce One in a strategic, technological, and financial alliance that could help boost sales of its new software. Under the proposed agreement, Commerce One, which provides online exchanges for businesses, would use SAP software to build and maintain new and existing exchanges. In return SAP would invest a significant amount in Commerce One, in which it already owns a 1 percent stake." Reading between the lines, SAP needs Commerce One to break into the online exchange business—the heart of the entire B2B transaction market. As the article concludes: "SAP introduced its marketplace products late in 1999—long after Ariba and Commerce One . . . and has been slow in signing up customers." Oh, really? Well they've gone to the right place for help.

Just two weeks earlier, *USA Today* prominently displayed Hoffman's smiling face in its cover story on the B2B industry. While reporting that "Many hail the exchanges as the 'killer application' of the Net, the Holy Grail of the electronic commerce revolution," they also warn that even though nearly a thousand online marketplaces in seventy industries have been announced, it may be years before all industries are fully brought into the Internet age. Even so, Commerce One is a star in the industry. As *USA Today* concludes: "Analysts say the early leaders appear to be Silicon Valley software start-ups Ariba and Commerce One, and high-tech giant Oracle, the world's number-two software company. . . . The deal-making reached a frenzied pitch earlier this year, when Commerce One landed GM for an auto exchange, while Oracle signed on Ford. Since then Ford and GM have told Oracle and Commerce One to join hands and build the grandfather of all exchanges in Detroit. Easier said than done. Ellison and Hoffman are bitter rivals, going back to Hoffman's tenure as CEO at Sybase, a software firm that threatened Oracle's dominance in the early 1990s. . . . A consultant, Diamond Technologies, was hired to evaluate Oracle and Commerce One's software suites. It recommended Commerce One. Oracle executives went ballistic, according to industry insiders." That behavior would be following the lead, no doubt, of their founder and CEO, Larry Ellison—one of the truly "socially challenged" denizens of Silicon Valley.

Even *Fortune,* two months earlier, got excited about the GM deal: "GM recently announced . . . a vast electronic marketplace called GM TradeXchange in partnership with Commerce One . . . GM is reaping billions from its investment in Commerce One. (And why not? GM is supplying much of the business that's driving up its partner's stock price.)" Very recently, DaimlerChrysler also expressed interest in joining the GM/Commerce One and Ford/Oracle online exchange. That became just too much for the trustbusters at the Department of Justice, so now they're taking a look at it. However it all turns out, it's a sure bet that Commerce One will have a big piece of this "grandfather of all exchanges." Why? Because, as Mark Hoffman says, he's simply got the best product for these giant customers.

How big is Commerce One's opportunity? How big is the B2B market? Nobody really knows. Forrester Research, the leading Internet forecasting firm, reports online business-to-business transactions could hit a jaw-dropping $2 trillion in three years. Another research firm, Gartner Group in San Jose, is wildly forecasting up to $7 trillion in total transactions, with $2.7 trillion of it going through B2B Internet software and platform companies like Commerce One. Whatever the truth, B2B will surely end up being the giant part of the e-commerce world. The business-to-consumer (B2C) sector will likely continue to plummet for the very old-fashioned reason that these companies can't figure out how to make a profit! Most of the B2C companies have too many products chasing too few customers. That's a problem Commerce One does not have.

How does one prepare to be a successful Silicon Valley entrepreneur? Well, as you might guess by now, Mark Hoffman's CV is solid. I'd call it Midwestern solid actually. The good news is that a "solid" CV can still take you a long way, even as a Silicon Valley entrepreneur. The "entrepreneurial portion" of the CV goes like this: He joined the predecessor firm of Commerce One in September 1996. It was then a small, twenty-person supply chain software developer. Hoffman changed the name, refocused the products away from sellers to buyers, and has made Commerce One the leading firm in the world for Internet-based B2B exchanges. The company today has over 1,200 employees and it carried out a very successful IPO in

July 1999. Before Commerce One, Hoffman had cofounded Sybase in 1984. As CEO of Sybase, he managed the company's dramatic growth from a software start-up to the number-two relational database management system firm and the sixth-largest independent software company in the world. When he left in 1996, Sybase had annual revenues of nearly $1 billion. Along the way he also found time to create another high-tech company, Intraware, where he still serves as chairman of the board.

So I asked him: "Tell me, Mark, how *do* you prepare yourself to become a successful Silicon Valley entrepreneur—three times over in your case? Was it West Point? Business school? The different jobs you held before you became an entrepreneur? All that fresh air in Minnesota? What's the secret?" He laughed and replied: "Well, the Academy provides a great undergraduate engineering degree. You get engineering in a lot of different disciplines there. So it gives you the engineering skills. It also gives you leadership skills. It gives you discipline skills. All those things that come into play sometime later. And, for me, business school was a great thing in that I hadn't really been exposed to business at all before that. The U.S. Army doesn't teach you that! And it's hard to build a business with zero business background. You'd better be bringing in some other founders along with you who have that kind of experience if you don't have it yourself because you're going to be in front of venture capitalists, you're going to be doing the financing, you've got to create and put together your business plan, so I think there are some advantages of business school, either at the undergraduate or graduate level. I think the skills that I picked up at West Point all kind of came together after graduate school. And going to graduate school, I don't know why it coalesced, but when I came out of there I at least felt that I knew how all the pieces of a business worked.

"After all that, the business I chose to work for was Amdahl. That was my first exposure really to an entrepreneurial style, and to the Valley in particular. I was at Amdahl a couple of years. There were a lot of guys there who had been fundamental in starting Amdahl and growing it. Amdahl back then was at the very leading edge of technology. So I got exposed to the Valley, got exposed to the entrepreneurs there, the entrepreneurs at Amdahl, and all of those things were of a lot of interest to me. I didn't come up here with the idea of starting my own company, but my jobs at Amdahl were very entrepreneurial. You know, they were kind of independent jobs where they threw me into situations. That was 1979 and 1980. Then the guy who had hired me at Amdahl, the first guy I had worked for, left Amdahl and went to a start-up company. He recruited me over there so I was like employee number forty going into that company.

"That company was called Britton Lee and they were making database machines. So I was brought over there as VP of operations to build up the manufacturing operation. They put me in this big empty building with one desk and said, 'Build us a manufacturing facility.' I learned a lot there but the VP of engineering and I weren't happy with the management. This was 1984. Even though we weren't happy with the management, we tried to present them with a business plan to change their business into a software company. The guys who were there had come out of the hardware industry. They just said *no*, they weren't interested; they were hardware guys. So at that point the VP of engineering and I resigned and began to build our own business plan. We said, 'Let's just go do it ourselves. We can do this. We can do it better. We can do it just pure software as opposed to hardware.' And we believed we could get funding at that point in time. So this was the beginning of Sybase in 1984.

"And then, I took over what was actually a very small group here. I was really restarting and repositioning this company in the marketplace and building it into what it is today. It's quite different from the initial, tiny company of about twenty people. The thing that happens along the way is obviously you get more confidence in building these companies, and you get more contacts for raising money or other expertise that's required. All of those things come together and help you move on to build another company. So in my case it wasn't just an immediate swing over to being an entrepreneur. It took a couple of moves that built up this entrepreneurial spirit. Starting up Sybase after Amdahl really exploded it for me. I think there were some things in my personality also. I'm a pretty independent person. And I'm a builder. I just like building things. I've always liked doing that since I was a kid."

Now we move to the crux of the matter in Hoffman's universe. Apparently starting up companies in Silicon Valley is the easy part. After all, if teenagers with no products and no capital can do it, how hard can it be? It appears that just about anybody can call himself or herself "an Internet entrepreneur." The tough part, however, seems to be lasting more than a year or two—and doing that very old-fashioned thing of actually making products that customers will buy—*and* making a profit at it! Mark Hoffman has done this, a couple of times. So I asked him: "Once you're up and running as an entrepreneur, particularly in this fast-moving Internet world, what separates the men from the boys, so to speak? What makes Commerce One successful, and a hundred other Internet or dot-com–type start-ups crash and burn?" His answers drove straight to the heart of the enterprise—making products that customers will buy—or as we like to call it, having customer/product vision:

- "First, you've got to have some background here in order to make these businesses go. And that means you come in and learn the industry very well in a larger company. To me that's extremely important. Some people have done start-ups where they haven't had a lot of experience in the industry, but they are technical guys with strong expertise. That is like Gates or somebody with a technical expertise that he brings to it. So you've also got to have some kind of expertise, or experience, that you bring to these businesses. You have to know something and be good at something!

- "You have to be able to recognize and put together great ideas in these marketplaces. But also I think, in some sense, ideas are cheap. The trick is to be able to pick out what ideas or what products are the right ones within this industry. And recognizing what the opportunity is—that's extremely important. Then as you begin to build on that idea, I think you have to be very flexible in these marketplaces. You kind of shoot and aim afterwards.

- "You've got to listen to the market, you've got to listen to your employees, you've got to still be thinking about the market as you learn more about it, and be able to adjust your strategy very rapidly. And then the ideas begin to coalesce into the bigger business that you're going to build in the end. And it may not exactly resemble what you started out to build up front.

- "So yes, it's focusing on the customers, and listening to the customers, because these are the guys who are building the applications. You've got to make them successful and listen to what they're saying about what works and what doesn't work and get that back into the product itself. So, for the next customer, you've taken it a step forward. But I think you've also got to be careful in this industry. You've got to listen and focus on customers, but you can actually overdo that to some extent in this marketplace. Customers can be very selfish in the problems that they're trying to solve. So you're looking at customer input, you're listening to other outside forces that can influence your direction, such as partners or whatever, but you also have to look at your own vision of what this market should become. You have to balance it all. I think, particularly in a high-growth company, if you're only focusing long term on the customer, and the customer has an inherent interest to see you propagate and grow your initial products, that may not be where the market's going. Let's say, for example, you're Sybase, and you've got your loyal Sybase customers. Well, they're only interested in the database part of the business. But at some point that levels off, and becomes a mature business. So you've got to not only look at that customer in that business, but you've also got to stick your head up and be a visionary, looking out to say: 'OK, what other products or businesses do I have to be in here to be successful?'

- "And you've got to be very determined about going after this thing. You know some of these dot-com companies spring to life and come to fruition pretty quickly. So you've got to be willing to commit a big chunk of your life to it to do that. If you're not willing to dedicate a very big chunk of your life to making it happen, being an entrepreneur is probably not a good solution for you.

- "And then I think, past all this, it's just get in there and keep doing the business. You know, failure is not necessarily a bad thing in this business. The business is forgiving of failure. But you've got to stay in there and do it!"

As a wrap-up question I asked Hoffman what he was most proud of up to this point. "To me, it's just building the businesses. It's having built companies that are substantial businesses today. You know Sybase, Intraware, Commerce One, they're still free, independent companies in this marketplace. They all have the ability to grow to well over a billion dollars in revenue, and they already are, or will be, major factors in the industry."

There you have it! Whether in cyberspace or in Windom—it's the customer/product vision of a true all-American entrepreneur.

LOVING CUSTOMERS AND PRODUCTS

No amount of management theory can replace the entrepreneur's old-fashioned adage: "My customer, my product, my self-respect." In the start-up phase, at least, they have to personally make the product and sell it to prospects. This two-step process gives rise to the most powerful emotion in all enterprise: the anxiety-producing, face-to-face trauma of customer judgment. The judgment is aimed right at the ego of the entrepreneur. It can send you to the heights of glory or it can shatter your self-esteem. Believe it or not, this is all good for you. It's what makes you different from the bureaucrats. So welcome it. Embrace it. Taking it personally is what's going to make you win!

This is really the secret. Entrepreneurs have no superhuman skills. They're not smarter than everybody else. And they don't even work harder than a lot of big-time executives. Their secret weapon is that they focus on customers and products and do it with obsessive consistency. We call it loving the customer and loving the product.

"LOVING" THE CUSTOMER

The entrepreneurial approach to customers is full of caring, common sense. You'll find no conceptual breakthroughs here. Loving customers is easy when you see them as the only means of putting food on the table. It's hard to hate people who do that for you. It's also easy to appreciate anyone who admires and uses your own creation: your product or service. It's just not normal to dislike folks who think your work is great. So as an up-and-coming entrepreneur, you will definitely have strong motivation to love and respect your customers. The really nice thing is that every minute you spend on this is money in the bank. Of all the ways entrepreneurs can show their love of customer, here are four of the most important.

➤ *Knowing Your Product*
Yes, the very first requirement in loving your customer is knowing (and loving) your product. After all, how can you take care of your customers if you don't know how your product works, how to fix it when it's broken, and how to squeeze more out of it to make life easier for your customer/user? And never forget this little pearl of wisdom: Nobody wants to see a salesman, but everybody is dying to see the person who can solve a problem. And that takes a product expert, not a salesperson with an order form. This little entrepreneurial twist, virtually forgotten by the marketing gurus of big business, could be the most powerful sales and marketing tool you will ever have.

➤ *Responding Immediately*
The most startling difference between entrepreneurs and big-company bureaucrats is the priority they place on responding quickly to customers. Fortunately for start-up entrepreneurs, most of the competition is just plain awful at it. It simply wouldn't occur to successful entrepreneurs that anything could be more important than responding immediately to customers' requests, questions, and complaints.

➤ *Being Courteous* **and** *Competent*
Some companies and their employees can be quite friendly but technically incompetent. They smile a lot but nothing works right. Others may be highly competent but far from courteous. The planes run on time but you're being served by cabin crews from hell. The great entrepreneurial advantage is that you have to be both courteous

and competent to survive. As an entrepreneur you will actually mean it when you say *thank you* to the customer who just spent $200. And if the product or service isn't right, you really can make amends on the spot. This double-barreled behavior, so rare in big companies and government agencies, is just another area where entrepreneurs and their young companies have a built-in advantage over the bureaucracies of the world.

Keeping Current Customers Forever

The priorities are clear when you're young and small. Your best prospects are current customers, always, always, always. Losing one or two existing customers is an unmitigated disaster—to be avoided at all costs. If you allow these things to be forgotten in your growing company, you will have committed the cardinal sin of entrepreneurial growth. You will not only be putting at risk the most profitable piece of your business, you will be a sitting duck for every new and hungry entrepreneurial competitor around. Don't let this happen. Remember, the most important marketing job in any business is to resell and expand those current customers. "Keeping current customers forever" is the first priority for continued growth, not the last.

"LOVING" THE PRODUCT

If you have to boil it all down to one thing, the single most critical element in any successful start-up is the entrepreneur's ability to come up with a better mousetrap. The mousetrap could take the form of a break-through product, an innovative new service, or even a new and improved version of an existing mousetrap. But the final judge of the worth of your efforts will be the market, not you. So, again, it's the bringing together of the scientist and salesman in yourself and your start-up team that is required to produce winners. Here, straight from the entrepreneur's handbook, are four of the most basic practices for loving your products—and getting others to love them, too.

Knowing Your Customer

Artists will tell you that no one values their work as much as they do themselves. They will also tell you that trying to sell their first work of art can be an ego-smashing exercise. All of a sudden, what matters most is not how beautiful the artist thinks it is, but rather, how beautiful the customer thinks it is. Both of these notions—loving your work and accepting that beauty is always in the eye of the beholder—are central to the entrepreneur's obsession with the product.

➤ *Feeling Old-fashioned Pride*

A lot of people say pride went the way of most old-fashioned things—down the tube. Well, that just isn't true. All entrepreneurs have it. I've never met an entrepreneur who didn't believe that what he or she was doing was important—beyond the paycheck. And that's key. You have to believe that your work is worth doing. You have to feel a personal sense of mission about the products you produce and the customers you serve. This is what creates old-fashioned pride, and it's an enormous advantage entrepreneurs have over the competition.

➤ *Making It Better Than the Next Guy*

You can succeed in beating the competition in one of three ways: providing products and services of higher quality, or lower costs, or both. You had better be able to do at least one of the three, or you'll simply be out of the game. But, to the entrepreneur, the really important word here is "competition." It's another reason why entrepreneurs are so focused on their competitors. Blindly pushing for ever-higher quality may get you the Malcolm Baldrige award, but it may also drive you into bankruptcy. And you can lower costs a lot if you're willing to make junk that falls apart in a week, but your customer base may also fall apart. But don't despair: The entrepreneurial method works every time—just make sure you're "making it better than the next guy."

➤ *Making It Faster Than the Next Guy*

Speed is truly the entrepreneur's secret weapon. And as Akio Morita, the founder of Sony, liked to say: "The best thing about it is it's free." This should be sweet music to your ears. It's no secret that entrepreneurs love to compete with big companies. The reason is simple: Breaking the tape first is practically guaranteed!

It almost doesn't matter which actions you take in "Loving the Customer" and "Loving the Product." It's hard to go wrong spending time on either one. In that spirit, let's take a little closer look at the company that thinks of little else *other than* customers and products. Welcome one last time to the beautiful sights and sounds of Taylor & Boody.

THE SIGHTS AND SOUNDS OF TAYLOR & BOODY

For those of you who believe the only vision future entrepreneurs will need will be from cyberspace, we'll close with a return visit to the sights and sounds of Taylor & Boody—master organ builders and new-millennium entrepreneurs. The hard part of interviewing John Boody was finding him. Just over the Blue Ridge mountains, a half-hour down County Highway 254, and then five miles east on Route 708, I found myself in the most beautiful countryside dotted with white farmhouses and cows. There were few signs. I drove right past an old, two-story, red-brick school building with no markings of any kind. After seeing nothing but more cows for another couple of miles, I backtracked and went to the school building to ask directions. I walked up the main stairs, opened two very large doors, and saw stretching upward through a large opening in the ceiling, the biggest, most magnificent organ I'd ever seen. Behind it was another one, about half the size, but equally beautiful. I figured I had found John Boody.

It turns out that mechanical pipe organs have a long history—dating back to the fifteenth century in Europe. They are among the oldest surviving technical inventions in the world. Many, built as long as four hundred years ago, are still in regular use and are revered for their superior aesthetics and dependability. But as happens to most treasures of earlier ages, human ingenuity moves on, finding "better" ways to meet the same needs. By the dawn of the twentieth century this certainly looked to be the fate of the historic organ-building industry. But something very different happened. A hundred years later, as we enter the new millennium, traditional, handmade pipe organs are a booming business. Organ builders call it the "tracker revival" and it's in full swing worldwide.

Taylor & Boody are very much in the forefront of this renaissance, so I asked John Boody to explain it: "First of all, as happened to a lot of small businesses, by the time the twentieth century came along, the old organ builders got bigger and bigger and they turned out to be big factories. So most pipe organs in this country were made by large companies—not large by some business standards, of course—but they weren't small craft companies anymore. And they converted from the traditional mechanical action to both pneumatic and electrically operated systems. They were able to spread the organs all over the churches and music halls from one end to another, because everything was hooked together by electricity. But along the way they kind of lost the point. They lost the handcrafted care that you can put into a product with a small company. A pipe organ, after all, is a musical instrument and it responds really well to the particular attention you can pay when you have a small, craft-oriented company.

"The rebirth started because so many American servicemen, who were musicians, ended up in Europe at the end of the Second World War. They discovered there were a lot of historically based organs still in Germany and Holland and France, and these organs had more musicality and more sensitivity than the big electric action organs that were being built in the United States. They said: 'Well, how can we get back to this music? How can we reestablish this craft in America?' The European builders had to rebuild a lot of these organs after the war. So they had the skills and techniques to build this kind of organ but these skills hadn't come to this country yet. So it took three or four individuals, who recognized what was happening, to create what we now call the 'tracker revival' in the United States. Trackers are the thin strips of wood that provide the mechanical connection between the keys and the wind-chest. They're more responsive to the player than the pneumatic or electric actions. The word comes from the Latin—'to pull'—as in tractor. Anyway, this started just after the war but it took a while to build. At first it was just imported European instruments, because they had the jump on us. But then, shortly thereafter, we started building instruments in the same way in this country. Now it's completely flipped around. There are about five companies, all in this country, that are leading the pack worldwide in the quality of the instruments that are being built."

Since George Taylor and John Boody's company is part of this elite group, an obvious question comes up. What does it take to reach the top of this unique and very demanding industry? Where do you even learn the business of organ building? I asked Boody how he and George Taylor got into such an enterprise in the first place: "George and I came at it in slightly different ways. George went to Washington and Lee in Virginia. He was a sociology major, but he was an organ student also. So he played the organ and was familiar with organ technology. The school had a Henry Irvin organ built just after the Civil War. The organ was threatened with a modernizing reworking and George went to the president of the university and said 'If you let them change this organ, you're doing the wrong thing.' The president was impressed and George basically got to oversee the work that was done. That was his introduction to organ building. Actually, we've just recently rerestored that same organ. After he graduated, George received a Ford Foundation grant to go to Hamburg, Germany, and do a three-year apprenticeship with Rudolph Von Beckerath, a very well-known organ builder. He got his German journeyman papers and then went on to get a Master Organ-builder rating. There are very few people who have done that—learning the organ-building business in the German way from top to bottom. He came back to the United States and began working in a partnership in Ohio for an organ builder named John Brombaugh.

"All through high school and college, I sang in choirs, a cappella groups, and even a barbershop quartet. I've also always been interested in making things, particularly in woodworking. I even took shop class in school, which none of the other college track kids were interested in. Of course, that was great training for a future organ builder. I liked working with wood well enough that I went to the University of Maine and entered their forestry program, which is one of the best in the country. It was good training for me, but after a year I decided my heart was really in music and I changed my major from forestry to music. I ended up getting a BA in music—with an emphasis on voice and choral conducting. That also turned out to be a great experience for becoming an organ builder. At the university, I worked for the FM radio station and two things happened: First I started a program called Organ Masterpieces and I learned there was a whole genre of European organs that were original, historic instruments. I got interested in that and wondered if anyone in the United States was building organs that way. Another thing that happened was I was given a couple of pipe organs that came out of old Maine churches that were getting electronic substitutes. I started putting the organs together and fooling around with the parts. Because of my interest, I even managed to spend my summers apprenticing with Fritz Noack, a great organ builder in Massachusetts. We have a saying that you can catch the 'organ bug,' and I really did. There's just something special about pipe organs being mechanical and musical at the same time. I graduated from college in 1968 and was quickly drafted into the Army and went to Vietnam for thirteen long months. When I returned home I got a job with John Brombaugh and Company in Ohio. Of course, the day I walked in, there was George Taylor."

So there you have it. Business 101 for entrepreneurial organ builders. It's a far cry from the management pap that business schools serve up. It's George Taylor's love of organs and his years in Germany and the United States learning to be one of the world's masters at building them. And it's John Boody's combining his love and skills in music and woodworking to give the business a worldwide reputation for the high quality of its wood and the fine decorative style of its organ cases. In true Disney style, this is how entrepreneurs who love their products and respect their customers prepare themselves for the business world. So then, why and how did Taylor & Boody Organbuilders get started? What was the impetus to take the entrepreneurial plunge and create their own company? Boody continued: "John Brombaugh was part of that group of organ builders who, after the Second World War, got interested in making historically based organs. They studied the old German organs and learned how to revive a craft that really had been lost for a hundred years in this country. So John was in the first generation of the revival—and George and I are a half-generation removed because we worked together with John for seven years. In Ohio we did a lot of pioneering work in metallurgy, metal technology, and pipe making and kind of returned to the historic mechanical action way of building organs. That time was the perfect incubation for us because we were young and inspired and wanted to change the organ world. And we were willing to work for no money—for the opportunity to learn. I think the first year we made 35¢ an hour. We built some really good organs and a number of those organs were very influential to other people.

"We were building a big organ in Eugene, Oregon, and while we were working out there Brombaugh fell in love with the West Coast. He just announced one day he was going to move the company to Eugene. John was a little bit on the crazy side, and he didn't worry about how much money he made. George and I decided we didn't want to do that. We had been starving for a number of years so we decided to try starting our own business. In 1977 we took one contract from our partnership with John as a start-up.

"When we started we were still young. I was only thirty-one. It took us more than a year to build that first organ. It was very low priced by today's standards, and we took progress payments to survive financially. Of course, we had a very slim organization. We actually built that organ in the garage behind my house in Ohio. George and I, with our bare hands, added on to the garage when we needed to set the organ upright. By the time we were through with that organ we already had secured another contract and since that time we've never, ever lacked for work. We've had one contract after another and right now we're running with a five-year backlog of contracts."

What? No business plan? No venture capital? No market research? How can you start a company without these things? Easy, according to John Boody—if you've just spent ten years becoming very, very good at what you're doing. One of the secret advantages of being a real expert on your markets and products is you might actually know more about them, or at least as much, as your customers do. This is a hard concept to grasp in an age when polls, focus groups, and reams of market data are used to tell companies what color to make the product and what shape to make the package.

In any event, it would be interesting to know exactly how Taylor & Boody got their second and third and fourth customers—leading up to their impressive five-year backlog of clients: "Well, people came and saw the first organ we were building and thought the quality was very good. And when we finished, organ people could go see it and hear it. We also had several contacts and consultants along the way who saw that we were going to be a good, sane alternative to some of the more eccentric people in the business. And, most important, we've lived up to our promises. We tell people when the organ is going to be delivered, and what to expect for quality, and we've been able to deliver. Sure, organs are very esoteric things, but a lot of times we're dealing with the business people in the churches or universities, and they respond very well to a kind of sane organization. They appreciate that we've been modestly profitable over the years, that we own our own saw mill and workshop, and that the buildings are attractive when they come to look us over. They're always impressed with our workplace: clean, well-organized, good-quality equipment, and all that.

"And we've been very fortunate that we've had some very prestigious jobs. We built the organ for St. Thomas Church on Fifth Avenue in New York, which is one of the premier music churches in the country. Now we're going to build a second organ for them, a small portable instrument, so we'll have two organs at St. Thomas'. We've also built for Christ Church in Indianapolis, which is very well known for its musical work. The Harvard organ is a small, portable instrument. The business school has a nonsectarian chapel which has three musical instruments—a very fine grand piano, a very good harpsichord, and now a Taylor & Boody organ. Then there is the huge organ we made for Holy Cross College, which has been recorded numerous times. And, of course, we're very proud of our five organs in Japan."

It was all sounding so uplifting, that I had to remind myself that Taylor & Boody had to compete with some very tough, high-quality competitors around the world. I asked Boody to describe the business and competitive climate: "Today we regularly compete with five to ten companies worldwide who are doing a very high level of craft organ building. In this market, the smallest portable organs are around $50,000—while the big jobs run over $1 million. We have a couple of $1 million–plus jobs in our backlog right now. The lower quality companies in the industry are falling out. Some of them have gone out of business. The largest one in the country turned into a brontosaurus and recently went belly up. Those guys are getting strong competition from the electronic organ manufacturers—which are all computerized now. There'll always be a market for the electronics because there are so many places that don't want to spend more than $20,000 or $30,000 for an organ. Most of those places we couldn't build for anyway, because they're not acoustically capable of holding a really fine instrument.

"As I said earlier, the whole direction of the trade is changing. The American companies are exporting to Asia and even Europe. In Japan, where we've had good success, Taylor & Boody is competing directly with the Europeans. The Japanese seem to like dealing with Americans, but, more important, they perceive that we can give them better quality and better musicality. We've even had several people from Europe come here to learn organ building from Taylor & Boody. Actually we have people from Germany here right now. After their training, they'll be in high demand back in Germany because people have seen what we can do.

"By now, we've kind of worked our way to the top of the heap. A lot of our contracts now come to us without any competition. People come to us and say: 'We want to buy a Taylor & Boody. When can you do it for us?' So I guess in business parlance we've developed something of a brand name. We've been able to provide the quality our customers are looking for and also the business structure that people have come to depend on. They know we will deliver the quality and service they expect."

It seems clear that no matter how much business success George Taylor and John Boody attain, they remain craftsmen to the core. Like all crafts people, they have to both make and sell. And like all successful entrepreneurs, they are very good at both. It's fair to say that they are indeed, masters at "loving" their customers and "loving" their products. My closing question to Boody concerned this point. I asked him to describe how Taylor & Boody's powerful customer/product vision is actually implemented in the day-to-day business. In other words, how does the *make* and *sell* process really work at Taylor & Boody? His reply: "It's not that we're reinventing the wheel every time we build an organ for a customer, but they *are* tailored to fit where they're going to go. The architectural design is different, the stop list is different, and the whole configuration of the instrument can be changed around. We start by going out and examining the customer's building or the drawings, do the acoustical analysis, and begin to design the organ. The mechanical and architectural design is produced on our computers from start to finish. We post the designs in the shop and our people make the parts.

"Everything is made to very strict specifications. For example, the facade pipes are constructed of 98 percent lead and are hammered, planed by hand, and lacquered. Lead is used because it gives a more mellow sound. And we've become well known for making instruments with a really wonderful, decorative look to them. So you have to have craft skills like hands-on woodworking and woodcarving and all those things. The only electric part we use is a small wind blower so the player can inflate the wind bellows electrically or the traditional way of foot pumping. George and I see how the parts are made on a daily basis so we're sure that everything is made just the way we want it. Then we put the whole organ together in our shop, and we test it for performance. So, again, George and I are working on and responding to how the organ is going together here in the shop. Then we take it all apart, pack it away, and depending on where it's going, put it on trucks or sea containers or air containers. The organ is transported to the site and our people go and put it back together so we're controlling how the assembly is done. Then two or three of us go and we listen to every pipe, and we tune it and regulate it so the organ is making the maximum amount of music for the given situation."

Boody neatly summarized it this way: "So from the first sales contact to the finished product, to the last pipe tuned, we pay attention to every step. One thing all this means is that we can't grow too fast. And that's fine with us. We feel where we are right now—about fifteen people—is pretty much ideal. We have enough power to keep everything moving forward but George and I can still work with every customer and have our hands on the products from one end to the other."

When you consider the customer/product vision for your own company, remember the Taylor & Boody model. You're going to need the same "absolute focus on customers and products" to survive and succeed in your own entrepreneurial venture. To help keep this in mind, we'll close with one of the most powerful statements of customer/product vision I've ever found. Here are the words of George Taylor and John Boody at the dedication of their twenty-fourth organ, back in 1994:

> In conclusion, one may well ask why we build organs in an age which is ever less interested in objects of lasting worth. Obviously the construction of traditional musical instruments is an anachronism in our time. Not only is a fine organ difficult and time-consuming to build, when compared with machine-made goods, it is costly indeed. Furthermore, learning to play an organ requires years of devoted practice. Given these facts, it is tempting to settle for less expensive alternatives to the traditional organ. But the truth remains that there is a value to the work done by human hands which is sacred. The spirit of those who have contributed to this organ will breathe through its music, a message of peace and good will. Herein lies the real meaning of this investment. In return, may it bring to life the musical treasures of ages past together with the talents of our time. Let it stand as a sign to future generations of our confidence and faith in God who has blessed us so richly.

HIGH-SPEED INNOVATION:
When Your Life Depends on It

We are studying the most sacred information that exists: the
information that goes into designing you.
— KARI STEFANSSON,
FOUNDER AND CEO,
DECODE GENETICS

In 1980, there was not one biotech company in the world. Late that year the U.S. Supreme Court ruled that genetically engineered organisms are patentable—and one of history's most important, fastest-growing, entrepreneurial industries was born. Today there are over one thousand biotech firms around the globe. *Fortune* estimates that total worldwide sales of biopharmaceuticals will soon surpass the traditional pharmaceutical industry's figure of $250 billion. And that doesn't even include the biggest potential market of all for biotech—agriculture. The only thing quite like it, where venture capital and entrepreneurial start-ups abound, is the ten-year-old explosion of the Internet industry—except biotech has been at it for twenty years, with arguably much *higher tech* and infinitely *higher touch.*

The biotech revolution is now moving from childhood to adolescence, or in our terms, from the start-up phase to a phase of sustained high growth. It's been a story of tiny, scientist-entrepreneur-led firms literally stealing a $100 billion market from right under the noses of the world's mature, cautious, and slow-moving pharmaceutical industry. And there's no end in sight to the growth of the biotech industry. By all rights, the existing giant companies, many of them with very deep pockets and a hundred years of global experience, should own this new market. But they don't. The "owners" are companies no one had even heard of fifteen years ago. Companies like Genentech, Amgen, Chiron—and now deCODE Genetics, a fabulously interesting and innovative member of today's biotech elite, founded in that far away Viking land called Iceland.

The year 2000 happens to be the 1,000th anniversary of Leif Eriksson's first voyage from Iceland to the shores of the Western Hemisphere. There is another exploration taking place in Iceland today, which may have as profound an effect on humankind as the Vikings' discovery of the New World. And in a very significant way, these two phenomena are inexorably linked. Iceland was and is one of the most homogenous populations in the world. It's made up entirely of the original Vikings from Norway and a few Irish slaves they brought with them in the ninth century. There has been virtually no new migration into Iceland since then. This twist of history is at the heart of Iceland's greatest entrepreneurial company—deCODE Genetics—one of the fastest moving and most innovative companies I've ever come across.

deCODE Genetics and its founder Kari Stefansson have certainly received great press. A *Wall Street Journal* headline read: "If This Man Is Right, Medicine's Future Lies in Iceland's Past." The *Financial Times* in London headlined its report: "Iceland Cashes in on its Viking Gene Bank." The *New Yorker* ran a full-length feature article titled "Decoding Iceland" with this lead-in: "The next big medical breakthrough may result from one scientist's battle to map the Viking gene pool." What's all this noise about? And just who is Kari Stefansson? And how did this happen in little Iceland—a country with a grand total of 270,000 people?

Well, here's the scoop straight from Reykjavik, Iceland, where Stefansson graciously submitted to a long interview with yours truly on a cold Saturday afternoon. To put the story into some context, it's worth noting that Kari Stefansson has become Iceland's richest person in just the four years since he left his post at Harvard Medical School. He's gone from living on a professor's salary to an estimated net worth of $400 million today. This is because his start-up firm has become Iceland's most valuable company with a market valuation of approximately $1.5 billion. Not bad for four years' effort. Yet, the underlying asset driving deCODE Genetics' amazing success has been a thousand years in the making.

That asset is Iceland's unique, homogeneous population. There are pockets of inbred populations around the world, but there is only one country—Iceland—with an entire population of homogeneous families. Since Iceland's genealogy is incredibly well documented, all the way back to 874 A.D., and there has been no new migration since, Iceland is a geneticist's dream laboratory. The whole premise that deCODE Genetics is based on is that the only way to discover the genetic basis of complex diseases like cancer, Alzheimer's, schizophrenia, and multiple sclerosis, is by finding the genetic mutations in a homogeneous population, thereby eliminating the wide genetic variability found among different racial and ethnic groups. Only by comparing the DNA of people with the particular disease to very similar people who don't have the disease, can we hope to isolate the disease-causing genetic mutations. Iceland is by far the best place in the world to do this. Not only is Iceland's population uniquely homogeneous, the country has also maintained extensive genealogical records dating back to the Viking days, it has a high-quality health care system, and serendipitously has accumulated an extensive bank of human tissues from biopsies and autopsies. On top of this, scientist-entrepreneur Kari Stefansson has assembled 300 top genealogists, geneticists, and DNA researchers in Reykjavik to work for him. They have identified and are currently working on finding the critical genetic mutations for twelve very tough diseases. Therefore, Stefansson is sitting atop a priceless array of assets for unlocking the secrets of the world's major diseases. They are also assets that make giant pharmaceutical companies drool and bring the international investment community pounding on the door. It's one of those rare and happy intersections in life of doing something really great and being able to make an honest buck at it. This is what makes a company like deCODE Genetics so interesting and so different from, say, the next band of dot-com zillionaires in Silicon Valley offering the world online solutions to shopping problems we didn't know we had.

Here's Iceland's high-speed innovation entrepreneur himself: "What I want to emphasize first is that there has been a paradigm shift in our society when it comes to value creation. It has shifted over to intellectual property and away from production and distribution. As a consequence of that, people are attaching much more monetary value to discovery, knowledge, and know-how than they did before. And as a consequence of *that*, there has been a shift in the center of discovery of new knowledge away from academia over to industry. That has led to some conflicts, but the important point of all this is that much more money has been put into discovery and knowledge. Also, industry always tries to do things more systematically than academia, which thrives on chaos—an important source of energy—but industry is trying to do this more systematically.

"If you think about it, there are two principal ways for mining knowledge out of laboratory data. One of them is the hypothesis approach. You put together a hypothesis and you test it. It's a wonderful method. It's basically the method the human mind uses best. It's an intuitive method. You start out with an unproven sentence—a hypothesis—and you select that hypothesis because it fits a rational sense in you. It cannot be totally rationally chosen, because then it would already be proven. This is a fairly interesting way, but it's cumbersome and it's very, very difficult to use when you are trying to examine complex phenomena. When you are examining complex phenomenon in society, be it in health care or whatever, the best way to do this is to use brute-force comparative analysis. You gather a large amount of data and that's folded into the embrace of informatics technology that looks for the best fit between data points. It does this by juxtaposing a very, very large number of data points with the sets of data that you are working with.

"I can give you an example of how this has been done very well. Fifteen years ago I could beat any chess computer in the world. Even after drinking a bottle of whiskey. Today, Deep Blue, the chess computer of IBM, beats the world champion every time they play. And how does Deep Blue do this? Deep Blue takes the chess that is in front of it, and takes a position on the board. And then it scans the database of all competitive games that have been played over the past two centuries, and it looks for the position that's on the board. Then it looks for the move in that position to win in the largest proportion of cases. There is no artificial intelligence, no weighting of observations, just pure comparative analysis. And this is an extraordinarily convenient, interesting, and important way of mining knowledge out of complex sets of data.

"Let's take my discipline, which is genetics. I mean what is genetics? Genetics is the study of information that goes into the making of man, and the flow of this information between generations. It is basically pure bioinformatics. We are studying the most sacred information that exists—the information that goes into designing you. So you could argue that what we are studying is the quintessential *IT*. And what we basically do is that we gather very, very large amounts of data on genetics, and we put it into the mechanism of modern informatics. And what we have done is that we have sort of approached our society as a system of data that we then mine with the use of the informatics technology. It is by far the most powerful way of looking for new knowledge in medicine and new knowledge in biotech, and it has worked wonders for us. And we are convinced that this is going to be the mechanism whereby we institute a new revolution in medicine.

"One of the things that you have read about a lot or seen a lot in the media in your country is the discussion of the Human Genome Project. This is Francis Collins and Craig Venter and all of those guys." I interrupted Stefansson to comment that Francis Collins's parents live just a few houses down the street from me and I've had the opportunity to meet him. I've learned that besides heading the U.S. Government's Human Genome Project, and being on the cover of *Time* and being interviewed all over TV,

Francis also rides motorcycles and plays a mean guitar. So he's sort of a biotech renaissance man. Stefansson laughed and continued: "Yes, and he's also quite religious, but the biotech scientists don't hold that against him either! Seriously, though, Francis Collins is very bright and he has been a wonderful leader of the Human Genome Project. But that project is focused on sequencing the entire system of the human genome. And once you have done that, how are you going to turn those data into knowledge? And that is where a company such as ours, deCODE Genetics, comes in. We take this human genome data, and look for the correlation between variances in the genome and variances in human nature. Variances like specific diseases, health problems, longevity, etc. So we are in an ideal position once the human genome has been sequenced. We can plough into it and we can begin to deliver knowledge that can be turned into solutions. We have already started doing this in fact."

I find biotech scientists fabulously interesting, beyond the impact they're having on my main interest, entrepreneurial enterprise. The science itself makes for a riveting discussion. So I stopped Stefansson again, to be absolutely clear on what he was saying. I wanted to know if he was actually describing the next phase in biogenetics, after the Human Genome Project was finished. It's been labeled in the media, at least, as the next great leap forward in medicine and it sounds terribly important. So I asked him: "Do you mean that your work is actually beyond the sequencing of the human genome. That when that is completed, your work really takes effect?" His immediate answer: "Exactly. Let's take the American company called Celera Genomics, which Craig Venter founded. The task of that company was to beat the Human Genome Project at its task—and finish the sequence ahead of them. So Craig Venter is going to be a few months ahead of the Human Genome Project. And so what? I mean the important thing is, What's he going to do with it? What happens next?"

My follow-up questions was this: "Isn't there a huge debate going on about who will actually own or have rights to this vital information? Whether it's proprietary to the Craig Venters or the world, or whether the U.S. government will distribute it freely, as Francis Collins says they should—or at least says they should with some legal and ethical strings attached." Again Stefansson's quick response: "Sure, everyone wants a part of this. But, in my opinion, that almost doesn't matter. The critical thing is how are you going to turn it into knowledge? And Craig certainly realizes that. He's on top of that and that's the reason why he's phoning us, not every day, but every other day it seems, wanting to work out an alliance with us— which we may do or may not do. I don't think it's terribly likely that we will, but it's possible.

"But, anyway, the basic approach to what deCODE Genetics is doing is to look at the society as sort of a system of information. And the Icelandic society has an advantage when it comes to that. One of the principal advantages is the wealth of knowledge on genealogy here in Iceland. I have the genealogy of the entire nation going 1,100 years back in time on our computer database. If you think about human genetics as the study of the flow of information, what the genealogy gives you are the avenues by which the information flows. And therefore it allows you to sort out what information goes where, what are the consequences of this variance and that variance. So we have an extraordinary resource in this genealogy database. Another resource we are beginning to construct these days is a centralized database on the health care of the entire nation. So you have the genealogy, which basically tells you who is related to whom, and then you will have the health care information on everyone. Then you can begin to figure out exactly what is inherited and what is not, what is transported and what is not. So I think that we are in a particularly interesting position in an exciting field and in exciting times—and we have exactly the right data."

At this stage of our discussion, I was already impressed that Kari Stefansson and deCODE Genetics were onto something significant. But the question that started bobbing up in my consciousness was, simply, How did this little miracle of a company get started? I knew that Stefansson's last job was teaching at Harvard, and, while prestigious, that seemed a very distant reality from the man I was facing—this world-class entrepreneur and the wealthiest man in the country! So I asked him how all this happened in just four years. Stefansson's personal story goes like this: "It happened in the following manner: I was a professor at Harvard Medical School and was sitting in Boston studying the genetics of multiple sclerosis when I first started to see the confluence of two very important things. One of them was the times—technology was being produced to allow one to study genetics in a systematic manner. And then I began to think about these incredibly important qualities of the Icelandic nation that would be possible to mine once this technology was in Iceland. Second, I began to sense the danger that foreign companies and universities would start to come to Iceland and do 'helicopter science.' By that I mean transporting the material abroad from Iceland for the studies.

"So I started to look at the possibility of setting up a facility in Iceland. And I put together a business plan and it took me a few weeks to raise enough money to start the company. We raised $12 million. We started the company in the fall of 1996—a little more than three years ago—and now the company is valued at about $1.5 billion. So things are going very nicely. When we started our company in the fall of 1996, we had 20 people and now we have in excess of 300 people. In February of 1998 we signed the largest corporate deal that a biotech company has ever signed in genetics. The deal, with Hoffman–La Roche in Switzerland, is valued between $200 million and $300 million. This is basically a research alliance where we are working on the discovery of genes that cause twelve common diseases. We share the intellectual property with Hoffman–La Roche and they pay us royalties and licensing fees and fund the work. So things have gone very nicely.

"The laboratory is absolutely fabulous. It is working extraordinarily nicely. Before you go back to America you should visit the company and let us show you around. We'll take you on a tour around the company. It's just marvelous to see these young people working. Let me give you an example of what I mean. There are totally different kinds of characters that become important. For example, we have some fabulous programmers and informatics people, who a few years back would have been classified as total social misfits. They do not abide by any rules of society that we would see as normal behavior. But these people have great ideas. They can contribute in that way. So there are identical twins who work in our company. They have been putting together marvelous software to deal with finding the variance in the genome that we're comparing to the variance in the people themselves. We call this genotyping and it generates an enormous amount of data. The question is, How do you extract that data and turn it into real information? This has been extremely arduous to do so. But these identical twins have written absolutely revolutionizing software to do that. But they are, indeed, strange guys.

"One day the head of bioinformatics came to me and said, 'Kari, we have to fire these guys. I mean they are never here. They are never here when anyone else is here. They come in at eleven o'clock at night and they are gone before we come in the morning.' So one day I sat down with the twins and said this was becoming serious. You have to be in at eight o'clock every day. They said, 'Yes, of course, if you want that, Kari, we'll do that.' So the next day I came at eight o'clock in the morning but they didn't show up. They were not there at nine o'clock, or ten, or eleven, or twelve, and so on. I happened to still be in the lab at eight o'clock that night when they came in with smiles on their faces. They said 'Kari, you see, we are exactly on time.' But these guys have done absolutely spectacular things. To gather this variance data from each unit in the lab, it took about four or five hours if we used the software from the company that produced that equipment. Then it took us about two or three hours to gather and enter the data with our own in-house software. Now these guys have written software that does this in ten to twenty seconds! They've revolutionized the work by several orders of magnitude. Yet they are guys who can hardly abide by any rules in society.

"Another very interesting thing is, you see, we are a part of this new wave, this new industry, this new paradigm, which is based on ideas, concepts, and discovery, rather than production and distribution. And there are many consequences of that. One of the consequences is that it isn't difficult to move an idea across boundaries. You just sit in your airplane and you carry ideas over boundaries between countries. It isn't like a production and distribution mechanism which doesn't travel very well. So, all of a sudden, you are in a culture that doesn't respect boundaries. When you talk to biotech people from Germany, England, Japan, or Iceland, and certainly from America, you see that everyone thinks in the same way. Everyone is marketing their products and themselves to the same markets. So this has become a fairly small world when it comes to this particular industry. And this is terribly important."

It's always interesting, I think, to find out what people think is responsible for their entrepreneurial success, and especially those people who don't really consider themselves entrepreneurs or even business people. Kari Stefansson fits this bill, so I asked him: "If a person who didn't know anything about starting a business, let alone a biotech business, came to you and asked the reason for your pretty amazing success, what would you tell him?" The surprising reply: "What I think characterizes the successful entrepreneur, or the successful start-up, which is the extension of the entrepreneur, is that in addition to having a good idea, and the willingness to work extraordinarily hard, you have to have a love of risk. It's not only that you shouldn't spend an awful lot of time avoiding risks, I think you should actually seek out the risk. It's the quintessential component of this—to thumb your nose at the risk. Sure, everyone is a little bit afraid of risk. But what gives you the courage to look risk in the face is the fact that you believe in your idea. First, you have to put together an idea or a concept. And the concept has to be good and you have to believe in it. Once you believe in your concept, the risk that others perceive is basically irrelevant. It isn't there. Because you believe that your idea is so great, you'll be able to go through anything.

"But it is also the willingness to sacrifice everything for what you're doing. And it's not because the amount of contribution you can make is in sort of a linear correlation with the amount of time you spend on it. It isn't. There is an exponential contribution when you begin to live the concept, rather than just work on it. You elevate yourself up to a higher level. You begin to see things in a way that no one else sees. You begin to understand in a way which no one else understands. I think it is the question of being able to put all of this intensity into it. And if you cannot do that, if you don't do that, nothing is going to come from even the best of ideas. Nothing can possibly come out. This is the modern crusades. This is the modern Viking, you know. You go in and sacrifice everything. And if you have a good concept, and you have good people, you come out a winner. If you don't the first time, never mind. If you are still consumed by your work, the following morning you rise out of the ashes like the Phoenix, and begin again anyway."

It was almost time to end the interview, but I really wanted to get Stefansson's thoughts on the notion of the organization life cycle. This should be particularly relevant to a company so dependent on maintaining its speed and innovation. I asked Stefansson the following: "Kari, our research shows that every company has a life cycle. They start, they grow big, they become bureaucratic, and most of them eventually die. What happens midway through is that the entrepreneurial genius that got them going in the first place eventually gets smothered by management techniques and bureaucracy. A primary casualty of this phenomenon is the company's ability to maintain its high-speed innovation—which you just happen to live and die by. Perhaps deCODE Genetics is too young to have faced this yet, but you will. How will you handle it?"

Stefansson thought for a moment and answered: "Everyone has to face this. And I will tell you, this is a particularly difficult task in a discovery based company like ours. Because the fact of the matter is, chaos is essential for the creative process. But this is the opposite of 'good management.' So I think what you basically have to do is do the same thing that people do in databases. One of the important tools in database management is the so-called wrapper. You can take data and put it into wrappers without classifying it, without doing anything with it, and put the wrappers in your database. Subsequently, you can take out the wrappers and begin to play with what is in the wrappers. And you can shift things between the wrappers. So you have to take our lab units, which we could call the wrappers of the laboratory, and leave some of them in the chaos. Of course, you have to manage them in a certain manner, so you know what resources this wrapper uses and that wrapper uses, etc. But you have to leave a unit, or units, within the organization that are allowed to maintain their creative chaos. The staff come in when they please, leave when the please, don't abide by the lab's normal rules, etc. You know you have to leave them alone for them to create. This is difficult to do but it is possible."

I noted that that's next to impossible for most professional managers to do. They're trained to do exactly the opposite. Managers are supposed to plan, organize, manage, and control activities—not leave them alone. Stefansson replied: "I recognize that. It is extraordinarily difficult to do what I am suggesting. I have seen an incredible number of organizations fail at this. But now I'm going to tell you a secret, which shows the importance of failing to do this. The only reason the biotech industry exists today is that the pharmaceutical industry failed terribly at doing this. We exist because the pharmaceutical industry has been incapable of maintaining a creative spirit within their labs' organizations.

"So I recognize the near inevitability of the failure to do this if you grow beyond a certain size. But these are exciting challenges to deal with. I am absolutely 100 percent convinced that we can succeed at it, but it's going to keep us up on our toes. My feeling is that in our 'stuff,' the products that we are developing in addition to gene discovery and intellectual properties, there may be a database that we will sell subscriptions to, and there may be software for medical decision making, etc. So we may, because of this very problem, spin off these things into smaller organizations to try to maintain this creative spirit which we know is so much easier to maintain in the smaller organization."

The following Monday I took up Kari Stefansson's offer to visit his offices and the "marvelous lab" he was so proud of. Joining me was my partner in Iceland, Arni Sigurdsson, and his associate, Olli Olafsson. Our tour guide was Laufey Amundadottir, who has a Ph.D. from Georgetown University and was doing research on breast cancer at Harvard before she returned to Iceland to join deCODE. She is currently the division head at deCODE for cancer genetics and personally runs the subprojects on lung cancer and prostate cancer. The first stop on the tour was the work station of Thor Kristjansson, deCODE's senior programmer and the architect of the firm's genealogical database. After a few introductory comments, he suggested that a simple demonstration might be the best way to understand his job. He turned to Olli Olafsson, a complete stranger to him, and said: 'Let's see how you and I are related. What's your complete name and date of birth?' Olli told him and Thor typed it onto the screen:

"Olafur Thor Olafsson—26, 11, 1953"

Next he typed in his own name and birthdate:

"Thordur Jon Kristjansson—03, 04, 1965"

Then he clicked on a few icons and the page began to scroll with separate columns of the names and birth dates of generation after generation of both his and Olli's direct line of ancestors until—bingo! A single name popped up, centered in a box, above the two lists:

Jon Thorsteinsson—born 1687/died 1762

Just beneath the name and dates were a couple of indecipherable lines of Icelandic, obviously giving some details about great, great, great,

great, great, great, great, great grandfather Thorsteinsson. "There," Thor proudly announced, "is my and Olli's most recent common ancestor!" Olli almost fell over. My partner Arnie was beside himself. And I, who have spent three decades trying to construct my own family tree back just two or three generations, stared at the screen in stunned silence. The computer had jumped 313 years and eleven generations back in ten seconds. Laufey, our guide and cancer expert, simply said: "This is why Iceland is such a good place to do genetic research."

High-speed innovation is obviously the name of the game in biotech. Kari Stefansson knows his company is racing against time with an insatiable need for innovation. He and deCODE Genetics have these two qualities—speed and innovation—in spades. And what about you? Here are the steps to ensure you will have them, too.

THE TWO GOLDEN RULES

A landmark study of California companies found that the cost of innovation, as measured by new products and patents, is an astounding twenty-four times greater at large companies than small companies. If you're the CEO of a giant bureaucracy, this statistic could keep you awake nights. If you're a start-up entrepreneur, it's the best news you'll ever hear. Few people today need statistics to convince them that speed and creativity are major competitive factors in our global economy. And even fewer would disagree that young, entrepreneurial companies, can and regularly do, beat the socks off their larger competitors. They are both faster and more innovative.

The questions, then, are these: How do you do that? What is it that makes entrepreneurs and their start-ups so fast moving and innovative? And can you keep it alive as your company moves along its life cycle—getting bigger and more bureaucratic year after year? These are terribly important things to know; we might call them the "genetic mutations" of the entrepreneurial company. Fortunately, unlike decoding the human genome, entrepreneurial practices are not so complicated. At the heart of all high-speed innovation are just two golden rules: Feeling the necessity to invent and having the freedom to act.

THE NECESSITY TO INVENT

Remember this bit of old-fashioned wisdom: "*Mater artium necessitas.*" If your Latin is a bit rusty, it means, "Necessity is the mother of invention." And we've all been saying it since the time of Caesar—because it's absolutely true. History is replete with evidence that anyone can be innovative if his life depends on it.

And nowhere will you find better illustrations of this adage than in entrepreneurial enterprise. Consider the six Minnesota miners who, in

1906, were facing bankruptcy after putting their life savings into a "worthless" gravel pit. They hoped it would yield valuable minerals but all they could find was sand. Out of desperation, they invented sandpaper—the first product of 3M—and the rest is history. To make sure the spirit of *Mater artium necessitas* stays alive in your business, here are three key points to keep in mind:

▷ *Feeling the Heat of Necessity*

The six miners in Minnesota felt it. It's knowing that winning is a necessity because your survival is on the line. It's called taking it personally and it's the most powerful force ever concocted to motivate people. Inside most bureaucracies, you can't find anybody who feels much heat about anything. From the sales clerks who shrug their shoulders all the way up to the executives who haven't talked to a real customer since 1975, absolutely no one seems accountable for anything. This would be unfathomable behavior to an entrepreneur. When it comes down to putting food on the table, succeeding with your business is a burning necessity, not a box to be checked off on the Performance Review form. When you and your people begin to lose this feeling, you'll know it's time to move on to the next point—and recreate a sense of crisis and urgency in the business.

▷ *Create Crisis and Urgency*

Akio Morita, the founder of Sony, said creating a little crisis in the company is a good thing. And so it is. Everyone knows that more innovation and action occurs in a day of crisis than a month of complacency. And few great leaps forward have ever resulted from careful planning. They almost always come on the wings of crisis. But creating a sense of crisis and urgency doesn't mean screaming at the top of your lungs (well, once in a while probably won't hurt) or threatening to fire everyone in sight. It does mean establishing deadlines and sticking to them. It does mean taking it very hard if a good customer is lost. And it certainly means that all your employees know you are dead serious about making the business a success. The trick is to deliver this entrepreneurial message in small, regular doses: a small crisis a day to keep complacency away.

▷ *Do Something—Anything—Better Each Day*

Thomas Edison, still the all-time record holder of American patents and the founder of scores of companies, was famous for this pearl of wisdom: "Invention is 10 percent inspiration and 90 percent perspiration." So what can you do to make sure the "perspiration level" in your business is high? For starters, you and every employee you hire has to believe that the most important task you have every day is to find a better way to do something. "Better" means more quantity, more quality, more speed, and less cost. It's called continuous improvement in human performance—and it's one of the most visible differences in behavior between the hungry entrepreneur trying to survive and the complacent bureaucrat counting the days until retirement.

THE FREEDOM TO ACT

Entrepreneurs have well-deserved reputations for high-speed innovation, in large part because they embrace the freedom to act. In fact, most entrepreneurs say action is much more important than innovation. A great idea with no action to implement it doesn't do much for the bottom line. If a person or company is very action oriented—trying this and trying that, going here and going there—most people would say: "Wow, look at all the things they're doing. That's really an innovative group." The fact is, if you try out a lot of new ideas, if you are willing to experiment, and if, when you make a mistake, you come right back and try again, you are an innovative group. The important brand of innovation in business has never been quiet, ivory-tower analysis to come up with a blockbuster idea. It has always been, and will continue to be, trying ten different things and hoping three of them work.

It's very much the old story about Amoco, which for many years was the top U.S. company in oil and gas exploration. When the crusty, long-term CEO was asked how Amoco beat all the other bigger oil companies in finding new oil, he replied: "We drill the most holes. You find a lot of oil when you drill a lot of holes." And so it is in all business. Here are three proven approaches to creating action in your organization.

➤ *Freeing the Genius of the Average Worker*

Who should be free to take action in your company? Who has the good ideas? How about the average workers? They're the people who will know the product inside and out. They'll also be the ones on first-name terms with customers. And it's the average workers who will have to deal with every new bureaucratic rule and time-wasting procedure future managers will dream up. In other words, they are the people with the most intimate knowledge of the workings of the business.

It's easy for growing companies to forget to tap into the "genius" of average workers. They're not superstars and they're not troublemakers. And if they don't do heroic things and don't cause trouble, busy managers can easily forget about average workers and their ideas. Entrepreneurs, fighting for survival, can't afford to silence what may be their richest source of new ideas to improve the way you do business.

➤ Action With Customers, Products, and Inside the Organization

Every single action directed at customers and products is a step in the right direction. You'll never go wrong by trying things to improve your products and better serve your customers. Of course, they won't all work, but there's no faster, cheaper way to learn. Entrepreneurs are often astounded by what they see in this regard when they get acquired by bigger companies. Numerous committees, dozens of meetings, and hundreds of e-mails and memos are expended on ideas and projects that have virtually nothing to do with the core business.

There is always serious work to do on fighting bureaucracy inside the company. Almost all of it involves getting rid of something, not adding something. Actions attacking dysfunctional procedures, out-of-date forms, and out-of-touch committees are all worth their weight in gold. It's called bureaucracy bashing.

➤ Bureaucracy-Bashing Bosses

Here's rule number one in bureaucracy bashing: Don't let it get started in the first place. Always remember that your fundamental mission is to beat the competition to market with better products and services. Every time someone suggests a new procedure, a new committee, another system, ask yourself how this is going to contribute to beating the competition. If you can't come up with a clear, convincing answer, kill the new idea. Don't worry, the company probably won't implode into a black hole no matter how passionately the champion of the new program pleads the case. The best approach in this crusade is: When in doubt, don't do it.

Now that you have all our suggested actions around "the necessity to invent" and the "freedom to act," let's return for a moment to Kari's Stefansson's Big Blue chess example. When I first heard his chess vignette, I asked Kari if he thought that biotech would ultimately be more important to people's lives than computers, or more specifically, the emerging Internet industry. He answered: "I think biotechnology is going to be very, very important in the twenty-first century, but information technology is going to be an integral part of all this. In fact, the company in biotech that is best equipped when it comes to informatics and producing knowledge out of the data will be the biotech company that's going to win."

So even if biotech and the Internet are the two great entrepreneur-ial industries of the future (as I think they are), biotech will, in fact, be very dependant on IT. Specifically, biotech needs great computing power for things like state-of-the-art genotyping, and rapid Internet access for send-ing and retrieving scientific research. So let's conclude this chapter on High-Speed Innovation by taking a look at that other "great entrepreneur-ial industry," which like biotech, operates in a race against time—with an insatiable need for innovation.

REINVENTING PR FOR THE NEW ECONOMY

In the course of working for other public relations companies, I learned more about what I wouldn't do than about what I would do in running my own company.

—Sabrina Horn
Founder and CEO,
The Horn Group

"We get probably forty calls a week now from companies that want to have us represent them. It's crazy. That's how many companies are out there. And you know, you pick up the phone and you basically decide which ones you want to meet with. And many of our competitors are in the same position. Forty leads a week just in San Francisco. In the Boston office they have about twenty. It is crazy. It's just, you know . . . 'Thank you God.'"

Welcome to the world of Sabrina Horn, wunderkind of the high-tech PR industry. Horn was still in her twenties when she founded the Horn Group, Inc. (HGI). In less than a decade,[1] HGI has become one of the fastest-growing PR agencies in the world. With offices in San Francisco and Boston, and agency partnerships in Europe and Asia, the Horn Group is a high-speed, innovative example of a totally new breed of business—the "new economy" PR firm. Or as the Horn Group likes to remind you with its registered service mark—"E-PR®"—a public relations firm totally dedi-cated to the emerging e-commerce industry.

HGI is currently on a superfast track. It is an *Inc. 500* company, making *Inc. Magazine*'s 1999 listing of America's fastest-growing compa-

---

[1] I'll have to repeat the disclaimer footnoted in chapter 3 about "never" profiling entrepreneurs and companies that haven't survived for at least ten years. That's technically true for Sabrina Horn. But as a disclaimer to the disclaimer, the Horn Group will soon complete its first high-ly successful decade, about the same life span of the industry it serves. And, after getting to know Sabrina Horn—who after ten years of entrepreneuring will still be quite young, I have no doubt that she and the Horn Group will be around a long time.

nies. It was also named "Best U.S. Employer" in 1999 by *Working Woman* magazine, an unheard-of accolade in an industry famous for its high pressure burnout rate. The firm has received numerous other industry awards and tributes. Most important for our purposes here, HGI is at the cutting edge of reinventing the PR industry. the Horn Group aims to be as high tech in the way it does PR as its clients are in their respective businesses. From the simultaneous distribution of a thousand virtual press releases to using hyperlinks for "streaming" video and audio trailers, to staging online press conferences, HGI's Internet-era PR services have become a largely paperless business—mirroring the cyberspace style of the clients it serves.

I recently visited the Horn Group in its totally wired, but warm and inviting, San Francisco offices. What follows is an incredibly honest and frank interview with Sabrina Horn: "The market is correcting itself right now. And that's a good thing because somebody had to let the air out of the balloon a little bit. But I think it's going to continue to be a massive growth area of innovation and economic development and prosperity. It was just the beginning of it and it just got so hot that the pressure valve needed to be opened up a little bit. So I think it's going to continue, but not at these crazy, crazy levels. You know, companies going public that have no business going public, that don't have the infrastructure, and with individuals running those companies who are more interested in personal wealth creation than building a company that will last. That is the downside to all of this. Because, let's face it, God created man with a couple of bad traits and one of them is greed. So, we ought to fight that. But I think the growth is going to continue for at least another ten to twenty years."

I was curious, given the furious pace of things in Silicon Valley and the industry nationally, how the Horn Group sorts out which companies look like winners and which are going to be losers. I asked her: "When all these companies call you, I would imagine that you try to pick good ones with a future as clients. So what do you look for in e-commerce companies to indicate future success or failure?"

It seemed that Horn had been thinking about this very question all her life. Her answer was quick and confident: "You know most often it's not the technology that fails. It's the people who run the companies. It's the management. The CEO has too big of an ego. Or the people they hire are not competent enough. Or they miss an opportunity to form a partnership with another company that could really take them over the top. It's all 'up here.' And you see the companies where there's a seasoned management team, with a CEO who's done it before, who's earned his stripes, so to speak, and he hires senior executives to help him. That company has a greater chance of success than a bunch of guys who are just out of college, or a couple of guys who came out of middle management who are trying it for the first time.

"What happens most often is, if you look at those companies, the people who started those companies no longer run them. They're in positions of strategy or technology vision but they're not running the companies. So we look at that. What's the quality of the management team? Have they done it before? Do they have good experience? Do they have their heads screwed on straight? Do they have realistic expectations? Are they committed to PR? Do they get it or do they just want to see themselves on the front page of the *Wall Street Journal?*

"The entrepreneur who isn't experienced in running a business can hire people who are. That's the smart thing to do. That's a really nice complement of vision and energy and entrepreneurialism with 'Wait a minute, what are we doing here? Is this what we *should* be doing?' And that's what you see a lot of. That's attractive. But if you only see a bunch of twenty-four- or twenty-five-year olds, you'd better look under the hood some more!

"The other thing that we look at is who's backed them. Who's on their board? Who's put money into them? Because everybody has got money these days. So it's not how much money they have necessarily or that they even have it. It's who put it in there. And when we meet with a company and they say, 'Well, we're backed by a lot of angel investors,' then we say well, who? Or if they say, 'We don't have any VC money yet,' we say, 'Well, when are you going to go get it? Who are you talking to?' That kind of thing.

"There's one other piece of advice I would offer. Never take anything at face value. Always look for what's not there. What are they not telling you? What's not on this piece of paper and what's missing? It's like when people want to hire somebody and they get references. The references are going to be very positive; otherwise, they wouldn't be references. So if you really want to know about a company or a person, you've got to do a little digging, and that's what we have to do."

Everybody knows that e-commerce companies move with the speed of light and live or die on relentless innovation. But there's another group of companies that has to stay one step ahead of the hurricane that e-commerce has become. Of course that's the very specialized, very high-tech PR firms that present them to the world. *USA Today* reported that the huge B2B segment of e-commerce, which HGI is in, has become "a war of press releases" in which "the corporate and media buzz over the exchanges has reached galactic heights." And so it has. Whether it's the unending string of new product launches, or new strategic alliances being signed, or make-or-break Initial Public Offerings, the PR agencies have to be ahead of the e-commerce industry curve—every day in every way. In fact, it seems there has never been an industry more dependent on public relations. It dwarfs anything the world ever saw in the old economy. And speaking of the good old days of the old economy, a really swift PR program was something like the famous United Airlines' campaign of sending a red rose every Monday morning to the (always female) executive secretary of the (always male) executive to nudge *her* to book *him* on United! Those were the days when PR was more about schmoozing and emotive half-truths than dealing with tough Wall Street analysts, knowledgeable high-tech editors, and the most technically demanding customers in the world. All of which led me to wonder what inspired Horn to adopt the life of an entrepreneur, especially in the high-pressure business of high-tech PR—and how she created and grew HGI into one of the premier companies in the industry.

Here's Sabrina Horn's story in her own inimitable style: "The biggest thing is the entrepreneurial spirit that I got from my parents who are both immigrants from East Germany—from before the Iron Curtain came down. My father was one of the first German research chemists who was hired by Union Carbide. He is sort of a self-made man several times over. He has about forty-eight U.S. patents, inventing various fibers and polyethylenes and other poly-whatevers. He also started a venture capital firm when he was fifty. He's actually had three different businesses, so I grew up with it in my blood, or at least in my heart and my brain. And that was a driving force behind wanting to try my hand at something that I had some knowledge of, to see if I could stand on my own two feet. But it was never to build a big business like this. It was just to have a few people, make a comfortable living, and you know, not too much stress.

"Secondly, in the course of working for other public relations companies, I learned more about what I wouldn't do than about what I would do in running my own company. So the collection of that knowledge gave me this inspiration to sort of set a new standard, or set the record straight, and try and do it right.

"And the last reason is probably that, at the time, in the early nineties, there wasn't nearly as much competition in my industry as there is today. So there was room for another operator. There was room for another player with the expertise that I had in the particular area of software that I knew about—and it was relatively easy, I thought, to set up my own shingle."

I then asked Horn specifically how she got into the PR field: "It was one of my first summer jobs when I was in college. I did an internship for an agency. And then I decided that I liked communications and specialized in that in my bachelor's degree program at Hobart & William Smith College. I went straight through to graduate school and got a master's degree in PR at Boston University. So I was very determined to be in PR and communications. And I started in PR early in my career.

"Then, through the company I was working for, I became exposed to a number of different software companies that all wanted to do business with one of my clients. I frequently wrote press releases for my client about all these different software partners. One day, one of those companies, called PeopleSoft, called me and said: 'Hey, that was a great press release. Can you do some more for us?' And I said: 'Well, no. You know I work for somebody else. You could come and be a client of my employer's company or I could hook you up with some freelancers who might be able to help you.' But I went home that night and I thought this could be it. This could be my ticket. But I wanted to be ethical about it so I was very, very careful about how I left my employer. I took two weeks of vacation to write a business overview to pitch PeopleSoft on my capabilities. I was competing with a firm that had thirty to forty people and was very well established. I did everything but dance on the table that day for the CEO and his management team. PeopleSoft was maybe a year old. They had $5 million in revenues and maybe fifty people. This was 1991.

"So I got home that night and there was a message on my answering machine that I had won this business! It was $7,000 a month and I thought I was queen of the day. The next day I walked into my employer and said: 'I'd like to go do this but I want to give you first right of refusal. It's the ethical thing to do. Do you want the account?' And they said, 'No, we don't know much about the business that PeopleSoft is in.' So I left. That was it. They were my first client. We had a long run with PeopleSoft—about six years.[2]

"As I said, I didn't originally intend to grow a company this size. I just wanted to have a couple of people, do a good job, go home at the end of the day, and have a balanced work-life arrangement. But I realized pretty quickly that PeopleSoft was a hot ticket and if I was going to keep them, I had better grow with them. So very quickly I started hiring more and more people and got up to ten people, and then I thought well, maybe we should grow to twenty, and then thirty. Ultimately, I had to grow the business by so much every year just to keep PeopleSoft under 30 percent of our revenues because they were such a big client."

That sounded almost too easy. So I asked Horn: "How did you do that? What are the things you've done to grow HGI, right up to today when you're being recognized as one of the fastest-growing companies in the country?" Again, she had the answers ready:

---

[2]Of course this is the same PeopleSoft that today is the fourth-largest software company in the United States, with revenues of $1.3 billion and 7,000 employees.

- "I initially built a franchise of clients around PeopleSoft's technology and that's a key thing. I think it's important for entrepreneurs to focus on an area of competence and not to get distracted by opportunities and by too much of a good thing. I think that was really good for us in the early days because we built a reputation for ourselves as being really good in one area of software. Everybody knew we did it and they all called us and we had our choice of the companies we wanted to work with."

"We've always had a focus within high tech. Business to business software is where we play right now. But as the market continues to further define itself, there will be such big segments of the B2B marketplace, we probably won't start working in all of them. First there was the Internet. And then there was e-commerce. And then there was business to business and business to consumer. So we took this B2B fork, and I think it will continue to split because there's just going to be so much. So many different ways of cutting the pie. For example, there's business-to-government software now to Web-enable the government. You know, we have so many great ideas. There are so many great companies out there to work for. But you just get so distracted. So we've actually developed a little model to help us get focused in the areas of technology that we want to go after. Anything outside of the dotted line—we're just not going to do it. And we're committed to not doing it. You always have to be looking at where the technology is going and where you need to go, but at the same time you need to have a core expertise.

- "In the service business, your product is your people. If we made a product like a TV, we'd have quality assurance, we'd have manufacturing, we'd have engineering, we'd have all this infrastructure to support making the product. And what services companies don't do enough of is support their 'product,' which is their people. So that's what we do. That's certainly our reputation and we've even won awards for it. We won this award last year for *Best Employer in the U.S.* For a PR agency to get that kind of recognition is big stuff because they're usually terrible shops that burn out people. So I think the second thing is, if you're an entrepreneur in a service business, or even if you're in a product business, it all starts with your people. If they're happy, then you have a better chance of having happy customers.

- "You know, it's shades of gray in PR. Because all of us offer similar services, it's in how we deliver the service that becomes the magic. I think we've always tried to be on top of, or one step ahead of, new ways of doing PR so that our services are never a cookie cutter. I'm always trying to reinvent the way we do things. And it's not just from using better technology in PR, but also in our processes. Just getting more efficient. Whether the client sees it or not, we are always retooling what we do. Currently, we call the vision for that "E-PR®." Because everybody has the 'e,' our registered service mark is now "E-PR®" for e-business.

"So I think that clients come to us because they are a fit with our focus, they appreciate our culture around people, and they like what we have to say about innovation and trying to do things differently. I think that would probably be the three key things supporting our growth."

I wanted to wind up the interview with Sabrina Horn's specific suggestions on how to become a successful entrepreneur, in e-commerce or any other industry. I asked her my stock question: "Sabrina, suppose some young people came to you and asked, 'How can we do what you've done? What do we have to know or do?' What advice would you give them to help them become successful entrepreneurs?"

- "Three things. First, it's not over till the check's cleared. You just cannot assume anything. You have to trust your gut and if they say, 'It's in the mail,' well, you know it's not there. You've got a new business deal? 'Yes.' Did you get the contract signed? 'No.' Well then, we don't have it. It's not over till it's over and you have it in your hand. I don't know any better way to package that up except to say, it's not over till the check has cleared the bank.

- "Secondly, you make your own luck. People say, 'Sabrina, you're so lucky. You've grown this great company. You've got all these people working for you and you're really lucky.' You know, there's a lot of blood, sweat, and tears that goes into every company that's successful. And you make your own luck.

- "The last thing is you should always know what you don't know. The second that you think you've made it, that's the day that you should give up your job because you've gotten too big for your britches. And then you stop worrying about the little things that keep people connected and keep the ball in play. So there's a lot of passion and a lot of energy and heartfelt stuff in here, but I think it comes down to those three basic things."

My last question was: "What makes you feel really great about what you've accomplished as you conclude your first decade as an entrepreneur?" Sabrina Horn's wonderful answer: "That there are about seventy-five people in the United States who work for the Horn Group who think that we're doing a good thing—and that they'll stick around. The best thing that could happen to me in a day of work would be that an employee would come to me and say: 'I love working here and I want to help you grow the company.' That would be the best."

SELF-INSPIRED BEHAVIOR:
Love What You Do and Get Very Good at Doing It

I promoted myself.

—Sarah Breedlove Walker
Founder, Walker Manufacturing Co.

Feeling disadvantaged? Try being poor, uneducated, black, and a single mother in nineteenth-century America. You can be sure that Sarah Walker never received an affirmative action promotion, a seminar on motivation, or a stock option—yet, somehow, she managed to become America's first self-made millionairess! And back in 1900 a million bucks was a phenomenal sum.

Born in 1867, the daughter of former slaves and orphaned at age seven, Sarah Breedlove never saw the inside of a school room. She was married at fourteen, widowed with children by twenty, and earned her keep as a washerwoman. In your great-grandmother's America, you couldn't get more "disadvantaged" than Sarah. Yet this ebony dynamo invented and manufactured health and beauty products for black women, created a 5,000-strong sales agent network, and became the most successful (and richest) woman entrepreneur in the country.

Madame Walker, as she liked to be called, set a whole new standard for self-inspired behavior: "I am a woman who came from the cotton fields of the South. I was promoted from there to the washtub and then to the kitchen. From there I promoted *myself* into the business of manufacturing hair goods, and I built my own factory on my own ground." And promote herself she did. By the time she died in 1919, annual sales were close to a million dollars a year, and Madame Walker had etched herself a place in business history. How do such impossible dreams happen?

Why do some people appear so self-inspired, while others spend their lives waiting for something to happen? Dig a little deeper into Sarah

Walker's history and some of her answers begin to emerge. Like many black women of her time, Walker's hair began falling out at an early age. Whether due to poor diet, disease, or whatever, there were certainly no special products to treat such maladies. Indeed, no manufacturers produced any products to meet the personal-hygiene or beauty needs of black women. In desperation she began concocting her own shampoo and hair conditioner to save her hair. Once successful, the word spread throughout her community and she couldn't make enough to satisfy the needs of other black women. She began selling door to door, with many of her customers becoming sales agents themselves. She attracted an army of other self-inspired black women, eager to move up from $2 a week as domestics to the $20-plus per week Walker agents could earn. Sold as the Walker System, her products were manufactured in factories and sold in hair salons across the country. This is self-inspired entrepreneurship at its finest.

HIGH COMMITMENT AND HIGH PERFORMANCE

If entrepreneurs like Sarah Walker are self-inspired, what exactly are they self-inspired to do? Do vastly different entrepreneurial personalities, such as Bill Gates, Soichiro Honda, and Anita Roddick, share any common practices as "workers"? Yes, they do, but it is a surprisingly short list. One characteristic of all entrepreneurs I've met is that they like what they do. They're *highly committed* to what they're doing. In addition to liking what they do, they're very interested in being good at doing it. At least as good, and hopefully better, than the competition. In personnel jargon, they're out to achieve *high performance*. So the self-inspired behavior of entrepreneurs rests on two pretty basic qualities—high commitment and high performance.

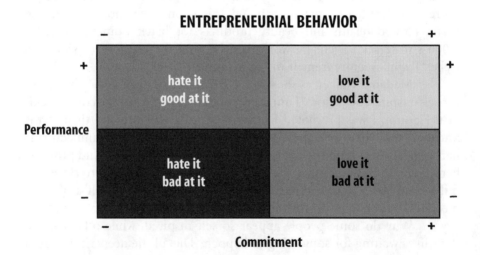

ENTREPRENEURIAL BEHAVIOR

You can actually find managers and workers occupying any of the locations on the graph. You've probably worked with all of them at one time or another. Here's a quick definition of each:

HIGH COMMITMENT/HIGH PERFORMANCE. The upper right hand corner is entrepreneurial territory. "I love what I do and I'm good at doing it" is the clarion call of all self-inspired entrepreneurs.

HIGH COMMITMENT/LOW PERFORMANCE. In the lower right hand area are those people who love what they do but aren't very good at doing it. It's not unusual to find new employees here. They can be bursting with enthusiasm for their new job, but they just don't have enough knowledge or experience yet to do the job well. Unfortunately, you can also find long-term employees occupying this spot. They're loyal and they do love the company—but they stopped learning and improving a decade ago.

LOW COMMITMENT/HIGH PERFORMANCE. The upper left hand area houses the exact opposite type of worker, and is much more common. This is home to those who may actually hate their job but are very good at doing it. They're usually highly skilled people who don't like the environment in which they have to perform. Commercial airline pilots come to mind. Flying tourists to Orlando has to be pretty dull stuff compared to combat missions over Iraq. You can see this type everywhere, especially in large bureaucracies, which can drive the commitment out of even the most highly skilled workers. Have you been to a government-run hospital lately?

LOW COMMITMENT/LOW PERFORMANCE. What can we say about workers who hate what they do and are no good at doing it? If you make such a blunder and hire this type in your business, don't compound the problem by wasting months or years trying to "fix" the person. Cut your losses and say sayonara.

Successful entrepreneurs, by definition, are squarely in the high commitment/high performance area of behavior. That's not the problem. Their big challenge is to pass on and instill the same behavior in their employees. The first mistake you can make is to wait ten years to get going on this. The time to start is with your very first employee. And the place to start is to make sure that you, as the founder, are doing everything you can to personally model high commitment and high performance for all your employees.

ENTREPRENEURIAL COMMITMENT: "I LOVE WHAT I DO"

Commitment comes from the belief that your company's mission has purpose and integrity, and that your role in it is both important and acknowledged. Entrepreneurs are extraordinarily committed to what they do. Their commitment borders on the obsessive. It comes from the *heart* and produces an abundance of pride, loyalty, and plain old hard work. Here are the four most important practices to foster entrepreneurial commitment across your company:

➤ Love What You Do

Entrepreneurs love what they do. They're proud of their enterprise. They see noble challenge in every mundane step they take. They love it so much, they'll work night and day to see it succeed. A little of this will go a long way in any growing company. Every job can be made important. Challenges can be created in the smallest of tasks. And companies can find noble purpose in almost anything—from landscaping services to finding a cure for cancer. The long-term payoff for getting this spirit instilled in employees is simply enormous. Through it all, never forget that the number-one rule in commitment remains: "You gotta like what you do."

➤ Give Autonomy, Demand Accountability

One sure-fire way to build commitment is to give people some autonomy and freedom to do their jobs. But the entrepreneurial approach is a lot more sharply focused than run-of-the-mill empowerment programs at *Fortune 1000* companies. In an entrepreneurial environment, empowering people, or giving them autonomy, means they own their job—and that means they're accountable for results. It's very much a two-way street. Employees not only understand this, they like it. For some, it may be the first time they've ever been treated like a responsible adult at work. Put this into practice. The results can truly be astounding.

➤ Share Fortune and Misfortune

Entrepreneurs have little choice but to pin their future on the future of their company. You will have to suffer the fortunes as well as the misfortunes of your business. And so it should be for your employees. If it's good for the company, it should be good for employees. Conversely, if it's bad for the company, there have to be some consequences for employees. It's called *shared destiny,* and without it, you can forget about a committed work force.

➤ Lead by Example, Never Compromise

How can you expect your people to care about what they do, if you don't seem to care about what you're doing? Leading by example is a rule everyone agrees on, but few practice. It's actually more critical for entrepreneurs to do this than it is for their managerial counterparts in larger companies. Everyone can accept having a cynical, uncommitted manager a few times in his career. It's the luck of the draw and you likely won't have to put up with him very long anyway. But if the creator of the company hates the work, or hates the customers, or whatever, who could blame the shipping clerk for some slippage in his commitment to the cause? Remember: Your people are watching you like a hawk—so never forget to show them you love what you do, even on a bad day. You owe it to your people and you owe it to yourself.

There are hundreds of specific policies and programs you can initiate to foster high commitment. Whatever you do, from major steps like employee ownership to the most mundane of personnel practices, remember that the underlying goal is to make people feel so important in their job and so proud of their company, that loving what they do will just come naturally.

ENTERPRENEURIAL PERFORMANCE: "I'M GOOD AT DOING IT"

Entrepreneurial performance is all about doing it better than anyone else. Performance depends on knowledge, skill, and working smart. It comes mostly from the head. Entrepreneurs look at performance as a matter of survival—not scoring points for the next merit review. Here are four key practices that define and deliver entrepreneurial performance.

➤ Get Better at What You Do

Continuous improvement in performance becomes a habit with entrepreneurs. This happens when you know you're in a competitive battle of survival. Working smarter takes on dramatic new meaning when it's the only thing standing between you and bankruptcy. If raising the bar to stay competitive is the lifeblood of enterprise, shouldn't it also be the lifeblood of everyone in the enterprise? Of course it should. And you can make it happen if it's crystal clear to everyone that "getting better" is every employee's most important job.

➤ Winning at Quality, Quantity, Speed, and Cost

The entrepreneur's shorthand for performance comes down to asking this: "How well, how fast, and how efficiently can I work?" And the performance standard on each is very clear. The bar is set just high enough to beat your best competitor. Just do this and you can forget about all the personnel consultants' systems for setting standards and measuring performance. These four common-sense parameters of performance are what you need. Instilling them in your people, constantly getting better at them, and measuring every employee by them will give you the employee performance you'll need to beat your best competitors and end up in the winner's circle.

▷ Save Your Best for Customers and Products

Entrepreneurs save their best efforts for making great products and selling real customers. It's called focus. As an entrepreneur, you will undoubtedly have this kind of focus in spades. It's absolutely essential to getting a new enterprise up and running. As always, the trick will be to pass this on to your employees. Time after time, we've seen promising start-ups lose their focus and blow their opportunity to become great companies. This often happens through the good intentions of employees who simply don't share the entrepreneur's original laser-point focus on customers and products. You begin to see time, energy, and money being spent on all manner of marginal activities and internal battles. The result? Your company gets diverted from its mission and becomes a prime candidate for early demise. You can avoid this fatal misstep by making sure that you and your people stay focused on the only performance that builds any enterprise—that which is aimed directly at making great products and serving great customers.

▷ Lead by Example, Never Compromise

If leading by example is a good way to foster entrepreneurial commitment, the same message applies here—in spades. Of course, you have to show the way on performance. As an entrepreneur, it goes with the territory. This doesn't mean that you have to be, or even should be, the top performer in your company. It does mean you have to be ready, willing, and able to roll up your sleeves and give it your all—side by side with your employees. Seeing the founder of the company putting the product together or personally delivering the service can be an inspiring sight to most employees. The biggest challenge will be to keep it up, especially after your company moves beyond the start-up phase. A million things will come up to keep you off the shop floor or prevent you from making customer visits. If this happens, watch out. You're about to lose your most powerful tool for fostering high performance in your people.

ENTREPRENEURIAL BEHAVIOR AND THE ALMIGHTY POWER OF CONSEQUENCES

The essence of self-inspired entrepreneurship still rests on an old, simple truth about human behavior. That is, people behave in their own self-interest—taking actions that they perceive will result in some positive consequence, and avoiding actions they perceive will result in negative consequences. However, this bone-deep law of behavior depends on the positive and negative consequences being accurate, timely, and powerful. The more the consequences fit this bill, the more self-inspired the person's performance will be.

This is the classic model of entrepreneurship—squarely based on the power of consequences.

THE ALMIGHTY POWER OF CONSEQUENCES

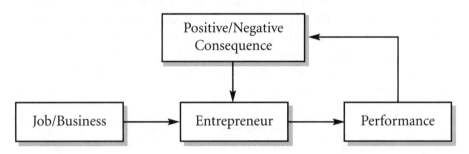

If you're looking for the number-one difference between entrepreneurs and bureaucrats, here it is. Entrepreneurs feel the consequences of their performance every Friday night when they count the money in the cash box. If it's full, they feel on top of the world. If it's empty, their kids won't eat. These are powerful, timely, and accurate consequences—which would affect anyone's behavior.

Bureaucrats, on the other hand, rarely feel any consequences—positive or negative. I learned how this works in my very first job, years ago, at American Express in New York. My salary was $1,250 a month, a princely sum to me at the time, and I was very excited to be working in the Big Apple. American Express was and is a great company, but it taught me a very frustrating lesson about consequences—or the lack thereof. It quickly became apparent that if I worked very, very hard for a month and brought in some big customers, I got $1,250. If during the next month I took it a little easier, more of an average month, I again got $1,250. And, finally, I understood that even if I did nothing for a month, just showed up and stayed awake at all the meetings, I got—you guessed it—$1,250. The message was loud and clear. The company was practically screaming at its employees: "It really doesn't matter what you do!" If this seems a far-fetched example to you—good. Hopefully, that means you'll never tolerate such a crazy system in your own company.

In spite of the best efforts of behemoths like American Express, enterprising managers can usually find a way to inspire themselves. The really hard part seems to be inspiring others. Ironically, entrepreneurs aren't much better than professional managers in using the power of consequences to foster commitment and performance in employees. They're usually on autopilot in pursuing their mission and don't worry about inspiring entrepreneurial behavior in future employees. They really expect everyone to behave just as they do. Such optimism (or naiveté) is the reason why entrepreneurs can sometimes be pretty lousy teachers. Unfortunately, by the time they recognize that they're leading an entrepreneurial mission that no one is following, the business may be well into its life cycle and careening down the "managerial" side of the curve. At this point, founders often become brainwashed into thinking that the only way out of this mess will be to create a super-duper personnel department and let them figure out how to motivate the troops. The company reaches into the bottomless pool of available "HR professionals," and it goes downhill from there. The power of consequences gets lost in a sea of personnel mumbo-jumbo.

As you grow your company and face the prospect of inspiring hundreds, if not thousands, of employees, is there another way this story could end? You bet there is. Meet Jannie Tay, entrepreneurial superwoman and Chinese mamacita to a sprawling watch and jewelry empire from Monte Carlo to Tokyo to Sydney.

IT'S ALL IN THE FAMILY

They become your corporate family and you have unconditional love for each other—you forgive and forget and you share the good and the bad.

—JANNIE TAY
FOUNDER, THE HOUR GLASS

Jannie Tay was recently named one of the the Fifty Leading Women Entrepreneurs of the World.[1] In the tough, discount-crazy Asian retail market for watches and jewelry, you have to be doing a lot right to hit $300 million in revenues after just twenty years in business. Today the Hour Glass has some fifteen retail outlets spread over Singapore, Australia, Malaysia, Indonesia, and Hong Kong. The company represents the world's top

---

[1]Tay was recognized as one of the Fifty Leading Women Entrepreneurs by The National Foundation For Women Business Owners as part of a global research project, funded by IBM.

brands, such as Cartier, Rolex, Christian Dior, Patek Phillippe, and Mondial Jewelry. They have also integrated backward with two joint-venture watch factories in Switzerland, as well as wholesale operations in Tokyo, Singapore, Hong Kong, Geneva, and Monte Carlo.

The Hour Glass has a strong public reputation based on two things: high quality products and exquisite, upscale service. They were the first watch and jewelry retailer in the world to be awarded the ISO 9000 Quality Certificate, solidifying their sterling reputation. What the outside world doesn't know, however, is that both the high quality and the great service are, in truth, driven by Jannie Tay's greatest personal asset: her amazing instincts for inspiring her people. It's her secret formula for making sure all 300 of her employees truly have that "all in the family" spirit.

Jannie Tay, always in a hurry, was several sentences into her story before I had even turned the tape recorder on: "So yes, my father was a very big influence on me. He was a physician by hobby and produced medicated oils as a small business. As a young girl, I used to go to trade shows with my father to sell this medicated oil and on the trips I remember stopping in all these little towns where we would visit his customers and have a cup of tea—so maybe early on I got the idea that business could be like a family activity. But you know, back in the 1950s, girls didn't have to work. All I really wanted to do was get married, have children, and have a good time, like all the girls in Singapore. But at sixteen I went to Melbourne, Australia, to study. The day I entered the university my dad died. It was very sad. In those days young Chinese ladies certainly didn't go off to foreign universities, and I always thank my father for that. My basic degree was in physiology and I got a master's in pharmacology. I also met my future husband in Australia. Henry was a Singaporean medical student.

"In 1971 we came back to Singapore. I taught at the University of Singapore in the Physiology Department for two years, but I was very bored by academia. After every lecture I'd say to myself, 'What am I doing here?' On the other hand, my husband's family had a small retail watch business. Henry said if I wanted to leave the university, why not work at his family's shop? So I became a salesgirl in my in-laws' shop selling watches. I loved it. I was very happy behind the counter, working with the customers. A lot of people said, 'You're a university lecturer, why do you want to be a lowly salesgirl?' But I was happy meeting customers, and I really liked selling watches to people.

"At that time in Singapore the big stores began moving out of our traditional retail area, and started opening on the more upscale and beautiful Orchard Road. I observed that those stores had a very good turn of business and all the tourists wanted to go to Orchard Road. The tourist market in Singapore was beginning to grow rapidly and our little shops in the more traditional Chinese areas were static and not growing. But when I told my mother-in-law we should move to Orchard Road, she didn't want to. So my husband and I decided to sell out of the family business. But it took a lot of money to go to Orchard Road and compete with the big stores. I went to Metro, which was the only retailer in town listed on the stock exchange, and proposed a joint venture with them. If they would provide the financial backing, we would provide the management for an upscale retail watch business. We were completely surprised when they said *OK*. It taught me a valuable lesson; you never get anything if you don't ask for it. Anyway, they took 51 percent and we had 49 percent, and we started the Hour Glass in October 1979. We opened with just one shop in Lucky Plaza, a new, fancy shopping area. After a few years, we bought out our financial partners, and owned the entire company—until we went public on the Singapore stock exchange in 1992."

The thing that people remember most after hearing Jannie Tay talk, is her passion for Hour Glass front-line employees. See if you agree: "The number-one lesson I have learned is that the value of the Hour Glass or any company is in its human resources. Everyone today talks about customer service, and it's true that customers demand good service from the people who work for the retailer. The truth is, if you develop and treat your human resources with respect, and I mean the front-line people as well as the management, you will win the customer's heart. I like the upside down triangle and initially some of my corporate staff were upset because they said I only think of the front-line people. But we have to remember, in a hierarchical situation, the people who are up here in the so-called head office are like gods. They are the ones who tell you what to do. They are the ones who pick up your mistakes. And they usually are the ones who get the most benefit from the company. In the Hour Glass, this is reversed. The front-line people who are closest to the customers are the ones who will benefit most and I support that. It's a complete culture reversal from most retail companies.

"Managers in a hierarchical system feel they have gone through the doghouse so to speak to get to the top, and now deserve to enjoy their position and their power. In my philosophy, I may have the title of managing director (MD), but I'm still that salesgirl first, and then I'm the MD. Some of my early managers could not buy this philosophy and they left. They even said it was 'morally demotivating' to them. I told them that, without the front-line people, we wouldn't even have jobs. We wouldn't be sitting here. But some people just can't accept that so they have to leave.

"I don't want any anti-entrepreneurial managers because that's the same as antigrowth in my opinion." This is Tay at full stride, describing exactly why and how the Hour Glass has become one of the most entrepreneurial companies in Asia—and I'm sure why she keeps picking up accolades like the Fifty Leading Women award. "Entrepreneurship means being challenged and wanting to do innovative things to keep growing—but a manager wants to be safe. You tell them what to do, they do exactly what you tell them, and they deliver the result—but no more. That's managing.

"I think Hour Glass is a very entrepreneurial company because we have developed as an entrepreneurial society in the company. I really believe you can help people change, you can develop them and you can support them. You can do this by letting them make mistakes, by nurturing them along, and giving them a second or third chance. And, of course, you do push them, you try to break their mind-set, all their limiting beliefs about themselves, and you keep pushing them. At the end of the day, if you do all this, you can bring the entrepreneurship out of anybody. But you have to do it all. People in their forties and fifties who join Hour Glass, do find it more difficult to be entrepreneurial because for so many years they were so set and structured in their minds. But I've found that they can be very entrepreneurial, once they get rid of their limiting habits. Even the accountants, who have been taught a certain way to do things, to be very responsible, to be careful—even they can be more entrepreneurial in their job.

"You see, when I say entrepreneurship, I mean allowing people to be creative, to be open minded, to test new ground, to be more motivated. Of course, you also want them to work as a team, to think first of the customer, to push for sales, but at the end of the day they should enjoy what they are doing, and be very committed to it. If you do all that, you will have more entrepreneurial people and you will be a more entrepreneurial and successful company."

The Hour Glass has the highest retention rate of employees of any Asian retail company. It is truly an amazing record. I was hoping to get from Tay some of the specifics on how this has been achieved. She didn't disappoint: "I realized that if I wanted the ten people who started with me to stay with me, I had to let them be their own bosses and be my business partners. I had to let them run their own businesses or else they would leave me for someone else who would take them away with a higher salary. So today those ten people, plus many after them, have been with me a long time. Now how did we do that?

- "First we develop them. Every Monday we still do training in the offices, particularly personal growth–type training. I know these things can help. When I first started I went to a lot of courses on building up my own self-confidence. I even went to an Anthony Robbins course once.

- "We all share our information completely. We share our experiences and how we tackle problems, and we discuss these things like owners of the business, not employees. I tell you, even though many of them haven't gone beyond high school, they have become more knowledgeable than MBAs.

- "All decision making is done by them in their stores and their departments. We support them, even advise them if they need help, but they make the decisions for their own areas of the company.

- "In our culture we want employees to feel like owners, and we do something very important about this. Everyone knows what the profits are and we share 10 percent of the company profit with all the employees—*every month without fail.* This monthly distribution is on top of their salary and commission. And at the end of the year, they are also eligible for a one-to-six-month bonus based on their individual performance.

- "All these approaches go right down to our front-line people—salesgirls and -boys just like I used to be. I know what motivates them because I did the same work.

"You know that more than 70 percent of our people have been with us more than five years, which is unheard of in retail in Asia. And 40 percent of our people have been here more than ten years. I truly believe this is because they are their own bosses and feel like part owners. At the retail level, we hardly ever have anyone leaving Hour Glass. I guess if someone would offer to double their salary they would leave. But really we have no one leaving us, which is very unusual for front-line people in retail."

And then we reached the concept that Jannie Tay is most famous for: an approach to employees that puts her somewhere between Mother Theresa and a Mother Hen, and never ceases to amaze outside observers. I think our own title of "Chinese Mamacita" may best describe the flavor of it all: "The key to everything we do is treating ourselves like a family. The employees all know my philosophy—that within a genetic family we love each other unconditionally and we share things with each other. If a member of our family upsets us, we're not political about it. We forgive them and we go on. But when you come to work, if your colleague does something to you, you become political and want to get him out of the company. So I say to our employees: 'Think a minute, and close your eyes. You know we spend more of our waking hours at work than at home. So what would happen if we feel everyone here is part of our corporate family? Keep your eyes closed and imagine yourself in your home environment, but surrounded by the people you work with. They become your corporate family and you have unconditional love for each other—you forgive and forget and you share the good and the bad.' It's an amazing exercise to go through with your staff.

"I'll tell you one thing that is happening just now, which so touched me. It's about one of our junior staff, a very nice young man really, at one of the outlets. I just found out yesterday morning that he took more than $100,000 of our stock, pawned them, and lost the money gambling. He obviously has a serious problem. He was confronted and he voluntarily went to the police and confessed. Now it turns out his wife also works for us and is expecting their first baby. If we could have found out about this sooner, I'm sure we could have stopped him. We could have minimized the loss and counseled him. Of course, now this young boy has to go to jail in Singapore. Well, today, I was so touched because a movement has started among our employees. They are saying we do not want him to go to jail because he is so young. We will all chip in and try to cover this loss, and hope the courts will not send him to jail and send him back to his wife with some kind of treatment for gambling. His manager even recommended that we hire him back, counsel him, and help him. You see, this is how a family would try to deal with a serious problem. Of course, this is a difficult example, but my point is that even in such a sad case, we can still try to be a corporate family and not turn our backs on each other.

"At the Hour Glass we do a lot of 'internal charity' work, and I insist that every employee must be involved somehow. We have cases where an employee has died or maybe gotten badly injured in an auto accident, and we keep helping the family. It sets a good standard for the employees, and they see that a company can treat its employees like a caring family."

And finally we got to the bottom-line businesswoman in Tay. Where the power of consequences always hangs in the air: "Of course, employees must understand that in a very dynamic industry, like high-end retail, doing business also means cutting expenses, being more productive, and always trying for a better response to customers. From all this effort, the profit or loss will come. Our people understand consequences. It's not a difficult concept. They understand that unless everyone in the company focuses on performance, on being a team, on sharing the ups and downs, we all lose. It's that simple."

Then in an almost-automatic return to focusing on the positive side of human nature, she ended the interview with these powerful words: "You know, just a few years ago, entrepreneurship was not recognized as something to be proud of. Entrepreneurs were wheelers-dealers. They were people who did not succeed in a job in a company. And they all had to be a little crooked. That was the image in Singapore. After all these years, I now know that being an entrepreneur is about integrity, honesty, truth, and credibility. And at the end of the day it's your relationship with people that counts most. It's all about people. It's how you deal with people. How you relate. It's a gut feeling, I guess—a common sense feel I have about what's important in my company."

Taking the cue from Jannie Tay's "common sense feel," what are some common sense rules you can use to inspire others? Can you really instill entrepreneurial commitment and performance in your employees? Of course you can. Tay cloaks her approach in her "all in the family" idea, and others have equally successful ways to get at it. But whatever the slogans or cosmetics, a few central principles run through every successful effort to create "mini-entrepreneurs" in a company. You'll recognize them all from Tay's own story: Individuals must run their piece of your company as their own business; satisfying customers is always the bottom-line; we're all in this together. The most basic rule of all is: Make sure that all employees feel the consequences of their behavior. This last one means you have to have rock-solid answers to the eternal question of every employee: "What's in it for me if I do and what will happen to me if I don't?" You have to put *powerful, timely,* and *accurate* consequences into the work life of all employees. They have to know there will be positive consequences for good performance and negative consequences for bad performance. Do these things and you'll be well on your way to creating an "entrepreneurial performance system" in the company—using the full power of consequences.

Try these common sense principles and you can forget most of the personnel jargon you ever learned and all those made-in-hell performance evaluation systems dreamed up by consultants. You can trust these basic entrepreneurial ideas, and you can trust Jannie Tay when she says: "If you do all this, you can bring out the entrepreneurship in anybody."

GOOD FOR THE BUSINESS, GOOD FOR THE SOUL

Entrepreneurs like Jannie Tay believe that self-inspiration, the indispensable human quality that underpins the entrepreneurial spirit, carries double-barreled power. Of course it's good for business. That's been true forever. But it may have as much to do with how you live as how you work.

Remember Sarah Walker? She proved this 100 years ago. Driven by her self-inspired entrepreneurial spirit, Walker became an important figure in American business history. She single-handedly exposed the huge economic potential of creating special products for the African-American market. In the process, she literally wrote the book on franchising and multilevel marketing on a national basis. And her indomitable spirit carried over into her personal life. She was the country's first black, woman philanthropist. She was tireless in supporting black social issues of the day. She was especially generous with financial contributions to educational institutions for black women. Through Sarah Walker's generosity and personal example, tens of thousands of similarly disadvantaged women have found the inspiration and knowledge to rise above their presumed place in society. They are all standing on Sarah Breedlove Walker's shoulders today.

This is the mission, isn't it? After a lifetime of effort, to make a difference in the world. I used to think only powerful people like corporate chieftains and government leaders could make a difference. Today I know that's not true. For the real purpose of being inspired is not to move mountains—but to move yourself. To motivate yourself to make your life matter. To believe, when all is said and done, that you did good work and gave it your best. It can make you a great entrepreneur, no doubt about it. But, even more important, it can make you a great person.

It's the power of self-inspiration that drove Sarah Walker and still drives people like Buel Messer, John Boody, Kari Stefansson, and Jannie Tay—and a hundred others that fill these pages. The truth is, when you go looking for self-inspired people, it's a sure way to get your standards raised. Take Messer, for example. It's hard to be too proud of yourself when a blind man outperforms you at every turn. You begin to wonder how your career would have gone if you had no eyes. You discover how much can be achieved with so little—and it makes you wonder at how little is sometimes achieved by those with so much. What does that say about the power of self-inspiration? It says to me that we'd better find out how to tap into it.

In the final analysis, why should you want to inspire yourself? Why should you like what you do and be good at doing it? Partly because you're supposed to—a fair day's work for a fair day's reward is still a fair obligation. But mostly because it makes your life worth living. At least the half to three-quarters of your life that you're going to spend at work. Psychologists call it *self-actualization*. Entrepreneurs call it doing something great with your life. Whatever you call it, you can be sure that self-inspired behavior is not only good for the business, it's also good for the soul.

6

What's Really Required to Become an Entrepreneur

Insanity is doing the same thing over and over and expecting different results.

—ALCOHOLICS ANONYMOUS

There must be a lot of insane managers and workers in the labor force these days. Just check the profile of the new American job seeker: forty-five years old with a résumé that already includes a minimum of four prior jobs. So halfway through your career, you're looking for company number five—at least. Over your entire work life this should work out to eight different corporations, or about seven more than your grandfather worked for.

The response to today's take-no-prisoners era of personnel management is mixed. Older workers dread it and pretty much give up on bettering themselves after their second or third downsizing or merger inspired restructuring. Most mid-career employees are trying to figure out what it all means and are spending more time honing their job-hunting skills than their actual work skills. Young Gen Xers, who have never worked any other way, view switching companies the same way the rest of us used to view switching departments or divisions. So one's reaction to the world of diminished company loyalty depends on where you've been. Still, the bulk of employees today (and their families) see all this as pretty bad news—another complication to make life more difficult. The worst reaction you can have is to do nothing and pray that it all goes away before you lose another job. Brother, that ain't going to happen! Even so, many loyal corporate soldiers keep trying to find the one big company that will still appreciate their good soldiering and long-term commitment—a twenty-first century variation of the AA insanity definition.

CORPORATE CHARLIE FINALLY GETS THE MESSAGE

My good friend Charlie Bishop provided an extreme example of this malady. Charlie's first problem was that he had an undergraduate degree in psychology and a Ph.D. in organizational behavior. Right off the bat, this would make him highly suspect to the great downsizers of the world. Here's Charlie's battle record over the past two decades:

- Federal Express (4 years)

- Baxter International (6 years)

- C&S/Sovran Bank (2 years)

- Nations Bank (2 years)

- Quaker Oats (3 years)

- ADT Security Services (2 years)

- Belize Holdings International. (1 year)

This is seven companies in twenty years, all at a director or VP level in human resource positions. It's approximately one traumatic career change every two and a half years. Charlie was never fired for poor performance. Every time he changed jobs it was due to a merger, a restructuring, a downsizing, or some other corporate reshuffling that left him no options but to move on. I know consultants who work for their clients longer than Charlie has been working for his employers. Maybe he should have seen it long ago: These giant companies aren't really employers—they're clients— and he's actually been in business for himself for a long time.

To be fair, I think Charlie knew this all along, but he just didn't admit it. Clearly, the reason he was able to keep resurfacing and surviving is that he had become very good at selling his product (himself), delivering excellent work, and then moving on to sell another big company. The bottom line is, you will never meet a nicer guy than Charlie. He's smart, hard working, and loyal to whomever he works for. But all this has not been enough to prevent him from getting bounced around like a ping-pong ball.

Up until very recently, my question had been: How many more times can this happen to Charlie before he gets the message? Well, I'm happy to report he has now gotten the message. Just a month ago, I received a brochure in the mail from a new firm called Chicago Change Partners. The cover letter was from none other than Charles H. Bishop, Ph.D., announcing the formation of his own consulting practice. Like any good entrepreneur, Charlie's offering a product he knows a lot about: "change." His letter says it best: "After being involved internally in large-scale, significant organization changes—Federal Express, Baxter International, Nations Bank, Quaker Oats and ADT—I decided to drop back and assess what it is that I have done in those changes that has made the most significant impact." So Charlie has come up with a couple of consulting services based on his own experience, and I say bravo for Charlie. He truly represents the profile of the new American job seeker: corporate castoff turned entrepreneur. Indeed it's true—in the Entrepreneurial Age the new entrepreneurs are us.

The good news today is that corporate castoffs don't have to get mad. They really can get even. There's a large and growing class of big business alumni for whom these changes are creating unplanned, yet wonderful, opportunities. They are rapidly becoming the largest part of the rising entrepreneurial class of the twenty-first century. They are highly skilled, highly motivated, and see working for themselves as a lot less risky than working for another big company. It's not an overstatement to say that all the turbulence at big business over the past two decades has given the entrepreneurial movement a double-barreled shot in the arm. First, experienced people, at relatively young ages, are being left no option but to fend for themselves. Second, with so many functions downsized out of companies, outsourcing has exploded to replace the necessary tasks. Over and over again we see the same good person who was downsized, like Charlie, hired back as a self-employed supplier.

THE THREE REQUIREMENTS

Becoming an entrepreneur may or may not be the right way to spend the rest of your life. But there are no wrong reasons for giving it a try. The days are long gone when, as Jannie Tay said, "Entrepreneurship was not recognized as something to be proud of." And the days are over when someone like Buel Messer, mowing lawns with his sons, was seen as the price you pay for making a mistake. So, whether you're a Gen Xer looking for your first billion, or a middle manager stuck in a Dilbertesque bureaucracy, or someone who just wants to make a few bucks on the side doing something fun, welcome to the "new and improved" world of entrepreneurial opportunity. But if getting entrepreneurial is the way to go, what does it take to actually get started? Assuming that you're now well armed with the four fundamental practices of successful entrepreneurs, the rest is pretty straightforward. There are essentially three things you have to make sure are in place.

A BIT OF MONEY

I was operating out of a spare bedroom and making only local calls. There was no capital involved. Zero.

—FRED GRATZON
FOUNDER, TELEGROUP

There's something about money that seems to brings out the worst anxieties in people. Many would-be entrepreneurs suffer a particularly bad case of this. Some never get beyond the first step because they just can't imagine themselves raising the money necessary to start their own business. Making it even more scary, the media hype about IPOs and young Silicon Valley billionaires has blown the public perception of start-up financial requirements out of all proportion. A dose of reality may help.

Our research shows that the average cost of starting a business in the United States today is about $14,000. Not a big deal when you consider the relative economic and social cost of some other ways you could spend your time:

- Five years of heavy smoking $15,000
- A year on welfare $17,500
- A year at Harvard $25,000
- A year in prison $30,000

Crazy comparisons aside, the point shouldn't be missed. On average, the cost of starting up your own business is modest. And, of course, everyone knows that the smart way is to get your ducks lined up as much as possible before you give up other sources of incoming cash. This usually means that you shouldn't quit your job before you're ready. Having said that, don't be afraid if the timing isn't quite so comfortable. There can be, ironically, great power in having the rug pulled out from under you. Akio Morita, the venerable founder of Sony, says "being obsessed with survival" is the entrepreneur's secret weapon. As he found out in war-torn Japan in 1945, people can and will do amazing things when their life depends on it.

Even if you agree that it's not a lot of money, you still have to come up with it. Where are you going to lay your hands on $14,000? According to a survey conducted by *Inc.* magazine, the multiple sources of start-up financing used by entrepreneurs breaks out as follows:

- Personal savings   73 percent

- Credit cards   27 percent

- Loans from friends and relatives   14 percent

- All other cash sources   14 percent

- Loans against personal property   7 percent

- Bank loans   5 percent

- Equity investments by friends and relatives   2 percent

One obvious lesson: For start-up financing, don't waste your time talking to bankers or equity investors. On the other hand, in a pinch, most people could come up with $14,000 on their various credit cards—so getting entrepreneurial seed money can't be too much of an obstacle. There are in fact, thousands of successful companies started for $10,000 or less.[1] Here's a diverse list of twenty bootstrapping start-ups, most from the same *Inc.* survey, to illustrate the point:

- Kodak, 1880 $5,000

- Coca Cola, 1891 $2,300

- UPS, 1907 $100

- Black & Decker, 1910 $1,200

- Clorox, 1913 $500

- Marriott (A&W Root Beer), 1927 $3,000

- Hewlett Packard, 1938 $538

- Johnson Publishing, 1946 $400

- Lillian Vernon, 1951 $2,000

- Domino's Pizza, 1960 $900

- The Limited, 1963 $5,000

- Nike, 1964 $1,000

---

[1] The sampling purposefully excludes more recent start-ups. We try to use examples with a decade of performance behind them. Also note that start-up amounts are not adjusted for inflation.

- DHL, 1972 $0

- Body Shop, 1976 $6,000

- Apple Computer, 1976 $1,350

- PC Connection, 1982 $8,000

- White Line Trucking, 1983 $300

- Gateway 2000, 1985 $10,000

- Telegroup, 1989 $0

- Fawcette Publications, 1991 $0

Just to counter the notion that, in the current Internet IPO age, every new entrepreneur has to have venture capitalists and investment bankers raising millions, the final two examples of "zero-based" start-ups are thrown in. Both their founders flat out declare they didn't need a penny of start-up money. Fawcette Publications, founded by Jim Fawcette in California, is an electronic and print publisher with over $25 million in sales. Telegroup, the brainchild of Fred Gratzon in Fairfield, Iowa (about as far away from Silicon Valley as you can get), is generating an amazing $300 million in revenues reselling AT&T long distance services. To be sure, starting a company with no money at all is rare and you would be well advised not to count on it. So most entrepreneurs do need some start-up money. But how much will you really need? Probably just a little.

But, lest we forget, while this list of successful and great companies didn't need or have a lot money to start, they all did have the one asset that is absolutely essential—a product or service that customers needed and were willing to pay for. This brings us to the second requirement.

A BIT OF KNOWLEDGE

General graduates of the university are twice as likely to start their own businesses as the MBA graduates of Wharton.
—PROFESSOR IAN MACMILLAN
WHARTON SCHOOL
UNIVERSITY OF PENNSYLVANIA

The number-one reason for new business failure is not a lack of money. It's more basic than that. It is, simply, you haven't come up with a product or service that anyone wants to buy. Or at least not enough people want to buy it to keep the business afloat. So you need to learn how to make something or do something that the world needs. And where are you going to learn that?

Apparently, one place you *won't* learn it is at the leading business schools of the world. Ian MacMillan, the iconoclastic British innovator at the Wharton School, developed the first entrepreneurial studies program at a blue-chip business school. And why did Wharton approve his pet project? Because MacMillan's research on how to educate entrepreneurs revealed huge shortcomings in the MBA program, powerfully summarized by his mind-bending statistic quoted above. Predictably, the broader business education establishment hasn't taken this criticism from one of its own lying down.

As an illustration, *Across The Board*, the respected magazine of The Conference Board, recently published opposing views in a provocatively titled article: "Do Universities Stifle Entrepreneurship?" Arguing *yes* was, ironically enough, another British professor. Adrian Furnham heads the Business Psychology Unit at University College London. In a wonderful example of the pot calling the kettle black, Furnham claimed that academic universities and their "anti-business, socialist" professors were killing off the entrepreneurial spirit in young people. His solution? Send everyone over to the business school.

Across The Board invited me to write the rejoinder to Professor Furnham's argument. I pointed out that his case is simply not supported by the evidence. The idea that business schools are in the business of creating entrepreneurs fails both the test of fact and common sense. It certainly failed Ian MacMillan's careful research at Wharton. At best, it sounds like more B-school nonsense on what entrepreneurs really need to know to succeed. It's an absolutely critical point for anyone who is thinking about starting a business—which, as noted earlier, is about 70 percent of the workforce.

Of course, it's great sport to blame academia for all manner of fuzzy and misguided thinking, but let's be honest. The educational institutions that have done the most damage to the spirit of entrepreneurship over the past fifty years are the business schools—not the broad-based universities around them. Universities may be guilty of benign neglect of entrepreneurship but at least they impart knowledge that entrepreneurs need, on everything from molecular biology and high-tech engineering to the social sciences and even the fine arts. In case the point is missed, these are all fields of study that teach young people about the technologies and needs of some of the greatest economic opportunities and challenges facing the world: biogenetics, aerospace design, computer architecture, reduction of crime and poverty, and America's fastest-growing export industry, entertainment. By contrast, for half a century, business schools (and their stepchildren, corporate universities) have majored in teaching theory after discarded theory about how to manage. Ask yourself this: How many entrepreneurs have ever been created by studying learning curve theory, matrix management, sensitivity training, reengineering, or the most current fad—leadership?

So entrepreneurial tip number one is to remember that there has never been a successful enterprise created out of a management technique. If learning management theories won't help, then what kind of education would be helpful? The bedrock essential of entrepreneurship (and all enterprise, for that matter) is being able to come up with a great product or service. This is the really tough part of business. Managing is kid stuff compared to being able to create a better mousetrap. Entrepreneurial tip number two, then, is to become very knowledgeable about something—to become very good at designing and making some product or service that answers a real need in the marketplace. It could be simple or complicated, high- or low-tech, but you must become expert at it. And where can you learn this? While not essential for every entrepreneurial possibility, a decent university can be a terrific place to get started. Let's look at a few real-life examples.

Take the case of Edward Penhoet, cofounder and CEO of Chiron, the hugely successful biotech company that discovered the vaccine for Hepatitis B. Where did Penhoet learn his trade? At a business school? Of course not. He learned it by getting a Ph.D. in biochemistry at the University of California. None of this is new. Bill Hewlett and David Packard never studied management. Like a thousand other computer entrepreneurs who followed them, they were engineering students. Andy Grove made Intel the "essential company of the digital age" with an engineering degree from then–tuition-free City College of New York. Or how about Clark Abt? He founded Abt Associates, the largest socioeconomic research think tank in the world. With 1,100 scholars and researchers on the payroll, Abt knows a thing or two about the value of intellectual capital in building an organization. His academic inspiration? A Ph.D. in political science from MIT. For an even more offbeat example, consider the career of Jodie Foster, arguably the most powerful woman in filmmaking today. Acting in, then directing, and now producing Hollywood blockbusters is big business by anyone's standard. Yet she's never seen the inside of a business school. She learned her "business" at the Yale Drama School. And on and on it goes—in an ever-spiraling coincidence of being highly knowledgeable and skilled at something that people want and need.

An even less-recognized source of essential entrepreneurial knowledge can be found far away from a country's institutions of higher learning. Ray Kroc, the great entrepreneur behind McDonald's and a high school dropout, had the right idea. He was notorious for giving large gifts to good causes but he drew the line at giving to most schools: "They will not get a cent from me unless they put in a trade school." He held that old-fashioned belief that young people ought to come out of school knowing how to do something practical, like grow a tomato, repair a two-stroke engine, or put up a wall that won't fall down. Kroc may have stumbled onto an even bigger socioeconomic idea. In America, a blue-collar education began to lose status in parallel with the mid-century notion that everyone had to have a full university degree to be socially respectable. Sending your children to a trade or technical school became downright embarrassing. It was somehow more honorable to hold a dead-end, middle-management job at AT&T than be a prosperous, self-employed electrician, plumber, or farmer.

This was not only a crazy elitist notion but it obscured a very important fact: Vocational and technical schools are a rich breeding ground of small business entrepreneurs—the driving force of every growing economy in the world. Today it's clear that whether you choose landscaping, auto repair, medical testing, construction, or graphic design, you'll be in a trade with great entrepreneurial promise in the twenty-first century. So don't get hung up on higher education being the only path to prosperity. Certainly, the list of world-class entrepreneurs who were university no-shows is very long, from Walt Disney and Soichiro Honda to Sam Walton and Richard Branson. There are also plenty of famous college dropouts like Bill Gates and Steve Jobs who tried academia and decided they didn't need it after all.

The important lesson in all the examples that fill these pages, from self-educated Sarah Walker to Harvard Ph.D. Ben Tregoe, isn't where and how they acquired their knowledge. The one mighty thing they do have in common when it comes to knowledge is that they all managed to become very good at *something*. They understood that what's required to produce high-growth enterprise is not becoming great at managing, but becoming great at making and doing something that a lot of people in the world need and will pay good money for. And that, indeed, takes a bit of knowledge.

AN ENTREPRENEUR-FRIENDLY CULTURE

*We've used the kids' college funds, we've used our insurance,
we've used all the equity we have in our home, we've got
everything including the lawn mower riding on this thing.*
—RON DOGGETT
FOUNDER, GOODMARK FOODS

Beyond acquiring the necessary "bit of money" and "bit of knowl-edge," entrepreneurs still have to play with the hand they're dealt in terms of the environment in which they operate. Or do they? Of course you can't, by yourself, change the macroeconomics of the day or control the political or social fabric of your country. But you can do a lot about the kind of cul-ture you design for your own company and the immediate environment you choose to work in. Some companies struggle to survive in depressing, anti-entrepreneurial environments while others flourish in supportive, entrepreneur-friendly cultures. Learning how to navigate these tricky waters could mean the difference between entrepreneurial success and failure.

This is the amazing story of Ron Doggett's "back to the future" flight from corporate America to the entrepreneurial life, with a soft (and prosperous) landing back in the corporate world. This may be the new American dream. Doggett and his products were the same for the entire round trip—only the ownership and the culture changed. The chronology of his career, up to his current overlapping roles between GoodMark and ConAgra, will put it in context:

- General Mills: professional manager—1961–1982

- GoodMark Foods: entrepreneurial owner and CEO—1982–2000

- ConAgra: advisor and (very large) stockholder—1998–2000

I've known Ron Doggett since we were at Harvard Business School together in the late seventies. I have also gotten to know many of the managers of his company GoodMark Foods. I love his story and he graciously offered to sit still for this long interview in North Carolina in early 2000. Beyond all his great entrepreneuring qualities, he is as friend-ly, sincere, and honest as the day is long. Ron is definitely one of the "good guys" in business.

As you read his Goliath to David and back to Goliath saga, you should feel dramatic examples of the power that different company environments can have on the entrepreneurial spirit. Ron Doggett certainly did.

General Mills' Corporate Culture—Conglomerate Merry-Go-Round

"I went to college in Minnesota on the GI Bill. While in college, I started a business of my own that I didn't do well at, so I thought it might be safer to go with a large company. Since I grew up on a farm, food and grains seemed to be a good match, and I went to General Mills and joined the treasurer's group. I was an auditor for a number of years, until I landed a job that no one else wanted. That was with Slim Jim, a meat snack brand, in Philadelphia. I was actually a part of the acquisition team of Slim Jim at the time from General Mills and they interviewed a number of people to take the job that I ultimately took. It was located in the slum area of Philadelphia. No one wanted to go to that area. It wasn't very safe. In fact, I was mugged the first night that I was there trying to get to my car, which was parked only thirty feet from the front door. Anyway, that was my start with Slim Jim. I joined as the controller and chief financial officer.

"General Mills at that time was buying a lot of companies and they were putting together a group called the Consumer Specialties Division so they were looking for a lot of specialty foods. Slim Jim was one of those. This was 1967. I asked myself many times: 'What am I doing here, how did I get here, and do I belong here?' But I was always attracted to the product. I was first introduced to the product when I was in the military. I thought it was a neat product but I never dreamed I'd be associated with it.

"I should back up. This is most interesting. General Mills acquired Slim Jim from the entrepreneurs who started the business. They had less than $400,000 in assets and were located in that slum area of north Philadelphia—and General Mills paid $25 million for the business of which $23.5 million was acquisition premium. That was substantial enough, but even more incredible, Slim Jim didn't even make its own product. The product was made by a contract packer outside Philadelphia. Well, shortly after General Mills' acquisition, this packer of the product said he didn't want to continue to make the product for us. So there we were, we bought this fine company, and we paid all this money for it, and we've got no one to make the product. So we scurried to find a company to make the product. General Mills acquired another company called Jesse Jones Sausage Company in North Carolina. That was the only reason we bought that small company. It was doing about $4 million to $5 million of business. The combination of those two companies became GoodMark Foods and North Carolina became the headquarters.

"General Mills continued to build its businesses. It continued to add to that division. That was the time when it also was growing the Fashion Division and the Jewelry Division, a Toy Division—businesses way beyond foods. It even owned some great furniture companies. This was indeed the era of the conglomerate. General Mills was going off into all kinds of different and unique businesses and, as usually happens, it lost focus. Of course, today it's strictly a food company again.

"I think you're interested in how they operated with our small business. General Mills was a huge company. It was what I called a company that could relate to boxcars: to boxcar loads of products, whereas we shipped parcel post. We shipped Slim Jims a case at a time. We don't anymore, but we did at the time. And we were a business that had to be highly responsive, because it was a product that competed in a broad snack category around the nation in a lot of unique outlets from bars and taverns to delicatessens and convenience stores, and a little bit in supermarkets. At that time there were no Wal-Marts, or Sams, or Costcos, those kinds of huge outlets. General Mills was eager to build the business because it had such great margins, but it couldn't relate to the business and it wasn't a product that fit well with its product lines. That's not being critical of General Mills, it's just how it was. At any rate, General Mills wanted to build this business through supermarkets. Well, it wasn't a product that was really ready for supermarkets. First of all, we didn't have the packaging or product that was suitable for supermarkets. Second, to give it to a General Mills salesman who was selling Wheaties, Cheerios, Bisquick, Gold Medal Flour, and O-cello Sponges—well, we were the last one on the sales order form, below O-cello Sponges. I know we were because we didn't get distribution and we weren't doing well. We couldn't get distribution and we couldn't get volume, but we had to get bottom line profit so we started to take it out of margins. We reduced the quality of the product by adding fillers and low-cost ingredients to improve the margins and we got away from what the consumer was used to getting—the standard, spicy Slim Jim. That was one of the factors that became clear to me in the later years of the General Mills ownership, and it was something that I knew we could change.

"Then General Mills decided to sell the business. The executives came to me in late 1981—it was October 11th at three o'clock in the afternoon—and said they had made the decision to sell the business and encouraged me to look around hard for another opportunity. Although there 'could' be something in General Mills, they encouraged me to look elsewhere. That moment was when I became most motivated to try to buy the business. It had occurred to me a number of times before. I had thought it might be a nice business to get because it was a good cash flow business, it had a tremendous brand dating back to the late forties, and I had thought if General Mills didn't want it maybe I could buy it some day. At any rate here was a product, Slim Jim, that I really liked, and which I knew had a great future.

"I went home and thought about it, and decided this may be an opportunity and why not try? So I talked to Mr. Hawkins Bradly, one of the original founders, and he ultimately became a partner. We decided to put a team together right then. After some discussion of who the players on that team might be, we agreed to keep the team small or we'd never get the job done. We couldn't do it by committee or by a consensus of fifteen to twenty, so we kept it to four people. Myself, who had an operational and financial background, another fellow who had an operational and marketing background, another one who had a marketing and distribution background, and another who had an HR and administrative background. They had all come from General Mills to work at Slim Jim. So over the holidays of 1981 and early 1982 we put together some plans and pro formas.

"On January 4th of 1982, when the President of GoodMark returned from vacation, I went to see him and brought the team in and we announced that we were putting together an offer to acquire the company. It was a big decision and we weren't very sure that we were going to be successful. The president told us that 'us little guys' were not likely to get the company so everybody should relax. I know that in the executives' minds we were not likely to succeed because they were confident they would find a better buyer. But the good Lord willing, they would not find a better buyer than us, and we could ultimately put together a deal.

"I should mention that by that time General Mills was getting out of all the 'less than boxcar load' kinds of businesses. It got out of bubble gum, potato chips, and nuts, Smith Crisps in the UK, Tom's Foods, which is still a very large vending company, and it got out of our meat snack and sausage business. It was getting out of all those kinds of small businesses and was going back to the mainstay, main-meal kinds of product lines. We were among the first to go in this big change of strategy. This was at the time that all the conglomerates were turning right around and shedding all the acquisitions they had just made. I think General Mills was having a difficult time managing them. They weren't growing. General Mills wasn't able to find businesses to add to the platform of Slim Jim meat snacks, for example. It was a small business that was taking more time than the conglomerate wanted to devote to it, and I really think General Mills realized it had lost focus and it wanted to go back to things that were more mainstream if you will—and easier to manage. Ours was not an easy business to manage. It's fairly unpredictable. Meat costs, our primary ingredient, were highly volatile. You could make a lot of money one year and three years later you could lose a lot of money, and General Mills didn't like that.

"We just didn't fit into a big company picture for all these reasons. There wasn't time to be responsive, there wasn't time to put a personal touch on it. There wasn't time to have one-on-one relationships with small customers. At GoodMark we dealt with one-man wagon jobbers up to distributors with a thousand trucks. It takes a variety of talent to work with these customers. It isn't like calling on headquarters accounts and covering the nation as a result of your headquarters call.

"So anyway, we had put together our offer. The offer wasn't accepted at first. We were told to hang on, they'd see how things went and if nothing better came along they would talk with us. That was the gist of General Mills's initial response. The fiscal year ended in May and they didn't have a better offer so they agreed to meet with us to talk about our plans. We had put together a pro-forma cash flow statement, but we didn't have enough really. They asked us what our equity input would be. I said I was able to come up with $50,000. Mr. Bradley could also come up with his $50,000. Our other two partners couldn't get that much so we would have to try and help them. We said we would come up with $200,000 of equity between us.

"Actually I did not have the money. We owned a $35,000 home and had only about $7,000 equity in the home. I went to one bank and they asked me what kind of things I owned. They sent a man out to make a list of the things I owned. And he asked: 'Is this all you own? Do you have a lawnmower, a wheel barrow, anything else?' Well, I'd already put up the college education funds for our kids, my life insurance policy, whatever I had, but I told him: 'Yes, I own a lawn mower.' And he said: 'Where is it? I want to see it.' He actually wanted to see the lawn mower! I couldn't believe it. I said: 'It's under the house if you really want to see it. It's a used Toro.' But then Jack Harris, the president of a new, start-up bank in Raleigh, North Carolina, who eventually joined our board, decided to take a chance on us and the prospects of the company and he loaned me and the other two partners our shares of the equity. I actually cosigned for one of my partners.

"The total financing package we put together was unique at the time. General Mills took some of the paper back but only after we found another way of financing the business. We got another loan from a local bank, and then we established a program for a stream of royalties over ten years based on revenues. So with the combination of General Mills paper, a stream of royalties over ten years, and some paper from a local bank, we were able to come up with an offer of approximately $31 million to acquire the business—and only $200,000 in equity. Of course, the worst case for General Mills was that if we failed they would just get the company back. That was General Mills' worst case really."

I interrupted Doggett at this point, to say that this looked to me like an early leveraged management buyout. And that it was like creating ownership value out of thin air. Ron Doggett admitted that that was true, except that he was on the line with personal guarantees for at least a hundred thousand dollars, which to him at the time was a fortune. If it didn't work out, he stood to lose everything he had, including his house—and probably even his Toro lawn mower!

GoodMark Foods' Entrepreneurial Culture—Back To The Basics

I asked Doggett: "Let's get some figures here for the record. What was the size and financial situation at GoodMark Foods when you took it over, and what did you do to turn it around?" His sobering answer: "At that time GoodMark was doing about $40 million in revenues and losing money. In fact, we had negative equity for the first nine months of our ownership. So we had to move fast. There were several things we did immediately to get the business moving in the right direction:

- "The first thing, that I mentioned early on, was that we had to restore quality. Fortunately, I knew exactly what to do about the quality issue. We immediately restored the Slim Jim to what it originally was. We took out the preservatives. We took out the fillers, the low-cost inferior ingredients, and restored it to what it was, which was costly to us. It cost us margins on the product. So the first thing we did was we fixed the product. We put it back to what consumers wanted.

- "Second, we had good people but they didn't have direction, they didn't have focus, and they didn't have respect for the vision of the company. I knew that we had to establish this. We had to give these people a sense of direction. We had to get them all marching to the same drumbeat, going the same way. And they had to know how committed we were to this. Obviously, signing personal guarantees for the ownership of this business was a pretty big commitment. We *were* committed. Our hearts were in it. Our souls were in it. So through communications, through putting the right people in the right places to do the right things, we got people motivated and committed, and feeling responsible for moving the company ahead.

- "One of the ways to go ahead was through marketing. The product was undermarketed. One of the reasons for that was that we never had a stable product. It was inconsistent. Quality was up and down. We couldn't deliver the product. So once we straightened out the quality issue, and we straightened out the people issue, we then straightened out some of the things that were lacking, which were marketing and sales support.

- "Beyond these things it was service to the customers. Our service to customers was deplorable. So we set up a basis for serving our customers within given hours. At that time our turnaround on orders had to be no later than seventy-two hours, which was darn good time in our business. But we got that down to where we were processing and shipping an order within twenty-four hours. That was a big key for us—being responsive. Because it's a niche product, it's very unique, you had to be different than the snacks that you were matched up against. You had to be better. You had to have a point of difference somehow in the marketplace to move ahead. We worked hard on being more responsive and faster moving than the competition. So we put that together with the other things that I mentioned to get GoodMark going."

I was wondering why such obvious things weren't handled long before. I asked Doggett to explain: "Without casting aspersions on anybody, if these were the kinds of things that were needed, why didn't General Mills do them long before? Doggett's response is a knockout punch to bigger-is-better thinking: "Well, they were the simple things. Easy things. Little things. Easy to identify but difficult to do on a consistent basis. General Mills' focus was a large corporate overview with a large structure. We spent most of our time there on developing reports, analyzing results, building plans. Our long-range strategic plan each year was about seventy pages long. And then we had a program review session which went on for three months of the year. We had program reviews, budget reviews, that sort of thing. We spent more time on management procedures than we did on creating and leading. I'm talking about little things that weren't working that we really needed to fix and make work. But you succeed at the things, I believe, that are important to you, that you are committed to, and that commitment was just not there for this business at General Mills. But as owners I can tell you that we were committed to it. We developed plans, thoughts, ideas, visions, and dreams for this thing. We also lost a lot of sleep and shed a lot of tears too. It took a long time getting this thing off the ground and getting it back to profitability. The result was that we started making a profit in nine months with the business.

"Larry, the things we did were very simple things, whether it was customer service related, people related, product related, operationally related, financial; they were all simple things. I'm convinced, and I often told our people this, the most successful businesses in this country don't do anything new, exotic, or dramatic. They're companies that are highly focused on their mission, just as you point out in your seminars. They're highly focused and they repeatedly do the simple things in their business that are most appreciated by their customers and consumers. Those are the kinds of things that we did here at GoodMark. They're customer-driven kinds of things and very simple: time, relationships, shipping an order, good quality, being responsive to needs, recognizing what stores need for displays or promotions, that sort of thing.

"We worked hard at these simple things. And to this day, it's recognized that's what made this business successful. We took it from a $40 million business at that time to a $225 million business today. And we've taken it from a business that had a small, fragmented market share to the dominant market share of the industry. And we've established a new category in the food business—meat snacks, including meat sticks, beef jerky, pickled sausage, etc.—and GoodMark Foods is number one in the category!"

At this point, the discussion shifted more specifically to the "culture" of GoodMark Foods. I said to Doggett: "I know we could spend hours on what you did for the next two decades owning and running the business. But one thing that would be most interesting, I think, is to hear how you changed the culture of GoodMark, going from being part of a giant—General Mills—to a much smaller, entrepreneurial-style company."

Doggett's response: "Well, Larry, operationally we just kept doing those simple things. We kept hammering away at certain fundamental issues with our people. And I think doing that is a big part of a company's culture. But on the broader aspects of the culture we created, there were a lot of things that I felt strongly about. But I should tell you first that the management team that we put together lasted only briefly. The day after we acquired the business from General Mills on May 16, 1982, two of the four partners came in and said, 'OK, we've got the business, now let's sell it.' I was absolutely stunned by that. I spent the next year trying to get these guys to march along on this thing. This wasn't the time to sell, we had to keep this together, we owed it to our employees to keep it together. I didn't succeed. Ultimately, I had to buy them out. I went to our bank to get money and the banker said *no, no, no!* Not a penny more! The bank's reaction was really because we had two unexpected settlements to make with General Mills over a dispute in the purchase price that cost us another $3 million or $4 million. Anyway, I managed to borrow the money from another bank and we bought them out over the next twelve to eighteen months. Much later, I also bought out the fourth partner on friendly terms. That was Mr. Bradly, the original cofounder. Bless his heart, he was in poor health and was a great guy to work with and a great support to me. Anyway, I had those difficulties to go through early on. It wasn't easy.

"But in 1983 things started to turn around for us. The business was going well, we were really getting some enthusiasm going for the business, the people were starting to have fun, they were enjoying what they were doing, the quality was restored, capacities were up, we had installed some higher-technology equipment, our packaging was better, marketing programs were coming together. It was getting to be fun. And the two of us, Mr. Bradley and myself, owned the business. But actually the banks and General Mills owned the business because we owed them a lot of money. And that was one of the reasons we decided to go public early. But the primary reason in my heart was that this is a big company and its going to be successful, and here's a way to share with the people. I assured them that when we took over the business that if we were successful, we'd share that success with them. I was careful not to guarantee that, but I said that as the business grows you're going to grow with it. We'll do this together. And as it turned out, we did do it together. I'll cover some of the things we did to create the GoodMark culture:

- "One of the first things we did was to establish an incentive reward system for our people. And establish pay programs for the people where they were compensated better than they were before. I believe strongly in the risk/reward theory; I think you call it consequences. I promised them if they took the same risk with me, that it would be beneficial to them and they responded to that. Everyone does.

- "And further to that we pushed the decisions down to the lowest level we could. We worked hard at that. We took it away from how it was in the large corporate culture down to our own culture. That was, you had to have the guy on the line, and on the shipping dock, responsible and accountable for what they did and if they did it well they got rewarded for it.

- "Back to the reason for going public, this was a way to share the business with employees. In addition to that, it was a way of increasing the leverage for the business to grow by going to the public for funds. We went public in November of 1985. Rather quickly actually. But the window was open in the market and we were ready. We put about 60 percent of the company on the market. Mr. Bradley and I still owned about 38 percent of the business. It was a successful offering on the NASDAQ exchange. I learned that credibility with the street is extremely important. So be honest. When things are bad, tell it like it is. When things are good, tell it like it is, and don't ever overestimate. Going public really made it possible for employees to become owners. Without going public that would have been very difficult, because there was no market for the stock. I want to build on this. We established a program where people got stock for years of service with the company, and they also got rewarded with stock for outstanding work to benefit the company. We could use stock to reward people, we had a stock-purchase program, and a stock-option program. And we have quite a number of people who became—it may stretch the word to say wealthy—but they made an awful lot of money by growing this business and getting options from the company. The stock-option program was quite large. Now it's a part of ConAgra's program—but they don't get nearly the amount of incentives and bonuses and stock options as we used to give out. It was a very big part of our success.

- "Another key thing we did was to maintain a high level of confidence and commitment, a sense of direction with our people. One of the most important things we accomplished, I think, during that time was obtaining and maintaining the respect and confidence of our people. You don't know our people very well, but they're a real team of people. That's a much overused word, but if you were to participate in our environment for a while, you would see a great deal of teamwork. These guys and gals are all pulling the rope in the same direction. They know how to get the job done and they're motivated to do it. People thought for a while, 'Ron is doing this just to cash in.' But over time the majority of the people believed—I believed they believed—that I was in this because I enjoyed it. That I could make something out of it with their help. I used to talk a lot about having fun. It's a fun business. You can do a lot of things with it and I wanted them to participate in the fun.

- "The other thing that I take pride in is that at first everybody was afraid of failing. They were afraid we were going to fail. They were afraid the company was going to be sold again, because we were going to fail at this. And we were losing money for a while. But honestly, probably from growing up with some of the things my Dad taught me, I never believed in failure. We continually communicated this. Don't be afraid to try things. When you made errors as part of the larger company, you got burned pretty bad. But with a philosophy of no failure, there's no such thing as failure. The only failure we can have is to not try again. You aren't going to succeed without making a mistake sometimes, but we never talked about failure. We talked about accountability and responsibility but nobody was going to be tagged because they made a mistake at something. So they're motivated to try again. If it does not work the first time, try something else. Or if we learned something from that, keep it up, we'll get there!"

ConAgra's Corporate Culture—Back to the Future

"My future always seemed far out in front of me. I really did not have a plan and a time horizon for myself in the business. I saw it going on indefinitely. I was having too good a time and it was growing so well and doing so well. I was asked by a dozen companies about my interest in selling my shares. I was now the major shareholder. Would we sell the business? And I had absolutely no interest in that because I had crossed all those bridges and repaired all those dams that we had over time and it was going so well, I thought, 'Hey, this is great.' People said, 'Why don't you retire and have fun?' and I'd say, 'Why? I've had more fun the last eighteen years than I've ever had in my life. I'd rather do this than play golf. It's my passion.' But my board encouraged me to think forward about an exit strategy. And the more I thought about it, I thought it's only fair to the people in the business and the shareholders that I have a clear exit strategy. So I said, 'OK, I'll have an exit strategy.' Well, one of the businesses that was chasing us for years was ConAgra. It went on for five years. They had a philosophy of operating with independent operating companies or IOCs. That philosophy would allow us to operate as an independent entity, which was important to us. The business could survive and do well and my people could be happy with that if they were fairly autonomous. We could operate as an independent operating company and we had every assurance that it would be that way.

"ConAgra is a huge company.[2] But it had a tremendous record. They had, I believe, eighteen years of compound earnings growth of 15 percent. That's pretty heady for one of the largest food processors in the world with some of the greatest brands in America. It was a record we could be proud to tell our employees and shareholders. So we came to an agreement in a short period of time at a good price for our shareholders. The company has operated fairly autonomously, as much as it can. And GoodMark has been a darling for ConAgra. It's a great business for them and it's growing tremendously. In fact in 2000, our second year with them, GoodMark revenues are up about 29 percent over last year.

"They paid $30 a share—which came out to about $240 million. It's all public information. My cost basis is 2¢ a share. That's public information also. It was about 8 million shares at $30 a share. I had bought out the last of the original partners in 1987, and I had also bought more stock in the company so at the time of the sale I personally owned about 34 percent of the stock." Doggett said this with no change in expression at

---

[2]The 1999 *Fortune Global 500* lists ConAgra as the largest food company in America and number three in the world after Nestlé and Unilever. Nestlé had just under $50 billion in revenue, while Unilever came in with $45 billion, and ConAgra recorded nearly $24 billion. ConAgra produces products and services across the entire food chain, from fertilizer and seeds to worldwide commodity trading, to a hundred famous supermarket brands such as Armour, Hunt, Wesson, Healthy Choice, Hebrew National, Chun King, Marie Callender—and now GoodMark. Even in this megabusiness, GoodMark Foods merited a nice accolade in the chairman's letter in the Annual Report: "In the first quarter of fiscal 1999, GoodMark Foods merged with ConAgra . . . . GoodMark's Slim Jim brand . . . will raise to twenty-five the number of ConAgra brands that chalk up over $100 million in annual retail sales."

all. I couldn't help but comment, as it was a much higher price than I had expected to hear: "That's pretty dramatic Ron, if you don't mind my saying so."

The ConAgra image, which represents the smart thinking in a lot of big corporations today, is that if you have good subsidiaries or good acquisitions—for God's sake, leave them alone. But does this ever really happen? I asked Doggett: "Well, ConAgra is struggling with that yet. They have changed the concept of IOCs from when they acquired us two years ago. They've broken them out into seven or eight large divisions versus eighty separate IOCs. They said they found that were too many IOCs. They could not get their arms around them so they've changed that. But they still have an underlying concept of pushing the decision making down. You come to them for approval of funds and plans, but other than that you still run your business. At least that's the concept."

On May 13, 1999, the first, very heavy ConAgra shoe dropped. ConAgra announced that it would be terminating 8,000 jobs and closing 15 plants. It was termed a "restructuring and consolidation plan," with across-the-board expense reductions to keep up its twenty-year record of earnings growth. Hello! Does this sound vaguely familiar? Could this be some of that same old corporate-speak that Doggett happily left behind two decades ago at General Mills? With GoodMark's sales booming and growing at 29 percent, it hardly seems the right time to go into a cost-cutting mode in the Slim Jim business. And it hardly seems to be the kind of entrepreneur-friendly culture Ron Doggett worked so hard to create.

And believe it or not, as I'm writing these very words, I'm looking at today's copy of my small town, local newspaper (May 31, 2000) and seeing the headline: "ConAgra Plant Closing Hits Valley Workers." The front-page story reports: "ConAgra Frozen Foods will close its Crozet plant as part of a company-wide restructuring and consolidation plan that will cut the giant company's work force by 8,000. The Crozet closing will idle 600 workers, many of whom have worked at the plant for decades. . . . The local union secretary said: 'This plant is the largest employer in the town. There are people who have been here forty years. The average is about sixteen years. This is a big blow to them.' . . . The company spokesman said: 'We appreciate the many contributions and the years of commitment made by our Crozet employees. In addition to severance benefits and outplacement assistance, we will work closely with our employees to help them through this very difficult time.'" Hmmmmm.

Welcome back to the future—to the culture of the giant, centrally controlled conglomerate! Ron Doggett was too nice to say this, so I will. The fact is, there are always tradeoffs to be made even in enlightened companies like ConAgra. Corporate has "corporate needs," and corporate needs will always be more important than the needs of each small part of the corporation. That's the way it's always been and that's the way it's always going to be. And that's the entrepreneur-*unfriendly* culture you should avoid like the plague in your own business!

Regardless of what happens to ConAgra and GoodMark in the future, Ron Doggett's record is already etched in granite—or should I say gold? And what a record it has been! Growing the old-fashioned way, not the ConAgra way of endless acquisitions, the compound revenue growth for GoodMark Foods over the eighteen years is about 12 percent. The compound growth rate for earnings is a whopping 19 percent. As an aside, I can't resist noting that these numbers beat both General Mills and ConAgra results over the same period—of course on a much smaller base. But the unspoken number in the interview is the one that stands out to me. You don't need a computer to figure out that Ron Doggett, the mild-mannered entrepreneur, the good guy from Minnesota, walked off with over $80 million. Not bad for eighteen years of having fun! Bravo, Ron!

Doggett closed our discussion with a great summation for any and all would-be entrepreneurs: "I'll never forget what my wife said when I went to her with the last straw on this thing. We had no place to go for equity when we bought the company—other than what little we had—and I said this means we've used the kids' college funds, we've used our insurance, we've used all the equity we have in our home, we've got everything including the lawn mower riding on this thing. Do you still think we should do it? And by the way I have some question about my partners and this business isn't doing well right now, so what do you think? And she said: 'Are you excited about it? Do you like it?' And I said, 'Yeah, I really do.' So she said, 'Well then, go for it.' She thought, and I thought, it was a great opportunity and I've often said it was the opportunity of a lifetime, and it was. So my message is to seize these opportunities. Seize the opportunity and leverage yourself to get it if you have to. Too many people pass their opportunities by in this life."

So, at the end of the day, what do you actually have to do to pursue your entrepreneurial dream? To be sure, as Ron Doggett's wonderful story shows, you'll need to acquire "a bit of money" and "a bit of knowledge," and create the most "entrepreneur-friendly culture" you can. But then you still have to get the business up and running, grow it, and fight off the competitors. The proven way to do that is to learn and apply the practices of the world's great entrepreneurs: *sense of mission, customer/product vision, high-speed innovation,* and *self-inspired behavior.*

If you're still not quite ready or convinced that you should try to become the next great entrepreneur, that's fine. A lot of very smart and happy people prefer to be part of a team in an organization. If this is you, read on to Part Two—Entrepreneurial Companies. It's all about developing the entrepreneurial skills of employees inside a company. The good news is that a large and growing number of companies are encouraging and rewarding exactly this type of behavior. We call it corporate entrepreneurship, and it may be a perfect fit for you.

part ii
entrepreneurial companies

*Reviving the Spirit of Enterprise
in Your Business*

7

The New Corporate Entrepreneurs

Today your career is your business.
—ANDY GROVE
CEO, INTEL

Andy Grove represents the new breed of entrepreneurial manager, who wants to instill the entrepreneurial spirit in every employee. Forget resting on your laurels. Forget lifetime employment. Companies are not security blankets and that's good for everyone. Get really good at something, work at it with passion, and you'll have ten good jobs waiting for you. Sit around waiting for a seniority promotion and a pension, and you're dead meat in today's do-or-die global economy.

Grove's most famous management dictum is this: "Only the paranoid survive." And who could blame him? After all, András Gróf survived both scarlet fever and Nazi pogroms as a boy. Then, at age 20, with the Red Army approaching, he fled Budapest after the failed 1956 revolution. With no money, little English, and a new American name, young immigrant Andy Grove hit the U.S. shores running. With a hard-won Ph.D. from Berkeley, he joined Fairchild Semiconductor where the legendary Gordon Moore became his mentor for life ("Moore's Law" correctly predicted that microchips would double in power and halve in cost every eighteen months). Grove was certainly no scientific slouch himself, running the team that purified silicon, a huge breakthrough that made the digital revolution possible. When Moore founded Intel, Andy Grove was at his side, putting him center stage in one of the most turbulent, unpredictable, and entrepreneurial businesses in the world.

Surviving mighty ups and downs, Grove has come out on top, building what *Time* calls "the essential firm of the digital age." Only thirty years old, Intel produces 90 percent of the world's microprocessors, ranks third in market value in the United States (behind GE and Cisco, as of this writing), and has given investors an average annual return of 44 percent over the last decade. Even so, this is an industry so fast paced, with such high stakes, that even Intel could be wiped out with a single strategic lapse. The 1994 recall of the Pentium processor, resulting in a massive $475 million writeoff, is a grim reminder.

Obsessed with the ever-present possibility of falling behind, Andy Grove and his engineers continue to push the frontiers of technology, squeezing 588 million calculations a second (at last count) out of each new Pentium II chip. Armed with their own ample share of paranoia, most Intel people behave more like start-up entrepreneurs than comfortable employees in one of the world's most successful companies. Grove's entrepreneurial management style clearly sets the tone. Intel employees know that when he tells them, "Your career is your business," he means it.

Managing and marketing one's own career has become the clarion call of twenty-first century corporate life. For those who bemoan the more entrepreneurial environment in corporations, it's all a matter of perspective. Sure, there are reasons to be sentimental about the good old days when company loyalty and lifetime employment were in vogue. But in an age of massive restructuring and downsizing, who can blame managers and employees today for getting more entrepreneurial in their approach to their careers? And also, let's not overromanticize spending forty years in the same company, doing the same job, and fighting the same battles. As Ben Hamper, the former GM assembly line worker turned author says, "Working at GM was like being paid to flunk high school the rest of your life."

Like it or not, most of us have to play with the hand we're dealt. Remember: We're living in an age when the biggest "employer" in America has become Manpower, Inc., a temporary help agency. Getting entrepreneurial is not really a choice any more for most of us. But don't despair. We have a great suggestion for you. It's a "don't get mad, get even" suggestion. How about learning to be a "corporate entrepreneur"? It's the new, smart, Entrepreneurial-Age strategy for people who really prefer being part of a large, world-class business, versus starting their own operation from scratch. There can be enormous benefits to you and your company. Big business may have had to reshuffle the deck a few times over the past couple of decades, but giant companies haven't gone away—they've just gotten a lot smarter. The fact is, big business has fallen in love with managers who can run their small part of the big business as if it were their own. All you really need are a few starter ideas and examples of how to become an entrepreneurial manager. If so, this section of *The Entrepreneurial Age* should be especially interesting and important for you.[1]

This is the Andy Grove message: Getting entrepreneurial will be good for your company, no doubt about it. But more than that, it will be absolutely great for your career. It's the win-win formula for reviving the spirit of enterprise in yourself and your business!

A good way to start is to recognize that it's possible—that entrepreneurial managers and entrepreneurial companies actually do exist. The story of Lincoln Electric exemplifies that message—in spades.

THE MOST ENTREPRENEURIAL BIG COMPANY IN THE WORLD

When workers are treated like entrepreneurs, they behave like entrepreneurs.

—FRED MACKENBACH
PRESIDENT (RETIRED), LINCOLN ELECTRIC

How many companies do you know that have to keep their gates locked before the morning shift to keep employees from starting work too early? Welcome to Lincoln Electric, the world's largest maker of welding equipment, and a company that stands conventional wisdom on its head. When I first heard this story, I couldn't believe it, so I checked it out personally with Fred Mackenbach, the president and COO, in Cleveland, Ohio. Along with the locked gates to keep workers out, Lincoln Electric also has some very strange ideas about compensating employees. Mackenbach says: "The company only gets paid by making good welding equipment, and we don't see any reason for paying employees for anything other than making that welding equipment." And they don't. They don't pay anyone for holidays, sick leave, lunch time, coffee breaks, trips to the toilet, or for poor quality product that no one will buy.

Then with a twinkle in his eye, Mackenbach let slip that the employees didn't seem to mind since they were all earning from $60,000 to over $100,000 per year, making Lincoln Electric employees the highest-paid factory workers in the world. Mackenbach said they had built the entire company on the following simple notion: "Lincoln can pay the highest factory salaries in the world because our people know that, like entre-

---

[1] Anyway, if this doesn't work for you, you can always throw in the corporate towel later and become a consultant or whatever. If and when you do that, please go back and reread Part I of the book to raise your odds—and hopefully figure out something more useful to do than consulting!

preneurs, the more good welding equipment they produce the more money they will make. And second, because entrepreneurs don't get paid for downtime or rejects, they're self-managing, which means we don't need to hire supervisors. So they work damn hard, and there's a lot of profit to be shared in that welding equipment." It's a modern version of nineteenth-century piecework pay, with two huge differences. First, all those savings go back to the workers in profit bonuses. In a good year, they average more than $20,000 per worker—an unheard-of figure in American factories. Second, the company guarantees continuous employment to its workers, and hasn't had a layoff since it was founded in 1895. The trick to guaranteeing employment is to instill the very entrepreneurial notion that, in slow times, managers and workers are expected to work reduced schedules. Over the years, Lincoln employees have been asked to temporarily cut their time by as much as 25 percent, but everyone in the company agrees that this is preferable to the standard industry practice of layoffs and outright terminations.

Other unusual things happen when corporate entrepreneurship takes hold. Mackenbach explains: "Our entrepreneurship springs from the willingness, and the ability, to take some risks. Large organizations are usually devoted to minimizing risks, not seeking them out. We are fortunate at Lincoln, because our strong pay-for-performance system forces us to take risks on a daily basis. We take a risk every time we make a new hire. We look for a strong work ethic and a burning desire to succeed. Evidence of that desire is the best predictor of success in the Lincoln culture. If we are wrong about a new hire, that person's substandard performance will adversely affect the productivity of everyone in that department. Since we are exactly staffed, the other employees will have to pick up the slack. So, at Lincoln, each new hire is a risky business decision.

"We also constantly take risks in our effort to better serve the customer, because of course the customer ultimately is our reason for being. We have a program called 'guaranteed cost reduction,' in which our sales representatives guarantee our customer, in writing, that by using Lincoln products and recommended procedures, they will save a specific amount of money within a certain time frame, or we will pay them the difference. As President of the company, I personally sign those guarantees. Is it risky? Sure. A couple of times the savings have failed to materialize and we had to cut checks for those customers. Has it been worth the risk? Absolutely. We've generated millions and millions of dollars of business by being willing to take this risk.

"We also take many risks by encouraging our employees to be self-managing. This means that we are willing to relinquish a certain amount of control, in exchange for the tremendous energy and initiative highly motivated people bring to our enterprise. Of course, the big benefit of having 6,400 self-managing employees is that we don't have to pay people to watch other people. Something that customers couldn't care less about is how much money we spend micromanaging our workforce. But the nonproductive cost of supervision could have a devastating impact on the prices we charge our customers. Now *that,* they care about!

"And of course our formal policy of guaranteed continuous employment entails an almost unheard-of risk. It is a risk we have continued to take, day by day, month by month, year by year, through recessions, and very hard times in our industry. But we believe the upside in all this is worth it. An example is the remarkable performance of our people last summer, when a sudden spike in demand for our products forced us to sharply increase production. Lincoln employees voluntarily deferred 614 weeks of vacation in order to meet that challenge. Their efforts broke all of our production and sales records. And I must tell you, our records were already high."

The most current financial results say Lincoln Electric's entrepreneurial approach is still working. On this year's *Fortune 1000* list, Lincoln is once again a star in its industrial category. You'll find the company listed in the Industrial and Farm Equipment category—about as "old economy" as it gets. In this most basic of basic industries, stalwarts like Caterpillar, Detroit Diesel, and Timkin are bigger and better known—but the Ohio manufacturer of welding equipment really shines when it comes to the key financial ratios. With $1.2 billion in revenue, it ranks only thirty-sixth of the thirty-seven companies in the category. But here's the entrepreneurial payoff: As percentages of revenue, it ranks number *two* in profitability and number *three* in total return to investors!

Of course, Lincoln Electric isn't General Motors, with half a million people to worry about. But it could very well be a General Motors billion-dollar division. And that's the best part of the story: Any big business in the world can operate like Lincoln Electric if the company wants to. There's nothing holding you back. As Fred Mackenbach concluded, "It's all pretty simple really. When workers are treated like entrepreneurs, they behave like entrepreneurs. Lincoln employees will do anything it takes to produce more welding equipment. It's just amazing." Then he chuckled: "That's why we have to lock the gates sometimes!"

8

Keeping the Sense of Mission Alive As You Grow

When it comes to setting up new companies, one of my advantages is that I don't have a highly complicated view of business.

—RICHARD BRANSON
VIRGIN GROUP

Richard Branson is Great Britain's most successful and famous entrepreneur since the days of William Lever, George Cadbury, and Jesse Boots. And he deserves every bit of his fame and his fortune. He's made Virgin a household name the world over with Virgin Music, Virgin Records, Virgin Atlantic Airways, Virgin Films, Virgin Direct, Virgin Megastores, Virgin Cola, and dozens more Virgin businesses.

But as terrific as he is, I'd hate to have to learn how to be an entrepreneur by listening to him explain how he did it: "To be successful, you have to be out there, you have to hit the ground running, and if you have a good team around you and more than a fair share of luck, you might make something happen." This is classic (and entertaining) "entrepreneur-speak." But you still don't know how in the world he became a billionaire entrepreneur or, more to the point, what you should do to become one yourself! Maybe in some deep psychological way that I also don't understand, that's just fine with Richard Branson. Regardless, this is a common characteristic of most great entrepreneurs: They're obsessed with creating and building businesses, not teaching others how to do the same.

Still it's impossible not to admire Branson and be motivated by his aura of success. And along the way, we can at least try to make sense of some of the pearls of wisdom he imparts. For example, it's just plain refreshing to hear him describe his approach to market research: "When I think about which services I want to offer on Virgin Atlantic, I try to imagine whether my family and I would like to buy them for ourselves. Quite often it's as simple as that." And some of his comments do at least sound like ideas a company could try: "Convention dictates that 'big is beautiful,' but every time one of our ventures gets too big, we divide it up into smaller units. By the time we sold Virgin Music, we had as many as fifty different subsidiary record companies, and not one of them had more than sixty employees." Finally, who wouldn't be inspired at least a little by this description of the core reason for The Virgin Group's meteoric rise: "More than any other element, fun is the secret of Virgin's success."

But just as you're beginning to think that Richard Branson is a teacher after all, he comes up with this "description" when asked about the future *mission* of Virgin: "I tend to either avoid this question or answer it at great length, safe in the knowledge that I will give a different version the next time I'm asked." What's that? How are you going to teach your people to be corporate entrepreneurs with a cryptic message like that? You're not—and that's why our *mission* has become to distill what these great people *do*—not what they *say they do*.

Now for the easy part when it comes to Branson's experience. There is one, absolutely clear behavior that he's demonstrated over the past three decades: Richard Branson has an all-consuming *sense of mission* about his work. He believes that what he is doing is important—and he is incredibly committed to doing it. So, we thank you, Richard Branson, for giving us an exciting, modern example of that old truth about entrepreneurs. And now we can move on to the business of figuring out how to put your brand of business, your sense of mission, if you will, into some simple, practical steps that any employee, in any company, can actually follow!

Sense of mission is the starting point for all entrepreneurs. They do truly believe they are doing something important. They see genuine value in their work: for their customers, for their employees, and certainly for themselves. They are convinced that their products produce needed benefits for customers. And without exception, they know the only way to stay alive is to produce products and services that someone, somewhere, will pay for. In this sense, at least, all organizations start off reflecting the goals, the philosophy, and the sense of mission of their founders. This is true in spades at Richard Branson's Virgin Group.

Perhaps none of this is terribly surprising. What may be surprising is the degree to which start-up employees also share in this sense of mission. In the young, entrepreneurial company, spirit or mission seems to come with the territory and is very infectious. But when you think about it, maybe it isn't so unusual. Consider your own career history. Most employees say the most exciting times in their working careers have been when they were involved with something new: launching a new product, opening a new market, fighting off a new competitor, and so on. In the final analysis, however it comes about, we know that having a sense of mission is a gift of enormous competitive value.

While it comes somewhat naturally for the original entrepreneur and his start-up team, it's going to be trickier to instill this powerful competitive advantage in an existing company with long-term employees and fixed attitudes about things. The first step is to have a clear understanding of exactly what sense of mission is all about. And the best way to do this, given the kinds of explanations offered by most of the great entrepreneurs of the world—such as Sir Richard—is to look beyond their words to their deeds.

If most entrepreneurs are not terribly articulate in verbalizing their mission, they are exquisitely articulate in their behavior; that is, in *what* they do and *how* they do it—day in and day out. These are the two essential elements of any mission. A person, a company, or even a country, has to know *what* its mission is, and *how* to achieve it. All entrepreneurs' behavior is highly focused on what they are doing and how they go about doing it— which we've translated into business language as "corporate strategy" (the *what*) and "corporate culture" (the *how*).

For entrepreneurs, the strategy really comes down to picking the right products and markets. And the culture has the specific role of making sure that you achieve that strategy. The entrepreneurial ideal is to be great at both. It's not good enough to have a strong strategy but a weak, nonsupportive culture. Conversely, a strong culture will never overcome a weak strategy. And, of course, you won't be around long if you know neither what you're doing nor how to do it!

SENSE OF MISSION

	−	+
+	weak strategy strong culture	strong strategy strong culture	**+**
"HOW" **Corporate** **Culture**		
−	weak strategy weak culture	strong strategy weak culture	**−**
	−	+

"WHAT" Corporate Strategy

The lesson that is so often lost in the bureaucracy of larger companies is that corporate strategy and corporate culture must be connected. You set the strategy, and then you determine those operating activities and skills that are most critical to achieving the strategy. One of the great modern examples of the power of that connection is 3M. Everyone knows 3M's reputation for product innovation. It has the highest ratio of new product revenue to total revenue of any big company around. First, 3M sets as its corporate strategy—and, on average, achieves—an incredible 30 percent ratio of new product revenue. Its definition has always been that any product invented within the past five years is classified as "new." So, how does 3M achieve this remarkable performance? First, by planning to do it—making new product revenue the core of its corporate strategy. And second— and here's the part so often missed by others—3M has built its entire corporate culture around product innovation. It has made innovation the number-one, in fact the only, corporate value of the worldwide company. This is both very smart and very effective. Would 3M hit its strategic goal year after year if it simply copied the values of, say, Wal-Mart, or Singapore Airlines, or Mercedes Benz—all great companies in their own right? Of course not! 3M hits its strategic goal by connecting its culture to its strategy. Failing to do that is the most common mistake that managements make in trying to instill an entrepreneurial sense of mission in their companies.

The challenge for you is to make sure that your behavior—and that of your employees—is also "obsessively focused" on these two fundamentals of successful enterprise. To do that, let's look at one of the great role models for creating an entrepreneurial strategy—Japan's greatest entrepreneur of the twentieth century.

CORPORATE STRATEGY À LA MATSUSHITA

Our duty as industrialists is to provide conveniences for the public, and to enrich and make happier all those who use them.
—KONOSUKE MATSUSHITA
FOUNDER, MATSUSHITA ELECTRIC

Konosuke Matsushita was a young salesman in Osaka. In 1918, he invested his life savings of 100 yen (about $50) in imported electric sockets from Great Britain. He was excited and very focused on getting the first batch sold and ordering more. He was certain this type of product would sell very well in the new, miracle age of electricity! He was wrong. None of the shops he called on were interested in stocking his electric sockets. Things got so bad that he went bankrupt. So the great Matsushita's first entrepreneurial venture was a bust. And in Japan, at that time, failing in business was about as shameful an act as one could commit. Then he did something that few sales people ever do—and it changed his life forever.

He went back to all the shopkeepers who wouldn't buy his product and asked them, "Is there anything I could do to change this socket so that you would want to buy a few for your shop?" Many of the shopkeepers gave him suggestions such as to make it bigger, make it smaller, change the color, do this or do that. He took all their suggestions and began tinkering with his sockets at home. He even fashioned a few prototypes of his own from scratch. He went back to the market with the customized versions and tried again. And again. And again. He kept repeating his routine of asking the potential customers how he could change the product so they would buy it. It was this process of back and forth customer/product strategizing, that produced Konosuke Matsushita's marvelous invention: the world's first two-way electric socket. With it, he began winning customers and the fledgling Matsushita Electric played a small, but critical, role in building the phenomenal electrical appliance industry in Japan. Now, a single electric line to a house could connect two appliances—an electric fan, a radio, a cooker, and so on. And as we know today, it gave birth to the world's largest producer of electric and electronic products. It also was a lesson in corporate strategy that Matsushita Electric never forgot.

By his own later account, Matsushita was unsuccessful at first because he was thinking too much about selling and not enough about what customers really wanted. So what was his successful "strategic process"? Simply this: "Ask the customers what they want, and then do that rare and unexpected thing: Give it to them!" When you're looking for simple, practical steps to follow, the no-frills, customer/product strategy of Matsushita is hard to beat!

In 1932, some fourteen years after start-up, Konosuke Matsushita again did something that most salesmen (and great entrepreneurs) never do. He started thinking about and putting on paper the principles of enterprise as he had lived them. It took him five years to get it down. The result was a very thin, twenty-three–page booklet titled *Matsushita Management Philosophy*. These twenty-three pages contain as much wisdom about enterprise as some entire business school libraries. The booklet provides a philosophical and strategic framework for any company, which, not surprisingly, all boils down to making products that markets actually need. It should be required reading in every MBA program in the world.

For eighty-five years, the *what* of the business at Matsushita has been driven by knowing very specifically, *what customers* want *what products*. Doing this better and more consistently than their competitors has always given Matsushita Electric—and its famous brands like Panasonic and National—the ultimate competitive advantage. In so doing, Konosuke Matsushita raised customer/product strategy from black magic to near certainty, and it all comes from those unsold electric sockets way back in 1918.

WHAT'S IN *WHAT*

Is there, then, an entrepreneurial strategy-setting approach that you and your people can use? Well, it may not qualify as a full-blown (and incredibly expensive) strategic planning process, à la McKinsey or Bain Consulting, but there are definitely some basics to keep in mind—whether you're creating a top-down corporate strategy or simply your own business unit plans.[1]

For starters, if the strategy is supposed to tell us what we are doing, we need to be crystal clear about what's included in the *what.* And it doesn't take 300 pages to figure that out. It only requires answering four straightforward questions. Listed below are the questions about the *whats* that matter most. If you know the answers cold, you're on top of your business. If you can't answer these basic questions, you not only don't have a useful plan, you may not have a business to worry about much longer.

> ### What Customers/Markets Will We Pursue?
> Are we really clear on what markets we will and won't tackle? What's the criteria for choosing? What do they really need? What will they really pay for?

> ### What Products or Services Will We Provide?
> What's the scope of the products and services we can and will provide? What's the criteria for picking winners? Will our products and services be better and cheaper than those of our competitors? Will they be better but not necessarily cheaper? Will they at least be cheaper?

> ### What Capabilities Are Required?
> What operating capabilities and resources are required to make, sell, and service our products and customers?

---

[1]Again, our description of the entrepreneurial approach to strategy is influenced by and in part modified from the original work of my friend and former boss, Dr. Benjamin B. Tregoe. These descriptions and modifications appear in Part I and more significantly in Part II of the book. We have applied his description of strategy to the entrepreneurial approach for one reason only—it so clearly illustrates why entrepreneurs do what they do. I highly recommend Ben Tregoe's (or Kepner-Tregoe, Inc.'s) own books and advisory services on the broader subject of corporate strategy.

> ### *What Cash Will We Have?*
Where will the cash come from and where will it go? Even if your company doesn't require it, thinking and planning in cash keeps your feet on the ground, right where they have to be in an entrepreneurial world.

CREATING AN ENTREPRENEURIAL STRATEGY

The best way to get a handle on creating an entrepreneurial corporate strategy is to recall the last big-company, strategic-planning session you attended—and then do everything as differently as possible. If your planning and presentation experience is anything like the ones most of us have had, it probably went something like this:

You're in an exclusive resort or the even more exclusive, corporate boardroom. All-powerful executives sit as judge and jury, while scores of nervous underlings parade to the front, making the projections they think the board wants to hear. Your soft estimates become hard facts as they get cemented into the overall corporate plan. The usual assortment of pin-striped consultants come and go, pitching their own version of your future. And, of course, there are the reams of research and planning books, piled high on the table, that nobody ever reads. Somehow, out of this surreal, big-business ritual, comes the big black book called the *Strategic Plan,* and everyone goes back to doing real work for another twelve months. If this doesn't ring a bell, be thankful. Because this is no way to pick products and markets.

I may have an more jaundiced view of strategic planning presentations than most. When I was just twenty-eight, I had the chance of a lifetime to impress the big brass of my *Fortune 100* employer, American Express Company. I was the marketing vice president for a really tiny, new acquisition that offered language training and translation services. Like all Amexco divisions and companies, we had to present our five-year strategic plan to the board, and I was asked by my president to accompany him. A couple of years earlier, American Express had embarked upon an aggressive acquisition strategy, hoping to grow faster by moving beyond its core products, which was all the rage at the time. The high-flying Amexco acquisition team had apparently thought that since American Express was the "company for people who travel," why not also teach them foreign languages? We all found out later that language training was a real mom-and-pop–type business—and even the world leader, Berlitz, had taken eighty years to get to only about $25 million in revenue from some one hundred schools.

Our subsidiary, which had just begun trading under the name American Express Language Centers, had only three schools in the whole world. To make us look as good as possible, we had really pumped up our projections for the board presentation. We all knew that, short of a miracle, we weren't likely to meet them, but we had convinced ourselves that we should present as aggressive a plan as we could to the board. Amexco had hired McKinsey Consulting to install a Strategic Planning System and I spent weeks with some of McKinsey's young consultants putting our plans into the right format and so on. Overall, our personnel had put months into the planning process, which we all believed was state-of-the-art stuff.

On the big day, I entered the old American Express headquarters at 65 Broadway in lower Manhattan and made my way up to the executive floor, which I had never even seen before. We were second or third on the list of presentations that day, but I was ushered into the boardroom through a side door while the preceding presentation was wrapping up. Upon entering, the first thing I saw was the giant mahogany board table— the biggest table I had ever seen in my life. The carpet seemed about two inches thick, and everything was beautifully polished. The room was huge, and everybody was there. The board members were all sitting around the enormous table. Seated around the edge of the cavernous room were various minions: the advertising agency folks, several of the strategic planning consultants, the PR people, lots of upper-middle–management executives with thick binders, and a dozen "go-fers" racing in and out of the boardroom. The group presenting before us was the Travelers Checques Division, a hugely profitable business. The highlight of that presentation was a prediction that by the summer of the following year, the "float" on Travelers Checques (the amount sold but not yet used) would hit a cool $1 billion for the first time in history. I'm sure it's many billions more today, but from my seat at the side of the room, I quickly calculated the interest per year on a billion dollars and winced. With this closing piece of good news, there was much guffawing and self-congratulation around the boardroom and, then, my president and I were up.

My boss had the somewhat redundant name of Jeffrey Jeffries. Jeffrey Jeffries was a long-term American Express guy, who was desperate to retire with his pension intact. After a brief introduction full of corporate platitudes, he turned to me and, as if he had just thought of it said, "Larry, why don't you give the board your projections." Even though I was extremely nervous with anticipation, I do remember thinking: "Why is Jeffrey Jeffries acting like we haven't been rehearsing this for days and, much more troubling, when did these become *my* projections?" So with my charts and, I'm sure in a trembling voice, I somehow got through the show and ended with the big number: the five-year-out revenue projection—which I knew we couldn't hit without an act of God—of $4 million. I sat down. A hush settled on the room. Nobody said anything. I peered up and scanned the board members who were all just staring at my

$4 million figure on the chart, saying absolutely nothing. It was as if no one had ever seen such a small number at a board presentation! After the long silence, the great and powerful chairman, Howard Clark (who's signature was on every one of those billions of dollars' worth of Travelers Checques) turned to Executive VP Hap Miller, my boss's boss's boss, and said: "I'm sure this young man you've got presenting here is a fine salesman, Hap, but I gotta tell ya, the salesman I'd like to meet is the one who sold us this damn company in the first place! He must be one hell of a great salesman."

I looked straight at the chairman, but all I saw was my career flashing before my eyes—until, that is, Jeffrey Jeffries, the guy with one foot in retirement and a veteran of "CYA" corporate maneuvering, sprang into the breach with the following gem: "It would be interesting to take a second look at the acquisition team's original projections and contrast them to the reality we now know we face." A masterstroke! There was a consensus grunt of approval and in the twinkling of an eye, Jeffrey Jeffries had shifted the blame from us to the guys who bought "this damn company in the first place." He leaned over to me and whispered: "Close call, but don't worry. You'll probably get a spot in corporate marketing, which will be better exposure anyway." I gathered up my charts and walked out of the boardroom, having learned an important lesson in strategic planning and career development at giant corporations: Successfully delivering your plan at the end of the year may not be nearly as important as successfully delivering the *presentation* of your plan at the beginning of the year!

Of course, all this flies in the face of entrepreneurial common sense. While the entrepreneur's strategy focuses on the survival of the business, traditional, big company strategy is often focused on creating financial projections to please the board and excite Wall Street. It's not so exciting, but creating an entrepreneurial strategy is still based on that old-fashioned business of picking the right products and markets. Trying to figure out how to survive is, after all, a pretty down-to-earth business. Here's how entrepreneurs approach it.

➤ It's a Matter of Survival

The goal is survival, not an affirmative nod from the board. And today it's career as well as business survival that we're talking about. If you get the plan right, you stay in business and you have a job. If you've picked the wrong products and markets, you don't get to try it again next year—you're history! At least that's the way it works for entrepreneurs.

➤ *Don't Make It a Big, Complicated Project*

Making up the plan is not the objective. Growing the business is. To the entrepreneur, creating the company strategy isn't a six-month project, or a conference in Bermuda, or an excuse for consultants to get rich. The entrepreneurs' method: Keep it simple, do it quickly, and get back to the real work.

➤ *Stay Focused on Customers*

The best partners you'll ever have in business are your customers. They know more and cost less than any market researchers and consultants you could ever hire. They'll tell you exactly what they need, what they're willing to pay for it, and how they'd like it delivered—if you'll only ask them. To create an entrepreneurial-style strategy, your plans have to be designed *with* your customers, not *at* your customers.

➤ *Stay Focused on Products*

The best product consultants you'll ever have are free. They're your customers and your competitors. In fact, there are three prime sources of great product and service ideas: you, your customers, and your competitors. Mining all three sources, all the time, is the entrepreneurial way to create a product strategy. And remember: While it's true that entrepreneurs "love their product," what keeps them in business is making sure their *customers* love their product.

➤ *Know the Criteria That Count*

Choosing products and markets is the name of the game. The information entrepreneurs want most is intimate knowledge about *market need* and their *competitive position* against the best competitors in the field. These are the two criteria that always count most!

THE CRITERIA THAT COUNT

As Matsushita told his managers, you can write your plan in a 200-page book or on the back of your hand—but always remember that the two things you must know are what your customers really need, and whether you have the best product to fill that need. So we think Konosuke Matsushita would agree when we say the criteria that count are market need and competitive position. To make the best choices about markets, you will practically have to live with your prospects and customers. And to make the best choices about your competitive position, you have to know everything you can possibly (and legally) find out about your best competitors. In short, you need the lowdown on "what, when, where, and how much" about both your customers and your competitors.

Here's a final word about "picking winners"—and the traditional planning cycle: The process of choosing products and markets has to go on all the time. It happens whenever ideas and opportunities present themselves. Most great market ideas aren't going to pop up in October just because you've started your planning cycle. And damn few great products have ever been conceived at a planning conference in Bermuda. So stay flexible and don't get locked into the notion that picking products and markets is a once-a-year job.

The chart below can be used to rate and then combine the ratings of the two criteria for all your markets and products. While entrepreneurs aren't big fans of matrices and charts, this one will give you a simple, easy-to-see method of evaluating any market or product you are considering. In other words, it will help you determine if you have picked a "Market/Product Winner" or not. As you may recall from Part I of this book, each quadrant in the matrix represents a unique market/product position.[2] And the actions required to improve your market/product position will differ greatly for each quadrant. The overall objective is to take those actions that will move your product or business in an upper-right direction—toward bigger markets and a higher competitive position.

THE CRITERIA THAT COUNT

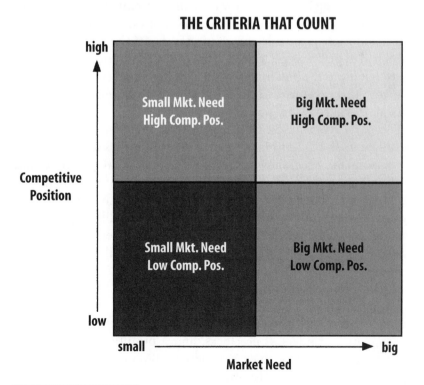

---

[2]To review the complete descriptions of the four market/product positions, see Chapter 2 in Part I.

So now you and your organization have a clear strategy for *what* markets and *what* products. And everyone should have a clear picture of *what* to do. The only thing standing between you and success is *how* well you can do it. This is where corporate culture, and the specific values that drive it, must get plugged into the business.

CORPORATE CULTURE À LA WATSON

The beliefs that mold great organizations frequently grow out of the character, the experiences, and the convictions of a single person. More than most companies, IBM is the reflection of one individual—my father, T. J. Watson.
—THOMAS J. WATSON, JR.
PAST CHAIRMAN, IBM

This could only happen to IBM: You're fourteenth in sales and sixth in profits on *Fortune*'s *Global 500* list but everyone keeps saying you're over the hill. In an odd sort of way, it's actually a tribute to the awesome power and reputation that Big Blue carried for most of the twentieth century. With the benefit of some perspective, one could make a strong case that IBM was the greatest and most profitable corporation in the entire history of business. If you had to pick a single factor at the core of IBM's long run at greatness, it was that it was the best in the world at doing those few critical things that were absolutely essential to the achievement of its business strategy. Tom Watson, Jr., called it the "power of IBM's beliefs."

Thomas J. Watson, Sr., founded IBM in 1914 and immediately began instilling in all IBMers his now-famous set of beliefs: Cultivate outstanding customer service, show respect for the individual employee, and put forth a superior effort in all tasks. History shows that these beliefs—or, as we call them, values—served IBM well for seventy-five years. Where did they come from? Did Mr. Watson take a vote among his employees or hire consultants to tell him what the IBM values should be? No, they came from Watson himself, as he figured out what IBM had to focus on to achieve its strategy.

T. J. Watson was an eternally optimistic salesman, and he didn't see IBM's strategy as a product leader and innovator—like 3M, for example. In fact, in the early days, IBM's products were fairly humdrum: butcher scales, meat slicers, coffee grinders, time clocks, and a primitive assortment of punched-card tabulating machines. Watson saw IBM's competitive advantage in providing outstanding customer service, whatever the product. This value was verbalized as a flat-out, uncompromising promise to the world:

"IBM will give the best customer service of any company, in any industry, anywhere in the world."

Watson set out on a lifetime mission to make that promise come true. For years, IBM's corporate advertising simply declared: "IBM Means Service." IBM sales people were trained like no sales force ever before. They spent as long as eighteen months in IBM schools before seeing their first customer. Early on, the company began recruiting sales trainees from college campuses, an unheard-of practice at the time. And Watson invented the idea of "customer engineers" being assigned to all sales teams—to ensure that customers had face-to-face contact with IBM's highest level of technical expertise. IBM schools were opened to customer personnel, further fostering interaction and good relations between IBMers and the people who paid their salaries. IBM sales and service teams were legendary for working weekends and round-the-clock to get client systems up and running on schedule or back in service after repairs. In a brilliant masterstroke to strengthen respect for customers, IBM publicly declared that 95 percent of all IBM product ideas came from customers. And, perhaps most powerful of all, everyone at IBM knew that the absolutely guaranteed way to get fired was to be rude to customers. These and a thousand other means were used to instill the "customer service belief" at IBM as the primary competitive advantage of the company.

Next, Watson strongly believed that giving the best customer service in the world required having the best employees in the world. Watson's belief was transformed into the second IBM value: "IBM will respect the dignity of every employee." This straightforward value has probably created more IBM folklore than any other single facet of the company's history. It generated the trim "IBM look": white shirt, dark blue tie, and close-cropped haircuts. Women employees also had to toe the company line, with white blouses and blue scarves. From this belief also came IBM's unique series of policies: having subordinates formally rate their managers; its famous open-door policy as a "deterrent to the possible abuse of managerial power"; an incredible amount of training for all employees; a strong promote-from-within policy; and, yes, even some company hoopla. Sixty-five years of a no-layoff policy—even during the darkest days of the Great Depression (yet inconceivable at today's IBM)—didn't hurt company loyalty and morale either. And, of course, IBM's consistent record of paying top dollar and top benefits cemented all the above.

Some of this "people stuff" may sound quaint in the entrepreneurial age, but the principles behind these policies are important. Take the IBM dress code, for example. Thomas Watson, Jr. explained it this way: "Our management has long believed that sharp contrasts between blue- and white-collar people in a business has to be avoided." And, in those early days at least, employees in all companies wore uniforms; they were just different uniforms. It was easy to tell who the first-class corporate citizens were: all the managers with their suits, ties, and starched collars. And it was obvious who the second-class people were: the factory workers with blue collars and dirty coveralls. At IBM, T. J. Watson said: "There will be no second-class citizens"—and that's why IBM made everyone, including factory workers, wear a white shirt and dark blue tie. That's not a bad principle even for today's entrepreneurial-style organization.

Value number three was where the rubber hit the road, so to speak. It was stated as follows: "IBM expects and demands superior performance from its people in whatever they do." T. J. Watson was an unabashed believer in striving for perfection, telling his people: "We believe an organization will stand out only if it is willing to take on seemingly impossible tasks. The people who set out to do what others say cannot be done are the ones who make the discoveries, produce the inventions, and move the world ahead." Reading between the lines, it's a safe bet that T. J., like many other great entrepreneurs, wasn't the easiest guy in the world to please! But this striving for perfection did feed into his natural optimism and can-do attitude. During the Depression, for example, Watson was asked how in the world IBM could still be hiring salespeople while the rest of the industry was cutting back. His answer: "Well, you know, when a man gets to my age, he always does something foolish. Some men play too much poker, and others bet on horse races, and one thing and another. My vice is hiring salesmen."

On the bottom-line message of why it's important to create and instill an entrepreneurial-style culture, the early IBM was crystal clear. The rationale for its belief about people is a good example. While recognizing his father as a compassionate person, Thomas Watson, Jr., once bluntly described the business purpose of the IBM value on respecting people: "Our early emphasis on human relations was not actually motivated by altruism, but by the simple belief that if we respected our people and helped them to respect themselves, the company would profit."

And, finally, compared to some of the nonsense today (beautifully framed mission statements and their ilk) that gets passed off as corporate culture, the most unique thing about how the values at IBM were implemented is the amazing fact that nobody even bothered to write them down for fifty years! The first written description of IBM's values came from Thomas Watson, Jr., in 1963, half a century after his father founded the company. As a matter of company history, Watson, Jr. produced a marvelous thirty-three–page booklet titled: *A Business and Its Beliefs—The Ideas That Helped Build IBM.* (This, by the way, would make a great companion piece to Matsushita's twenty-three–page booklet!)

The fact is, IBM's values were instilled and kept alive by T. J. Watson's unremitting personal commitment and example. He had no culture consultants telling him how to do it. He had no Corporate Culture Department producing long lists of motherhood and apple pie slogans. And no one was racing around the IBM offices plastering framed copies of his beliefs on every wall. We call it "corporate culture à la Watson"—and it's the best advice you'll ever get on how to create and instill a powerful and competitive culture in your organization.

CREATING AN ENTREPRENEURIAL CULTURE

The primary value at 3M is product innovation. At Singapore Airlines, it's safety, then customer service. At Mercedes-Benz, it's making the highest-quality machine in the world year after year. And the plaques on the walls at McDonald's still say its values are quality, service, cleanliness, and value, but, in its increasingly global marketplace, the overriding company value may have become "worldwide consistency" in delivering those four fine virtues—which would seem to be just fine with Big Mac fans everywhere.

So whatever your values are, and however they may evolve over the years, remember that their real purpose, as with Mr. Watson's beliefs at IBM, is to focus your effort on those few things that will make your strategy come true. This is the crucial connection between the *what* and the *how* of the business so casually missed by many big companies. You can't afford to miss it—if you want to give your people and your business a more entrepreneurial sense of mission.

Creating an "entrepreneurial corporate culture" isn't a completely unstructured task. All cultures are based on a discrete set of core beliefs or values that the bulk of the society agrees with and commits to. Doing this successfully in large, modern organizations depends on putting a few basic ingredients in place. Whatever you do and however you do it, you must focus on *competitive advantage* and *personal commitment*. These are the only *musts* on the list. The overarching reason for fostering change in the company culture is to improve your competitive position. And the change must have the binding, personal commitment of management. To create a culture that maximizes your competitive prowess, consider the following.

➤ *Competitive Advantage*
To the entrepreneur, this is not another drill in dreaming up slogans and banners to paste on the office and factory walls. This is the deadly serious business of identifying those things you absolutely, positively have to be great at in order to achieve your strategy. The objective is to

get very, very good at those few operating factors that are most directly related to the success of your customer/product business strategy. And once you've determined what those two, three, or four critical factors are, they must become the operating *values* of your business. This is not a one-size-fits-all exercise. The values can come from a wide variety of possibilities: innovation, cost control, global distribution, product quality, employee relations, and so on. The values that would make an automobile company successful, for example, may have little impact on a biotech firm, and so on. The test is this: If they don't maximize your competitive advantage, they may sound nice but they aren't entrepreneurial business values.

➤ Personal Commitment

If the values you choose are indeed those few things that will make or break your business, you'd better find a way to get people committed to them. Allowing people to shrug off the company's declared values is worse than not having them in the first place. This clearly will require the full and active commitment of all top managers—no exceptions. This is buy-in-or-get-out time for the executives. For the rank and file, you must have a critical mass who are committed to the values. Keep in mind that employee commitment to the company's values is one of the few factors that really does need to be "controlled" at the top of the business.

➤ Behavior, Not Words, at the Top

Your behavior is more eloquent than your words—always. Believe this if you believe nothing else in this book. The moral for management: Don't announce the *new culture* until and unless you are living it yourself. There is nothing more devastating to employee commitment than the CEO who preaches that "The customer is king" and hasn't seen one for thirty years.

➤ It's Not a Big, New Project

As with setting strategy, the entrepreneurial approach to creating culture is not about setting up a *culture staff,* hiring consultants, or packing the executives off on a corporate retreat to create new wall plaques. Remember: Nobody at IBM even bothered to write the company's beliefs on a piece of paper for fifty years. This is truly a day-in-day-out, on-the-job task.

➤ Few and Simple

How many things can you be best at? Two or three? Well, if you're lucky, maybe one! But the good news is, that's all it takes. 3M doesn't try to be all things to all people. The company tries to be great at one thing. And you can do the same. OK, try for three if you want, but be absolutely certain that you hit the bull's eye with one. There's another important and related reason to keep the list short. The culture of the company has to be carried around in the minds and hearts of employees. It can't be a list of twenty-five different things they have to look up in the policy manual to just remember.

➤ *Never Compromise*

Here's the really hard part. You just can't go around changing your principles because you're having a bad day, or even a bad quarter. Unfortunately, compromises are often more habit-forming than principles. One well-placed compromise can reverse years of principled effort. So never means *never*. However, this doesn't mean that you can never change your values. You can and should change them if your strategy changes or the conditions for achieving the strategy change. Sticking to the same values and culture too long may well have been what IBM did wrong back in the seventies and eighties. No, what we're talking about here is shipping junk to make your numbers while all the wall plaques say "Quality Is Number One."

KEEPING IT ALIVE

> *A philosophy is not only preached but also practiced at the very top of a company . . . sound principles vigorously applied.*
> —LORD CHARLES FORTE
> FOUNDER, TRUSTHOUSE FORTE HOTELS

Creating an entrepreneurial culture and values is not so tough. The hard part is keeping them alive for decades. In too many companies, slogans and shifting priorities begin to replace the original culture. The deeply held convictions and inspiring personal examples of the founding group just disappear over time. The unhappy fact is, corporate culture can, and often is, trivialized beyond recognition. This all flies in the face of the entrepreneur's hands-on, lead-by-example style. Great entrepreneurs like Watson, Matsushita, and, yes, Richard Branson, maintained their corporate cultures for decades by serving as the best example of the values themselves.

It's not easy. I learned from firsthand observations of eighty-five-year-old Lord Charles Forte just how tough and frustrating it is to be the last entrepreneurial role model in the company. The energy he and other great entrepreneurs have to put into keeping their corporate cultures alive is awesome. The good news is this: If you do it hard enough and long enough, you do get very good at it.

To keep your values alive for decades, which means keeping your competitive advantages alive, here are the three most important practices to follow.

▶ Daily Behavior of Senior Management

Lord Charles Forte, the founder of Europe's largest hotel chain, Trusthouse Forte, is right. Maybe it's not a fair world after all. The top management of any company is "on stage" every minute of every day. In this regard, it's very important to remember that to the lowly clerk on the shipping dock, his supervisor is "management." So whatever your level, the people below you are watching you like a hawk. Your most insignificant behavior is of intense interest to employees—as well as to other interested observers, like customers, suppliers, and shareholders. While this may give you a feeling of great power, it also carries serious responsibilities. For example, if customer service is a core value of the company, you had better be first in line to show love for your customers. If product quality is the value, you have to be the one who never, ever, allows junk to go out the door. The single most powerful factor in keeping any company's values alive, is management's daily behavior. So if you violate the company's values, you may as well pack up your tent. The culture is already dead.

▶ Organization Rituals and Practices

Suppose you decide that innovation has to be value number one in your company. You announce it in your annual message to the staff, and it's even noted in the Mission Statement posters hung around the premises. The initial hurrahs are all good. But for the next five years the rank and file don't hear about it again. Innovation isn't a line item in their annual plan or budget. It's certainly not written into anyone's job description or annual performance review. It's not discussed in meetings. The company newsletter has never had an article about innovation. There's not even an active suggestion program in the company.

These are important things—because any company's values reveal themselves not in the policy manual but in the mundane rituals and practices that get woven into the fabric of the business. If the values are not part of the daily life of the company, and don't impact the ongoing routine of employees, they will be as dead as yesterday's newspaper.

➤ *Reward and Penalty Systems*

The most frequently violated practice in keeping values alive is whether or not they are part of the reward and penalty system of the company. What do people really get rewarded for around here? And what do they really get penalized for? To employees, the answers to these two questions absolutely define what the company values really are. Say, for example, "loving the customer" is the big value in your company. Employee "X" is widely recognized as "Mr. Customer Service" who will do anything to satisfy the customer. Employee "Y" hates customers and everyone knows it. At the end of the year, X and Y both get a slap on the back and an across-the-board 8 percent raise. Good-bye "loving the customer" as a value.

Dramatic changes in a company's strategy and culture can and do occur. The effect on customers, employees, and shareholders can be extraordinary. This is the important, final point about reinstilling a sense of mission in your organization. As you've seen, doing it the entrepreneurial way—the Matsushita and Watson way—requires a lot of hard work and old-fashioned common sense. This approach doesn't have the cachet of going off to Bermuda or Hawaii with the consultants to forge strategy, or floating sets of freshly minted *corporate values* posters down through twenty layers of management. But it does have one redeeming quality: It does indeed reawaken your—and your company's—sense of mission!

9 ▶ *Reinstilling Customer/Product Vision in Every Employee*

The inclination of my life—has been to do things and make things which will give pleasure to people.

—WALT DISNEY

Every book ever written about entrepreneurs says they have *vision*. But vision of what? The simple answer is this: All entrepreneurs are blessed and obsessed with a clear vision of a set of customers who need and will pay for a set of products or services. Walt Disney had it right in his famous quote, cited above. When he said, "Do things and make things which will give pleasure to people," he wasn't talking about the latest management theory or granting more stock options. He was talking about the two most important ideas in enterprise—products and customers.

At the core of Disney's philosophy was his belief that he had to be good at both making the product and selling or servicing the customer. Remember the "scientist-salesman-bureaucrat-entrepreneur" classifications from Part I of this book? Disney, like all great entrepreneurs, was squarely in the entrepreneur's box on the chart. Focusing on, caring about, and being an expert on customers and products simultaneously—these are the *essentials* of entrepreneurial practice. It's the art of the craftsman—the original make-and-sell enterpriser. After fifteen years of looking, I haven't found one great entrepreneur who didn't have this integrated customer/product vision.

THE FUNCTIONAL ORGANIZATION: DEATH OF THE CRAFTSMAN

However, it hasn't been easy to remain a craftsman in modern times. Along the way, we got the Industrial Revolution in the nineteenth century, which produced companies of a size and scope never before seen in history. And then, in response, the twentieth-century managerial age began inventing all manner of tools and rules for dealing with the increasing size and presumed complexity of corporations. The result? Enter the twentieth-century answer to growing bigger and more efficient forever—the modern, functional organization.

The aim was noble enough. As companies grew bigger and bigger, it just wouldn't do for everyone to do everything as it was done in the good old days. That sounded like chaos, the one thing, above all, that both the industrial and managerial revolutions couldn't tolerate. The solution was to specialize *across* the company, and create a command and control hierarchy *up and down* the company. It was at this apocryphal time in business that the organization chart was born. The beauty of the organizational chart, as everyone soon found out, was that it showed everyone exactly where they fit: in which company silo they belonged and how many rungs up and down the corporate ladder they could climb—or fall. It all looked terribly rational and efficient, as our fathers and grandfathers were all herded into the wonderful world of the organization man.

Aside from whatever else the modern functional organization achieved, it, quite literally sounded the death knell for the craftsman. The entrepreneur's integrated vision of customer and product was simply organized out of existence in the functionalized corporation. The quest for organizational control and efficiency created unnatural barriers in companies. Some employees—sales people, service personnel, market researchers, those more or less focused on customers—were put on one side of the company. Others—scientists, product designers, assembly-line workers, those more or less focused on products—were put on another side. And rather amazingly, the huge numbers of workers who weren't focused on either—the folks who cut the payroll, write the leases, handle personnel—were all lumped together at headquarters and called the administration. So today's large, rationally designed organization, ends up with more or less three super-functions. And, in the process, employees have been transformed from entrepreneurial business people to *product people,* or *customer people,* or *administrative people.*

THE MODERN (DYS)FUNCTIONAL ORGANIZATION

The supremely efficient (that is, the most highly functionalized) companies find themselves in the absurd situation of having product people who have never seen a customer, customer people who know nothing about the product, and administrative people hopelessly out of touch with both customers and products.

Breaking up real business units into functions and then centralizing everything from R&D to market research may look like a good idea in theory. However, the hierarchical and specialized organization has given us instead a very large, very rigid, and clearly *dysfunctional* form of enterprise. In the real world, it's a proven prescription for creating boredom and bureaucracy for average employees. And, for our purposes here, it has dealt the single most devastating blow ever concocted to the entrepreneurial spirit—in even the best of employees. Simply put, it killed the craftsman.

XEROX

The most famous case in all business of the disastrous effects of functionalizing and separating product people and customer people belongs to Xerox. Its Palo Alto Research Center (PARC), founded in 1970, virtually paved the golden road to the modern computer industry. The only trouble was, none of the gold ended up in the hands of Xerox. You may recall that, in the seventies, PARC invented the Alto, the world's first personal computer, and never marketed it. Not so well remembered is the fact that Xerox also invented the world's first fax machine, called the Telecopier, and just let it die. The complete list of technologies created by PARC that made others rich is truly astonishing. The *New York Times* sampling is enough to make any Xerox shareholder weep:

A SAMPLING OF TECHNOLOGIES CONCEIVED AT XEROX PARC[1]

Technology Invented	Later Developed By
Personal computers	Apple/IBM
Facsimile machines	Canon/Panasonic
Modern chip-making technology	VLSI Technology
Silicon compilers for chip design	Silicon Compilers
Portable computers	Grid Systems
Bit-mapped screen displays	IBM/Apple
Mouse- and icon-based computing	Apple
Laser printers	Hewlett-Packard/Apple
Drawing tables	Koala
Ethernet office network	3Com
Graphics computing and computer animation	Pixar
Database retrieval systems	Metaphor Computer
"What you see is what you get" word processing	Microsoft
Small-talk language, object-oriented programs	Park Place Systems/Digitalk
Postscript language used in high-end printers	Adobe Systems

[1]The *New York Times,* 6 October 1991, Sec. 3, p. 6.

How could this possibly happen? Easy—if you completely separate your product development and marketing functions. It didn't start off that way of course. Back in 1946 in Rochester, New York, Chester Carlson made and sold the world's first photocopier and founded Xerox. By the 1960s, Xerox produced only two major products, but dominated the world in both: photocopiers and electronic typewriters. Being dependent on just two products, albeit the market leader in both, seemed risky. So Xerox came up with a smart new strategy on *what* to do instead. The company would launch an all-out attack to develop new technologies and new products. Unfortunately, it wasn't quite as smart in determining *how* to go about it. Xerox, like most other blue-chip companies at the time (RCA, GE, IBM, AT&T), got caught up in the "lab in the woods" theory of doing product innovation. That was to set up large research facilities in remote, serene places, far from the annoying interruptions of people like company salesmen and customers. They were also caught up in the wonders of functionalization and specialization—and couldn't imagine that the great and mighty Xerox couldn't gather together the great scientists and researchers to come up with blockbuster products.

They were right, of course. They created PARC, located it in sunny Palo Alto, and stuffed it full of young, bright, and very hip Californian scientists. They only forgot one thing: They left all their young, bright, and very pinstriped marketing people in their Stamford, Connecticut, headquarters. These two groups were not exactly made for each other. The *product people* were the brilliant, hippie scientists with long hair and gold chains in California. The *customer people* were the high-flying, two-martini, marketing and sales chiefs with their Ivy League MBAs—sitting 3,000 miles away. The two groups not only didn't share the same company culture, they didn't seem to come from the same universe. The result: The Palo Alto scientists came up with one great idea after another, which the marketing people in Stamford mistrusted and just never got around to selling. If R&D and marketing couldn't get together on personal computers, the hottest electronic product since TV, the outcome for the rest of the list is easy to understand.

Tens of billions of lost sales later, Xerox is making a huge effort to make up for lost time and get everyone marching to a new drumbeat. Or should we say old drumbeat? Today you will find marketing people on all product development teams at PARC and R&D people assigned to follow through with marketing groups introducing PARC's twenty-first–century product ideas. We call it "reinstilling customer/product vision."

TOYOTA MOTOR

Xerox could have hired Eiji Toyoda as a consultant and saved itself a lot of grief. Toyoda (with a "d") was the founder of Toyota (with a "t") Motor, arguably the best all-around car maker in the world. It's certainly become the most valuable. The 2000 *FT Global 500* ranks Toyota number one in market value at $180 billion. Trailing far behind are DaimlerChrysler at $76 billion, Ford at $58 billion, and GM slipping to $44 billion. Toyota's operating margins are the highest. It can assemble a car in thirteen hours versus about twenty for Honda, Nissan, and Ford—GM is even further behind. It regularly matches or beats Mercedes in quality, using one-sixth the labor of its luxury class German competitor. And a completely built-to-order car can be in the hands of the customer in an amazing week to ten days. Nobody else even comes close.

What's the secret of Toyota's success? It can all be laid to the customer/product vision of founder Eiji Toyoda. He started making cars in 1933 and assumed that the car business, like any other enterprise, had to be built around customers. From design to after-sale service, the customer called the shots at his company. But he still didn't have the right framework or organization to be as responsive to customers as he thought the company should and could be. That would soon change.

In 1947 Toyoda and his legendary production boss, Taiichi Ohno, visited America for the first time. They went to Detroit to learn how the Americans made cars, but they didn't see much there that they didn't already know. What they did happen to see, which just amazed them, were American supermarkets. At that time, and still today in some sectors, distribution methods in Japan were archaic and agonizingly slow. By comparison, Toyoda saw in the U.S. supermarkets a distribution system that operated with lightning-fast speed, especially with perishable foods. He described the rapid resupply of fresh milk at the dairy counter, for example, as a system where customers literally pulled products through the company. He saw this delivery of fresh milk from the cow to the supermarket to the customer, often two and three times in twenty-four hours, as a great idea for the car-manufacturing business. Toyoda and Ohno went back to Japan and designed their own *customer-driven production* system for making cars. They established complete business units, putting design, production, marketing, and sales together under the same boss. They called it *kanban,* or *just-in-time,* production and started a counterrevolution in the auto industry against the slow, unresponsive, functional method of organizing.

Their famous *chief engineer system* became the organizational method of choice. This method dictates that all new car models have a chief from start to finish. Thus, the chief engineer has enormous authority from design to production through marketing for a specific model. Once in place, it's practically impossible for design people to disregard production people, and for production people to disregard marketing people. Obviously, Toyota is "organized." People and groups of people have specific tasks to perform. But the kanban culture, constantly tracking the customer, overrides the entire organization. Sure, *kanban* is just a technique, but it's a technique driven by an integrated customer/product vision. It's a vision that says we all jump together when the customer speaks. The point is that nothing could be further from the coast-to-coast mess Xerox found itself in.

DELL COMPUTER

Kanban has been brought to a new level in the twenty-first century by companies like Dell Computer, Amazon.com, and Commerce One.

For example, let's take a look at entrepreneur Michael Dell's amazing company, which he started in his dorm room while still a student at the University of Texas. Even a cursory look shows that Dell Computer is driven by maintaining an integrated customer/product vision. Michael Dell is the guy who eliminated the middlemen and put his entire company into direct contact with its customers—who are primarily sophisticated, corporate buyers. He literally invented selling computers direct to customers and enabling them to custom-design their purchase—over the phone and now via the Internet. Talk about bringing your product and customer functions together: It doesn't get any more integrated than this. You can't be just a salesman and still expertly help every customer to custom-design his computer. Conversely, you can't be just a scientist and spend eight hours a day talking to customers. Michael Dell himself says the company's mission is to bring to bear all its human and technology resources to better serve customers: "We're always looking to see what we can do to make our customers' lives easier or save them money. It pervades every part of the company."

Like *kanban* before it, Dell's approach, which the world now knows as the "Dell direct model," is revolutionizing how business operates in many key areas—particularly in B2B selling. The Internet, which Michael Dell calls the "ultimate direct model," accounts for 20 percent of Dell's sales today and that percentage is growing rapidly. Dell predicts that it won't level off until it hits at least 50 percent. Dell's model of selling custom-made machines directly to buyers gives it some hard-to-believe competitive advantages. Aside from obvious things, like tons of direct customer feedback and no resellers to deal with, it also means Dell carries no finished-goods inventory. Dell's total inventory costs are running less than 2 percent of sales! What old-line manufacturer wouldn't die for that kind of inventory management? Dell has not just taken Toyota's *just-in-time* game to a new level, the company has created a totally new ball park in which to play the game. When you hear Dell people say "Our only religion is the direct model," you know they mean it!

All this is pretty radical stuff when you think about it. Even *Fortune* magazine, not prone to hyperbole, recently called Dell "customer obsessed" and the "stock of the decade." Dell's innovativeness when it comes to reconnecting traditional customer and product functions does appear to be good for Dell's clients—and very good for Dell. For the full decade of the nineties, Dell Computer racked up some eye-popping records among the *Fortune 500* companies: It ranked number one in total return to investors (79.7 percent per year!) and number one in earnings per share growth (51.3 percent per year!) Now that's the way to close out a century!

DISNEY

And, finally, we end up back with our old friend Walt Disney—who also could have put Xerox back on track—had Xerox executives asked. In the theme parks, at least, the Walt Disney Company today still tries to follow Mr. Disney's customer/product vision. The Disney training manual at Disney World in Orlando says: "While a department may not deal directly with the public, it is imperative that each department within an organization view its customer or 'public' as the person or people who actually benefit from the service of that department. For example, at the Walt Disney World Vacation Kingdom, the wardrobe department's actual 'client' is not the guest, but the host and hostess who will be interacting with that guest. Or, the accounting department can view its 'clients' as a variety of internal departments. The people in any department might be three or four layers removed from the guest who purchases a Magic Kingdom Park passport. Nonetheless, their attitudes toward service will ultimately affect the quality of service the guest receives—a real domino effect!"[2]

All employees in every company can pay more attention to the quality of their own products and the needs of their own customers. A 10 percent change in attitude could have enormous impact against your competition. There is one step any company can take anytime. It's a step practically guaranteed to produce that first 10 percent change in attitude. It will require treating employees as businesspeople—not salespeople or scientists or clerks. It's straight talk, designed to get managers and workers out of their functional pigeonholes and back to the business of enterprise. Here's what you do:

Start by axing all those convoluted, five-page job descriptions. They just confuse the issue. Replace them with an entrepreneurial job description, containing only three questions. They are the questions entrepreneurs live and die by: Who are my customers or users? What are my products or services? And what exactly do I have to do to satisfy my customers?

Every employee in your company should be able to answer these three simple questions. In some organizations, however, the number of employees who can't answer them can be shocking. For many managers and workers, defining their positions in terms of their customers and their products can create a totally new mind-set concerning what their job is all about. Of course, that's the whole point. This first, modest step may not instill the customer/product obsession of Eiji Toyoda or Michael Dell or Walt Disney in your organization, but it could be a giant leap forward away from the chokehold of the anti-entrepreneurial functional organization. For sure, this is an effective start to developing mini-entrepreneurs in any company. The following is a sample of the Entrepreneurial Job Description":

---

[2]Service Disney Style, Walt Disney Company (undated), p. 5.

MY ENTREPRENEURIAL JOB DESCRIPTION

	Internal Customers	External Customers
Who are my customers or users?		
What are my products or services?		
What are my customers' or users' exact requirements? • quality • quantity • timeliness, etc.		

CREATING AN OBSESSION FOR CUSTOMERS AND PRODUCTS

What bureaucracies desperately need, and entrepreneurs have in spades, is passion for the firm's products and customers. Entrepreneurs go to sleep at night thinking about customers and products. They dream about them. They wake up thinking about them. They are truly obsessed about customers and products.

Instilling this obsession in the average worker—and making it stick—is the key. This usually requires a big change in organizational priorities. And since it's you, not your workers, who determines what's important, the changes have to start at the top. When senior management really gets serious about customer and product priorities, things do start to happen. Simple things, which everyone talked about for years and didn't do, take on monumental importance. For example, providing an immediate response to all customer requests. Not "Tomorrow" or "I'll get back to you soon," but right now! And old-fashioned courtesy will no longer be a rare event—it will be the only way customers are ever treated. Really listening and really doing something about customer suggestions will change from a slogan to a daily reality. Individual worker responsibility for quality will become the norm, not more wishful thinking by the Quality Assurance department. Compromises on quality won't even be suggested, let alone tolerated. Endless product planning will be replaced by a sense of urgency in producing innovative new products that meet market needs. And, ultimately, losing a current customer will become the one unforgivable, cardinal sin in the business.

You don't need a Ph.D. to figure out that these are the kinds of behaviors you must inspire in your people to become a company with entrepreneurial zeal for customers and products. They're all common sense ideas. They're things entrepreneurs do all the time. Large companies do some of these things some of the time. In the entrepreneurial organization, employees do all these things all the time. Here's what it takes.

STEVE JOBS

The greatest modern symbol of entrepreneurial passion for *both* customers and products may very well be the Steve Jobs story of developing the Macintosh—right up through the advent of the iMac. With all the management drama that occurred at Apple Computer over the past two decades, it's easy to forget that Jobs is the original "user friendly" computer guy. He's the pure example of an entrepreneur who loved his product—but loved seeing it used by customers (especially school children) even more. Jobs founded three great companies, Apple, NeXT, and Pixar with the same obsession. Do you really need any more proof of the almighty power of customer/product vision? I'm sure you don't, but here it is anyway. When Jobs returned to Apple as chairman and "top manager," it was a shell of the great company it once was, and had been written off as dead by all the pundits. You know what happened. Jobs reinstilled the same customer/product passion of bygone days, reawakened Apple's dormant spirit of enterprise, and singlehandedly brought it back from the dead. Steve Jobs never wanted to be a manager, and he would probably hate the term, but now he has earned the title of the Great Entrepreneurial Manager!

ESTÉE LAUDER

Josephine Esther Mentzer grew up in a poor immigrant family in New York City. As a young girl, she yearned to be one of the beautiful high society women she saw in salons and department stores along Fifth Avenue. She became a salesgirl in several of those same stores—until she recreated herself and started her own small cosmetics business. The company had one overriding mission: to make women beautiful—Estée included, of course. For years, she personally applied her products on customers, honing both her product knowledge and her considerable customer service skills. Eventually, she employed 7,500 "beauty advisors" (not salesgirls) and trained them incessantly to give the same personal attention to customers that she did. The one lifelong lesson she learned: "Women really do want to be beautiful—and helping them do that is the way to succeed in the cosmetics industry." Up until her eighties, she gave final approval on all new products after testing them on herself and her friends. The intense focus on customers and products has paid off. Today Estée Lauder, Inc. is the world leader in fine cosmetics, with $3.6 billion in revenue and over 15,000 employees. It accounts for an amazing 37 percent of all cosmetics and fragrances sold through department stores. Not bad for a poor immigrant girl who only dreamed of being beautiful—and helping other women to do the same!

RAY KROC

Getting passionate about customers and products could require a bit of the traveling salesman's instincts of Ray Kroc, blended with his personal obsession for delivering "quality, service, cleanliness, and value" a million times a day. From a lowly salesman of milk-shake machines to an absolute zealot of the clean bathroom, Ray Kroc epitomized the value of keeping your eye on the customer and the product at the same time. Visit the top-volume McDonald's in the world on spit-polished Orchard Street in Singapore: spotless bathrooms. Visit McDonald's in one of the grimiest neighborhoods in America at the entrance to the Lincoln Tunnel in Manhattan: spotless bathrooms. We'll never know how many billions of Big Macs have been sold just to get at a clean bathroom for the kids—but you and I could retire on it. It all comes from knowing what customers really want and delivering it over and over again. Ray Kroc used to loved to say: "You gotta see the beauty in a hamburger." And that, it turns out, is the secret to getting millions of others to do the same.

SOICHIRO HONDA

And it may even take some passion, Japanese style. Soichiro Honda was passionate about racing cars and high-performance engines. He was no less passionate in his self-anointed mission of providing postwar Japan with much-needed, cheap, and reliable transportation. Designed down to the simplest of machines, the Honda scooter still stands as the modern symbol of giving customers exactly what they want. Meeting very simple needs, perfectly, may be the first *passionate* lesson of customer/product vision.

There are literally hundreds of great ideas for reinstilling customer/product vision in your company. If you are serious about creating an entrepreneurial organization, getting everyone to "love" their customers and "love" their products, is a great place to start. Here are the basics for doing just that.

LOVING THE CUSTOMER

I solemnly promise and declare that every customer who comes within ten feet of me, I will smile, look them in the eye, and greet them, so help me Sam.

—SAM WALTON, FOUNDER, WAL-MART STORES
(EMPLOYEE PLEDGE)

Here's the prediction: Sometime during the first year of the new millennium, Wal-Mart Stores, headquartered in Bentonville, Arkansas, will become the biggest company in the history of the world. In the last year of the twentieth century, General Motors, the world's largest corporation for fifty years, pulled in sales of $173 billion. Wal-Mart was $8 billion behind at $165 billion. Since Wal-Mart is growing at more than double the pace of GM, it's a very safe bet that this remarkable, customer-friendly company is going to be the world's biggest in the twenty-first century. And there's more: Wal-Mart, which isn't even forty years old, still covers less than half of the U.S. market, and only a tiny fraction of the global retail market. It's gone from one store in 1962 to over 3,500 today, and it's just getting started. As amazing as it sounds, this is a company with a lot of room to grow!

How did all this happen? How could a five-and-dime retailer from Arkansas become the biggest business ever? We've all heard about Wal-Mart's super-duper information systems and its hard-nosed purchasing. But those are not the reasons I go to Wal-Mart. And they're not the reasons why millions of others go, either. After all, Target, K-Mart, Costco, and a dozen other discount chains have similar information and purchasing systems. What I, and I suspect the millions of other customers, really like about Wal-Mart is: It's the one big company that really and truly makes you feel welcome. Like the famous Wal-Mart employee pledge quoted above, everyone and everything at Wal-Mart says: "We love our customers!"

Take the official Wal-Mart job of "People Greeter." The idea, which came from an employee, is that when you visit a Wal-Mart store, it should be like visiting a friend's home. So there's a People Greeter to greet every visitor, at every door, of every store. Essentially what they do is smile, say hello, give you a cart and wish you a good visit. Each of the 3,500 big stores must have at least five or six People Greeters. That's about 20,000 employees standing around, doing nothing but saying hello to people who enter the stores. They don't sell, stock, check out customers, or even sweep up. They just say *hello.* Can you imagine how long these jobs would last with the great cost-cutters and downsizers of the world? You're right. Not one day!

Loving the customer, along with loving the product, is the *sine qua non* of entrepreneurial behavior. But it's become a cliché in so many companies. Imagine what it would be like if all the employees actually behaved as if they loved customers. It would be like, well, it would be like Wal-Mart. To create this highly entrepreneurial approach to customers, here are some simple but powerful lessons your people will have to start following.

> ### Knowing Your Product

The number-one complaint about sales people today is that they don't understand their products. What's the message you're giving to customers when you can't even explain how and why your product will solve their problem? This opens up an enormous competitive opportunity for those organizations willing to inject their marketing, sales, and service people with a strong dose of entrepreneurial customer/product vision.

Think of the last time you chose a doctor. Or wanted to buy a car. Or needed to acquire outside help to solve a business problem. Who did you want to see? An expert, of course. Someone who really knew the ins and outs involved in solving your problem. Certainly not a salesman—no matter how friendly he might be, or how many lunches he might buy you.

The truth is, most people will clear their calendars in a second to get their hands on a real product expert. This is entrepreneurial territory. It gives the entrepreneur—or the entrepreneurial team—an enormous opportunity to outshine the competition. It all goes back to that integrated vision of customer and product exemplified by Disney, Benz, Matsushita, and other standard-setters. The opportunity to do what the highly functionalized and specialized corporate types could never do is the best reason why *knowing your product* is the first step to really loving your customer. So toss out all those business cards with titles like "Salesman" or "Marketing Rep" and replace them with cards that say "Product Genius." And then cancel the sales training courses for the next five years and put every sales and service person in the company into intensive, ongoing product training.

> ### Responding Immediately

The number-one complaint about service people is they are always so busy with other things that you have to wait and wait and wait. Think about the last couple of times you checked into a big, busy hotel. Did it seem that the staff behind the counter knew every trick in the book to avoid making eye contact and getting sucked into waiting on you? If you had a dollar for every minute you've waited at airline counters, hotels, department stores, gas stations, on the phone with parts or service departments, not to mention renewing your driver's license, you probably wouldn't be reading this book. You'd already be sitting on the Riviera! I've come to the conclusion that most of these "service" people must have broken necks or fused spinal cords. They actually seem physically incapable of raising their heads too quickly. Maybe this is what keeps them frozen in place staring down at their desks and computer terminals. Whatever the reason, what's the message the customer gets? "I've got something a lot more important to do than wait on you."

Responding promptly to customers is a standard part of all customer service training. It's taught over and over again, yet nothing changes. Why? Because giving customers an immediate response is not a training problem or a systems problem. It's a deep-seated problem rooted in the priorities of the service giver. Waiting on customers is simply a pain in the neck to most people in most companies.

But, what wonderful news all this is for the entrepreneurial-style company! To entrepreneurs, responding immediately to customers is one of the greatest weapons ever invented to beat the competition. This is why Sam Walton insisted that every employee take the Wal-Mart pledge. It's also why he put Wal-Mart People Greeters in every store. It's not very scientific, but this is the kind of immediate customer response "stuff" that's made Wal-Mart the fastest-growing retailer in history. And it can do wonders for you too—if for no other reason than you'll probably be the only place in town doing it.

▷ *Being Courteous* and *Competent*

"When we answer the phone, we're very courteous. That's the good news. The bad news is we don't answer the phone." Famous last words from Ramon Cruz, former CEO of Philippine Airlines, lamenting the lousy telephone system in Manila. What he was really saying was that courtesy without competence will get you nowhere. The most courteous airline in the world (which PAL may well be) can't overcome chronic lost baggage problems and reservation systems that don't work. The opposite is also true. Competence without courtesy isn't exactly going to get you in the winner's circle either. Lufthansa will get you and your luggage where you're going on time, every time. In fact they usually have the best on-time performance of any airline. But, oh, those concrete-hard leather seats. They seem to actually tilt forward slightly, forcing passengers to do perpetual isometrics to keep from slipping onto the floor. And while we're on the subject, an occasional smile, perhaps just one per flight to break the ice, would be a welcome add-on to this airline's unrivaled reputation for technical competence.

Bigger companies often voice sterling intentions when it comes to courtesy and competence, but it's tough to put those into practice. The folks who made this little machine that doesn't work are never the ones you see. The young sales clerk may smile, but he doesn't know diddly about the gas-powered garden tiller you need—or what software is really best for the kind of graphics you produce. At another level, it's just not easy to always be courteous to thousands of people you don't know and will probably never see again. And it's really tough if you know in your heart of hearts it makes damn little difference to your company—and no difference at all to you personally. This is the real nub of the entrepreneurial advantage, where a lack of courtesy and a lack of competence can drive you out of business. Where coming to work means you have to do more than just show up.

➤ *Keeping Current Customers Forever*

Everyone *says* that current customers are important. That repeat business is what we want. And we know with the sky-high marketing costs of acquiring new business, all of the profit for the year sits in the current customer reorder base. However, all these entrepreneurial notions seem to get lost in the shuffle as the company grows large.

If current customers are so important to us, why does everyone scream and cheer over every new customer? And why does everyone just shrug their shoulders and say nothing when one of the current customers quietly slips away? Why do 99.9 percent of all sales compensation systems pay a premium for new business and nobody gets penalized for losing old business? Why are the best people thrown at new clients and the ten-year-old client ends up with the "B Team"? And why, in so many companies, is new business marketing the champagne and caviar side of the business while spare parts, repairs, and ongoing service feeds on a diet of warm beer and grits? None of this is an argument against new business. It's just a common-sense reminder that the best and most profitable way to grow most businesses is—"keeping current customers forever!"

LOVING THE PRODUCT

Daimler was completely possessed with the idea of equipping every conceivable vehicle with Benz's engines.

—FRITZ NALLINGER, BIOGRAPHER
GOTTLIEB DAIMLER AND KARL BENZ

Karl Benz was the "product man" of one of the greatest teams in the history of business. He was the inventor and product genius behind the first commercially viable automobile. Historians rank his contribution alongside electricity, antibiotics, computers, and space travel as one of the most profound scientific and technological advances of the twentieth century. We can say that Karl Benz was one businessman who truly loved his product.

He would likely be shocked to see himself identified as a seminal thinker or inventor. At heart, he was, a relentless tinkerer, totally dedicated to making his engines the best in the world. He believed customers deserved real improvements in the automobile products he and Gottlieb Daimler produced. He felt this so strongly that the notion of turning out a new model every year never occurred to him. For him the rule was to produce a new model if and when you had significant improvements to offer the customers. He would have been confounded by the concept of "planned obsolescence," that nifty marketing plot hatched in Detroit many years later. Benz was essentially a car maker who could sell if he had to. This made him the perfect partner for Daimler, the first of the great car salesmen and tire kickers.

Which leads to the following set of entrepreneurial practices for loving the product. To awaken the spirit of enterprise in your organization, loving the product, along with loving the customer, is the place you really do have to start.

➤ Knowing Your Customer

Gottlieb Daimler was a salesman who could make cars. It was Daimler, more than the technical genius Benz, who understood that knowing your customer is the essential first step in producing great products. He was technically competent to be sure, but for him the whole point of making cars was to please and even astonish the customer. In 1900, the largest distributor for the Daimler automobile was in Vienna, Austria. When this distributor threatened to switch to another manufacturer, Daimler rushed to Vienna and promised him that the company would do *anything* to keep his business. As a joke, the distributor told Daimler he'd only stay with the Daimler car if they put his eleven-year-old daughter's name on the hood. And what was her name? You guessed it. Her name was Mercedes, and the rest is history.

Now, no one will expect you to put your customers' names on your products, but then again, maybe you should. Or at least find a dozen other ways to show that you really want to know what your customers want and need. Gottlieb Daimler was hailed as a great producer of engines and cars. In reality, he was simply a near-fanatic about knowing exactly what his customers wanted. And so it should be with the product people in your business.

Feeling Old-fashioned Pride

I like to tell the true story of the retired Honda worker in Tokyo who shined the chrome on any Honda he saw parked on the street "because I can't stand to see a dirty Honda." Now that's taking real pride in your product, as much as any entrepreneur could. Which just goes to prove that some big companies can instill old-fashioned pride in their people. It's easy for entrepreneurs to take pride in their own products, but how many people working in today's giant bureaucracies really feel that kind of enthusiasm and love for the products their companies make? Entrepreneurial pride is clearly based on believing that what you're doing is important and that your particular job is an essential part of making the enterprise successful.

So how many of your employees feel that what they're doing is important? That their job is essential to the company? How many even know how their job affects anything at all? These are the things that rip the pride out of work, and these are the things the aspiring entrepreneurial organizations have to guard against. A lot of techniques have been invented to put pride back into employees' jobs: job autonomy, quality of work life, psychological ownership, and the like. These are not wrong ideas; they're just not central ideas. Having autonomy, quality, and ownership in a dead-end, unimportant job won't make one bit of difference.

In my experience, the best way to keep old-fashioned pride alive and well is to make sure that everyone knows how and why his or her role in the business is important—from making the product right up to face-to-face interaction with customers. As any entrepreneur will tell you, there is really no substitute for getting praise from happy customers—and getting yelled at occasionally by unhappy ones.

Making It Better Than the Next Guy

Lord Charles Forte grew Trusthouse Forte (THF) from one sweet shop on Oxford Street to over 800 hotels worldwide. He knows something about entrepreneuring and how to make it better than the competition. When I first met him several years ago, he gave me the best definition of "making it better" that I've ever heard. Forte said that when his managers proposed opening a hotel in a new city or country, which they did all the time, he asked them just three simple questions:

- Can we make that hotel cheaper and better than the competition?

- If not cheaper, at least better?

- If not better, at least cheaper?

If he didn't get a convincing yes to at least one of those three questions, Trusthouse Forte didn't erect a hotel in that spot. The simple system seems to have worked rather well over the years.

Most entrepreneurs, like Charles Forte, don't get caught up in academic and arcane definitions of quality. They typically see popular concepts like the ISO 9000 certification process as a lot of bureaucratic poppycock. The missing link in many theories and techniques on quality is the word "competitive." The entrepreneur makes his living by beating the competition. And as Charles Forte knows, you can beat the competition three ways: by offering higher quality or lower costs or both. And lower costs can be just as good a way as higher quality. This very competitive approach explains why THF is equally content to own low-cost chains like TraveLodge in America as they are to own some of the ritziest properties in the world like the Savoy in London.

In an age when the life cycle of thousands of products can be six months or less, we may have to add one more question to Lord Forte's simple list: Can we make it faster? And that leads us to the final entrepreneurial practice involved in loving the product.

➤ **Making It Faster Than the Next Guy**

Ed Penhoet, the founder of Chiron, is one of the superstars of the biotechnology industry—and a man in a hurry. He says the entire biotech industry has been a horse race: "Everyone in the industry is smart, so you don't get much of a competitive edge with just brains. The winners are the ones who get to the finish line first with FDA-approved products. So it may be that speed is even more important than cost." So in the super high-tech field of biogenetics, speed appears to confer a bigger competitive advantage than brains or low costs. This is a lesson no twenty-first–century company can afford to forget.

Naturally, "making it faster" is just as important for big, mature companies as it was for Chiron in the race to patent and win FDA approval of the first Hepatitis B vaccine. Ross Perot, that quintessential entrepreneur from Texas, really hit the nail on the head on this point. After selling EDS to General Motors and becoming its largest stockholder, he was stunned and dismayed at how slowly everything seemed to happen in the biggest company in the world. He went public with this famous complaint: "I just don't understand it. It took us four years to win World War II—but it takes these people seven years to produce a new Buick." Touché!

A FINAL THOUGHT: GROWING THE OLD-FASHIONED WAY

Here's a final thought about growing your business, which was inspired by that all-time master of keeping it simple, Buel Messer. You'll recall him as the blind cattle rustler–turned–landscaping entrepreneur in Part I. It just struck him one day that the most important reason to focus on customers and products is that they hold the key to *all future growth* in the business. He wasn't thinking about growing through mergers and acquisitions, strategic alliances, or fancy accounting techniques. Messer and virtually all entrepreneurs grow their businesses the old-fashioned way: making more products and selling to more customers. Since there are only four possible ways to achieve real growth in any business, this concept isn't all that complicated. Here are your choices:

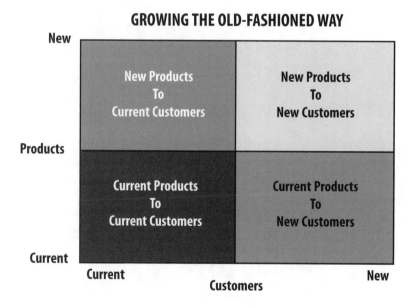

GROWING THE OLD-FASHIONED WAY

	New Customers
New Products	New Products To Current Customers / New Products To New Customers
Current Products	Current Products To Current Customers / Current Products To New Customers

This and a thousand other good ideas abound when you focus on customers and products. A few of the ideas may have been around for years, merely waiting for a champion. Many will come from customers, competitors, and innovative workers. Others may come to you in the next five minutes, just as "growing the old-fashioned way" came to Buel Messer.

Here's a closing suggestion that might help you and your people to focus more and to gain more momentum when it comes to the two most critical elements in your business: Take just one hour a month to brainstorm with your people about ways that you can dramatically increase "loving customers" and "loving products" across the company. It could very well become the most important sixty minutes of the month to keep your business growing and ahead of the competition. It will certainly be a mighty step forward in reinstilling customer/product vision in your people.

10 Fostering High-Speed Innovation

Anybody can be innovative if his life depends on it.
— AKIO MORITA
FOUNDER, SONY

Akio Morita was the right person to ask about action and innovation. The company he founded, Sony, is still recognized today as Japan's most innovative large company. Morita learned firsthand in postwar Japan that anyone can move quickly and creatively if his life depends on it. It's a lesson he never forgot. And it's the central lesson to learn in transforming any bureaucracy into a fast-moving, innovative, twenty-first–century competitor.

Most people probably think that Sony's first product was the transistor radio. Hardly. In Japan in 1945, products had to be much more practical. Akio Morita was a young, Japanese Navy lieutenant who had served in World War II. He obviously had to start looking for a new career. What he and everyone else discovered upon returning from the war was shocking. Tokyo was a devastated, burned-out city after 400 straight days of Allied bombing. There were no jobs, no money, no raw materials to make anything, and little food. Surviving was a day-to-day challenge. In this chaos, Morita thought that making something for sale or barter might be the best thing he could do. He and a small band of friends asked themselves, "What can we possibly make that the Japanese people still need and will be able to buy?" Everyone ate rice. But they weren't farmers. They were unemployed engineers. They eventually came up with the idea that since everyone was still eating rice, people would have a need for something to cook the rice in—like an electric rice cooker. But they faced an immediate problem. There was no finished metal available. And they couldn't afford to go to the black market, which was the only possibility they knew of—until they remembered all those American B-29 Superfortress bombers that had flown thousands of missions over Japan. The B-29s had American fighter escorts which, because of the great distances, had to carry extra fuel tanks under their wings. Before returning to the American bases, the fighter pilots would release the empty, extra tanks, which fell to the ground. So there was actually a lot of metal available all over Japan. The group scavenged the hills around Tokyo and brought back all the discarded fuel tanks they needed. They then heated and reformed them. By early 1946, Sony had its first product, which was—you guessed it—a Japanese rice cooker made from the fuel tank of an American fighter!

Sony's first hi-tech product came to market in 1950. Morita wanted to make a giant leap forward and propel the company into producing more sophisticated products. He was keen to try producing magnetic tape, which, he reasoned, at least he could sell to the Ministry of Education for classroom use. Again he encountered a major roadblock when it came to finding raw materials. There was no plastic available in Japan and making recording tape without plastic seemed impossible. Morita and his colleagues tried cellophane, but it didn't work. They tried standard newsprint and found it was more stable. On their hands and knees, Morita and his team cut long strips of the paper. They coated them with ferric oxide, a compound they found at a local chemist—and lo and behold—it recorded sound. By 1965, just fifteen hectic years later, this little-known Japanese firm had gone from making recording tape from newsprint to becoming the great IBM's biggest supplier of magnetic computer tape.

Morita always chafed at the criticism that Japan is a nation of imitators, not innovators. In his view, there are three types of creativity: "creativity in technology, in product development, and in marketing. To have any one of these without the others is self-defeating in business." After World War II, all Japanese companies—Sony, Honda, Matsushita, and the like—concentrated their creativity on simple product development. This decision grew out of market and economic necessity. They couldn't worry about researching future technologies or implementing global marketing strategies while they were still using American fighter-plane fuel tanks for raw material. Over time, however, Sony's record of high-speed innovation expanded to encompass the other two areas. A quick glance at some of the company's early achievements illustrates tremendous wellspring of action in all three areas of creativity cited by Morita:

- 1950—First recording tape in Japan.

- 1953—Founder Morita works in the United States for four years as a Sony company salesman to learn the market.

- 1955—First transistor radio in the world.

- 1957—Discovery of the "electron tunnel effect" by Sony employee Esaki, for which he became the first scientist in Japan to receive the Nobel Prize.

- 1959—First transistorized TV in the world.

- 1960—First VCR in the world.

- 1964—First desktop calculator in the world.

- 1970—First Japanese company to be listed on the New York Stock Exchange.

Of course, there are hundreds of other great innovations pioneered by Sony. One of the most famous, the Walkman, was personally invented by Masaru Ibuka, Sony's homegrown technical genius. He designed it in his spare time simply because he loved to listen to music while he worked, and his old phonograph and tape recorder were too heavy to carry to the office. So much for sophisticated market research and focus groups. And, to be sure, they've made mistakes—like pushing their technically superior Betamax VCR for too long when VHS technology was capturing the market instead. But this happens when you're innovating like crazy. Morita was happy to absorb the occasional mistake to keep up the torrid pace of innovation.

In any event, I'm sure you get the message. Morita and his company know a thing or two about high-speed innovation. Sony was born out of necessity and required fast, creative action to survive. And in the fifty-five years since, Morita recognized how difficult it was to keep that competitive advantage alive as Sony became too big, too rich, too secure, and, in his own words, too complacent. He fought this complacency all the way, trying to keep the entrepreneurial spirit alive in the company: "It is said that the creativity of the entrepreneur in Japan no longer exists. I disagree. Big companies like Sony are doing all they can to think small. From a management standpoint, it's very important to know how to unleash people's inborn creativity. My concept is that everybody has creative ability, but very few people know how to use it. We try to promote entrepreneurship right within our own large company by the way we manage. For example, as an idea progresses through the Sony system, the original presenter continues to have the responsibility of selling his idea to technical, design, production, and marketing staffs, seeing it to its logical conclusion whether it's an inside process or a new product going to market. Sony has even funded the businesses of former employees, who originally presented their idea to Sony but for one reason or another it was not taken up. This is quite opposite actually from the Western practice of tying corporate researchers up in knots with noncompete agreements."

Which brings us back to the powerful and most basic lesson of Morita's entrepreneurial experience: Innovative action is not a mark of genius. It's not a skill you learn in management school. It is a normal human reaction to crisis and challenge—and it can vanish in a hurry if people and organizations lose their sense of urgency and crisis. In your own organization, your gravest threat may not even be coming from your competition—it may be coming from your own growing bureaucracy and self-satisfied complacency. Recognizing these internal threats, and knowing how to beat them off has to be your first line of defense in keeping high-speed innovation alive in your company.

THE SEVEN DEADLY SINS AGAINST HIGH-SPEED INNOVATION

Everything that can be invented has been invented.
—CHARLES H. DUELL, DIRECTOR
U.S. PATENT OFFICE, 1899

Charles Duell is one guy you wouldn't want running your new product development unit. On the other hand, the very agency he was trying to kill a hundred years ago is now a twenty-first–century example of how even the best of ideas can be transformed into a bureaucratic nightmare.

The history of the U.S. Patent Office is instructive. The first patent issued in the United States was on July 31, 1790. The three examiners who approved that first patent, a process to make potash for fertilizer, were none other than Thomas Jefferson, Henry Knox, and Edmund Jennings Randolph—respectively the secretary of state, the secretary of war, and the attorney general of the United States. This was a high-powered team, underscoring the enlightened and even noble premise behind the founding of the U.S. Patent Office. The original mission was to encourage innovation by giving inventors a twenty-year commercial monopoly in exchange for sharing their inventions with a world thirsty for machines and processes that could improve the way people lived. In an era of nuts and bolts devices, the rules for obtaining patent protection were very strict. The invention couldn't just be an idea or the discovery of a law of nature. It had to be a unique machine or process that the inventor—the genius in the garage—had indeed invented. And, to be fair, the Patent Office had its share of Charles Duells who saw it as their mission to make it tough, not easy, to get patents. In that world, Thomas Edison's light bulb was clearly patentable, and Albert Einstein's Theory of Relativity clearly wasn't.

Apparently, it's not so clear today. The confluence of twenty-first–century technologies, like cyberspace and biotech, combined with a 200-year-old culture of bureaucratic survival at the Patent Office, has produced a Brave New World where almost anybody can get anything patented. The numbers tell the tale. It took fifty years for the patent office to award patent number 10,000. Nowadays 10,000 patents are awarded every three weeks.

A *New York Times Magazine* piece, titled "Patently Absurd" (March 12, 2000), cites Amazon.com's successful battle to gain a patent for its *One Click* method of placing a book order ("wherein the single action is depressing a key on a keypad") as the beginning of the end for any rational approach to what can or should be patented. While e-commerce first movers like Amazon capture the patent headlines, the mania for patents is pervasive. How about these landmark inventions that have recently been awarded patents: a technique for measuring women's breasts to determine bra size (Pat. #5,965,809), a method for walking your cat with a laser (#5,443,036), and instructions for swinging your tennis racket while wearing a knee pad (#5,993,366)? And, by the way, if you ever want to start a company manufacturing mailboxes shaped like football helmets, don't. There's already a patent on them! As the *Times* article says, "The system has begun to disintegrate—by growing out of control. The United States is issuing patents at a torrential pace, establishing new records each year, and it is expanding the universe of things that can *be* patented."

Why is this happening now? Is it because America has just recently turned into a nation of commercial inventors, cranking out nearly 200,000 inventions a year, each one worthy of a twenty-year government mandated monopoly? No, the wild increase isn't because American industry has become exponentially more inventive. Many great digital-age success stories—Microsoft and America Online, for example—have had virtually no patent protection to propel them forward. Microsoft, in fact, didn't even apply for its first patent until 1986, eleven years after it was founded.

The primary reason for the explosion of patents has less to do with the patent seekers than it does with the patent grantors—those well-intentioned bureaucrats who review and approve the applications at the Patent Office in Washington, D.C. In one of the great ironies of Reaganomics and its efforts to make government more "businesslike," government funding for the Patent Office was cut off in 1991. It was decreed that, henceforth, the agency had to survive on patent fees. The clever bureaucrats quickly got the message and figured that the only way to survive was to make damn sure they received and approved a lot of patent applications. In an understandable yet unfortunate miscalculation, they determined that the patent applicants, who, after all, were paying their salaries, were their "customers." It apparently never crossed their minds that Mr. and Mrs. Average American, who were never going to submit a patent application, might actually be their real customers.

As the *Times* article concluded, "The voices heard daily at the patent office belong to people who like patents, want patents, and rely on patents for their living; their creed is, *the more the better*. Officials measure their own performance in terms of their output. It's as if they were a manufacturing company turning out products. . . . Examiners know that their year-end bonuses depend on their productivity. Each morning, as Commissioner Dickinson arrives at his Crystal City office, he walks past a framed poster bearing the motto 'Our Patent Mission: To Help Our Customers Get Patents'."

Hello bureaucracy, good-bye common sense! Self-serving and unchecked bureaucracy is completely overhauling the mission of the U.S. Patent Office before our very eyes. If this can happen at an agency charged with protecting American innovation and exerting a strategic impact on the entire U.S. economy, what do you think could be happening at other organizations—your own, for instance? Of course! There will always be a thousand "good" reasons for any organization to create its own bureaucracy—and all of them will detract from getting people's innovation and action focused on the right things—the things that will make you more entrepreneurial and more competitive.

Allowing bureaucracy to creep in is just one of the factors that can paralyze high-speed innovation in your organization. All the way from hiring a "Mr. Duell" to run your company R&D efforts, to permitting an organization to lose its focus à la the Patent Office, there are a lot of ways to kill innovation and action. We call them "deadly sins" and here are seven that an entrepreneurial organization has to avoid like the plague.

➤ *I'm OK, You're OK*

Mr. Duell's "I'm OK, You're OK" complacency is at the top of the list. Insisting that we're all OK—another gift to business from the psychologists—produces terminal inaction for companies in the heat of competitive wars. Mr. Morita's point is that we're *not* OK; we're *never* OK! Crisis and stress may have become politically incorrect in business, but they do at least scream out that we're probably not OK, and we'd better fix what's not OK in a hurry!

➤ *One Best Way: Silencing Workers Forever*

If you really want to silence workers, there's no better way than to instill a "one best way to do the job" mentality in your company. This ranks as the original sin of "scientific management" and comes straight from the granddaddy of all industrial consultants, Frederick Taylor. Way back in the 1890s, this Philadelphia cost cutter popularized the idea that there is one best, optimum way to perform every task. Whether it's turning a screw on a motor mount or timing the toilet trips of assembly-line workers, everything could and should be optimized.

This could be great news for mass-production fanatics, but it's the death knell of worker innovation. The bottom line? "One best way" managing can do wonders for uniformity, but it's not much help in inventing products, beating deadlines, hitting new levels of quality, or fostering employee commitment.

➤ *Out of Touch With Customers and Competitors*
There are three proven sources of innovative customer/product ideas in any business. The most obvious lies within your own organization. Tapping the collective genius of all your people has to be an ongoing, internal process. The other two sources, however, are found outside the company. In fact, the odds are very high that the next great idea for a new product or service will come either from a customer or a competitor. Thomas Watson, the founder of IBM, used to say that the idea for 95 percent of all IBM products came from customers and competitors—not from inside IBM. This is why being out of touch customers and losing sight of competitors is so damning to successful product and service innovation.

Whatever the ratio for your particular business, you can't afford to miss any sources of new, good ideas. This means you have to virtually live with your customers and know your competitors like the back of your hand. Being close to customers and competitors comes with the territory for the entrepreneur, and you have to create the same behavior in your company if you hope to stay ahead of the "great idea" learning curve.

➤ *Centralized Everything*
The argument for centralization rests on two shaky assumptions. First, centralizing will give us the economy of scale to do things more cheaply. This is the usual argument for centralizing purchasing, personnel, R&D, even production facilities. The second assumption is that centralizing authority will ensure that things are done right.

But does centralizing actually achieve economies of scale? Are big factories really more productive than small factories? Does a company really get things more cheaply through central purchasing? Is the big

R&D center the most efficient (or effective) way to invent products? And what does a headquarters personnel department really contribute to the bottom line? Every company has to make these judgments for itself, but be careful. The evidence to date reveals that bigger is rarely cheaper and centralized is almost never more efficient.

"Making sure it's done right" is a heavy statement about who knows better and who performs more responsibly. At its core, it's about who trusts who to do what. But *controlling* is not actually the problem: It's what's getting controlled that causes concern. Too often, the wrong things are being centralized and the things that truly need some corporate control are left to the discretion of any employee who happens to be there. Being true to the values of the company is an obvious example of this. You may have elaborate systems for financial reporting, but nobody is bothering to track employee commitment to the core values of the company.

Whatever the merits of centralization, you can be sure that fostering high-speed innovation is not one of them. Remember that wherever and whatever you centralize, the tradeoff will be innovation and fast action. Therefore, for companies trying to operate in an entrepreneurial mode, the wise rule of thumb is: When in doubt, decentralize!

➤ Lab in the Woods

This is the big bang theory of product innovation. It's the story of Xerox's Palo Alto Research Center, RCA's Sarnoff Center in Princeton, GE's 600-acre R&D facility in upstate New York, and a hundred other corporate research facilities hidden away in the woods—far from the hustle and bustle of the marketplace. The idea that corporations would need such idyllic spots to do research and invent products came shortly after World War II. Big business was impressed with war-era achievements like the Manhattan Project, the U.S. effort to manufacture and produce the atomic bomb. Since this work was being done in great secrecy in the middle of the New Mexico desert, building your own research center in the middle of nowhere became all the rage in corporate America.

It turned out that building an atomic bomb in the middle of a war to drop on your enemy wasn't the same as building products that customers will buy. Over the decades, it became painfully apparent that a lot was going into these labs in the woods, but not much was coming out. At least not much that could be manufactured and sold. And virtually nothing that would qualify as a "first mover" innovation, to borrow the Internet's in-phrase for blockbuster ideas. It turns out that the big bang theory of R&D was launched on a false premise.

Remember that frightful statistic—the cost of innovation is twenty-four times greater at big companies than at small ones? Maybe all those stories about inventors in garages are true after all. Certainly, you don't need a giant research center in the woods to be innovative. Some of the best product and service innovations in the world have emerged from the floor of a noisy factory, or from a brainstorming session with a bunch of salesman, or from face-to-face meetings with unhappy customers. At least give all these more entrepreneurial approaches a try before you sink untold millions into your own lab in the woods.

➤ *Marketing Takes Over*

The antidote to the lab in the woods is not to go to the opposite extreme and expect your customers, all by themselves, to come up with your next great product innovation. But this is exactly what often happens. The marketing argument goes like this: "If our scientists and engineers can't come up with the new products our customers want, why not give us a crack at it?" Some CEOs, particularly those who inherently distrust R&D anyway, buy this argument hook, line, and sinker. After all, it's marketing people who know what the market really wants. They do all the market research. They conduct the focus group sessions. They're the ones "in touch with the customer." In the past, this approach gave the world such memorable products as striped toothpaste, instead of plain white, and giant fins on already oversized cars.

Marketing's product innovation role really picked up steam when *customer service* began to be recognized as an integral part of the *product.* With this new opening, marketing departments everywhere went into overdrive, coming up with product-service "improvements." They were typically little more than cosmetic embellishments, often with a distinctly "California feel." Take, for example, the near-obsessive insistence in some companies that all customers get called by their first name. What's the point here? Is it really more courteous to use first names for people you don't know and who are twice your age? In the same vein, consider the mandatory script followed by that perky waitress in many "marketing-driven" restaurant chains. You've heard it a thousand times. The memorized cant, delivered with the frozen smile, turns out to be a sales pitch for exotic drinks and dishes you know you don't want. And, most recently, some marketing innovations have taken a decidedly tricky turn, especially on the telemarketing front. Here, half-truths and outright lies are replacing direct, straightforward product offers. It's as if they know you'd never buy their actual product in a hundred years, so the marketing ploy is to get you to buy it without really knowing you've bought it. Telephone companies, adept at tricking consumers into switching long-distance carriers, are the undisputed masters of this innovative approach to product marketing.

What's wrong with this picture? Plenty. It seemed to be working until consumers discovered that striped toothpaste doesn't clean teeth any better than the old white stuff. And while the fins were impressive, buyers found the engine was still a piece of junk. And now we realize that the waiter's hip approach and memorized script don't make the cold T-Bone any warmer or the weak coffee any stronger. No, giving marketing full rein on product innovation is a great concept—until your customers begin demanding *real* product improvements.

So why don't marketing-inspired innovations go right to the core of the matter and make fundamental improvements in products and services? *Because marketing people are not product experts!* Conversely, why don't R&D folks, toiling in their idyllic research centers in the woods, come up with the product innovations that customers want and need? *Because product people are not customer experts!* There's no one to blame for this dysfunctional mess. Marketing and R&D are both prisoners of the artificial functionalizing of contemporary business. A lifetime of separating product/customer innovation has given us too many specialized experts and too few Disney-style craftsmen. This doesn't have to happen in your company. Simply defunctionalize and put your best "scientists" and "salesmen" back together on the same team. You will significantly raise your odds of coming up with the new products and services the world wants and will pay for.

➤ Senior Management Disconnected

A recent survey of CEOs asked: "What functions in your company do you trust the most and the least?" Dead last on this list was R&D. Show me a company where upper management distrusts or disconnects itself from the innovative processes of the company, and I'll show you a company where nothing new is going to happen for a very long time. Of course, moving at the speed of light and living with uncertainty— the hallmarks of great R&D—unsettle most rank-and-file executives. Yet encouraging rapid experimentation and even tolerating some chaos are central to fostering action and creativity. But who can blame the executives, really? For one hundred years, the business schools where they all got their MBAs have been teaching nothing about chaos and unpredictability except that they must be stamped out.

The irony here is that most senior managers got to be senior managers precisely because they were able to "beat the system" throughout their careers. The play-it-by-the-rules type almost never rises to the top. Much more often, it's the guy (or gal) who turned several divisions upside down, broke some rules along the way, and carries battle scars from hand-to-hand corporate combat who rises to the upper echelons in most corporate settings. They most definitely are not wallflowers. They *are* human, however—and, once at the top, the last thing they want is a lot of unpredictable chaos roiling beneath them. It's as if they decide that they will be the last rule-bending innovator in the company! Whatever the reason, when a company's top management stops practicing and fostering high-speed innovation, bureaucracy and slow motion can't be far behind. The solution? Make sure your senior managers are the most dedicated practitioners and biggest cheerleaders of high-speed innovation in the entire company.

THE GOLDEN RULES OF HIGH-SPEED INNOVATION

Sony may be Japan's most innovative big company, but the world champion in this category has to be the great Minnesota Mining and Manufacturing Company, known around the world as 3M. From the very beginning, when six miners invented sandpaper to avoid going bankrupt with their "worthless" gravel pit. This has been a company built on a single-minded strategy—to grow by inventing new products year after year. With $15 billion in revenue and 58,000 different products, this is a tremendous record. How does 3M do it?

It's important to note, up front, that by throwing massive amounts of money around, 3M's R&D budget as a percentage of revenue, for example, is only average for its industry. The company does it, first and foremost, by *aiming* to do it. The most important strategic goal each year is hitting the 30 percent new product revenue target. Next, 3M executives have created a focused corporate culture, in direct support of their strategy. 3M's culture has one overriding value: *product innovation.* And after nearly a hundred years, the culture of innovation at 3M is pervasive. You can't avoid talking about it, thinking about it, and practicing it. It's obvious to everyone that the way to get ahead at 3M is to invent something. The company is run by people who love science and products, not by MBAs. All senior executives push for new products in their divisions. If you invent a product, you get first crack at running that product business, a highly unusual and motivating factor for company scientists. Every corporate ad talks about innovation. It's the basis of the most important employee awards, including being invited to present your ideas at the 3M Inventors' Forums held around the company. And "daydreaming" is an officially sanctioned activity. Engineers and scientist spend 15 percent of their time daydreaming about new and different products, away from their official, current project. Perhaps most important of all is the company mantra that "Failure is a good thing." At 3M you don't get demoted or fired for making mistakes in your efforts to invent new technologies and products. 3M learned this crucial lesson long ago.

If you ask many 3M people for the real secret of their success in inventing new products, they're likely to come up with some truly vague things like "accidents and mistakes." They'll tell you about the laboratory accident that led to the discovery of Scotch Guard. Or you'll hear about the repeated attempts to make a super-light glue that kept failing to stick permanently—and ended up as one of 3M's greatest all-time products, Post-it Notes! But, of course, all companies have accidents and make mistakes. What makes 3M inventors and executives different from their competitors is that after their accidents and mistakes, they ask themselves a naïve question: "Have I come up with something here that anyone in the world might need?" They then put together a makeshift marketing team and find out if anyone wants to buy this unplanned concoction from the 3M lab. The answer comes back yes often enough to give 3M the greatest record in the history of business of inventing new products and getting them to market in a hurry!

When you look objectively at innovative and fast-moving entrepreneurial organizations, you will see that it's not a system or a process or a management technique that is producing their high-speed innovation. Rather, you'll find a crazy collage of policies, beliefs, and practices, like those that underpin 3M's success. But if you look at enough of these companies, and peer just a little below the surface, it's crystal clear that all of them are being propelled by at least a couple of powerful forces: First, they all have a passion for, and belief in—*the necessity to invent*. For them, innovation is not *icing* on the cake. It *is* the cake. And second, they are simply brimming over with the *freedom to act*. From the CEO to the average employee, experimenting and trying new things are inherent to the job. It's expected of everyone. These two simple practices are the entrepreneur's "golden rules of high-speed innovation."

THE NECESSITY TO INVENT

We did it because we believed we had to.

—LARRY HILLBLOM
COFOUNDER, DHL

A great way to capture the spirit of invention as a necessity is the amazing story of Larry Hillblom.[1] He was a young law student in California who did freelance courier work on weekends. He discovered that hand-carrying important shipping documents and bank travelers' checks to Hong Kong or Sydney was a great way to spend a weekend. He got a lot of studying done and pocketed a few bucks. He also began to wonder why no company provided this valuable service. It was all freelance and very disorganized. So on one of his twenty-hour flights he came up with the idea to create an international courier company. He got two of his law-school buddies to join him, they called it DHL (for Dalsey, Hillblom, and Lynn), and they literally invented an industry.

There was certainly a need. Everywhere Hillblom went, he found interested prospects. After all, he was offering something unheard of. Sending business documents from Tokyo to Milan could take ten days. From Lagos to Mexico City forever. In a world where postal delivery times between Philadelphia and New York had gone from three days by Pony Express to seven days by plane, overnight delivery anywhere in the world had terrific appeal. But as they got started, they quickly found out that big banks and shipping firms weren't about to contract out their worldwide courier needs to three students who didn't have business cards, let alone a single overseas office to serve them. Hillblom saw that creating a DHL global network was an absolute necessity to getting the business up and running. In fact, they had to have most of the network in place *before* they could get the big clients they desperately needed. A half-built network wasn't very interesting to the Deutschebanks and Toyotas and IBMs of the world. DHL had to be everywhere they were. This meant everywhere that they had put an office over the last fifty years, and DHL had to be there *yesterday!* But how could three students with no business experience and no money possibly do this?

---

[1] Larry Hillblom was killed a few years ago while flying his own plane. It disappeared without a trace into the Pacific Ocean near his home on the island of Saipan. Larry shunned publicity all his life and became a virtual recluse by the time he was forty. He died as he lived—doing his own thing in his own way. I didn't know him well but, like everyone who met him, I was fascinated by this remarkable business innovator.

Hillblom told me later they pulled it off for one reason only: "We did it because we believed we had to. No network, no business. And we didn't know there was any other way than bootstrapping it, which was lucky. If we had spent our time writing business plans, lining up bank financing and venture capital, and using headhunters in fifty countries, there would be no DHL today." And what a network they built! They opened offices in an amazing 120 countries in the first ten years of DHL's existence—the fastest international expansion of any company in history. Their method was pure *Mater artium necessitas*."

They started in Asia. On every courier trip each of them took, they signed up somebody to be their local partner—a taxi driver at the Sydney airport, the manager of an A&W Root Beer stand in Malaysia, a toy salesman in Hong Kong. Using this *literal* seat-of-the-pants approach, the DHL Network began to grow country by country, gaining momentum with each new location. By the late seventies, it was like a thunderbolt roaring across the globe. There were no plans or systems or procedures. Handshakes were the principal contracts. The owner or manager in each DHL outpost was, by default, king of her territory. Each fiefdom had one overriding obligation: "Whatever comes in, and whatever goes out, handle it with the speed of light." Thus was born a world of DHL mini-entrepreneurs—all based on high-speed innovation bordering on the unbelievable.

Yes, Larry Hillblom and his two young friends created quite a network, without resources or experience—because they had to. In the process they also created a $3 billion company with 40,000 jobs. These things happen when you truly feel the heat of necessity.

➤ Feeling the Heat of Necessity

The necessity to invent that Larry Hillblom felt came from his observations as a freelance courier on twenty-hour plane rides across the Pacific. Creating the DHL global network of offices was his bricks-and-mortar response. In other cases, feeling the heat of necessity can lead you to a more cerebral—or should we say virtual—result. Take the incredible case of Jerry Wang and David Filo, cofounders of Yahoo. They were Ph.D. students and buddies at Stanford in the early nineties. At the time, they and their friends were all experimenting with a remarkable new research and information source called the World Wide Web. But Wang and Filo could see that the variety and quantity of information on the Web was becoming so immense that it was impossible for anybody to really know what was out there. And there was no categorization of topics which made using it for research a real hit-or-miss proposition. As users, they feared that this wonderful new information access system was imploding into a chaotic mess. *Fortune* described their response this way: "So the two went to work building software that could organize Internet sites into categories. Within a few months the site, which initially was called Jerry's Guide to the World Wide Web, was renamed Yahoo and took on a life of its own. Yang and Filo found themselves working round the clock, and Stanford's computer infrastructure began to creak under the traffic. In late 1994 university officials asked them to find a company that was willing to host their service, and Yang and Filo finally admitted they were onto something." What they were onto, of course, was the fastest-growing Internet company in the world—all thanks to their finely tuned feeling of a necessity to invent.

Great companies like 3M and Sony work very hard at keeping this feeling alive and so should you. Whether your organization is in bricks and mortar, or cyberspace, you have to keep innovation and creativity alive. You must make the necessity for invention very visible to all your people. The best way to do this is to make sure they know they're an important part of an important competitive battle. Beating the competition is a powerful entrepreneurial motivation, so why not make everyone a part of the contest? Another critical step for many organizations is to simply tell their employees why invention is a necessity and why it's an important part of their job. Of course, you should back this up with performance goals and rewards for being innovative. And don't forget the all-important 3M lesson: that failure in the pursuit of improvement is part of the deal and no one gets fired for trying. Making sure everyone in the company personally feels the necessity to be innovative is the first necessity.

➤ Create Crisis and Urgency

The entrepreneurs I know would not do well in a business school course on Personnel Practices. One particular lesson they would surely fail would be the one on reducing stress in the company. I've never known an entrepreneur who operated without stress. And I strongly doubt if they have any skills at reducing stress in their people. This may be politically incorrect in some quarters, but it turns out to be a huge entrepreneurial advantage—at least when delivered in reasonable doses. Entrepreneurs have a very tough time not getting upset when things go wrong. They also find it impossible not to get excited when things go well. They are impatient people who love winning and hate losing. These are not characteristics normally associated with stress reduction but, in an odd, behavioral twist, they do seem to inspire enormous commitment in rank-and-file employees.

Some great entrepreneurs really stand out in this category: Steve Jobs, Richard Branson, and Soichiro Honda spring to mind. They are all well known as masters at instilling a sense of urgency and crisis in their companies. They are also company leaders who are unabashedly idolized by their workers. It may not always be pleasant working for hard-driving entrepreneurs but, at the end of the day most employees love and admire leaders who really care and don't mind showing it.

➤ *Do Something, Anything, Better Each Day*
Wouldn't it be wonderful if every employee you ever hired came to work each day thinking, "What can I do today a little bit better than yesterday?" But they won't—unless you tell them that's the most important part of their job. Most corporate managers don't tell their people to do this because they don't think about doing it themselves. In the typical bureaucracy, everyone comes to work ready to do the job exactly as it was done yesterday and last week and last year. The entrepreneur can't afford this. Finding a way to do something better, faster, and more cheaply every day is the core competitive advantage of any entrepreneur. And making sure this philosophy finds its way into the daily performance of all employees is the only way to keep this advantage alive. The once-a-decade grand strategic stroke is always welcome, but it's the day-in-day-out improvements by everyone that really keep you ahead of the pack.

To convey this idea in your organization, there are a dozen common-sense things you can do. First, get this notion into every job description. You might then put real teeth into it and make it part of everyone's performance goals and evaluations. I would even be so old-fashioned as to run a half-day meeting or a workshop on why it's critical and provide simple examples of exactly what you want people to do. It's much too important to just announce along with the daily blizzard of e-mails, so try it face to face. Remember: If every single employee truly came to work every day and actually improved something in his job or area, you are talking about a miracle in companywide improvements. It just may be worth a try!

THE FREEDOM TO ACT

The trick is to get to the finish line first.

—ED PENHOET
COFOUNDER, CHIRON CORPORATION

I went to see Ed Penhoet, cofounder and CEO of Chiron, to learn the secrets of success in biotech. Armed with his Ph.D. in biochemistry, Penhoet is the scientist-entrepreneur who guided Chiron to its lofty position as one of the top five biotech success stories of all time. I had assumed, given the incredibly high-tech nature of the industry, that success primarily depends on how smart your scientists are. It turns out that I was in for a very big surprise.

Penhoet, one of the true superstars of biotech, is perhaps the industry's most articulate spokesperson: "The competitive advantage Chiron has is overall speed. But I'm measuring speed from the point where somebody conceives of a new piece of biology and it gets commercialized at the other end. It's one thing to move an opportunity which is obvious, but it's another to recognize a new opportunity. So I think where we have special skills is, first of all, recognizing new opportunities very early on, grabbing those, and then running with them in a very aggressive manner. The large companies have difficulty competing in a rapidly moving field like biotech. In large part, it's because their bureaucracy requires too many levels of review. By the time you've educated everybody in a large organization about the advantages or disadvantages of a new program, somebody else who has a more light-footed organization has already moved the product so far along that the large company is no longer in a position to compete.

"Whenever people have visited Chiron over the last fifteen or twenty years, the number-one impression they've left with is a feeling of energy. When you walk by the lab, you feel the energy, people are busy, things are happening, so energy is an extremely important part of our success without question. So it's that sense of urgency, feeling of energy, knowing the competition is there—it's our whole culture if you will."

And what about my assumption going in that the smartest people in biotech are going to be the winners? Penhoet continues: "By the time you get to people who have Ph.Ds. from Harvard, UC Berkeley, or UC San Francisco, it's a given that they're smart. They were in the ninety-ninth percentile on their SAT scores and all the rest. So while being smart is obviously necessary to get in the race, it isn't what gives you *competitive* advantage. It isn't the factor that's going to get you into the winner's circle at the end."

Wow! Who would have imagined that speed and energy are actually more critical than IQ in winning the biotech race? After all, this is an industry where even junior staffers have a couple of Ph.Ds. Penhoet's inside analysis aside, he and his scientists at Chiron are plenty smart. They've been smart enough to discover and get to market one of the first biotech blockbuster products—the vaccine for Hepatitis B, followed by treatments for kidney cancer and melanoma, pediatric vaccines, and blood tests for HIV. And they're smart enough to be the third-biggest biotech firm in the world (after Amgen and Genentech) with revenues of $800 million. Still, Penhoet's words carry a powerful warning to us all: "In biotech we all know what products are needed and what research has to be done. The trick is to get to the finish line first."

If it's true in biotech, what are the odds that high speed is a critical competitive factor in your business? If you're thinking about 100 percent, you're probably right on the mark. So is it possible for the management of any bureaucracy to match the speed of smaller, more entrepreneurial competitors? Of course, it's possible. There's no rule of law or science that says they can't. Entrepreneurs aren't action oriented because their genes are different. They move fast simply because they personally feel the need to act and they don't have to ask six layers of management before they move off the dime. To create such a bias in favor of action, and to keep it alive in your company, your people have to have the freedom to experiment, the freedom to make mistakes—the freedom to act. It's no more complicated than that. Here's how to make sure that happens.

➤ *Freeing the Genius of the Average Worker*

Sochiro Honda was never part of the blue-blood establishment in Japanese industry. Indeed, he was the "working man's man." Tetsuo Chino, the former president of Honda USA and a lifelong friend of Mr. Honda, told me a wonderful story about how Honda got along with the rank and file:

"The young people idolized him. For example, when Mr. Kume was introduced as the new president, replacing the founder, we had a big party. Thousands of employees came. Mr. Honda stood up to introduce Mr. Kume. It was emotional and a little tense because the great founder was stepping down. Mr. Honda started this way: 'This company, Honda, we always seem to have a kind of sloppy person for president. A person just like me. Have you noticed? Well, this time again. Tadashi Kume is a very sloppy person and that is why he now becomes the president.' Then he turned straight to the audience of several thousand employees and said, 'So I'm sorry but because you have such a sloppy president, you will have to work harder or the company will collapse.' And you know, the young people just cheered and cheered. They loved it."

On the point of who in a company should be "trusted" to innovate and take action, Chino concluded: "Mr. Honda really thought the genius of the company was in the workers. And they knew that he trusted them. This was appreciated by the employees and it's very unusual in famous Japanese companies."

Who are the geniuses of your company? Who in the company needs to have freedom of action? Who has the ideas and should be encouraged to experiment? Honda often said that in any group of one hundred workers, 5 percent will be superstars, 5 percent will be bums, and 90 percent will be average. And he really did believe the average workers were the geniuses of the company. They were the ones who built the cars and literally made the company go. As Mr. Honda saw it, the problem was that his managers spent most of their time with the superstars and the bums. They were always trying to keep the superstars happy and make the bums more productive. They literally forgot about the average workers. Because *average workers* didn't do anything so special and they didn't cause any trouble, management didn't think much about them or even talk to them. Yet, they had the bulk of the knowledge and ideas about what needed to be improved and how to do it. Honda's idea was simple: If you got just one good improvement action a month from each one of the 90 percent of the workers, company performance would go through the ceiling. The moral of the story: Free the genius of the average worker and you may create a miracle.

▶ *Action With Customers, Products, and Inside the Organization*

Where should you aim your high-speed innovation? The entrepreneurial answer is simple: on the core of what keeps you competitive. In other words, on your customers and products. You can never go wrong taking action to improve your customer service and make your products better. The other area that's a sure-fire winner is action directed at improving the internal workings of the company. Not marginal activities like who gets the corner office or planning the company picnic. Every day spent improving core processes of the company—such as employee development, product innovation, and customer research—is money in the bank.

It really all boils down to taking action on the things that make or break the company. Kathy Prasnicki, a soft-spoken thirty-five-year-old from East Texas, learned this on day one in the tough, "man's business" of wholesale gasoline. She figures if you can't outmuscle them, you can always outthink them: "Every day I have to find things to improve and ways to save time and money. It's the only way to win in a 3 percent margin business." And win she does. She constantly finds ways to do things better than the competition, whether it's promoting from within or building a day-care center for employees' kids—both unheard of in the rough-and-tumble world of wholesale gasoline. Being relentless in attacking "the little things" that eat up time and money has worked wonders. Sun Coast Resources, the $250 million company she founded at age twenty, has become the largest distributor of gasoline in the state of Texas in just fifteen years.

▷ Bureaucracy-Bashing Bosses

At most organizations, the real battle is to wipe out fifty years of bad habits and misplaced priorities. Only bosses can clean up this mess. Mid-level task forces just don't get the job done. What's really required is to take a sledge hammer to the bureaucracy. It isn't pretty but it may be the most heroic act any CEO can ever perform. Getting everyone's attention is a necessary ingredient in successful bureaucracy bashing.

Robert O'Brien, past president of the old Carteret Bank in New Jersey, once told me the all-time secret to cutting down on the time wasted in meetings. His complaint was that most of his managers seemed to spend most of their time in meetings—instead of doing something useful like visiting clients. So he took the bold step of removing all the chairs from the many conference and meeting rooms in the bank. He told me: "Larry, it was a miracle! Today we have very few meetings and they never last more than five minutes. What I found out was that our people loved to sit for hours in those big, comfortable leather chairs—but they just hate stand-up meetings. Put this one in your next book, please—because it's something every company in the world should do." No doubt about it, Bob came up with a winner with the "stand-up meetings" idea. A little extreme maybe, but just the kind of eye-catching action you'll need in your company to keep the creeping bureaucracy at bay.

The most insidious thing about bureaucracy is that it's almost always well-intentioned. Bureaucratic practices, rules, and procedures are never introduced to destroy the business. They're put in place to resolve some earlier glitch or to make sure things are done correctly in the future or to ensure equal treatment of all employees, and so on. Unfortunately, after several years of implementing these bureaucratic procedures with all good intentions, the place starts feeling more like a police station than the innovative, fast-moving company it used to be. The way to prevent this from happening is never to let it get that far. From day one as an entrepreneur, institute five-minute meetings, one-page memos, periodic crusades to cut down on e-mail, and regular "bureaucracy audits" to weed out unneeded practices, procedures, and forms. And never forget: It only takes three people to create a raging bureaucracy.

Just as you must bash bureaucracy from the highest echelons on down, it takes top-down action to instill all forms of high-speed innovation in a company. Keeping an organization creative, flexible, and fast moving are all areas where the CEO and the top team must lead by example. As a short, final story of how one great entrepreneur does this, here's a real-life example I'll never forget. Jimmy Pattison is the founder and the sole owner of The Jim Pattison Group. With over Can$4.6 billion in revenues and over 22,000 employees, it's Canada's largest company owned by a single individual. As you might guess, Jimmy Pattison has a knack for getting people's attention. A couple of years ago, he called my office (from Frank Sinatra's house in Palm Springs, which he had just purchased!) to invite me to address his annual company conference—to be held in a couple of months at a beautiful site in British Columbia. Naturally, I agreed.

Several months later, upon arrival at the conference site, I noticed that the printed schedule showed that I was to open the conference the next morning with my talk—at the bewitching hour of 7 A.M. At dinner that night, to make sure it wasn't a misprint (which I secretly hoped it was), I asked Jimmy if 7 A.M. was really the starting time. He said matter of factly: "Yes. We like to start all our meetings by 7:00. And by the way, would you mind showing up a little early because I really don't like to start late." I said, "Of course," went to my room, and set the alarm for 5 A.M. to be safe. I got to the large meeting room about 6:40 the next morning and noticed that everyone was already seated, waiting for the conference to begin. I'd never seen that before. Jimmy grabbed my arm and started escorting me to the stage, saying, "I think everyone's here so let's just start now." I cleared my throat the best I could with a quick gulp of water and started presenting to the 150 managers in the audience. I glanced at my watch one last time. It was 6:41 A.M. and The Jim Pattison Group annual conference was rolling! Jimmy was center aisle, front row, taking notes. I'll never forget it as long as I live.

And that's the whole point. What I later learned that makes this little tale worth telling is that Jimmy Pattison never starts a meeting on time. He always starts them early. He's sending a powerful message. One of his VPs told me: "It's Jimmy's way of getting our attention, of telling everyone we have to keep moving—that we all have a lot to do and we can't sit around wasting time! I can tell you one thing: Nobody in this company ever shows up late for a meeting." Well, Jimmy certainly had the attention of his top 150 managers—and he had mine too. So whether it's fostering innovation, speeding up action, or wiping out bureaucracy, this is what we mean when we say: "Getting everyone's attention is a very necessary ingredient . . ."

Making Self-Inspired Behavior the Organization Standard

Get rid of the committees and consultants and MBAs. Stop showing contempt for your dealers, your employees, and your customers. Give up the corporate dining room, the chauffeured limousines, the hefty bonuses. Get back to the trenches. Listen to the troops. Take care of them first, and they'll take care of you.[1]

—H. ROSS PEROT
FOUNDER, EDS AND PEROT SYSTEMS

I first became intrigued by Ross Perot back in 1979. But it wasn't because of this Texas entrepreneur's business exploits—even though he had already made a name for himself as the founder of Electronic Data Systems. I had a more personal reason. Like many other Americans working in Iran around that time, I had gotten trapped in the wild and woolly Iranian revolution. Yes, that would be the same revolution that brought down America's pal, the Shah of Iran, and declared America the Great Satan.

I was in Teheran to close down an office I had myself opened just three years earlier. On my arrival, I saw a very different Teheran from the one I thought I knew. The ride in from Mehrabad Airport had been an eye-opener. It looked like a war zone. We were stopped and searched every few blocks.

Tanks, nervous soldiers, and sandbags clogged the streets, while a million demonstrators screamed anti-Shah and anti-American slogans. It was an angry and eerie sight in a country where such behavior had been unthinkable for decades. Everyone in the country seemed to be on strike except the troops loyal to the Shah and the Ayatollah's demonstrators. At the Sheraton Hotel, where I was staying, the windows were all broken, the staff was gone, and we few remaining "guests" helped ourselves to what food was in the kitchen.

---

[1] From Ross Perot's very public and, by most accounts, very well-deserved attack on the General Motors Board. After Perot sold EDS to GM, he became GM's biggest shareholder and loudest critic. GM eventually paid him another $750 million to get him off the Board and to shut up about the company's "contempt" for customers and employees.

Over the next week, the situation went from bad to worse. I won't bore you with the details but it evolved into a surreal mixture of "voluntary" house arrest in the Sheraton lobby and being glared at by a lot of wild-eyed Iranians, all swept up in the revolutionary fervor. One thing seemed certain—there was no way to get out. That is, until a young Frenchman, an employee of Air France, came to my rescue. Because Ayatollah Khomeni had been given political refuge in France for many years, the French were still free to come and go as they pleased. Anyway, this brave young man offered to help me escape if I were willing to try. I was—and he did. I'll never forget our back-street ride to the airport, trying to avoid both the very nervous soldiers and the frenzied demonstrators. What was normally a thirty-minute drive took about five hours. It didn't really make much difference, since the airport was closed and everyone was on strike. No planes were allowed to land or take off. I did have lots of company, however. There must have been 10,000 Iranians and all kinds of foreigners at the airport trying to leave the country.

Once inside the airport, my French host and helper seemed particularly encouraged about my chances when I told him that I had no preferred destination. "This means you will go any direction?" he asked. "Yes, any direction, any country," I responded. "This is good. Just sit or sleep on the floor near the Air France counter, and I will find you when the right time comes." So I took up my spot on the floor just like any other refugee. Over the next thirty-six hours I waited.

In the middle of my second night on the floor, like a shining knight in blue, the Air France agent leaned over and whispered: "Come with me. There's an Air France 747 out at the end of the runway. She's been allowed to refuel but cannot discharge or take on any passengers. But I think I can get one person on." He shoved an Air France jacket toward me: "Put this on, it's safer." In a bit of a daze, I followed him behind the counter, through the office area, down several corridors and—Presto!—we were on the tarmac. There was no ticketing, no passport control, no customs, nothing. We got in an Air France jeep and shot across the runway heading for a beautiful, blue and white bird with Air France emblazoned across its side. The agent was yelling as we drove: "I can give you no ticket. Everything is broken. I will tell the purser you have to buy your ticket when you arrive." Just then it dawned on me that I didn't even have the foggiest idea where I would be arriving!

At the plane, the agent directed the mechanic's ramp ladder to the front cabin door. Up we went, the door opened, and a rapid-fire exchange in French took place between the agent and the purser. The agent turned to me, stuck out his hand, and said those wonderful words in French that even

I could understand: "Bon voyage." The purser led me to a seat and asked, "Monsieur, where do you want to go?" I replied, "I want to go wherever you're going." "We're going to Bangkok, is that OK?" was the polite response. Without thinking I sputtered, "That's wonderful. I've never seen Bangkok before. Let's go to Bangkok."

After I returned home, one evening I happened to be watching the news on TV when Perot's face popped up on the screen with the incredible story of how he had rescued two EDS executives from Evin Prison in Teheran. The news story reported how Perot had organized and paid for a commando team of ex–Green Berets, a couple of planes and helicopters, and plenty of guns to bring his two employees home. It seems that when Perot became convinced that President Carter couldn't or wouldn't rescue his people, he decided to do it himself. Naturally, I was fascinated by this daring exploit in a place I had just escaped from on my own. And I was stunned that a company CEO would put so much on the line to save a couple of employees. I remember turning to my wife, Julie, and musing: "Do you think my company was going to send commandos to rescue me?" We both knew the answer, of course. Perot's heroic mission seared into my consciousness a question I still ponder, and one you might want to ponder as well: If you ever get thrown into a foreign prison, whom do you want to be working for?

All of this made great headlines and even a great book and movie, *On Wings of Eagles.* Perot has become a larger-than-life character with his unique brand of example setting. Over twenty-five years ago, he personally went into Laos to try to get supplies to American POWs being held in North Vietnam. He bought the Magna Carta for $1.5 million and promptly gave it to the U.S. National Archives as a national reminder that individual liberties only come from individual action. Amid great controversy, he headed a commission to lift Texas education out of last place in the country; his thanks was the eternal resentment of the education establishment.

Like most people willing to take strong stands on controversial issues, he has ended up in the love-him-or-hate-him category of opinion polls. But in the opinion poll that counts most with Perot, there's no ambivalence. There's no CEO in the world who has earned more respect and loyalty from employees than Perot. The commitment of some of his people borders on the unbelievable. One executive gave up $900,000 in GM stock to go back and work for Perot Systems. The corporate motto at Perot Systems is "One for All and All for One." It may sound corny to some, but, if history is any guide, this slogan really means something when you work for Ross Perot.

Yes, Perot's style makes great headlines. It also makes great people management, if you're looking for extreme commitment and performance from your people. Just imagine what it would be like to work for a CEO who built a company worth billions, but set his salary at $68,000 in 1965 and never gave himself a raise? When Perot launched his take-no-prisoners attack on mighty GM in defense of their workers, can't you just see the GM "rivetheads" stomping and screaming their support for a Board member saying the things they had felt all their lives. And, perhaps most dramatically of all, what would you do in return for the CEO who hires commandos to rescue you from a foreign prison?

Here's a closing reminder that Ross Perot isn't finished yet. He may never become president of the United States, but his entrepreneuring days are hardly over. In 1999, thirty-five years after starting EDS, he took Perot Systems public and added another cool billion dollars to his personal war chest. So there's another billion for whatever "crazy," self-inspired idea he comes up with next!

CREATING HIGH COMMITMENT AND HIGH PERFORMANCE

SELF-INSPIRED BEHAVIOR OF ENTREPRENEURS

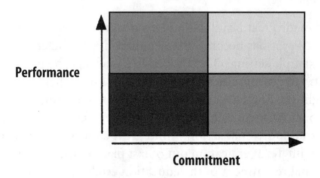

Remember this chart? Pretty simple stuff, right? High commitment and high performance are easy to describe, but they can be hard to achieve. How many people in a typical company really love what they do—and are really good at doing it? How many work as hard as they can and as smart as they can all the time? Certainly some, but probably not most. Yet high commitment and high performance are the fundamental behaviors that produce successful enterprise. Think about it—competing against a band of people who absolutely love what they do and are very good at doing it—well, that's going to be one tough competitor!

So how do you create and maintain both these highly entrepreneurial qualities in your company? While carrying overlapping effects, the distinctions are important. Training, for instance, is an action to improve performance. It presumes a lack of knowledge or experience. If someone hates his job, training him until hell freezes over won't raise his commitment.

To create inspired employees, you don't have to become a larger-than-life character like "public figure, Ross Perot." But in your own world, and in your own way, you do have to do some things like "company manager, Ross Perot." You have to personally demonstrate self-inspiration in whatever you do. You have to show that you really love what you do. And you have to work darn hard to do it well.

Of course, being a corporate entrepreneur yourself may be the easy part. Getting 10,000 workers to act like entrepreneurs is the real trick. Creating a company full of highly committed high performers may the biggest and toughest challenge facing entrepreneurs and managers alike.

HIGH COMMITMENT: GETTING EMPLOYEES TO LOVE WHAT THEY DO

> *No employer-capitalist with a true feeling of brotherhood can be happy in the enjoyment of wealth without feeling a strong sense of dissatisfaction with present industrial conditions and a strong desire to improve them so that employee-workmen may be raised to a much higher level in social well-being.*
>
> —WILLIAM HESKETH LEVER
> FOUNDER, LEVER BROTHERS (UNILEVER)

This is William Lever in 1909, announcing the Lever Co-Partnership Trust, the world's first employee stock ownership program. By 1925 an amazing 18,000 employees were members of the Trust. Was Lever a man ahead of his time? Probably. If nothing else, he put his money where his mouth was in urging workers to cast their lot with his company.

Lever was an early believer in entrepreneurial "tough love," doubly inspired by entrepreneurial passion and the belief that workers should get their fair share of the pie. In 1900, Lever Brothers was the largest company in the world. Today, Unilever[2] ranks forty-third in global revenue and 32nd in profits. With $50 billion in sales and 267,000 employees, it is also widely recognized as a great place to work. This amazing one hundred–year performance gives Unilever the best record of any large twentieth-century

---

[2]Unilever was formed in 1929 through the merger of Lever Brothers and several smaller Dutch companies. It operates today as a Dutch/UK group, with headquarters in both countries.

company in maintaining its global ranking. Company management must have done something right.

When it came to business, Lever was a very tough competitor, indeed. Aggressive and expansive, he literally overwhelmed traditional competitors. He traumatized the gentlemanly world of London commerce with massive and outlandish American-style advertising. He literally invented brand recognition, the concept of market niches, and the production of multiple brands to compete against each other. By 1888 he dominated the British market and by 1910 Lever Brothers had 60,000 employees in 282 operating companies spread across five continents. He also demonstrated an autocratic model of leadership, demanding hard work and high morals from employees, insisting they were the root of all success in business and in life.

But we also find caring words and radical deeds in his commitment to employees. Creating the first employee stock and profit-sharing program was truly revolutionary for the times. Taking this giant step toward the creation of mini-entrepreneurs within the organization was among his proudest achievements. Beyond the Co-Partnership Trust, Lever instituted many employee benefit programs we all take for granted today. Unilever was the first company on record to provide company training, sick leave, annual paid holidays, and pension plans. These were all radical steps.

The most famous example of Lever's commitment to employees is Port Sunlight, the model community Lever Brothers built for its employees in 1889. Working-class Britain at that time endured living conditions equivalent to the worst modern-day slum. Port Sunlight eventually housed 3,500 people and became a model of company-sponsored living unequaled to this day. A less famous example, but in some ways more telling, was Lever's battle with the trade unions over the length of the work day. No, management wasn't pushing for more and the union less. Quite the opposite. Lever proposed to reduce the standard work day to six hours and provide two hours of "self-improvement" classes for workers. His fellow industrialists thought he had lost his mind. But the real surprise came when the union leadership opposed the idea of "compulsory education" and that was that. Talk about being ahead of your time! Perhaps the capstone of Lever's efforts to honor the dignity of the common man came late in his life while serving in the House of Commons. In 1907 he was the author of Britain's very first legislation to provide old-age pensions for its working-class citizens. Not exactly the act we'd expect from a soap tycoon.

So what are we to make of this self-inspired entrepreneur and his lifelong commitment to workers? The legacy of Lever's "tough love" approach to employees is clear: The company has enjoyed a high commitment/high performance workforce for over a century, and it is still overwhelming the competition! The bottom line may be, as with most things in life, that commitment is a two-way street. The underpinnings of creating high commitment may seem obvious, but they are worth reciting. Here are four of the most important:

➤ Love What You Do

OK, it's not a fair world. Everyone can't "love" every job they will ever have. I haven't and you haven't. But that doesn't change the principle. People aren't going to get committed to jobs they hate and companies they're not proud of. It starts with hiring people who are interested in what you do, trying hard to enrich the boring jobs, and really letting people "own" their piece of the business. Generously rewarding those who are highly committed to the mission doesn't hurt either. And, in some cases, it may have to come down to saying good-bye to those who just don't give a damn.

➤ Give Autonomy, Demand Accountability

We're forever controlling the wrong things. Imagine the production line supervisor who's responsible for ten workers and a million dollars worth of equipment—but can't spend $50 of company money to take his team out for a beer to celebrate a good week. This story gets re-played in a thousand ways for factory supervisors and any other employees who don't have the status to be "trusted to do the right thing" with a few bucks. The message is: You're responsible for the productivity of the ten people and the million dollars worth of equipment, but we don't trust you to spend $50 to celebrate with your people. It wouldn't be so awful, if we didn't also realize that one unnecessary first-class air fare by an executive can cost $5,000 and nobody thinks twice about it.

The point isn't the $50 or even the $5,000. It is simply that to get the commitment of people, a little freedom goes a very long way. And everyone understands that with freedom comes the responsibility to perform. We call it giving a little autonomy and getting a lot of accountability in return. That happens when you begin to treat people like mini-entrepreneurs, responsible for their piece of the business.

➤ Share Fortune and Misfortune

Nowhere in the world will employees commit to a company that isn't committed to them. This is just simple common sense. In practice, this means that your people have to believe the following: "If it's good for the company, it will be good for me. And if it's bad for the company, it's going to be bad for employees." This is the ultimate entrepreneurial mind-set—sharing fortune and misfortune. Of course, it's easier to share the good times than the bad. But no employees will be ready to share any company misfortune if they haven't experienced, along the way, a fair share of the company's good fortune. Unfortunately, at many companies, the first real sharing employees are asked to participate in is a cost reduction program, a downsizing, or some other equally unpleasant edict from corporate headquarters. And in other organizations—the government comes to mind—it seems that neither fortune nor misfortune has ever been shared with employees.

All these examples illustrate why handing out million-dollar executive bonuses while lowly employees are being downsized is guaranteed to destroy commitment. Such actions may not be immoral—but they're certainly stupid. These are all bad habits from an earlier age that need to be broken, fast. The absolute, a priori requirement for creating entrepreneurial commitment to the cause is a full sharing of both the good and tough times with your people.

⟫ Lead by Example, Never Compromise

Leading by example is a given for most entrepreneurs. Many of them believe it's also their most powerful people management tool. It can and should be the same for every manager in a company. To not lead by example will deal a fatal blow to employee commitment. To put it squarely on the line—it's the height of arrogance to expect more of subordinates than you can personally give. This doesn't mean you have to be the best salesman or the greatest product developer in the company. But you cannot take a back seat to anyone in terms of commitment to the mission if you hope to create entrepreneurial high commitment in your own staff. It just won't work any other way.

So never be shy about showing that you love what you do. Openly demonstrate your pride in the company's products. And never, ever forget that the customers pay your salary too. Leading by example, and never compromising, could be your most powerful people management tool too.

HIGH PERFORMANCE: GETTING EMPLOYEES TO BE GOOD AT WHAT THEY DO

> *If I can't sell better than anybody in the company, I don't deserve to be president.*
>
> —JOHN JOHNSON
> FOUNDER, JOHNSON PUBLISHING

Would the Harvard Business School hire a professor who said he believed the most important management principle of all is hard work? You doubt it? Well, that means they wouldn't hire the entrepreneur who founded, and ran for many years, America's largest black company. Meet John Johnson, whose grandmother back in 1946 hocked her furniture to loan him $400 to start a magazine in Chicago. Against great odds he created *Jet* magazine, and then *Ebony*, and ultimately built the great empire we know today as Johnson Publishing. He also said he only had two important jobs in the company. First was to know exactly what his employees thought of their jobs and the company, so he personally interviewed every new employee and every departing employee. His second job was to sell a lot of advertising space, which he learned on day one was the only way to stay alive in the magazine business. He actually believed presidents of companies are supposed to be able to sell their products. What a novel idea that would be to most young MBAs coming out of business schools! He took it even further with his motto, cited above, that if he couldn't sell the product better than anyone else, he didn't deserve to be president. This is performance aimed squarely at the heart of the enterprise—the only kind that interests entrepreneurs.

All kinds of managerial techniques and training programs have been invented to improve the performance of your employees. Some of them may even be useful, if your people first understand the entrepreneurial mandate that says moving the business forward is the goal—not writing long memos that nobody reads or looking good at staff meetings or attending another management seminar. In other words, you want your people to perform like entrepreneurs.

To the entrepreneur, performance is a fight to the finish—not trying to look good at the weigh-in before the fighting even starts. Their performance is also highly focused—on making products and selling customers. In this arena, your employees' job descriptions and performance reviews are probably useless. They rarely deal with customers and products and almost never help you "get better at what you do." Here are four key steps to getting your people started on the road to entrepreneurial high performance:

➤ Get Better at What You Do

Seeking continuous improvement in product quality has been been a mantra for American business for decades. But how about applying the same idea to people? We need to tell employees that their most important job is to improve something every day. This may or may not require working harder, but it surely means working smarter. Show me employees who are seeking out new ideas and methods to improve their performance, on their own, and I'll show you a corps of high-potential mini-entrepreneurs for your company.

➤ *Winning at Quality, Quantity, Speed, and Cost*

How good, how much, how fast, and *how efficiently* are the entrepreneur's base parameters of performance. The challenge for entrepreneurial managers is to make sure that your people are better than the competition at these four things. That will spell the difference between winning and losing the competitive battle. You don't need to make it any more complicated than this. Attitude surveys, high-priced seminars on "managing performance," and fancy performance appraisal systems dreamed up by personnel consultants can be tossed overboard if you simply consistently measure, improve, and reward these bottom-line performance factors. This may not have the cachet of some new-age HR management systems, but it does have the redeeming value of helping you beat the competition in the marketplace!

➤ *Save Your Best for Customers and Products*

In some organizations, employees seem to concentrate their best efforts on winning internal turf wars and impressing the brass. Enormous effort and expense can go into these side issues. Yet this only happens if the top brass allow it to happen. If employees believe that making a great board presentation will get them more kudos than coming in on Saturday to make sure the right product was shipped to their customer, you've already got a huge performance problem on your hands—and a dangerous lack of focus on what's important to the enterprise. To an entrepreneur fighting for survival, devoting resources to such nonsense would be akin to having a corporate death wish. If you really want to transform your people into mini-entrepreneurs, you simply must keep them focused on customers and products. And there is no better way to do that than being focused yourself—which we call leading by example. This is the last point to make on achieving organizational high performance. So, please, read on.

➤ *Lead by Example, Never Compromise*

Above all, entrepreneurs are high performers. They have to personally set their company's standards of performance. Corporate entrepreneurs have to do the same. Now you don't have to be a better performer than anyone who works for you. But you do have to be the first in line to pitch in and get a job done, and the last to leave after it's finished. In plain-spoken English, you've got to set the standard on effort and hard work. What you don't need to offer is another seminar on the meaning of leadership. Leading your people to higher levels of performance is actually pretty simple. As John Johnson believed when he was building *Jet* and *Ebony* into the world's leading black magazines, you can't achieve anything in life without hard work. This may mean different things in different settings, but getting out of the office and doing real, front-line work every so often would be a terrific way to start. You can get away with a lot of things as an up-and-coming entrepreneurial manager, but being lazy isn't one of them.

INSPIRING OTHERS: CREATING MINI-ENTREPRENEURS

The genius of the Honda Motor Company is in the average worker.

—SOICHIRO HONDA
FOUNDER, HONDA MOTOR COMPANY

Most of us can figure out how to inspire ourselves. But can we inspire others? The successful entrepreneur as well as the successful manager has to be able to do it. But it's a lot easier said than done. Most entrepreneurs and managers have a spotty track record when it comes to fostering high commitment and high performance in others.

The entrepreneur's excuse rings a familiar bell. Like great, natural athletes who make lousy coaches, entrepreneurs are often unaware of what they do. They don't think about it much and thus have a hard time passing on their "natural" ability as self-inspired enterprisers. For company managers, it may be even more of a challenge. Not only do they have to "learn" entrepreneurial behavior to model it for subordinates, but they also usually have to fend off a whole host of professional personnel people—both inside and outside the company—giving them a lot of really bad advice. Even today, fostering mini-entrepreneurs in big companies can easily get overrun by a lot of loony HR programs and theories.

But it's far from hopeless. We can't *make* employees more entrepreneurial, but self-inspired commitment and performance can be fostered in 99 percent of all people. As with everything else in this book, the best answers for getting people to "love what they do and be good at doing it," come from knowing how entrepreneurs behave—or, more precisely, knowing the circumstances and environment that inspires their behavior in the first place. To a large degree, this environment can be duplicated in any job in any company. So the best way—maybe the only way—to inspire others is to get them to inspire themselves. The single most important thing you can do is to show the way through personal example. And you'll never find a better example of this than Soichiro Honda.

Soichiro Honda was, hands down, the most interesting Japanese entrepreneur of the twentieth century. His death in 1991 was greeted with the greatest outpouring of grief and respect by employees ever accorded a Japanese corporate leader. Honda was an outsider to Japan's industrial establishment. He was the son of a blacksmith, who at sixteen began his working career as a mechanic. He moved on to auto racing but, after a near-fatal accident, decided to try producing scooters and eventually cars. With only a third-grade education, he was the working man's man.

He was also a master of the carrot and stick, and never hesitated to use them. He understood that inspiring others fundamentally boiled down to answering the question: "What's in it for me?" Honda answered by showering attention on good performers, always promoting fairly (Honda's relatives were not even allowed to work in the company), and putting his money behind his compassion (such as building entire factories just for handicapped workers). He also carried a big stick. He demanded top performance from Honda's engineers as well as from the engines they made. His temper flared when they failed. In one crushing outburst he could devastate a misperforming engineer or production team. The next morning however, he was back, sleeves rolled up, working together until they solved the problem.

Tetsuo Chino grew up with Soichiro Honda in the car business and knew him well. Chino was president of Honda USA from its startup in Marysville, Ohio, in the late seventies all the way through its record-breaking decade, the eighties. He was the first man to produce Japanese cars with American workers. And he was also the man who pushed the Accord to become the number-one selling car in the United States. I met with Chino at Honda Headquarters in Tokyo. He had recently entered semiretirement, a phase in Honda known as "soft running." He had enthusiastically agreed to meet with me to tell me the "inside story" of the real genius of Soichiro Honda.

"The Honda Company is probably most famous for its attention to customers. It also has a reputation of being the automobile company run by real automobile lovers," Chino says. "But maybe the untold story of Honda is how the founder inspired his people—even those American auto workers who everyone said couldn't make a competitive car anymore. Everyone, that is, except Mr. Honda."

So what kind of man was he? "On the one hand, Soichiro Honda was tough. He was a self-made man and he didn't like to be guided by somebody else. You know our MITI (the powerful Ministry of International Trade and Industry), which is full of Japanese bureaucrats? When Mr. Honda tried to enter the auto business from motorcycles, MITI said *no!*

They told him: 'Japan has enough auto makers already. You keep making scooters.' So Soichiro Honda fought the government. He told them: 'MITI is not our shareholder. You cannot decide my destiny. I want to make automobiles and certainly you cannot make that decision for me.' This was a famous fight in Tokyo. So he entered the auto business in spite of MITI. This was not done in Japan. Soichiro Honda was a very unique Japanese.

"On the other hand, he was a humanistic person. He always said the technology is just a means to make people happy. The company was founded as a people-oriented company. And even though he was the founder, he didn't allow his heirs in the company and none of the top executives were allowed to have their heirs in the company either. This was appreciated by the employees and is very unusual in famous Japanese companies. He was interested in the people in the community also, like the handicapped. Do you know he founded two plants in Japan specially designed to employ only handicapped people? Anyway he was very people oriented himself. Very easy to talk to. He was kind of an entertainer actually. He played music for people and entertained them. When you met him, he tried to have you enjoy the time. He tried to make everybody happy. When he was inducted into the American Automotive Hall of Fame, all the dealers came. They said they appreciated his efforts and his products. But Mr. Honda said, 'It's not me, all the merit has to go to you, the dealers.' Then he disappeared from the head table. He asked for a wine waiter's uniform. He dressed in the uniform and reappeared. He served wine to every dealer. He was saying to each one, 'Thank you, thank you. It is only because of you I'm even in this Hall of Fame.' I know that no other Japanese CEO would behave this way. And I doubt that any of the American CEOs in Detroit would either. But that was the type of man Soichiro Honda was.

"Mr. Honda always liked the workshops and the plants best. He went there a lot himself and discussed things with the workers and the technicians and the engineers. He discussed things in detail. He would make his comments and he listened to their ideas. He strongly inspired employees about the product. Of course, when he was young, he raced cars. He had a very bad accident and quit, but he was always keen to develop race cars. This is an important thing at Honda. It's not just for promotion purposes. It's very good for the engineers in developing new ideas and new technologies. Working on racing engines is very serious and is very good for timing, for faster learning. He always said, 'Beating the clock is the most important factor to becoming number one.' That kind of spirit about high-performance cars was very inspiring to the engineers and even the production workers. You can foster a good spirit in the automobile business through racing. Honda people in Japan, in the States, everywhere, are very proud of our Formula One championships. You see, Mr. Honda believed technology has no end. You can always improve it. For example, that's why we produced the all-aluminum-body car and we're now testing the 100 mpg engine. It's also why Honda was the first company to meet the tough U.S. emissions standards. There are many difficulties in doing these things, but our engineers are always encouraged to challenge limits. Automobile employees are very motivated by making machines no one else can make!

"Of course I must also say he was a very serious-minded person. If you made any mistake in the business, he could get so mad. His anger was not just emotional. He used it as a kind of teacher too. He really wanted all of us to learn to do better. The next day he would recover and come back to us and ask how we could all improve the situation. He always did this. He was aggressive about the business but he would always try to help us. He did this especially with the young people. They knew he was serious, but also there to help them. As I said, he was a very unique Japanese."

One can argue that Soichiro-san wasn't out to create "mini-entre-preneurs." Surely he wouldn't have put it that way himself. But he *did* inspire Honda employees to extraordinary levels of commitment and performance. Extraordinary commitment to the business of making the best motorcycles and cars in the world. And extraordinary performance in product innovation and customer service. At the end of the day, call it what you will, this is what entrepreneurial leaders are supposed to be able to do—whether it's firing up employees in a factory in Japan or a business in Marysville, Ohio.

Honda clearly understood the power of positive and negative consequences. He knew that the key to inspiring employee commitment and performance ultimately comes down to one question: "What are the consequences to employees for good performance and what are the consequences for poor performance?" This is the question you'll have to answer too—if you ever hope to inspire your employees to become mini-entrepreneurs in your organization. It's all about understanding the "power of consequences."

THE POWER OF CONSEQUENCES

There really is no mystery to why people behave the way they do. The platinum rule of human behavior is that people behave in their own self-interest. They avoid doing things where they perceive the personal consequences will be negative. And they do other things where they perceive the positive outcomes will outweigh the negatives. This applies to everything we do, including work. It applies in spades to the entrepreneur. The performance of entrepreneurs is dominated by the "life and death" consequences of meeting or not meeting customer demands—pure and simple!

The reality is that entrepreneurs are self-inspired by the immediate, often severe, and always personal consequences of their actions. There is no place to hide. There are no six-month probation periods. Your kid's next meal is on the line. On the upside, there's no supervisor stealing your glory—or otherwise deciding whether you did well or not. If you do well, you'll get immediate and powerful feedback from the folks who really count—your customers. Entrepreneurs work in an environment where their performance really matters and the consequences—positive or negative—are razor sharp.

Bureaucrats just don't live in this world. Big, modern bureaucracies are notorious for their ability to insulate employees from both the positive and negative outcomes of their work. This is probably bad psychology—it's certainly bad business. Too many companies, with too many personnel theories, are hopelessly stuck in neutral—no personal positives, no personal negatives, just the clear signal that individual commitment and performance really don't matter much. Managing employee consequences would seem a reasonable thing for bosses to do. Everyone knows that just giving a little personal feedback can be powerful—and it doesn't cost a cent. For any bureaucracy, instilling strong consequences is the fastest, surest, and cheapest way to transform themselves. The great mystery is why so many can't seem to figure this out.

Not managing consequences—or mismanaging consequences—can produce some really awful results. Some company managements operate in total denial. They behave as if everyone's doing their best—nobody's performing poorly—even if the company is on a collision course with bankruptcy. The cruelest and dumbest scenario comes with the inevitable layoffs—when every single employee says, "Gee, why me? I got a great performance evaluation last year!" At the other extreme, somewhere along the line we've convinced ourselves that sales people like special recognition but no one else really needs it. Elaborate sales commission schemes and trips to Hawaii are devised to recognize the sales force, while the factory workers and clerks get to read about it in the company magazine. The biggest travesty in the management of consequences, is the wacky and wonderful world of executive compensation and privilege. In the United States, at least, many CEOs and their top lieutenants seem to work in a performance system with only three levels of consequences: high financial reward, higher financial reward, and highest financial reward!

But there is hope. Any organization can start giving its employees straight, meaningful answers to the eternal question: "What happens to me if I do, and what happens to me if I don't?" For some companies, this may only require some fine-tuning. For others it will require a major overhaul in their performance systems from top to bottom. What it takes is re-creating the real-life environment of entrepreneurs. This means creating rewards and penalties in all jobs and departments. And these rewards and punishments must be tied to real results. Creating a more entrepreneurial environment, with specific performance standards, sends a very direct message. Both good fortune and misfortune are felt by everyone, starting with top management. The bureaucratic notion that no one is responsible has to go. When a client or market is lost, no one can just stand around and shrug. And when a new client or market is won, everyone wins. Not just the salesperson, but the factory worker and the processing clerk too. And top management, just like entrepreneurs, will live and die on how well the company satisfies customers! This is the power of consequences at work.

Finally we get to the crux of the matter—the missing link in this business of inspiring others and creating mini-entrepreneurs. Transforming bureaucrats to entrepreneurs is a tall order. What if they just don't want to be transformed? What do you do then? Is there some fail-safe button to push? Believe it or not, there is a button to push. In fact, there are three. They're each covered in the next section, so read on!

THREE PROVEN WAYS TO INSTILL CONSEQUENCES

Our folks don't expect something for nothing . . . they want to win so badly, they just go out there and do it!
—SAM WALTON
FOUNDER, WAL-MART STORES

Even a charismatic, entrepreneurial leader like Sam Walton, arriving at each store in his old Chevy pickup and leading the troops in the Wal-Mart fight song, found that hoopla can only take you so far in the business of inspiring employees. Walton got more mileage out of company hoopla than most, probably because he was so darn good at doing it. But even Wal-Mart, the fastest-growing, and now biggest, retailer in the history of the world uses carefully thought-out policies to help answer the "What's in it for me?" question. Wal-Mart's most prominent effort is an across-the-board employee stock ownership program for its 910,000 employees. The one-two punch of having a leader like Perot, Lever, Johnson, Honda, or Sam Walton, combined with solid, ongoing policies that foster a spirit of enterprise in workers, is a tough combo to beat. But companies don't get to have their founders around forever. Since Mr. Walton's death several years ago, the policies and programs he implemented have probably become even more essential to keeping that spirit alive. And, certainly, in giant companies like Wal-Mart, which recently surpassed the U.S. Postal Service as the biggest employer in America, it really would be impossible for any leader to "lay hands" on every employee.

So most of the efforts around the world to foster corporate entrepreneurship are being driven by managers in large companies, not entrepreneurs. Which brings us face to face with the challenge of creating more entrepreneurial employees without the help of a Sam Walton or a Ross Perot. In our experience, the only way to do that is to figure out how to instill entrepreneurial-style consequences throughout the organization.

Fortunately, there are at least three proven ways to inspire more entrepreneurial behavior in company managers and workers. They can become owners or shareholders of the company. They can create a new, little piece of the business as an "intrapreneur." Or they can be the entrepreneur of their own job or department—by working under an "entrepreneurial performance system." All three ways will help you answer that first big question on everyone's mind: "What's in it for me?" Here's a brief description of each.

➤ *Workers as Owners*
Miracles do happen! In recent years, many companies have become completely employee owned, with incredible results. Every year you can read about workers buying their company and miraculously saving it from bankruptcy! They perform this seemingly impossible turnaround with the same products, the same customers, and the same people. How can that be? It's not because they get smarter or more skilled. It's because, for the first time, they have a personal stake in the success and failure of their company. That does seem a bit like a miracle, doesn't it?

There is no question that the older, more common "partnership" form of organization has always produced incredible levels of commitment and performance. Regardless of what you think about lawyers, auditors, and consultants (I certainly confess to being a critic of consulting firms), we have to admit that the senior partners, the junior partners, and the wanna-be partners usually work circles around their own clients—which are mostly large, public corporations.

Less radical forms of employee ownership have been around for years. These include all the various types of employee stock-ownership programs. Even these efforts, where employees may only own a small number of shares, have a positive impact on results. All the studies in the United States clearly show that companies with employee shareholders outperform their competitors with no such employee involvement. The example of Wal-Mart is a good one. Company management believes so strongly that employees should be shareholders, that they've made the level of participation by workers a factor in every manager's annual performance review and consideration for bonus.

Whether it's Wal-Mart, United Airlines, Anderson Consulting in North America, Thomson/RCA in Europe, or privatized state industries in China, the result is always the same. It's just common sense that any form of employee ownership simply has to have some positive effect on the behavior of employees. There's no mystery to it. The only mystery is why 80 percent of companies around the world still don't do it.

▷ Intrapreneurship

This is an old idea with a new name. Give a small group of highly committed, top-performing managers a little seed money, a lot of autonomy, and participation in the financial results, and ask them to create a new business for the corporation—but outside the corporation. For some big companies, such as Xerox and Levi Strauss, this strategy is providing the chance to create new entrepreneurial businesses and not lose the entrepreneurs. The only downside of intrapreneuring is that only a few can play. The other 99 percent of your people will not be involved. Below are the major steps commonly followed in implementing an intrapreneurship project.

- Everyone in the company is invited to participate. Nobody is left out at this stage. Small-team submissions are usually encouraged.

- A customer/product vision or plan is submitted by any employee or team that wants to be considered. The plan goes to a panel of respected company managers. At least some panel members must have had direct experience in starting up new products or businesses.

- A full evaluation of the proposed venture is conducted by the panel, and an initial go or no-go decision is rendered.

- For those plans receiving an initial go-ahead, a "contract" is agreed to by the corporation and the intrapreneur team. The "contract" covers key elements such as start-up capital needs and an equity/compensation arrangement.

- Other corporate resources and assistance that may be required is also agreed to by the corporation and the intrapreneur team.

- The start-up phase begins with agreed-upon deadlines for the development of product/service prototypes and the securing of prospect/customer commitments. Actual or even trial use of the product/service prototype by prospective clients is strongly encouraged.

- The start-up phase is evaluated by the panel and the venture is either killed, significantly modified, or approved for full-scale start-up.

➤ *The Entrepreneurial Performance System*

If making workers into owners isn't for you, and if intrapreneurship affects too few people, what can you do? How can you get thousands of employees to behave more entrepreneurially right now, in their current jobs? Here's the answer! We call it the Entrepreneurial Performance System, the third proven way to foster the spirit of enterprise in your people. In my experience this is a practical step any manager in any company could take tomorrow. To help get you started, a full description follows.

CREATING AN ENTREPRENEURIAL PERFORMANCE SYSTEM (EPS)

The Entrepreneurial Performance System deals with all the causes of subpar performance, but relies most heavily on consequences as the primary people-management tool. In so doing, the EPS focuses on the most critical factor in the real-world performance environment of entrepreneurs. In fact, when creating entrepreneurial people is the goal, managing the *consequences* can be more important than managing the *people* per se. To implement the Entrepreneurial Performance System in your company, a few basic ideas have to be in place. The four most important are:

➤ *Consequences Determine Behavior*

Every employee has to know the answer to the "What's in it for me?" question. Positive and negative consequences are the most powerful influencers of behavior. The key is to make sure every employee feels them.

➤ *Everyone Has a Business to Run*

Every employee has a business within the business to run. All of them have products or services to offer, and customers or users to serve. Like entrepreneurs, the final test of their performance has to be based on how well their products satisfy their customers.

⟫ Customers Give Consequences—Bosses Give Feedback

The important consequences always come from customers. The boss' job is to give workers feedback regarding the positive or negative consequences of their performance and to make sure that something happens because of them.

⟫ The Company and the Workers Have a Shared Destiny

The consequences to workers and the company must be in sync. What's good for the company should be good for the workers—and vice versa.

The Entrepreneurial Performance System diagram below expands on the simple *Power of Consequences* model illustrated back in chapter 5. The EPS depicts the complete performance system in which we all work. The system itself never changes, and it applies to entrepreneurs, bureaucrats, and everyone in between.

THE COMPLETE ENTREPRENEURIAL PERFORMANCE SYSTEM

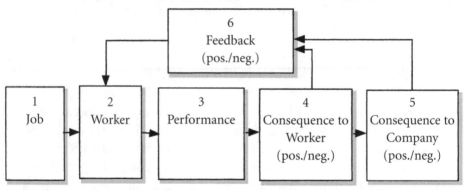

This diagram is a slightly modified version of the original work of my good friend and mentor on human performance, Dr. Geary A. Rummler, in Tucson, Arizona. He began his landmark work on Human Performance Systems many years ago at the University of Michigan. Rummler refined and greatly expanded his research over the years while founding three separate consulting and training firms. We have adapted his early, and admittedly simple, view of human behavior for one reason only—it so clearly illustrates why entrepreneurs do what they do. I highly recommend Geary Rummler's own books and advisory services on the broad subject of human performance.

The EPS's first fundamental assumption is that 99 percent of all human behavior can be explained with two words: stimulus and response. The clerk sees a customer and responds with courteous service, for example.

But while the system and its component parts are the same for everyone, individual performance may actually be quite different. Some clerks are courteous to customers; others aren't. More to the point, the entrepreneur responds to almost everything at work in a very different manner than a bureaucrat does. What determines that response (or performance) are the *components* in the system. Those components of the performance system are the following:

1. The job or task at hand—this is the stimulus or "input" to the system.
2. The worker—whether a self-inspired entrepreneur or an entrenched bureaucrat.
3. The performance of the worker—whether it's entrepreneurial or bureaucratic—is the response or "output" of the system.
4. The consequences to the worker—the effect of the performance on the worker.
5. The consequences to the company—the effect of the performance on the company.
6. Feedback—making the consequences known to the worker in a timely way that has an impact.

A breakdown in any of the major components of the system can cause performance, or commitment, problems. And this leads to the EPS' second fundamental assumption: The greatest influencer of human response or performance is the person's perception of the consequences— positive or negative—to her performance. I'll spare you the tedious details of all the things that *could* go wrong in your performance environment, and stay focused on consequences, the area that really counts for our purposes here: creating mini-entrepreneurs in your company.

The most common cause of a breakdown in the EPS—meaning that people are not doing what they "should"—is that the consequences are totally out of whack. They are either nonexistent or even the reverse of what they should be. The second-greatest cause is that the boss never gets around to feeding back the information on consequences to the workers. These are breakdowns that occur over and over and over again in most organizations. But, as we've stated before, practically by definition, this never happens to entrepreneurs. The biggest study in the United States on the causes of employee performance problems concluded that poor management of consequences accounts for an amazing two-thirds of all poor performance!

This is why we say consequences represent the biggest single difference between entrepreneurial and bureaucratic behavior. Entrepreneurs live and die on the direct feedback of consequences. The consequences are powerful and personal and the feedback is immediate. In bureaucracies, it's exactly the opposite. The consequences are out of balance, they rarely come from customers, and the feedback only comes once a year at your annual performance review. The feedback step is the manager's job. The trick is to make sure the employee actually feels the consequences, courtesy of the manager's timely, accurate, and fair feedback.

So if you're looking for the place to start, you've found it. The key to creating entrepreneurial performance is to put in place strong positive/negative consequences—and make absolutely certain that those consequences are fed back to all performers. It's the sure-fire way to change your employees' behavior—and awaken the spirit of enterprise in your company.

GOD HELP YOU AND YOUR EMPLOYEES

At the end of the day, why should people care about being self-inspired? And what does it really matter if they love what they do and are good at doing it? We know these entrepreneurial traits help the business, but they may have an even more important value. Think about it. Most people spend more than half their life at work. They spend more time at work than with their family, or with their friends, or enjoying a hobby. They spend more time at work than on any other activity in their entire life. This is why it's important to love what you do. It's your *life* we're talking about! And God help you and your employees if you spend your lives doing something you hate.

12 What's Really Required to Create the Entrepreneurial Organization

Developing better managers is not the answer to turning around a company. You have to get beyond managing. Every employee has to learn to behave as if the company is his own—as a true entrepreneur.

—HERVÉ HANNEBICQUE
SENIOR VICE PRESIDENT, ENTREPRENEURSHIP,
THOMSON MULTIMEDIA, S. A.

How many 120-year-old companies do you know of that are showing the level of growth noted in the table below? This is the kind of explosive rise we've only seen with a few Internet start-ups. Do the math. It's pretty staggering.

Total Market Value in French Francs
1996: FFr 1[1]
1998: FFr 6 billion
1999: FFr 13 billion
2000: FFr 100 billion[2]

This is Thomson Multimedia, S. A., the giant French electronics company, with revenue today at $8 billion. It is actually a marriage of two old and great companies—Thomson Electric and RCA—which had both been kicked around and mismanaged for years. The comeback of this merged company almost seems like a miracle.

From year-end 1996 to year-end 1999, operating income rose from a *loss* of FFr 640 million to a profit of FFr 2 billion. The improvement in net income, over the same four years, was even more dramatic: a FFr 3 billion *loss* was transformed into a FFr 1 billion profit. The new shareholders, includ-

---

[1]French Government's "symbolic" asking price in the proposed sale of the nationalized company.

[2]Actual market value at the time of this writing—March 2000.

ing over 17,000 employees, saw their stock value skyrocket from the IPO price of 21.60 Euros in October 1999 to 130 Euros as I write in March of 2000. Not bad for a company that, for years, had been the laughingstock of French industry. That is, until 1997 when Jacques Chirac, the president of France, hand-picked a new, entrepreneurial management team to turn this national embarrassment into the pride of French industry!

First the history: Elihu Thomson was born in Manchester, England, in 1853 and moved to Philadelphia as a young man. He began his working life as a high school chemistry and mechanics teacher. He teamed up with Edward Houston in 1882 to form Thomson-Houston Company in Connecticut. Ten years later Thomson-Houston merged with Thomas Edison's company, Edison General Electric, to form General Electric Company, the same GE that is going strong today. Thomson smartly kept his international rights, relocated to Paris, and "refounded" Thomson, where it is still headquartered today. Elihu Thomson was also a prolific inventor, eventually earning over 700 patents. The fate of the company in France was not rosy, however. After surviving two world wars and the Great Depression, the socialist policies of the Mitterand government finally did the company in. As a nationalized French company, things went from bad to worse. Finally, in 1997, the pro-enterprise Chirac government determined to privatize Thomson along with many other famous French companies struggling under government control. This, of course, is where Hervé Hannebicque's story is going to begin.

Radio Corporation of America (RCA) was originally set up, prior to World War I, as a subsidiary of the British Marconi Company. The man often called the founder of RCA was long-time CEO David Sarnoff. Actually, he started out as a junior employee but rose through the ranks to lead the company to its greatest triumphs over nearly five decades. His first brush with fame involved the radio, way back in 1912. Sarnoff was the operator of Marconi's transmission station on the roof of Wanamaker's department store in New York. On the fateful evening of April 14, 1912, and for three horrible days afterward, his was the only radio in America receiving transmissions from the *SS Olympic,* the first ship that reached the sinking *Titanic* and provided the names of the 750 passengers rescued from the icy water. After World War I, the U.S. government became alarmed that the fast-growing radio industry in America was owned by a foreign company. At that time, radio was viewed not only as a potentially huge commercial activity, but also as a strategic defense asset. In 1919, under U.S. government pressure, RCA became an American company with the General Electric Company (yes, the same GE) initially holding the major ownership and dominant control. Eventually, of course, RCA became a fully independent,

Fortune 100 company. It led the worldwide growth of television and created famous subsidiaries like NBC. By the 1970s, however, RCA was losing ground to its Japanese competitors and seemed to be losing its focus. It then tried to become a conglomerate, which only made things worse, and, ultimately, the company fell on very tough times. Ironically, the company that came in and picked up the pieces was none other than General Electric. GE stepped in and purchased the core businesses and sold off unrelated activities such as the Hertz auto-rental business.

By the early nineties, the fortunes of these two companies, with common roots going back a hundred years, had been connected once again. Thomson, now owned by the French government, realized it had to obtain entrée to both American technology and American markets if it ever hoped to compete with the likes of GE, Matsushita, Sony, and Philips. So where did it look for help? That's right. The General Electric Company with all those RCA assets. After much negotiating, Thomson bought most of the RCA patents, products, and manufacturing plants it wanted from GE. It also got a respected American brand name, thousands of good RCA people, and, perhaps most important, a presence in America.

Let's pick up the story here from Hervé Hannebicque, an original member of that new team assembled in Paris. I asked him what he and the privatization team found when they took over Thomson, which they had renamed Thomson Multimedia (TMM). In his very French, French accent Hervé didn't mince words: "At Thomson, when we came in March or April of 1997, we had inherited a company in large trouble. Large trouble in terms of results. The operating results showed a loss of FFr 640 million. It was even worse for the net results—a loss of FFr 3 billion for 1996. So there was no time to do anything but to engage in actions which could affect the profitability. It was a survival situation. We needed to do something, because if we didn't, we were against the wall. It was difficult to progress and move forward. So we needed to make decisions quickly in order to put this company on another track."

I then asked him how in the world Thomson had gotten into such a mess? He seemed to be choosing his words carefully: "I think, and it's only my feeling, that it came from the previous management. I don't want to blame them or their program really. Because we know that at any given time in a company, there's always a specific team with specific answers for specific problems. But at Thomson I think the major problem was much more the aim of the process, rather than specific tactics. I mean, the former chairman came from the 'right schools' in France, such as ENA (the prestigious National School of Administration), and so on and so forth. He was a clever guy, but he had organized this company in a highly functional way worldwide.

"If you remember, it was Marketing & Sales America, Marketing & Sales Europe, and Marketing & Sales Asia, but with no links between the product managers and the factories. No links between the factories and the sales people. At the time, one of my colleagues, an American, was in charge of all the factories everywhere in the world, whatever the products. It was a huge activity. It was a combination of a worldwide expertise center, and a lot of factories that all thought they were 'winners.' Of course, the objective for Marketing & Sales in Europe or America or Asia was only sales. They did not worry about inventories. It was not their problem. And at the same time, the factories were in charge of producing the inventories and they were not thinking about whether these products could be sold or not. OK, so one thing was a functional, disconnected worldwide organization. And there were three headquarters following the organization of Marketing & Sales. There was one headquarters in Boulogne near Paris, one in Indianapolis, and one in Singapore. There was really no global P&L of products and services or lines of products. So organization was the first part of the problem we saw.

"The second part, I think, was the style of management. As I heard it, the former chairman was very authoritarian and nobody could give the headquarters an idea. There was a kind of corporate terrorism, frankly speaking. This was the feeling we got when we joined the company. The people just said, 'OK, I need to do my job in my corner, and I don't want to show my head or give an idea.' This style had completely cut the origin or the source of imagination and innovation, right?"

I interrupted Hervé at this point to ask him the obvious: Since Thomson had been a government-owned company for so many years, wasn't that part of the problem too? This part of the saga, as Hervé began to unfold it, was worse than I had imagined: "In fact, before we arrived on the scene, the government had tried to privatize Thomson Multimedia. But the solution the prime minister of France, Mr. [Alain] Juppé, wanted to implement, became another part of the problem we inherited. I mean, to propose all of TMM—even with its debt—to the Korean Daewoo Company, and to ask Daewoo to pay just one symbolic French franc—that was a scandal within the company. And especially for the Americans. Remember: The Americans *are* RCA! They had just been acquired by TMM and were representing more than 65 percent of our global sales. So to hear from France, from the prime minister of France, that the value of their company was only one French Franc—it was an insult, of course, to the RCA people! And for the TMM Asian employees, to be told that the Koreans would be the masters, the owners of their company, for a single French franc, well, that was a problem also. And in Paris, if I remember the stories, the Korean managers were already coming to the TMM headquarters and deciding, 'This will be my office' and 'That will be your office' and so on. You can't imagine the turmoil that we inherited. We faced a very real risk of an LMBO (leveraged management buyout) by the Americans saying: 'OK. Good-bye, our French friends, we're leaving.' And TMM, at the beginning, without the Americans, was nothing. You can't imagine the situation.

"Next, there were a lot of demonstrations in Paris by labor unions and so on. What I heard later inside TMM, was that the former chairman even asked the management to demonstrate in the streets against the government solution of selling to Daewoo. And when the managers refused to demonstrate, he fired them. It was quite dramatic. But the last straw was that the French Privatization Commission thwarted the whole plan. They are in charge of proposing to the government the value of companies to be offered on the stock exchange or sold outright. It is an independent commission and they decided to not follow the French government plan about Daewoo. This Commission told the government *no*—we are refusing to support the Daewoo sale. So for TMM there was no future. The company was supposed to be privatized. The Privatization Commission is saying *no*. There are demonstrations in the streets of Paris. The Asians aren't trusting anything we say in Paris. The Americans are talking about an LMBO. And remember, this wasn't the socialists. This was the right-wing government! It was in 1995 or '96 and Alain Juppé was the first prime minister of President Chirac. What could possibly happen next?"

I was almost sorry I had asked. Just recounting this earlier fiasco seemed to insult Hervé's common sense and possibly his national pride. But I really wanted to hear the end of the story, so I asked about what finally happened. "What did happen?" repeated Hervé, pausing, it seemed, to recollect the sequence of events. "Well, I'll tell you. President Chirac finally had to step in personally and the French government ended up taking the right approach. First, the former chairman, Mr. Prestat, was fired. The government, which was still the 100 percent shareholder, then came up with a new plan. They would bring in the strongest management team they could find to completely reenergize and improve TMM, make it as profitable as possible—and then take it public. This was very different from the previous strategy, which more or less was to just give up and get rid of it for a Franc. So President Chirac appointed Thierry Breton as the new chairman of TMM in March 1997. I knew Breton from Bull of course.[3] We were both

---

[3]The giant French computer company, which had been privatized earlier by a specially appointed management team that included Breton, who was in charge of Mergers and Acquisitions, and Hannebique who was senior VP of human resources. All these recent privatizations of nationalized companies are part of post-Mitterand (some would say postsocialist) France coming to terms with putting French business back on the global commercial map.

there for the successful privatization of Bull and the merging of Bull with Motorola, NEC, and France Telecom. Thierry is a very good guy for mergers and acquisitions. He's very gifted at organizing this kind of marriage, or alchemy, between a three-pronged alliance of Americans, Asians, and Europeans. He has a worldwide vision. I was senior vice president of HR at Bull so Thierry and I became friends. At Bull, we had implemented a complete turnaround of the company, which had about the same financial figures as TMM, by the way. We privatized the company, and organized an internal shareholding process, and so on and so forth. That had been done and was very successful.

THE THREE REQUIREMENTS

So the pieces were starting to fall into place at Thomson Multimedia. With this background out of the way, the rest of the interview with Hervé was devoted to the "how to's" of actually transforming a struggling bureaucracy into a thriving entrepreneurial organization. It's not a coincidence that Hannebicque's ideas fall nicely into the three areas we call the Three Requirements. Over the past couple of years that we have worked together, a few good ideas were bound to rub off in either direction. And, naturally, there is always the possibility that there really *are* three critical requirements and anyone who digs deeply enough into the subject will figure them out! In any event, the added value that Hervé brings to the table is that he has been on the front line, actually doing what we're talking about.

The three requirements to create an entrepreneurial organization are: a bit of money, a bit of knowledge, and an entrepreneur-friendly culture. In discussing these three, Hannebicque starts off with culture, which makes a lot of sense given that existing, large companies, as opposed to start-up ventures, have developed a deeply embedded culture over the years. So the first requirement here really has to be changing that existing organization culture.

AN ENTREPRENEUR-FRIENDLY CULTURE

This is Hervé Hannebicque on creating an entrepreneurial culture at Thomson Multimedia: "So Thierry asked me to join him at TMM. The first decision was we needed to completely change the mind-set, the habits, the behaviors, and the processes of this company. We analyzed what we did with Bull. The good things and the bad things. Because we had shared the same experience at Bull, we did not need to spend a lot of time just talking about what to do. My first proposal to Thierry was that we needed to split the HR function away from my entrepreneurship role. I told him: 'I don't want to become your HR guy. I'm fed up with dealing with the trade unions. I'm fed up organizing the social plan (employee severance packages) to shut down all the factories. I've done this for the past twenty years. You know I'm willing to do it, but I think we need to develop a new way.' So the first idea was we needed to separate this function. At Bull I was in charge of the classic HR function but at the same time promoting an entrepreneurial program for employees. But how can you be credible and tell to your worldwide management network: 'I will help you become entrepreneurs at the same time I'm organizing your area's downsizing.' It's very difficult. We could do it. I did it at Bull. But I think it's not very efficient.

"So we decided to create a specific function of entrepreneurship to make it much more of a focused mission. I'm also a member of TMM's Executive Committee because I need to participate in those big collective decisions. But basically I'm in charge of TMM's 'managing to entrepreneuring process.' So what does it mean? I'm part of the hierarchy of this company but at the same time I'm a kind of maverick—outside, as a teaser. Well, I've learned it's a very good idea in a big company to find somebody to promote new ideas, and to implement very different programs in order to instill a spirit of enterprise. But you can only do that as an ambassador of the chairman and a member of the executive committee. Anyway, the first thing I did was to split the classical HR function away from this idea of promoting a spirit of enterprise. We thought this was the way to create the entrepreneurship mission."

At that point, I joked to Hervé that in all my experience around the world, he was the only senior vice president of entrepreneurship I had ever come across. So, if nothing else, he at least got to adopt a very unique title. His answer was dead serious: "But, you know, Larry, there was a lot of skepticism, especially coming from a lot of my headhunter and consultant friends. They just cannot understand the job. They look at my card and say, 'Hervé, it's only a position organized for you by your friend Thierry. After you are gone, it's gone, finished.' I tell them, 'No. You are wrong.' Still today, Thierry Breton is selling this concept to TMM colleagues everywhere in the world. He always tells our people: 'TMM needs this kind of position. It's not for someone to be a jet setter, a diva, a fool, or the king. No, we need someone to help us vision and manage the transition—the mutation we must pass through. Someone who is *part of,* but at the same time *out of,* the organization. It's very important to TMM.' Really, the first point about changing a company culture is that it's impossible to organize this kind of process without a very strong confidence between the chairman and the person managing the process. And this is not about creating another department or bureaucracy. I have no one working for me. I am able to do things because I am Thierry's ambassador. And all the work I am doing goes through the management networks we have set up across the company. This is a mission for me, not a career.

"As I said when we arrived, the need for urgency was very clear. Thierry told me: 'Hervé, we have ninety days to change the organization of this company. So you go where you want, you meet who you want, you are free. But in ninety days I want a blueprint for changing this crazy organization we have inherited.' So for the first three months I was traveling everywhere in the world, meeting the people, knowing little about the company really. My conclusion after ninety days was very simple. We needed to immediately organize the company as a series of autonomous businesses. As you Americans call it, by SBUs (Strategic Business Units).

"We had to restructure around this idea of the global P&L. It's common sense isn't it? We looked at our products, our distribution channels, and we decided to reconcile the product manager with product development. To reconnect the sales people with the factory. It's what we needed. We said: 'Look, we have the products, CTV, VCR, audio, and communications. The value is moving upstream and downstream with this idea of multimedia products and services. Tomorrow I don't want to sell just a TV to Mr. Larry Farrell. I want to promise you all your controls for cable and satellite, and in your living room at home give you a common platform with specific applications for everything—financial services, interactive TV, education, and a clear connection with the worldwide web.' We were never going to be able to do that as long as we were functionally organized across the world. We needed businesses with product people and customer people all on the same team.

"So we organized our business into six SBUs. First, we have three worldwide SBUs, each with a global P&L. These are businesses where the value is in core competence on a worldwide basis. In these SBUs, all the sales people, product managers, product development and factory personnel, are all dedicated to the specific global business, with a common accountability. And we also have three local SBUs: one in Europe, one in America, and one in Asia. Each of these SBUs is responsible for our CTV and VCR business, which are much more local market businesses.

"To support this new structure, we needed to promote a maximum of decentralization. We must be much nearer our customers. This has been a revolution at TMM. A lot of people, especially at HQ, were shouting about it, but we did not care. We simply had to organize ourselves around the customer so the priority became a maximum of decentralization. And at the same time our corporate functions had to promote a maximum of consistency. Because of our combination of companies, Thomson, RCA, several smaller brands and so on, while we were decentralizing we also needed to reinforce corporate consistency. We needed consistency inside the company and also in the marketplace—like Sony, for example, with one name, one brand, and one image. This was all happening in July of 1997 and the task was to maximize decentralization, to be closer to customers, and at the same time maximize the consistency of corporate identity and culture. So my second organizational emphasis was to promote this balancing of maximum decentralization and maximum consistency. It's not a binary problem—it's a balancing act." We used to call this the "loose–tight" organization. The trick, of course, is knowing what to centralize and what to decentralize. Hannebicque's program of decentralizing to organize around and get close to customers, while centralizing to achieve consistency of TMM's name and image in the market sounds like he knows exactly how "loose–tight" is supposed to work.

So the first major attack on the old culture of TMM was to abolish the industrial-age functionalizing of the business, and replace it with a series of customer/product driven SBUs—reinforced by a flexible loose–tight system of management. It all sounds very entrepreneurial so far. The next area covered by Hervé was TMM's no-holds-barred reliance on loose networks of employees around the world to implement changes as opposed to the bureaucratic turf fighting that multilayered hierarchical management systems always produce.

"At the same time that I was working on these big organizational changes, my next task was to create worldwide management networks. If we hoped to promote our multimedia products, we had to organize our company through networks. If we wanted to be close to our customers, we needed networks outside the hierarchy. If we want to compete in the digital age, and move quickly on a global basis, we could do it best through networks. So I designed and proposed three worldwide management networks. First was the Executive Committee of thirteen top people who meet every Monday via worldwide video conference, and every six months at a two- to three-session gathering to deduce the lessons of the former period and prepare for the next period.

"Next we organized a second worldwide management network, the Operations Committee, with sixty people. It's made up of major project managers and the P&L managers. We meet quarterly for two days. The Operations Committee is the secret of our success. To avoid the LMBO danger after Daewoo, we needed to rebuild the corporate culture at this level. At these quarterly meetings, the words have been very clear: 'You are receiving the same level of information as the Executive Committee, we are all promoting transparency, you are the engine of this company, you are changing and the company is changing with you.' The specific messages have also been very clear. First it was about turnaround. Next it was partnership. Today it's entrepreneurship and innovation. The words again are very clear: 'We used to tell you what we want to do, and you used to do what you were told.' No more! No more! You can check this with anybody in the company. They will tell you the same. And it works. Today when we announce a new product or project, it will be done. That is a very clear change at TMM. For instance, when we announced the employee shareholding program, people were very skeptical. Well, it is done. As for the promised new partnerships with Microsoft and so on, they are done. The successful public offering of TMM shares on the New York Stock Exchange. It is done. It's these actions, not our words, that are really changing the culture of TMM.

"And then we launched a third worldwide network. The network of entrepreneurs. For this we decided to break away from the so-called 'Hay Method'[4] of ranking jobs. We did not want to meet only the managers of the company. We wanted to meet every six months with the top-performing people from everywhere in the world. So the invitation to be in this network of 300, which we call the Entrepreneurs Network, is based completely on performance, not on hierarchy or management level. So we have tried to break this bloody concept of hierarchy and the company entrepreneurs' role is to demonstrate and spread the new TMM culture and the entrepreneurial spirit into every corner of the company. We do not depend on management alone to pass these messages down. They are too important. So the task is clear: to change the structure, the practices, the hierarchy, and the beliefs of the old culture. And to replace that culture with the spirit of entrepreneurship across the company."

We don't usually think about things like structure, SBUs, "loose–tight," and networks as the *stuff* of corporate culture. But, of course, they are. And they're a thousand times more powerful in changing a culture than plastering copies of the latest version of the mission statement on the walls. Hervé's summary of this phase of the "managing to entrepreneuring" process is blunt: "When you think about it, these big organization and management changes were really designed to kill the old, bureaucratic culture. I think today everyone will agree that we have been successful in doing that—in completely changing the culture of TMM."

---

[4]The widely used system for setting salary ranges, devised by Hay Consulting in the United States.

A BIT OF MONEY

This requirement doesn't necessarily mean the company has to spend more money. It most likely will mean, however, dividing the pie in a new way. So let's move on to how TMM handles the "bit of money" requirement. This is Hannebicque again: "We learned from Bull that we need to have a culture of progress, not a culture of budgets. A culture of budgets means nothing. The budget is just the train. What does it mean to organize a beautiful budget? It's only dreams. When you see month after month that you are not achieving your budget, or you are achieving your budget but it is below last year, it means you are retreating. We cannot accept that. So promoting a future of progress is very, very important. Even if it is only a little progress. So today we say to our people in these three worldwide networks, please show us that you are making progress versus last year. And we don't mean just internally. We must also have a culture of comparative progress against the best of our competitors. It's a kind of annual benchmarking. There is no progress if we are unable to compare ourselves vis a vis our best competitors. We don't compare against the average, but against the best, because we need to be the best in class. This culture of comparative progress has been a beautiful concept for us.

"So we designed a new incentive compensation plan for all of the 6,500 managers in the company. It's called a Contract of Progress. All managers have a Contract of Progress, which is designed and negotiated with their boss. We also decided to manage the company by semester periods—every six months—to keep the Contract of Progress very timely. In the survival situation we faced, a full year was too long. There are three short-term goals for the half year, which are always comparative goals promoting our culture of progress. They must be very concrete, based on facts and numbers, to be sure to promote the changes we want in terms of results. Another goal is in terms of behavior, and there is one long-term goal. Even when we were in a survival mode, we couldn't afford to not think about the future. These Contracts of Progress are now the basis of our incentive compensation plan, which is given every six months. We know this has changed a lot of things. It's a kind of backbone for our culture change. We know that our 6,500 people, who are managing the other 50,000 employees, have been very consistent in trying to meet the three short-term goals. So this has been a good tool for us. It has certainly been a dramatic change from the days of nationalization, when all the employees were treated like government bureaucrats."

If the incentive compensation plan was a dramatic change, the TMM employee ownership initiative delivered the *coup de grâce* to the old bureaucratic days. I can personally attest to the intense interest TMM/RCA employees have in the company's stock price. It's the first thing they ask about at meetings and seminars. And I can guarantee that in Indianapolis, TMM/RCA's North American headquarters, there are a whole lot of people who know the daily exchange rate of the euro to the dollar. So, once again, in terms of creating an entrepreneurial organization, it's hard to beat the impact of employee stock ownership.

Hervé, who was responsible for installing TMM's worldwide stock ownership program certainly agrees: "Yes. Of course. Thierry Breton got it started by getting the French government to agree to open our stock to our four industrial partners—well before the Thomson IPO on the New York and Paris stock exchanges. As you know, TMM has created a global alliance with four prestigious, high-tech partners—Microsoft, Direct TV, Alcatel, and NEC. The deal with our partners was that each of them bought 7.5 percent of TMM equity. That means the four companies, collectively, bought 30 percent of the company. As part of the original deal Breton worked out with them, each of the partners agreed to sell back a part their TMM shares to the 370 members of the management networks. This was important, since we had no stock options while we were nationalized and we needed to keep these people to grow the business and create value. The arrangement was also to ensure that we were all sharing the same goals and, for sure, to convince the partners that we would and could successfully privatize, implement the IPO, and create value for them. So they agreed to sell back, collectively, 2 percent or 0.5 percent each to the three worldwide management networks. You can imagine the infusion of lawyers and bankers between the USA and France and Japan to get all this done quickly, but it was worth it. The name of the shareholder program for the 370 members of the networks is the Contract For Value Creation. Ninety percent of the members are today shareholders. So the stock became a very key tool almost from the beginning.

"We were also deeply convinced that we needed a full internal shareholding process in tandem with our IPO. So we designed an employee shareholding program for 3.25 percent of our equity. Today 30,000 employees all across the world are eligible to become shareholders. And only a few months into the program, more than 17,000 have signed up. But you cannot imagine the difficulty of implementing a worldwide shareholding program. I spent most of 1999 on this from France and the United States, where it was straightforward, to China where it was unheard of. Only in February of 2000, did we get government approval for our China managers to join through a Hong Kong vehicle, which completed the coverage for TMM's global operations. What a job but what a joy at the end of the day. We have Polish, Mexican, American, French, and Chinese employee owners today. And as you have seen, Larry, they are all talking about the stock. They are excited. And why not? Look at the price. The stock has gone from 21 euros to 80 euros in just the four months since the IPO. That's why they're excited!

"With the 2 percent coming from Microsoft, Direct TV, Alcatel, and NEC, and the shares reserved for stock bonuses as part of our incentive compensation, we have a total of 6.12 percent of Thomson Multimedia equity for employees. And the value has quadrupled. Not too bad for a company that was 100 percent–owned by the French government two years ago. And not bad at all for a company that the government wanted to sell to the Koreans for one bloody French franc!"

A BIT OF KNOWLEDGE

Hervé prefers to label all training and education activities as "communication programs." I think this is because he desperately wants to keep his entrepreneurship mandate as far away as possible from the long shadow and iffy reputation of most Human Resource departments. However he labels it, he's a big believer in disseminating new, useful knowledge. Here is how he describes that part of the managing to entrepreneuring process at TMM: "We have pushed at least two major knowledge activities in TMM. The first is to just learn about entrepreneurship. That means to teach what entrepreneurship is and really push the TMM entrepreneurial concept down through the company. My job was to instill entrepreneurial behavior in the company, but a lot of people were saying to me, 'OK, Hervé, but what do you mean by entrepreneurship?' Well, I'm not going to give you a lesson on that, since you're our teacher! But the point is, it's time to stop speaking about managers and the techniques of management. We very much need real entrepreneurs in TMM. As you know, we have started the communications program on this which we simply call *Managing to Entrepreneuring*.

"The second knowledge activity is to learn Value-based Managing, which means managing the P&L versus managing this or that. It is also a reinforcement of the shareholding program. In the old company, the focus seemed to be more on administrative management. Now we are promising P&L management, which means our focus has to be much more dedicated to the customer. At the same time, because we are now shareholders, it's very much in our self-interest to promote value-based management. So the question is how can we forget the old administrative management ways and become P&L managers? Well, one thing we can do is teach all our managers value-based managing. This training can at least make it faster and easier for TMM managers to move from being political, administrative managers to real businessmen and value creators.

"There are, of course, other areas where new knowledge or ideas were needed. They were quite specific things. We implemented several global education programs at TMM on such things to increase the company value. The first one was to communicate the need to drastically cut our costs. We called it the 'Stop the Bleeding' program. The idea was to eliminate anything not useful to the customer. This was one of our early successes. Another program was directed at using reengineering ideas specifically to boost productivity. Another was a very concrete program on protecting and leveraging the GE/RCA patent portfolio TMM inherited. We launched all these big corporate programs in the first two years. Training and communication programs to improve specific operational areas can be a very strong way to improve company performance. To move from managing to entrepreneuring, this kind of targeted knowledge is so much more important than the typical courses on leadership and general management principles."

I imagine all prospective corporate entrepreneurs will buy into the need to acquire relevant new knowledge. Of course, the key word is *relevant*. How do you sort out the pap from the good stuff that you really need to know to grow the business? Hannebicque's story parallels our general suggestion on this. To instill entrepreneurship in your company, two kinds of knowledge are certainly needed. First, your people have to have a solid understanding of what entrepreneurial behavior actually is—and how it can be applied in a corporate setting. Second, your people must have state-of-the-art knowledge on their products, their markets, and the key operating processes used by the company. In short, they have to be trained "experts" in the basics of their business—and constantly seeking to learn more. Most other training, as intellectually stimulating and entertaining as it may be, should be deferred to another time and place.

The last question I put to Hervé was this: "What are the lessons? If some other big company team came to you and said, 'We see you've been through this a couple of times. We're thinking about creating an entrepreneurial-style company and trying to get the kind of financial results you've gotten. What are the three or four most important things we need to be thinking about to make this happen?' So, Monsieur Hannebicque, what would you tell them?"

- "I tell you frankly, the first thing you have to check is their own behavior. This tells you their seriousness to change. For example, all during this time, everyone in TMM from the chairman on down is flying coach to save money. Believe me, it's true. So I would want to check if they are just status guys. If they are, I would say: 'Please, if you want to change your company, are you ready to change yourself first? Are you coming here on first class while your company is losing money?' And just to check deeper into their personal practices, I would ask: 'Are you coming with the usual big company ways? Are you creating a bureaucracy? Are you pushing a lot of reporting? Do you have the mind-set yourself? You must check all this in yourself. Because you will have to set the first example in this process.'

- "Second, I would ask: 'Do you have the courage to do this? Because it is very difficult and you will be struggling against the tide for several years.'

- "Third, you must find out somehow if they are innovative people, willing to try new things and abandon old habits.

- "And finally I would have to say: 'Do you have the ethics for this?' In this process you cannot lie. You must be completely transparent. For example, if you are speaking about shareholding, it's vital. This is not business as usual, paying employees at the end of the month. During just two weeks, we had more than 17,000 people investing their own money in the company. Try to imagine that you are working in a TMM factory in Mexico. The share price can represent more than half your monthly salary. So if you don't have ethics, if people are suspecting that you are lying, or that you are organizing a coup, then creating an entrepreneurial company is not for you. It's clear, it cannot work."

THE THREE REQUIREMENTS: A SUMMARY

This topic is so important that we have pulled out and summarized the key ideas in Hervé Hannebicque's interview. Below is a listing of the critical subpoints or actions taken under each of the Three Requirements. We hope the summary is useful to you.

Summary—Entrepreneur-Friendly Culture

- CEO and senior management commitment is critical. A focused and rapid-fire implementation, perhaps guided by a trusted executive outside the hierarchy, is the process of choice.

- Do away with the old hierarchical, functional organization structure. Replace it with customer/product driven business units.

- Reinforce the new structure with a flexible loose–tight organizational approach. Maximize decentralization to be closer to customers while maximizing the consistency of corporate identity and culture.

- Learn to communicate and implement through "flexible networks of employees" versus the bureaucracy of a multilayered management hierarchy.

SUMMARY—A BIT OF MONEY

- Kill your "culture of budgets" and replace it with a "culture of progress." Compare progress against yourself *and* your best competitor. Innovative actions, such as managing by quarters or half-years can be useful in obtaining short-term progress.

- Institute incentive compensation, or "pay for performance," for everyone—*yesterday!* Any incentive program, no matter how rudimentary, is better than operating with no consequences at all.

- Institute employee ownership—*yesterday!* Again, any form you can come up with is better than nothing. Cover all managers and as many workers as legally possible. At minimum, aim for a critical mass of your workers.

SUMMARY—A BIT OF KNOWLEDGE

- Provide communication and training on *why* you want the company to become more entrepreneurial, *what* entrepreneurial behavior really is, and *how* employees can use it in their job, day in and day out.

- Provide communication and training programs to improve specific, high-impact operational activities. Most product and customer training would qualify. Value-based managing and the Stop the Bleeding programs at TMM are excellent examples as well.

A FINAL THOUGHT FROM LINCOLN ELECTRIC

"People are amazed when I tell them that some Lincoln factory workers earn in excess of $100,000 a year."
—FRED MACKENBACH
RETIRED PRESIDENT, LINCOLN ELECTRIC

Let's go back to Lincoln Electric for a final thought on creating the entrepreneurial organization. Lincoln is that truly amazing business with the most entrepreneurial work environment I've ever seen in a big company. Remember: This is the company with no paid holidays or sick leave or even coffee breaks, where very demanding productivity standards are the order of the day. In the face of all this, the workers are extraordinarily committed to perform. They defer vacations to meet heavy client orders. They come early and stay late voluntarily, all the time! How can this be?

President Mackenbach's answer: "Well, it's not very complicated. The key issue is if we are going to encourage entrepreneurship in large organizations, we must drive home the point that in order to get a commitment *out of people,* management must first make a commitment *to those people.*" And what a commitment Lincoln has made! For starters they are simply the highest-paid factory workers in the world. And Lincoln has lived up to its guarantee of continuous employment for over forty years. Perhaps even more to the point, Lincoln's CEO and president earn just five to six times the average employee's salary, far below Germany or Japan's ratio and miniscule compared to the 150:1 ratio American CEOs at other *Fortune 1000* companies make.

Fred Mackenbach sums up the Lincoln experience with a challenge all company leaders should think about: "People are amazed when I tell them that some Lincoln factory workers earn in excess of $100,000 a year. Well, why shouldn't they? They are, in fact, dedicated entrepreneurs. Think about it: They are the true foundation of our free enterprise system." Now that's worth thinking about, if you truly want your company to join the Entrepreneurial Age.

part iii
entrepreneurial countries

*Creating an Entrepreneurial
Economy to Win the Twenty-first
Century Global Economic War!*

13 The Great Unanswered Mystery of Economics

The most important question in economics: why are some countries richer than others?
—THE *ECONOMIST*

In its classic cover feature, "The Mystery of Economic Growth," *The Economist* stated: "Understanding growth is surely the most urgent task in economics. Across the world, poverty remains the single greatest cause of misery; and the surest remedy for poverty is economic growth." But then to underscore the crisis that has plagued a majority of the world's population for a thousand years, the article sadly concluded that "to its shame, economics neglected the study of growth for many years. . . . [W]ith a few exceptions, the best brains in economics preferred not to focus on the most vital issue of all."

The *Economist* optimistically suggested this may be changing as we enter the new millennium: "Citizens of the world who sensibly keep an eye on what economists are up to can at least take pleasure in this: the profession has chosen for once to have one of its most vigorous debates about the right subject." If so, it's not a moment too soon, since the economic evidence is crystal clear that the gap between the richest countries and the poorest is wider now than at any time in history. But will a "vigorous debate" on economic growth by economists at Oxford, Harvard, and the World Bank actually lighten the load of the world's poverty-stricken masses? Or shed any light on what you can do to ensure rising prosperity for your kids. Or even create a single job anywhere in the world? Don't hold your breath.

If economists haven't spent much time over the past several hundred years pondering why some people are rich and others are poor, has anybody? How about elected government leaders? Surely they think about it. Well, think again. On a flight from Washington, D.C. to Los Angeles recently, I found myself sitting next to Congresswoman Jane Harman of California. It's not every day that one gets to chat with a political rising star. My initial reaction, I admit, was to silently wonder how many U.S. citizens realize our that elected representatives (Ross Perot called them "our employees") fly first class. Fortunately, that awkward thought quickly left my mind and after a bit of conversation, it came out that I was on my way to Singapore to give a speech on creating entrepreneurial economies. She expressed polite interest so I asked her my favorite interview question on the enterprise of nations: "If you could be the absolute economic czar of the United States, or any other country for that matter, and you could implement any policies or programs you wanted, what are the first three things you would do to ensure that country's economic prosperity in the twenty-first century?" There was a very long pause, then: "That's really a good question. . . . I'll have to think about it."

She seemed truly surprised by such a question, as if no one had ever brought it up before. I was a little taken aback. I had naively imagined that our leaders in Washington were thinking about things like this all the time. It can make you wonder what politicians *are* spending their time on in Washington or other capitals of the world. Now I believe that Ms. Harman is a hard-working representative for her constituents in California, and she certainly doesn't owe an airline-seat companion an answer to anything. But, in an odd sort of way, I think she was probably being quite truthful. Perhaps she really *hadn't* thought about it.[1] Perhaps no one in Washington thinks about it much. Maybe the *Economist*'s editors are more on target than they know. Could it be that nobody is thinking about it? The mind reels . . .

But hold on. If you look long enough and hard enough, there may be some light at the end of the economic growth tunnel. I actually did find someone who has thought about this. In fact, he spent most of the twentieth century thinking about it. His name is K. T. Li.

THE TWENTIETH CENTURY'S GREATEST MINISTER OF ECONOMICS

> *The greatest advantage I had as economic affairs minister was I never had a course in economics.*
>
> —K. T. LI
> MINISTER OF ECONOMIC AFFAIRS, MINISTER OF FINANCE,
> REPUBLIC OF CHINA ON TAIWAN

K. T. Li, the "father" of Taiwan's economic miracle, is simply the world's most successful economics minister over the past hundred years. I

---

[1] That wouldn't exactly be out of character for Congresswoman Harman, according to *Time* magazine. During her unsuccessful bid to become governor of California, *Time* said of her campaign: "It might have worked—if she had been ready with a coherent plan for the state. But she wasn't. A former political aide, lawyer, and lobbyist, Harman has spent most of her adult life in Washington . . . but wasn't up to speed on the issues and spent months offering little more than platitudes."

had the honor and delight of interviewing him in Taiwan, which was something akin to taking a crash course on the history of the twentieth century. There were many important voices in the shaping of Taiwan's economic development, but K. T. Li is widely recognized as the primary architect: the person most consistently and centrally involved over the past fifty years.

The venerable, Cambridge-educated physicist arrived on the former Japanese colony of Taiwan in 1950. He came with Chiang Kai-shek and 1.6 million mainland Chinese following their bitter defeat at the hands of Mao's freedom marchers. His role in the Taiwan economic miracle began as the president of the Taiwan Shipbuilding Corporation. He ultimately became minister of economic affairs and in 1969 added the title of minister of finance, the only man to hold both jobs simultaneously. He retired from the cabinet as minister of state in 1988 at the ripe young age of seventy-eight, and today carries the honorary title of senior advisor to the president, Republic of China. From the many honors framed on his wall, I learned that he's the only Chinese ever admitted as an Honorary Fellow of Emmanuel College, Cambridge University. And in 1990, Harvard instituted the K. T. Li Lectureship at its Center for International Affairs.

Nearing ninety, he still likes to shock visitors with quips such as these: "The government's most important job is to make the people rich" or "The best policy is to keep the smart people out of government—and in the private sector." As the architect of the twentieth century's most amazing economic success story, Li is particularly proud that he never studied economics: "Of course the economic and finance minister has many economists as advisors, and they all thought I should be helped. I took their ideas with due respect. But in the end, it only requires someone with common sense to make the judgments." That common sense has produced some staggering economic results.

This small island in the South China Sea has the fifth largest foreign reserves in the world—after the United States, Japan, Germany, and China—a stunning feat when you consider that Taiwan's population is only 21 million. It also has the highest GNP growth (9 percent per annum) of any country over the past fifty years, producing a seventy times increase in per capita GNP. And defying all economic theory, it has achieved these record-beating results with practically zero inflation and one of the most even distributions of income in the industrialized world.

If your country is facing financial meltdown, or if you just want to know what actually works in economic development, learning K. T. Li's secrets for creating economic miracles may be a lot more useful than asking the IMF. Since Li believes common sense, not arcane economic theories, will get the job done, not repeating the same mistakes over and over is a good place to start: "First, we determined that runaway inflation and rural poverty were the main reasons for the rise of communism on the mainland. We were determined to avoid that in Taiwan. So our policy was to do the opposite." His overall philosophy for creating national prosperity is distilled below into five broad principles. Here, in K. T. Li's own words, are the ideas that created the economic miracle in Taiwan:

➤ The Starting Point Has to Be Population Control

"This is more important than any economic theory. When you have such a large number of young people, you have to create jobs for them. So you have to be practical. People growth and economic growth have to be together. I think this is the most important thing. By the 1960s, our population's birth rate reached thirty-eight per thousand. We could not sustain such a high rate. Now birth control is definitely against the Chinese philosophy. Confucius says that if you do not have descendents, then you are a failure. Well, we did it without laws. We talked quietly to the people. They know really. They know that at the third or fourth child the situation is bad. Their house is bad. Not enough food. Today we are at fifteen births per thousand. Below 2 percent. Look around. Whether it's Catholic, Muslim, Buddhist, where you find too many people, you find poor countries. No work, no opportunity, no hope."

➤ Never Print Money You Don't Have

"Fighting inflation all the way was also a big part of the policy. And we never took the easy way on money. We even had to sell our gold, but we never printed money we didn't have—never. We thought this was the way to avoid what happened on the mainland. We've gone from $130 to nearly $10,000 in per capita GNP and controlled inflation to the point that the wholesale price index in Taiwan has actually fallen six out of the last ten years. Taiwan's domestic inflation rate has been just 2.2 percent over the past fifty years. That's what happens if you never print money you don't have."

➤ Government's Job Is to Make the People Rich

"The policy has been that all the individuals—the farmers, the domestic businessmen, the exporters—should become prosperous. As the government, our job was to do everything in our power to help them. Farmers, for example, were the largest part of the labor force. Increasing the earnings of the farmers would be the best thing to keep the economy stable—that's very important. We wanted to make sure that if farmers worked harder they made more money. So land was sold at only two-and-a-half times the fixed value of the yield. As their yield went up, it became easier and easier for the farmer to pay off the land. This we wanted. We wanted owner farmers, not tenant farmers with great, rich landlords. Another thing about agriculture—countries have to be able to feed themselves. Especially poor countries. They go broke if they have to import food. So everything we did in the early days was to help the farmers prosper. If they increased output, they prospered. Farmers will do that if you let them. It worked very, very well. We are now of course big exporters of food like rice and sugar."

➤ *Timing Is More Important Than Ideology*

"We believed that everything we did should foster private initiative, be highly pragmatic, and be implemented in some logical order. This last point—the right policy at the right time—is very important to development. The country's life cycle, or stage of development, should determine economic policy, not a particular ideology. To us, timing was everything. First, we had to concentrate on agriculture, with strong government intervention in land reform to create owner farmers. Next we focused on domestic business. We actually implemented a policy of import substitution with high tariffs—admittedly an anti–free-market policy—to help our local entrepreneurs get up and running. But, unlike socialists countries, we understood that protecting local businesses should not be a permanent policy and we got rid of it as quickly as we could. Then we understood that Taiwan had to export to grow so we opened the borders and embraced free trade to the fullest. In this phase, which continues until today, we have done everything we can to facilitate exports by both local and international companies producing products in Taiwan. So doing things in some logical order, in phases, is more important than following the dogma of a particular economic theory. Of course, in all these phases, we wanted the individuals—the farmers, the domestic businessmen, the exporters—to become prosperous. This was our most important goal—not pushing one economic idea or another as many politicians and economists seem to do. Anyway, we thought that was the best way to avoid what happened on the mainland."

➤ *Create and Honor the Entrepreneurs*

"From the beginning, we believed that entrepreneurs were the backbone of any growing economy and the government should do everything in its power to help them succeed. We knew that if we helped create one entrepreneur, he could create fifty more jobs. In the beginning, we inherited from the Japanese a lot of state-owned enterprises. We decided to break these up and sell them as smaller businesses to our people. All these could be handled by the private sector better, so we sold them at very reasonable prices. We encouraged a lot of the former landlords to become investors for the first time in small enterprises. We wanted to create entrepreneurs. Y. C. Wang, the "famous plastics king" of the world, started this way, as did many others. The government sold the plants cheaply, helped find the private investors, did everything we could to create domestic entrepreneurs."

What does all this have to do with the *Economist*'s unsolved mystery: "Why Are Some Countries Richer Than Others?" For one thing, you might be getting the idea that the *Economist* is asking the wrong people for the answer. It turns out that the world of economics isn't so different from some other "expert" professions—where having to produce practical results often seems just beneath their level of dignity, but just above their level of competence. It's hard to avoid the sinking feeling that in economics, common sense can easily get lost in the theoretical shuffle. So this is the connection: it's important to get a reality check from someone who has actually done it—such as K. T. Li.

The economic results clearly show that Li and the Taiwanese know a lot about avoiding poverty and inflation, the two big lessons they learned in losing the Chinese mainland to the communists. At its heart, the Taiwan miracle is a story of unadulterated, uncomplicated, all-out enterprise. The one absolutely clear fact about this tiny speck of land in the South China Sea, is that it didn't get rich by browbeating its entrepreneurs. On that happy note, we will further explore K. T. Li's final point: "creating and honoring the entrepreneurs." Learning just what it takes to create entrepreneurs and build an "entrepreneurial economy," may be the first step in creating your own economic miracle for the new millennium.

THE PROSPERITY CYCLE OF NATIONS

> For Japanese young people, factory work and blue collar work are out. Our fathers did those jobs but we want something better like planning or public relations.
>
> —KOJI SHIMA
> ASSISTANT TO THE CEO, UNI-CHARM CORPORATION

The prosperity of individuals and companies has always depended on the larger, national spirit of enterprise around them. In the post–cold war world, this reality has moved center stage in government policy making. Competition among countries to win the global economic wars of the twenty-first century has become the number-one political issue of our time. Countries may have turned their swords into plowshares, but a new kind of Armageddon awaits us. From the economic tragedy of Africa, to the industrial chaos threatening Russia and much of its former empire, to a global angst over a new, tough, and very competitive China, the world is facing an economic slugfest the likes of which we've never seen. For the foreseeable future, economic power is the name of the game. There are close to 200 players, some very powerful, some dangerously weak, all bound together by a single ambition: to end up in the winners' column in the battle for prosperity. Of course, the question is how to do that.

The history of prosperity is easy enough to recount—it shows a continual coming and going of winners and losers. The ever-shifting positions in the relative prosperity of Europe, North America, and Asia illustrates the point. The nineteenth century belonged to the Europeans, spearheaded by the Victorian Liberals of Great Britain. The twentieth century winner was clearly dominated by North America, with the United States emerging as the richest nation in the history of the world. The twenty-first century is up for grabs, but the smart money and the trends are on the side of Asia, led by over a billion hard-working Chinese. South America could be a sleeping giant. If its growth trends hold, and Brazil provides the economic horsepower, South America could match European (West plus East, of course) levels of prosperity by 2050. In this global race, Africa lags far behind all the other areas. It holds the awful distinction of being the only continent actually growing poorer.

Within these broad regions, individual countries can experience enormous ups and downs, often in a very short span of time. For example, what really caused the dizzying decline of Great Britain, the world's wealthiest and most powerful nation at the end of the nineteenth century? By 1970, not a long time in Britain's thousand-year history, it had to go hat in hand to the IMF for emergency loans to pay its debts![2] Or what really created the economic miracle of Taiwan? Poorer than Albania in 1950, today it has the highest per capita foreign reserves of any country in the world! There is no economic, political, or management theory to explain either case. The point to ponder is this: What really causes the rise and fall of a people's prosperity? Is there an immutable law of the universe that says it has to be this way? Can we really do anything to change the course of history? These questions are worth considering.

---

[2] For the past twenty years, the UK has been back on a strong and highly entrepreneurial growth track. To many pundits, the rebound seems to be just as big a mystery as the steep decline!

THE PROSPERITY CYCLE OF NATIONS

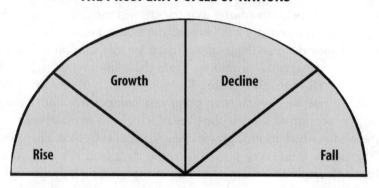

Nations—like companies, and people for that matter—have a definite life cycle. The names are a little different, but you'll recognize the four phases from "The Life Cycle of All Organizations" presented in the Introduction. The similarities are most striking when comparing countries' economic cycles, and not just their ongoing existence. That's why we've labeled it "The Prosperity Cycle of Nations." Clearly, there are differences in the pure life cycles of companies and countries. The time frames are very different, the stakes are very different, and, in one of the most obvious differences, countries don't just go out of business if they can't satisfy their customers— or citizens. They probably *should,* but they don't! Even with these important differences, most countries, or societies, will ultimately pass through most of the phases in the prosperity cycle. When you think carefully about the prosperity cycle of countries, history shows that only three things can possibly happen: The poor get rich, the rich get poor, and some poor stay poor forever. Staying rich forever is potentially a fourth possibility, but it's never yet happened in all history. We'll come back to that later. For right now, let's explain the three possibilities that every country faces:

THE POOR GET RICH

This is the Taiwan story. It's actually the normal story of all prosperous nations, on the assumption that no rich country or society was rich from the day it was founded. It's interesting to note that in recent memory, say, the second half the twentieth century, most examples in this category have been small countries. Minister K. T. Li's warning, "Where you find too many people, you find poor countries," appears to be sound. With the notable exceptions of Japan and Germany, over the last fifty years, *small* seems to translate into *strong* for high-growth countries, as it has for high-growth companies. This is an early warning that we believe entrepreneurial characteristics are very much at work in high-growth economies. In fact, the evidence strongly supports this belief. *The Economist's* current ranking of countries on a scale of Global Competitiveness is instructive: In rank order, the most competitive countries are:

1. Singapore   8. Taiwan

2. Hong Kong   9. Malaysia

3. United States   10. Norway

4. Canada   11. Luxembourg

5. New Zealand   12. Netherlands

6. Switzerland   13. Chile

7. United Kingdom

Actually, even I was astonished when I first saw this list. Eleven out of thirteen of the world's most competitive economies are small countries! Even if Canada, with its 30 million people, is labeled mid-sized, the list is still amazing. The *Economist* defines Global Competitiveness as: "the ability of a country to achieve sustained high rates of GDP growth per head." We listed the odd number of thirteen countries, just to reinforce to our Latino colleagues, that world-class competitiveness can and does exist in South America too!

THE RICH GET POOR

We call it the disease of the rich—or national complacency. Japan may be at the beginning stages. According to Koji Shima, the country seems hell-bent on destroying its primary strength, which has been the extraordinary commitment of Japanese workers to do whatever it takes to push their company (and country) ahead. Mr. Shima, the young assistant to the CEO of Uni-Charm (Japan's Procter & Gamble), cited above, was quoted fully as follows: "For Japanese young people, factory work and blue collar work are out. All young Japanese call it KKK work. *Kitanai* means dirty, *kike* means dangerous, and *kitsui* means hard. Our fathers did those jobs but we want something better like planning or public relations." Hello, industrial decline!

Countries in the "rich get poor" category have an old familiar ring—one we've heard from the fall of Rome to the decline of Britain. It's that same old inward-looking complacency, the muddying of the national sense of mission. It's the loss of urgency, with too many people waiting for someone else to do the work. It's the ring of a people beginning to see prosperity as more of a right than a reward. In short, it's an entire nation watching its spirit of enterprise slip through its fingers.

SOME POOR STAY POOR FOREVER

Like start-up companies that don't make it, some countries just never rise economically. They don't even get into the cycle. Bangladesh, for example, has been poor for a thousand years, and nobody seems to think its situation will ever change. Other unfortunate examples of countries stuck in this terrible no-man's land include Haiti, Albania, Yemen, Mozambique, and Cambodia. The only good news is that these countries do not have to accept this fate.

Other places with fewer resources and more inhospitable environments have become extremely prosperous. Read the following interview with President Olafur Grimsson of Iceland if you want proof. And in today's global economy, there's no reason why the next Microsoft or Genentech can't come from one of those "poor forever" countries. Look at Nokia of Finland. The *Financial Times Global 500* shows that Nokia is now the eleventh most valuable company in the world. Its market value of $208 billion is more than Royal Dutch Shell, IBM, Toyota, or Citigroup. Now that's just amazing! Or go to tiny Uruguay, stuck between two very big and very tough neighbors, Brazil and Argentina. You'll see why this highly prosperous country is called the "Switzerland" of South America.

As mentioned earlier, while nations can and do remain poor forever, the even more compelling point for us is that no nation has ever stayed rich forever. Not the grandest of China's dynasties. Not the Romans, the Persians, the Ottomans, the Spanish, nor the British. It's never happened. And the United States, the twentieth century's economic powerhouse, which is still going strong, has experienced a 30 percent decline in its relative share of world markets since 1950. So don't think for a minute that the United States is immune to the prosperity cycle of nations!

Does it have to be this way? Of course not. There is no law of nature or rule of behavior that says rich nations can't stay rich; that they must lose their spirit of enterprise and become poor. Anyway, you don't even have to worry about "staying rich forever." All *you* have to do, all any generation can do, is to make absolutely certain that you leave your country in better shape than you found it. But how do we do that? Are there any lessons to learn, or rules to follow, in the noble effort to create and maintain national prosperity?

Yes, there are. But those lessons will never be found in the stuff of trickle-down economics or in endless debates over the perfect capital gains tax. You won't find the fundamental principles of enterprise in an IMF report, at the London School of Economics or the Harvard Business School. In fact, governments, business schools, and the science of economics may be the worst places to look for answers. Certainly, a textbook economic analysis would show that Zambia, rich in natural resources, should be more prosperous than Taiwan, with no natural resources. Or that frozen Iceland must be an economic basket case compared to richly endowed Paraguay. Or, for that matter, that "east" German workers should be as productive as "west" Germans. And that today's young generation of working Americans, like every generation before them, will retire more economically secure than their parents and grandparents. Since none of these textbook conclusions seem to be true, maybe it's time to look elsewhere for answers—to discover what really causes the rise and fall of a people's prosperity—and what, if anything, we can do about it.

It's hardly a theoretical issue. The stakes are high and time is running out for many countries. In Africa, things are getting so bad that the only alternatives may be a complete bailout by the world's rich nations or a whole continent going bankrupt—two unthinkable results. And what about the "sleeper" continent? With the highest birth rate in the world, what can South America (and especially Brazil), really do about its 200 million poverty-stricken citizens who live side by side with 100 million prosperous citizens? And can the new and enlarged European Union really just sit by and watch Russia and much of eastern Europe slip into the third world? In Asia, the battle for economic supremacy between Japan, China, and even India is just beginning. But what will be the economic role of the smaller, prosperous countries like Singapore, Taiwan, and even Australia? Who will lead and who will follow in Asia is a very old question. In the past, life could be tough for the followers. Will history repeat itself?

And, last, in the Western Hemisphere, what is it going to take to transform Mexico into a first-world economy? And will super-prosperous Canada and the United States ever solve their deep problems of regional and inner-city poverty—or will we someday just accept that 5–15 percent of any group of people are going to be poor, uneducated, living on welfare, and committing most of the crimes? Can that really be an acceptable outcome amid such national riches? The twenty-first century and the Entrepreneurial Age would seem like a perfect time to answer, finally, the longstanding question: What can be done to create that rising tide that will truly raise all boats?

A few things seem certain at the outset. First, at the dawn of the twenty-first century, the ups and downs of national prosperity are coming at a faster and faster clip. The rise and fall of the wealth of nations is being measured in decades, not centuries. Second, this economic slugfest is truly worldwide, and countries must be prepared to compete globally at a world-class level to survive. And finally, there's one very old lesson worth taking to heart. It really does come from *us!* The prosperity of countries, like the profits of companies, still depends on the enterprise of people. You can be sure that when enterprise goes, decline and fall can't be far behind.

The same underlying basics that propel growth and decline in business are very much at work in the rise and fall of economic states: Pursuing a purposeful mission, producing goods and services a little better than your neighbor, feeling some urgency about it all, and being supremely self-inspired are the characteristics of all entrepreneurial and enterprising people. They are the day-in-day-out attitudes and behaviors that produce prosperity for individuals, for companies, and for countries.

What's always been interesting to me, and I think appealing to others, is that these principles are so simple, common sensical, and obvious. But what's puzzling is that the obvious doesn't seem to be obvious at all to so many "experts" around the globe: not to most of our political leaders, not to the education establishment, and certainly not to the economists of the world. The experts' notion of creating national prosperity seems to be that things are terribly complicated and we need Ph.Ds., computer models and more congressional hearings to figure out what to do.

Well, things aren't quite that complicated in the small and highly prosperous country of Iceland. And we even persuaded the president of the country to tell us why.

COUNTRIES: HERE COME THE VIKINGS!

> *I would argue that Iceland . . . offers an inspiring example of what can be done if the potential that is in everybody for progress, for work, for initiative, for creativity, for entrepreneurship is allowed to grow.*
>
> —Olafur Ragnar Grimsson
> President, Republic of Iceland

"I think if you look at the history of the Icelanders, in the twentieth century, it's in many ways a remarkable story. At the beginning of the twentieth century, we were less than 100,000 mainly poor farmers. But everybody could write and read and everybody was culturally trained in the spirit that there were no limits to what you could do. You could go on a boat and fish and earn a living, you could start a farm, buy a few sheep, and grow them. If you were energetic, prepared to work, you had a great chance at life. But it was also a society where people relied on each other in a positive way. If an accident happened, they helped each other. If a farming family lost the sheep, the neighbors would help. So it was a combination of what we would call today an entrepreneurial spirit in each and everyone as well as a cooperative culture where everyone saw it to his advantage to benefit from the progress of others."

This is President Grimsson of Iceland. We were meeting at his official residence, thanks to the indomitable entrepreneurial spirit of my partner in Iceland, Arni Sigurdsson.[3] Among Arni's many talents, he knows how to fix a Sony tape recorder that won't work, which occurred at the beginning of this interview with the president. There are few things in life more embarrassing than sitting down to begin an interview with the president of a country, and realizing that your damn tape recorder isn't working. Even President Grimsson tried to get it to work. He then called an aide to bring batteries, but that didn't help. While Arni was feverishly working on it, I tried to break the embarrassing tension by joking to the president: "If you had your room wired the same way Richard Nixon did, we wouldn't even need my tape recorder." The president looked me straight in the eye, smiled, and replied in a very presidential tone: "If I did have my room wired, I wouldn't tell *you*—now would I?" Before I had time to figure out the next dumb thing I could say, Arni yelled from across the room, "It's working now!"

Here's President Grimsson continuing: "So when technology came in the beginning of the century, this cultural root of entrepreneurship and self-awareness and the belief in oneself and the possibility that one could do things started to create a remarkable progress, which, by the end of the century, made Iceland one of the richest countries in the world with the highest standard of living, a high-tech economy, and an extensive system of education and health services available for everybody. And in addition to

---

[3]Arni Sigurdsson, tall and imposing like most Icelanders, has redefined for me the definition of entrepreneurial behavior! I had asked Arni if he thought it would be possible to arrange an interview with someone in Iceland who could talk about the nation's entrepreneurial style. I suggested it could be a respected economist, someone working in the government, or even possibly the minister of finance, if he would agree. A day later Arni said to me, "I called the minister of finance for your interview, but he's out of the country. So I called the president and he's agreed to see you at 5 o'clock today." This is something new and incredibly entrepreneurial—if you can't see the minister, don't ask for his subordinate, ask to be transferred to the president! This is the great lesson from Arni, the Viking entrepreneur: Stop *going down* the pecking order of life's opportunities—and start *going up!*

that we have a remarkable culture. In terms of publishing books, we have the highest rate of book publishing per capita in the world. We have a world-class symphony orchestra, and every week twenty to thirty theatrical productions and art exhibitions in the capital area."

The president isn't whistling Dixie with those claims. The numbers are impressive. Iceland ranks eleventh worldwide in GDP per capita, ahead of such economic powerhouses as Canada, Great Britain, Sweden, Italy, Singapore, Hong Kong, and even our showcase example, Taiwan. It's number eight on the *Economist*'s Quality of Life Index. It ranks second in the world behind Japan in high life expectancy and low infant mortality. The only reason it's not in the top ten or fifteen in Global Competitiveness (see the listing earlier in this chapter) can be found on any map. Iceland borders the Arctic Circle in the middle of the North Atlantic. Even with this huge logistical challenge, it still ranks 38th out of nearly 200 countries.

The president again: "When you look at all of that and you bear in mind that we are only 270,000 people, then you can see the potential for other parts of the world. Wherever you take an assembly of 270,000 people—whether it is in New York, Los Angeles, Tokyo, Delhi, London, or wherever—and you challenge those people by showing what 270,000 Icelanders can do, you're entitled to ask them: 'Why can't you? Why can't you?' I know that some of my countrymen have this theory that we are very special. That we are almost unique. And we have great discussions today about genetic science and capabilities based on genes. But I fundamentally believe that we are not that different from anybody else—or that this could only happen in Iceland. So I would argue that, in terms of the potential for other people in the rest of the world, Iceland offers an inspiring example of what can be done if the potential that is in everybody for progress, for work, for initiative, for creativity, for entrepreneurship is allowed to grow. I have said to leaders of other nations, in discussing the prospects for the twenty-first century, perhaps the greatest contribution Iceland can make to the rest of the world is to demonstrate—by what we are and what we have done—the huge potential that exists in the rest of the world for every community, large and small.

"If you analyze Icelandic history and even if you go back to the old Viking Sagas, written in the thirteenth century, that deal with the history of this country from the tenth century up to modern times, there is this great belief in the capability of the individual. It's a belief in one's own worth and one's own capabilities—not necessarily in a negative competition, but in cooperation as well. I sometimes think that modern marketing theories and theories of competition have put it wrongly. They emphasize that the condition for advancement is somehow a negative competition between people where you try to destroy the competitor—instead of seeing entrepreneurship and competition and growth and progress as a result of one's own drive in a positive relationship with others. So Icelanders have, at the same time, a strong sense of individuality and a strong sense of community. Sometimes these have been thought too contradictory, but I think the Icelandic experience shows that they can go together fantastically well and can produce one of the most successful societies in the world.

"We have allowed individualism to grow but we've also had a deep-rooted sense of community. It's even in the way we express ourselves. If you ask Icelanders, 'Who are you?' they will give you an answer that tells you who they are as individuals but at the same time expresses who they are as Icelanders. They never see themselves in isolation from others. They always see themselves as part of a whole.

"In addition to this, I think the old Icelandic society of farmers and fishermen forced this individual entrepreneurship in a very interesting way. And since all societies are inherently rural historically—the United States, Europe, certainly Latin America and Asia even today—this is not especially Icelandic either. It means that all of us in the modern industrial world can go back to our cultural roots in the farming community and the fisherman's community and transfer that culture over to our modern high-tech society. Certainly in looking at modern Iceland, it is a challenging question to ask: 'How is it possible for only 270,0000 people to create this phenomenon, a cosmopolitan city like Rejyavik, full of restaurants, and theaters, and cinemas, and shops and enterprises? I think the answer lies, as I have told you, in the combination of a very strong sense of individualism and entrepreneurship, and also a very strong sense of community."

Bear in mind, these are *deep* roots President Grimsson is talking about. Iceland's one-two punch of individual entrepreneurship and sense of community have been a part of the culture for a long time. If you recall the earlier interview with Kari Stefansson, the biotech entrepreneur, Icelanders measure their family trees in millenniums, not centuries. Iceland is also, as Dr. Stefansson made clear, one of the most homogeneous societies in the world. All this makes having a shared national mission practically a given— as the president's words clearly show. The rest of us may have to work at it a little more. We can't put our national mission on autopilot and just assume that it will stay on course for a hundred years—or even a decade, it seems. Given this, I asked President Grimsson how he sees the role of a president or a government in fostering individual entrepreneurship and creating a more entrepreneurial society. Is that something the president of a country should be involved in or is it just something that either happens or doesn't happen in a national economy?

The president leaned forward and I detected just a slight shift from Chief Executive to Chief Politician, as he obviously relished this kind of question: "No, no—I think you can certainly create the conditions in many ways:

- "First of all, education is essential. An open, innovative, creative educational system is essential.

- "I think secondly it is important to emphasize, both by the leaders of the country and by the educational system, that everybody has the potential within himself or herself to achieve great progress and to make a difference. It's just a question of training yourself and developing your skills.

- "I also believe, thirdly, that what we call *creativity,* this ability to do new things, to find within yourself and your mind new ways of doing things, is a very important element. It's important whether it's in the workplace or in the arts or in research or inside a company.

"On the third point, the leadership of a country can do a lot to encourage creativity. I know it's a new way of thinking for government, because the tendency of a bureaucracy is always to universalize everything instead of fostering creativity. Also, I fundamentally believe that both the laws of the land as well as the ways in which corporations work, must be based on the principle that as many people as possible should be given the chance to start their own company, do their own thing, or make their own contribution. Unfortunately, in many spheres of the modern economy, there are all kinds of regulations and laws that limit these possibilities. Some of them are relics from the industrial age.

"It is important for us to realize that we are now in such a different setting that nobody has a formula for how the future is going to be. There are lots of people who are prepared to tell you—whether they're in government or elsewhere—but the fact of the matter is nobody has a formula. Nobody knows where the initiatives are going to come from that will change our technology or our way of life. They may come from somebody in a garage in Seattle like Bill Gates or an Icelandic scientist like Kari Stefansson doing important things in biotech. It means that anybody can influence the world in a fundamental way. And the role of the government or the corporations is to make sure that we allow this big potential to have the impact it can have. If this means changing the operations of the corporations and the laws of the land to make it possible, so be it!"

Since about three-quarters of the world's countries don't have a successful and prosperous economy, as Iceland does, I asked the president what specific advice he could offer other nations: "As you travel the world and meet other heads of state, let's say from some desperately poor country, what advice would you give these poor countries? It just seems that some of them stay poor forever. How do they break their cycle of poverty and suffering?"

His reply: "The advice I have given to some of them, which I also discussed with Kofi Annan at the UN when he came here is this: 'If you will come to Iceland, instead of talking to me or meeting the ministers, or listening to experts, I will take you to one of the small towns or villages here in Iceland. I will show you the standard of living in the private houses, the excellence of the schools, the excellence of the sports forum and the swimming facilities, the health care center, the football ground, the harbor, the ships, the companies, the workplaces, and then I will show you a picture of that poor village fifty years ago, or even thirty years ago.' After that I would tell them: 'None of this was created by the government or by the president. This was created by the people who live in this town. It was through their own initiative, entrepreneurship, energy, and dedication. And you can do exactly the same in your own country.'

"I think this is very, very important. When leaders of countries travel, they go to the capitals. They go to Washington or New York, they go to London, Paris, Berlin, which are marvelous cities—I like them all. But if they really want to understand the potential of growth, of what can be done, I will take them into the small Icelandic villages and townships and show them how the people create a uniquely high standard of living, and try to inspire them by example of what they can do in their own country.

"We have some old books here of travelers who came to Iceland in the seventeenth and eighteenth centuries from England, Germany, and France. They were learned people, since only highly educated people traveled such distances during those centuries. And they all witnessed, almost in awe, the Icelandic farms and the Icelandic farmers who could discuss with them literature and world events, and learned philosophies and theories. They couldn't comprehend how farmers could be so educated and so inspiring in their discussion—because they thought such capabilities were limited to a small elite of people in society. Here in Iceland, we have always assumed, whether you are president or a farmer or a fisherman or a clerk, that you have the same right and the same potential to say clever things and be inspiring as anybody else. In fact, in my own country, I have to come to terms with the fact that if you are a great poet, the country will respect you much more than they respect the president."

I thought we were coming to a good place to conclude the interview, and I knew that President Grimsson had other activities scheduled, so I said: "Thank you very much, Mr. President. I know you have a busy schedule but is there anything else you would like to say on anything we've discussed?" He surprised me—very pleasantly—by wanting to talk a bit longer. I got the sense that he was enjoying this and was really warming up to the subject at hand: "Yes, indeed. It's a very interesting subject. I think it's a fascinating subject. Because what you call entrepreneurship, and I would call entrepreneurship or creativity, is the key element to progress in the twenty-first century. I have come to the conclusion from my own thinking and my discussions with corporate leaders in the world and the leaders of nations, that it doesn't really matter how much financial strength you have, or industrial base, or high technology, or big bureaucracies in your government ministries. If you lack the vibrant element of, shall I say, entrepreneurial creativity among your people, your staff, and your workforce, you're going to lose out. Only those that encourage creativity in their own right, whether it's a nation, a corporation or an individual entrepreneur, are going to be successful in the twenty-first–century economy. And in that notion of creativity is the inherent sense that everybody's capable of making a difference, of being an entrepreneur, of driving progress.

"I understand the term *entrepreneur,* in its essence, to be somebody who can create progress and drive it forward and maintain it in whatever setting he chooses to work. And you can't do that without being a creative person. And therefore the big corporations of the world, and even the powerful nations of the world, have to understand that if they want to maintain their position in the twenty-first century, creativity is the key thing. And I think that is inherently good, because creativity is a very democratic phenomenon. You cannot really have creativity in societies that are not open and democratic and free. In oppressive societies you just don't have a big element of creativity or entrepreneurship. And therefore I believe that the driving force of the twenty-first–century economy, the force of creativity, is also a strong force for democracy and peace in the world. So by encouraging the process of creativity or entrepreneurship throughout society and the economy, one is also working for democracy and a more peaceful and secure world."

There was one last question I just had to ask: "Thank you again, Mr. President. And now I have a last question. Isn't this the thousand-year celebration of Leif Eriksson?" Well, if the entrepreneurial spirit is "a very fascinating subject" to President Grimsson, you can only imagine how fascinating the story of Leif Eriksson is to any Icelander. Here's President Grimsson's own wonderful and entertaining Icelandic Saga:

"It is indeed. We will celebrate, together with America and Canada, the one thousandth anniversary of Leifur Eriksson's so-called discovery of America. And I'm very pleased about that because I brought the proposal to President Clinton, in our meeting in July of 1997, that we should commemorate these events. It's not just because they are interesting historical events, but also because by looking at these stories, which are described in detail in the Icelandic Sagas from the thirteenth century, we can gain an understanding about ourselves. We can use the history of Leif Eriksson and the other discoverers to look at ourselves and challenge ourselves. It must have taken a great spirit of discovery or entrepreneurship to sail across the unknown ocean and be willing to go into unexpected lands and discover new continents. I believe we need that sense of discovery and exploration in the twenty-first century. We need this cultural root of daring to go into the unknown. Whether it is science, the genetic essence of man, space travel, or whatever else the future may offer us, we need some roots and heritage to gain and maintain our balance. Therefore, we are celebrating these big events with the United States and Canada to draw a lesson from the Vikings' journeys and prepare ourselves for what is ahead in the new millennium.

"I think we should also realize that Leif Eriksson and the other discoverers came from the only democratic commonwealth that existed in Europe at that time. It was the old Icelandic Commonwealth—founded by the establishment of the Icelandic Althing (Parliament) in 930—the oldest Parliament in the world. So they came from a democratic community. They were also Christians, which many people are not aware of. So these discoverers of America, one thousand years ago, had been influenced by the two greatest cultural strands of the Western world—democracy and Christianity.

"We can see that perhaps more clearly in the life history of Gudrídur Thorbjarnardóttir, who was first married to Leif Eriksson's brother and when he died married another discoverer. A few years after Leif Eriksson discovered the new continent, she sailed with her new husband and settled in America and lived there for a number of years. She had a boy there, the first child of European origin to be born on the American continent almost a thousand years ago. Then she came back to Iceland. After having been here for some years she traveled to Rome to inform the Vatican of this new continent across the ocean. Then she came back to Iceland and lived here until she died an old woman. She was the most traveled woman in the world for over 500 years—and she is, I maintain, until somebody can show me otherwise, the greatest woman explorer of all time!

"That brings us to a final element which is worth looking at from your point of view. Maybe one of the explanations for the Icelandic success is that we have always been a society of very strong-willed and determined women who have always played an equal part in our society. All this, by the way, is aptly described in the Viking Sagas."

So, does President Grimsson convey a sense of national mission for Iceland? Do the country's economic results indicate that Icelanders are successful in producing products that customers want? Are the people innovative and creative? Do they appear to be self-inspired? Anyone who has spent more than thirty minutes in Iceland knows the answer to all these questions is *yes*—in spades. And you will certainly recall these four points as the same simple, basics of enterprise that entrepreneurs and their companies live by.

We know that abandoning those simple basics hasn't worked for companies—and it won't work for countries. It doesn't pass the test of history or of common sense. Nations need to learn and start practicing some old truths, not new theories, about fostering and maintaining prosperity. We call it creating an entrepreneurial economy.

14

The Entrepreneurial Economy

We were charged with promoting entrepreneurship through-out the country. But neither I nor my senior staff had any idea what entrepreneurship was.

—MUSTAPA MOHAMED
MINISTER OF ENTREPRENEURIAL
DEVELOPMENT, MALAYSIA

Go back to K. T. Li's common sense principles: Population control, fight inflation, make people rich, don't get hung up on ideology, and create an entrepreneurial economy. Of special interest to us is the final, underpinning principle, which K. T. Li carefully labeled "Create and Honor the Entrepreneurs."

That was exactly the mandate given to Mustapa Mohamed in Malaysia, the only minister of entrepreneurial development in the world. There's something else about Minister Mustapa that is even more unusual than his title. He's that rarest of rare "experts" who will actually admit to what he doesn't know. After acknowledging that no one at the Ministry had the foggiest idea what entrepreneurship was all about, a rather serious concern given his Ministry's mission, he went about educating himself and his senior staff (with a tiny assist from us, I should add). This is one of the small, but useful lessons that most government leaders never learn: If you openly admit that you don't know everything, it makes it smart, not embarrassing, to go back to school and learn what you need to learn. Anyway, Minister Mustapa went on to develop valuable policy initiatives and support programs to keep entrepreneurs and small business high on the priority list of the Malaysian government. This focus on entrepreneurial development has often been cited as one of the reasons Malaysia has rebounded so well from the Asian economic crisis of the late nineties. As the minister liked to say, when you're competing with the likes of Taiwan, Hong Kong, and Singapore, you'd better know what you don't know—because you won't be getting a second chance against those Asian tigers!

So how does someone like the minister of entrepreneurial development foster a high-growth, entrepreneurial economy? What exactly does it take to "create and honor the entrepreneurs"? Hopefully, he can do more than engage in a "vigorous debate" as the economists are doing today. Certainly he needs to offer a more promising response than the politician's: "That's really a good question. I'll have to think about it." Well, the good news is that we actually do know a lot about how to go about this. Let's return for a minute to the basic entrepreneurial practices of entrepreneurs and see how they work for a city, a state, or the economy of an entire country.

THE ENTREPRENEURIAL BASICS: APPLIED TO THE ECONOMY

Instilling the entrepreneurial spirit across an entire economy may sound complicated, but the fundamental questions to ask aren't. You'll recognize them all. Let's examine them one by one:

➤ *Creating a National Sense of Mission*
Let's return to those simplest of words that have a profound impact. *What* is your country's mission for the twenty-first century? And *how* are you going to achieve it? Is your economic *strategy* smart or stupid? Does your *culture* support your national strategy or block it? Do your values maximize your competitive position or erode it? If you can't answer these fundamental questions or, worse, if your answers all point to roadblocks standing in the way of prosperity, you're probably living in a country headed for tough times. The good news is that it doesn't have to be this way. Over time, any country can develop a competitive strategy and a powerful culture. For sure, all nations will need these qualities, in spades, to successfully compete in the global economic wars facing all of us! So whatever you can do to invigorate your national, regional, or even local sense of mission, will be well worth the investment. You owe it to yourself, and your children's children, to at least give it a try!

➤ *Creating Customer/Product Competitiveness*
Does your country produce superior goods and services at lower prices than your best foreign competitors? Do you have the competence to produce the highest-quality products in the world? Do you provide better service than your best competitors in every field? Do you have the smartest and hardest-working labor force in the world? Making and selling products and services the world needs—whether they be

automobiles or Internet portals—that's what still matters most. These are the qualities that will continue to determine the competitive position of your country and your future national prosperity!

➤ *Creating a National Urgency to Improve*

Do you have a national sense of urgency about solving old problems and exploring new frontiers? Do you encourage innovation and action in all facets of national life? Do you hate bureaucracy? What are you doing to wipe it out? If you're stuck in a poor country, does every single person understand that "improving something—anything— every day" is the fastest and surest path to national prosperity? If you were lucky enough to have been born in a rich country, what are you doing to avoid complacency? Will yours be the first rich society in history to conquer complacency? This is what it's going to take. Entrepreneurial countries, like companies and individual people, are fast moving and innovative—always.

➤ *Creating a Nation of Self-Inspired People*

What is your country or state or city really inspired about? Are you and yours focused on the day-in-day-out high performance and high commitment it takes to be the best in the world? Are you working smarter and harder than your best competitors? Are the consequences in place to make all this happen? If your people, especially the young, do the right thing, what happens to them? If they do the wrong thing, what happens? If the positive and negative consequences are not timely and powerful, do you have the social and political will to change them?

Let's take a more in-depth look at how just one of these Entrepreneurial Basics applies to an entire economy. We've selected *Sense of Mission,* but note how this overarching principle also impacts customer/ product competitiveness, the urgency to improve things, and fostering self-inspired people.

CREATING A NATIONAL SENSE OF MISSION

Does your country know *what* to do and *how* to do it? Do you have a *strategy* of high purpose and a supporting *culture* of high standards? A few countries around the world certainly do. Unfortunately, most people and their governments do not have a winning, national sense of mission. They fall short of one or both of the two fundamental variables: the *what* and the *how* of the national mission. Their economic strategy, to the extent that there is one, may be neither smart nor focused. Instead, it typically promises something for everyone and is presented with a lot of feel-good political rhetoric. The popular culture and values being propagated across the country are coming from God knows where, and they will most often have absolutely nothing to do with achieving the nation's economic strategy. If this sounds even vaguely familiar, you'd better hope your country gets the message soon. Creating a powerful and competitive sense of mission is exactly what it's going to take to reach the winners' circle in the twenty-first century. To illustrate, here once again is the "What/How" matrix, adapted to countries, and highlighting two of my favorites—Brazil and Taiwan.

To get a grip on this seemingly simple, but profound analysis of a nation's well-being, it may be helpful to look at extremes. Brazil, that beautiful country with beautiful people and an amazing national appetite for having a good time, spent most of the twentieth century redefining economic chaos. It was, until very recently, the classic example of a country with a great and colorful culture, along-side a truly unfathomable economic strategy. At the opposite extreme, Taiwan is the country with the most successful economic strategy of the twentieth century, but would be dead last on anyone's list of places to go to have fun. It's the archetypal example of a country with a great enterprise strategy but existing within a grim, nose-to-the-grindstone culture.

WE'RE GOING TO HELL, BUT WE'RE GOING FIRST CLASS

Several years ago a Brazilian executive who was attending my seminar, delivered one of the great quotes on "national sense of mission." When he first saw the "What/How" matrix above, he said: "I've found Brazil's spot, upper left-hand corner! Our sense of mission seems to be, 'So what if we have a crazy economic strategy? We've got this great culture and we're having such a good time, who cares?' It's like we're going to hell but we're going first class!" Only a Brazilian could show such loving tolerance of his country's split personality.

Up until the late nineties at least, that Brazilian's humor was the perfect definition for this bigger-than-life country. I fell in love with Brazil twenty years ago and ever since have been over-awed by its people, its culture, it's enormous potential, its unbelievable poverty, and it's absolutely loony economic history. Brazil's global image has always been that it's a country full of talented people—pursuing a grand but unfulfilled national mission. It is true that Brazil has embarked on a heroic effort, based on the directives of the so-called "Washington Consensus," to implement a more sane economic strategy the past five years. But looking into its lop-sided sense of mission over the past hundred years is an economic lesson worth remembering. It has been, after all, the world's premier example of how a nation can have a good time while going broke.

To illustrate this in as benign a way as possible, I will go back to the early nineties to a lunch discussion I had with Olavo Setubal, former Foreign Minister of Brazil, Mayor of Sao Paulo, and elder statesman of Brazil's ruling elite. When I met him, he was Chairman of Bank Itau, Brazil's second largest bank, which just happens to be owned by his family. I had thought this gregarious power-broker, with his vast experience in government and business, would be a good person to ask about Brazil's national mission. I even hoped with his high profile political days behind him, he might provide an inside view of Brazil's economic strategy. Over lunch at the bank's private dining room, I asked the most obvious question that comes to mind when visiting Brazil: "With your tremendous economic potential, what's the plan to eradicate Brazil's poverty? What's going to happen to the 95 million poor people?" There was a long silence while we were served a delicious Brazilian hors d'oeuvre—and finally the answer: "Nothing is going to happen to them. There is no plan. The world has always had, and always will have, poor people." Well, that seemed clear enough: nothing will happen to Brazil's 95 million poor people—ever! Then I asked about the country's crushing foreign debt, at $100 billion the largest in the world at the time and growing daily. It was the same sort of answer: "No one in Brazil seriously thinks we will ever repay our foreign debt." It was on to the main course and a long, pleasant conversation that somehow never returned to the more awkward topics of poverty and the national debt.

Mr. Setubal certainly didn't make these rather shocking comments with any hint of malice or even cynicism. They seemed, rather, to be self-evident truths to him. And who knows? Perhaps they are and he was just stating the obvious. After all, eradicating poverty and getting completely out of debt would be a tall order for most of the world. But it just sounded so—how to put it—so "missionless." And so different from the upbeat, determination in Taiwan, for example, where they did exactly that: eradicate poverty and become debt-free.

Maybe none of this would matter, except happy-go-lucky Brazil has the fifth largest population and the eighth largest economy in the world—and, as noted earlier, is expected to be the economic engine that pulls all of South America into the developed world in the twenty-first century. And it turns out that whether it's self-fulfilling prophecy, coincidence, or just plain bad luck, having a great culture and a lousy economic strategy has left Brazil with some pretty nightmarish socio-economic results:

• Carrys the second largest foreign debt in the world at $160 Billion, while the debt servicing eats up 38% of all foreign exchange earnings.[1]

• 50% of the population—about 80 million people—live below the poverty line. The Government benignly calls it "living on marginal activities."

• 33% of the people have incomes of less than $100 a month.

• Suffers one of the highest infant mortality rates (51/1000) in the world outside of Africa.

• At 1.6%, the annual education investment ranks 7th lowest in the world as a percentage of GNP.

The real problem may be this is also a country that ranks first in the world in wanting to have a good time—that is, holding the world's greatest party every year during Carnival, dancing the samba, going crazy over their beloved fútbal, making babies, and going to Disneyworld—where Brazilians rank number three (after the Canadians and British) on Disney's roster of foreign visitors. Unfortunately this obsession with having a good time hasn't done much for the national prosperity index.

One is always left to wonder if things are getting better or worse in Brazil. Is national prosperity just around the corner? Are they closing the income gap? Happily there are some very encouraging signs today. First among the encouraging signs is that Brazil's best Finance Minister of the

---

[1]Mexico, another country with a wonderful culture and a wacky economic policy, takes top honors in the world in the foreign debt race, with a staggering $165 billion.

last hundred years, has been elected, and reelected, President. Fernando Henrique Cardoso did what everyone said was impossible. He broke the back of inflation. *The Economist* put it bluntly: "Before Cardoso, to outsiders, Brazil—to be frank—was a joke. Since he arrived on the scene, Brazil and its 160 million people have gone through a headlong economic revolution. And whatever its faults or problems, no outsider today sees Brazil as a joke." Here's a list of encouraging signs upon which President Cardoso could create a new prosperity in Brazil:

• Brazil ranks eighth in the world in total GDP, and should soon become the first South American member of the elite Group of Seven club comprised of the major industralized nations. It could soon become the "G-Eight" club.

• Brazil has finally learned how to cut inflation. It's currently running at 5 percent to 10 percent, a far cry from the 1000 percent to 2000 percent range of the past.

• The country ranks first in the world in self-sufficiency, importing only 6 percent of GDP.

• They can feed themselves! It ranks seventh in agricultural production and tenth in agriculture exports.

• The country has vast quantities of natural resources just waiting to be sold globally.

• They have no political or military enemies.

The truth is, Brazil is actually two economies in one country. The working half of the economy would look like any European country. The other half lives in abject poverty with little hope for improvement. And the working half, no matter how industrious they are, cannot produce enough to lift the other half out of poverty. This has to mean it's time to look for completely new solutions. Of course, one that comes to mind here would be to unleash Brazil's entrepreneurial power, right within the half of the country with little means and little hope. Given half a chance, several million new Brazilian micro-entrepreneurs could stand all past economic history on it's head.

But nothing fundamental and lasting will ever change if the national sense of mission becomes hostage again to the economic values and beliefs espoused over lunch. The current leaders who set the nation's economic strategy have to stay the course and bring to Brazil what JFK called a "rising tide that lifts all boats." That tide is just beginning to hit the shores of Brazil today. Let's hope it continues—and that all those talented Brazilians finally fulfill their grand national mission.

WE'RE GOING TO HEAVEN, BUT IT'S HELL GETTING THERE

If you don't believe in economic miracles, then you haven't been to the Republic of China on Taiwan—the reigning champion of national enterprise. If nothing else, Taiwan is a country with an overpowering national mission—to create prosperity for its citizens. Here are a few of its record-breaking achievements that are virtually guaranteed to not resemble absolutely nothing going on in your homeland:

- Average 9 percent GNP growth for fifty years—number one in the world.

- A seventy-fold increase in per capita GNP since 1950—tops in the world.

- $104 billion in foreign reserves, joining the United States, Japan, Germany, and China as the only countries in the world with more than $100 billion in reserves. Taiwan beats them all by a wide margin on a per capita basis.

- Average domestic inflation rate of only 2.2 percent for five decades.

- Near 100 percent revaluation of its currency over the past decade, while still increasing exports each year. Now that's hard to do!

There are fifty years of hard work, personal sacrifice, military intimidation from China, and political ostracism from the rest of the world in those numbers. Yes, Taiwan may be going to heaven, but they've truly gone through hell getting there.

Turning conventional economic theory on its head, Taiwan has long mystified international economists. Strapped with a huge twin surplus in foreign trade and dollar reserves, it should be suffering from what economists call Dutch Disease—industrial stagnation due to earning more money than you can reinvest. A country is certainly not supposed to maintain the same record-setting 9 percent GNP growth they've had for fifty years. Exactly the opposite has happened. Of course, the notion of Dutch Disease is a hard one to prove, since Taiwan is about the only country that actually has the disease!

Taiwan not only mystifies but infuriates the world's left-of-center social engineers. They keep asking when the politically incorrect Taiwanese are going to fall into the famous *Kuznet* trap, that old socioeconomic chestnut that says rapidly developing economies always produce a widening of the gap between rich and poor. Again, exactly the opposite has happened in Taiwan. The ratio of the average income of the top 20 percent of Taiwanese to the average income of the bottom 20 percent has dropped from 15:1 to less than 5:1 today. This gives Taiwan one of the most equitable distributions of income in the world. So much for modern economic theory!

As a point of interest and by comparison to Brazil, our other sense of mission example, Taiwan has a near zero rate of poverty and no foreign debt. In fact, it is one of only two countries in the world (Finland being the other) that has repaid, in full, every penny of economic aid it received from the United States. The final portion of that debt was paid off amid great fanfare in the early 1960s.

Outsiders have to remember that the mainland Nationalist Chinese had been ravaged by war with Japan from 1931 to 1945 and were then driven out of their homeland in a bloody civil war with Mao's communists, that lasted until 1950. They ended up on a mountainous island, one-tenth the size of California, with few assets and virtually no natural resources. How, then, did this small group of people, beaten and broke in 1950, accumulate a $104 billion surplus in foreign reserves by 2000? And, just to drive the point home, how can this occur in a country with almost no diplomatic recognition around the globe? To most observers, it all sounds impossible. However it sounds, the causes of Taiwan's skyrocketing prosperity since 1950, turn out to be pretty basic things—starting with the economic beliefs and strategy of the ruling elite in the government. In the following discussion, see if you detect any similarities with the ruling elite of Brazil. I doubt you will.

The top academic economist in Taiwan is Dr. Chi Hsieh. K. T. Li told me that Hsieh was "a very practical man for an economist," so I went to see him. As the chairman of the Economics Department at National Taiwan University, Hsieh gets a lot of questions from foreign countries on what they should do to create their own economic miracle. In his polite but blunt answer, he says it comes down to a matter of will more than brains: "Knowing what to do and having the will to do it are separate universes. Go back to the late forties, early fifties. Taiwan faced a very tough situation in the domestic economy, as well as a dangerous international political situation. Taiwan's economy was dominated by state enterprises inherited from the Japanese: maybe 70 percent of the economic output. But the government restrained itself to reverse the expansion of the public sector. The government privatized most of the public enterprises. To a great extent, the government encouraged the private entrepreneur. Also, the government picked a very tough way to deal with inflation. Most countries take the easy way, printing the money and behaving like really big government is really good government. Taiwan has always been very, very conservative financially. Even though the popular thing was to spend, the government did not spend. They had strong will. And up to today, they still stick to this policy.

"My theory is I don't believe anyone in the government could forecast what was going to happen from these policies. For example, no one believed Taiwan would become a big exporter. Well, maybe someone like K. T. Li believed, but most didn't. But the leaders were ready to give many things a try. And when something worked, they really pushed it. For example, when exporting began to work, the government moved in with all means to promote exports. I mean they did everything possible. Here is the key point for policy makers. You don't have to be so intelligent—a genius. You just have to be smart enough to see changes. You don't have to be brilliant, or a great man to do this. But you have to remain alert. If your policy is working, push it 100 percent. This is my theory of what our government really did.

"Of course, this requires hard work by the people. But I believe this is also economic, not just a cultural thing. It's a famous debate in the textbooks. Any country has to decide where to keep its best people. In some countries, especially in the developing world and the socialist countries, the best people went to the government. That is where they could do the most good, become famous, and so on. In Taiwan, the government never expanded the public sector. All the opportunity was in the private sector. So for the young people, the people who have the very strong desire of achievement, what you call the entrepreneurs—they will say to themselves, 'I will not join the government. I will go to the private sector.' This is just common sense.

"So the important point for all countries is you have to find a way to let the people taste the development. Participate in it. That means if they do certain things, they and their family will be better off. Government's job is to stand by and watch and try to create a lot of these kinds of opportunities for the people. It's all common sense. But as I said, the hardest part is sticking to the common sense. Maybe this has been the most important capability of Taiwan's government for fifty years—not deviating from common sense principles."

So doggedly keeping your eye on the enterprise ball does require some tradeoffs, or at least some patience. The original tradeoff that Chiang Kai-shek and his defeated government made was economic freedom for political freedom. The wide-open national elections in Taiwan, which recently (and peacefully) brought the opposition party to power for the first time, is a rather clear sign that those days are now over. The other tradeoff was in the quality-of-life area. This is a country that tops the world in foreign reserves but isn't even listed in the *Economist*'s annual rankings of the top eighty countries in the world on the Quality of Life Index. The most persistent criticism of Taiwan's government is that they haven't paid enough attention to infrastructure, social issues, and quality-of-life issues. Anyone who's suffered through a traffic jam or a typhoon in Taipei would certainly agree.

For these critics, it should be welcome news that the Taiwan government is in the midst of the largest public works program ever undertaken by a country. Taiwan has budgeted a whopping $300 billion for 779 separate projects to improve services throughout the country. Few countries in the world could afford this, but, naturally, Taiwan can. Perhaps Taiwan's robust democracy and its current attention to quality-of-life issues are just more examples of K. T. Li's belief in "the right policy at the right time!"

Taiwan and Brazil are both great countries, but for very different reasons. I'm sure you get the picture, even from these sketchy illustrations. Such enormous differences really come from the differences in the national sense of mission being promoted by each country's leadership. This reveals itself in both the country's economic strategy and its operating culture. In the examples of Brazil and Taiwan, it is clear that both countries are trying hard to improve areas of their national mission they have neglected in the past. This is good news for their people.

And what about the people of your state or region? What will it take to create an entrepreneurial economy in your own backyard? We'll end with a close-up view of one man's mission of creating an entrepreneurial economy—in the beautiful, bluegrass state of Kentucky. This is the story of Kris Kimel, good friend and amazing guy, who has been mining this field for fifteen years—and just hit the mother lode.

STATES: KENTUCKY'S ENTREPRENEURIAL CONSCIENCE

> *We're pleased and proud of the fact that creating an entrepreneurial economy has become . . . a part of public policy in Kentucky.*
>
> —Kris Kimel
> President, Kentucky Science
> and Technology Corporation

"Basically, in our work at the Kentucky Science and Technology Corporation (KSTC), it became evident that the key for development for communities and states and regions in today's world was really contingent upon their ability to grow and expand new knowledge-driven companies. That came, certainly, from looking at the literature and the research, as well as our own experience and the work that we had accomplished. It was in a sense an emerging thing that came out of ten to fifteen years of work within KSTC.

"It was based on what we saw happening globally. And, specifically in Kentucky, despite progress over the prior decade or so, we found ourselves still lagging behind many states in such critical areas as new firm creation, research and development, availability of risk capital, and so on. And given our belief that the key to developing this region was contingent upon creating what we termed the entrepreneurial economy, that having weaknesses in those critical areas—at least in our minds—created a greater sense of urgency to do something."

This is Kris Kimel, or as we like to call him, the state of Kentucky's "entrepreneurial conscience." How does one get into this line of work anyway? What's the prerequisite for leading a campaign to create an entrepreneurial economy in a state? In Kimel's case, it began with a couple of senior-level government appointments when he was quite young. Here's Kimel again: "Well, first I was the executive assistant to the Kentucky attorney general for eight years, but it really started when I became the chief of staff for the lieutenant governor of Kentucky starting in 1983. It was in that capacity that I became very interested in the whole issue of technology policy, entrepreneurship, and the innovation of those things in creating economic growth. Then I started the Kentucky Science and Technology Corporation in late 1987. So you could say I've been at it, seriously at it, since 1983."

From my own experience, there is no more knowledgeable person on this subject than Kris Kimel. A few years back, when I first met him, he was already several years into his crusade, which he called "Kentucky, Inc.—Creating an Entrepreneurial Economy." And he's at his entrepreneurial best when he delivers his compelling argument for doing just that in the Bluegrass State. According to KSTC's research, Kentucky had (and still has in many areas) severe shortcomings in key entrepreneurial indices. For example, among all fifty states of the United States, Kentucky's rank in a few key indices is:

Key indice	*Rank*
• World Wide Web hosts per 1,000 persons	50th
• Percentage of adults with high school degrees.	50th
• Percentage of adults with university degrees	46th
• Start-up "incubators" per million population	43rd
• New firm creation.	42nd
• Equity capital available.	40th
• Industry R&D investment	40th

Given these dismal entrepreneurial indicators, I asked Kimel to say a word or two about the general economic strategy and culture of Kentucky. What would creating an entrepreneurial economy do to enhance that strategy, which run of the mill economic development might not do? I think he had been asked this question a thousand times. His finely tuned answer: "Well, historically, Kentucky's economy has been, like a lot of states, based on plentiful and fairly inexpensive natural resources and labor. In our case, it was agriculture and tobacco. Over the past several decades, we've seen a profound shift away from those types of things. Kentucky then developed a reliance on larger industries and outside industries. As a consequence, there has been a lack of emphasis on entrepreneurship and creating companies. Of course, one could argue that farmers are one of the earliest entrepreneurial groups. But by and large there has been an overdependence on larger and outside companies as opposed to creating knowledge and wealth within the state. That has made the challenge a bit more difficult. Kentucky has certainly benefited from the relocation of some very good manufacturing plants into the state. The big Toyota plant, for example, is a very nice thing to have, but it's not a long-term solution to economic development in Kentucky. They could be gone tomorrow. So what we have to do in Kentucky, as do all states, is to focus more on creating our own knowledge and our own expertise and our own value, because that's where the real payoff comes from—those kinds of companies and those kinds of long-term, well-paying jobs."

I asked Kimel what kinds of specific activities KSTC has undertaken to create an entrepreneurial economy. His response: "We have focused our attention in a fairly systematic way. We focused both in the areas of education and also economic development and competitive economy issues. We've done a number of things. We produce and issue an entrepreneurial capacity report. We issued our third report in 1999. We have developed and implemented initiatives to help companies develop and grow. We do an annual entrepreneurship and commercialization institute in Kentucky, again geared toward the start-up and growing of knowledge and technology companies. We've also created a program aimed at college and university students. It's basically a Web-driven program to provide information and advice to students who have an interest in starting companies. We run a monthly competition with those students—in which we hold a business idea competition and award $1,000 every month to students who win based on their business idea and plans. The winner can be one student or a group of students. We're also involved in helping to expand the research and development capacity of the state. We believe that a lot of the energy for creating these new companies is going to come from universities.

So we have really a variety of things that we're currently involved in: both helping to educate people about entrepreneurship as well as helping people to actually start and grow companies."

Kris Kimel knows the political and governmental landscape in Kentucky very well. That's surely been a factor in KSTC's success, and it offers a lesson for others trying to refocus a statewide economy. Anyway, I wanted to ask him his views on the proper role of government in this whole process. His answer: "Well, the government has an important role. I think the government's role is to help create the conditions under which this type of economy can thrive and grow. I don't think it's necessarily in managing programs or those types of things. It's more in terms of creating conditions. For example, looking at different kinds of incentives that the public sector might offer to encourage high-growth technology companies. Or possibly making some capital available in the precompetitive phase of entrepreneurial development—like in the early R&D areas that some governments do now. Perhaps some very, very early-stage, pre-seed capital that might be made available to help stimulate growth. But, again, it's primarily in helping to create the elements for these companies to succeed and grow. To help create the environment in which this can happen as opposed to directly involving themselves in trying to manage actual programs. You have to be very careful in having public organizations getting too involved—because they respond to a very different set of conditions. We just don't want or need government getting involved in making business decisions. On the other hand, making public officials aware of the real meaning of entrepreneurship, what it really represents, and that it goes beyond just someone starting a company—all these are terribly important."

Touché! And to cap it off, I wanted to hear specifically what advice Kris Kimel might give others who wanted to create a more entrepreneurial economy in their own states. So I asked him what tips he would offer to an economic development team from, say, Maine or Oregon or Puerto Rico. These economic development officials might say to him, "Look, we've heard you've been doing this for a decade or so in Kentucky. We're ready to do the same in our own state. What advice can you give us to raise our chances of being successful?" Kris thought for a moment, shifting a bit perhaps into more of an official "advisory mode" and responded with several important points:

• "First, we've learned that creating an entrepreneurial economy is as much about changing the culture as it is about influencing some of the economic institutions and factors in a state. Changing that culture is somewhat of a slow process but it doesn't have to take forever. We tried to walk the walk in the sense that we tried ourselves to be entrepreneurial in creating the type of programs and initiatives that we thought could jump-start this. I've also talked again and again to everybody in the state about the three or four things that characterize an entrepreneurial economy. One is knowledge. Entrepreneurial organizations recognize the value of knowledge and are driven by knowledge. The second is to be highly innovative. Certainly coming from your first book, I know you agree that relentless innovation is a big part of it. And third, is to be fast. To understand the importance of velocity, and speed, and moving quickly.

• "Second, as we recognized that these things are vital in an entrepreneurial company or economy, we certainly tried to behave that way ourselves. So we were, I think, somewhat aggressive. We worked with people where we could, but certainly we were fairly aggressive in trying to stimulate and work with other partners to get as many things going as we possibly could. We also recognized that this wasn't going to happen in a linear way. That's why we tried to get as many things going as we could, recognizing that some would succeed and some would fail and that we wouldn't know where the successes were going to come from at the beginning. It was always very important to us to get as many things going as we could and that has been our driving philosophy.

• "In addition, I think another key strategy for any state or region wanting to foster this kind of economy is addressing the issue of risk capital. And I mean at all stages—in everything from research and development, to pre-seed, through early-stage venture, and mezzanine financing. And this requires some working together between the public and private sector. The public sector has a role in the very, very early stage of development, where the commercial marketplace probably isn't going to be particularly interested because of the risk involved. And then as you move down the entrepreneurial pipeline, the private sector has to step up to create angel networks, venture funds, early stage funds, etc., that are going to provide the different stages of capital that new and growing companies need. This has certainly has been one of the bigger problems historically in states like Kentucky, where we have not had that kind of strong, indigenous risk-capital industry. And while it is now starting to emerge, we have found ourselves, in many respects, playing catch-up because we haven't had a venture-capital industry. In a sense, that's the thing, not the only thing, but risk capital is certainly a major part of the fuel that drives the development of these kinds of companies.

- "At the Kentucky Science and Technology Corporation, we crafted our own definition of entrepreneurship to try to illustrate it to public officials. Our working definition is 'the unrestrained pursuit of new ideas resulting in an innovative creation.' From that definition, you can draw several key points. One is that while entrepreneurs are certainly cognizant of the barriers and the problems that exist, they aren't constrained by them. They're not letting those things discourage them at the beginning. Another key point is that an entrepreneur or an entrepreneurial organization is not only searching for new ideas, but they are also creating something. It could be adding value to an existing process or the creation of a whole new company. The important part of the definition is they're actually *creating something!* You know, you can be creative and not create anything. But we stress to everyone, especially in the public sector, that the definition doesn't only apply to people creating new companies. Creating an entrepreneurial economy is about all of the institutions and all of the companies in an economy, coming together and striving to become entrepreneurial in their operations."

- "Also I think you have to bring people together—and you've all got to be relentless in coming up with ideas and ways of implementing strategies that can lead toward the creation of this kind of economy. Perhaps the key thing, as part of the definition, is that you've got to move fast. We have found that there's not much time to think about these things. You have to act and be prepared to adjust as you go along. As someone once said, you have to be willing to jump off the building and grow your wings on the way down. Obviously, it's not about having everything figured out up front at the beginning. So I think really it's certainly being clear in what you're trying to accomplish, being very strategic, acting quickly, and doing as many things as you can and recognizing this is not a linear process. This is not A plus B equals C. And if you move along in a very linear process, you're still going to be doing it thirty years from now, while everybody's kind of passed you by."

- "A final important point is that, as you know, KSTC is an independent, nonprofit company. We work very closely with government, but we're not part of government. I think that's been an advantage. It gives us a lot more flexibility not only to do things, but it gives us more flexibility to make mistakes. And we've certainly made our share of mistakes. But learning from those mistakes, and not being afraid of making mistakes, I think, has aided us a great deal in helping to accomplish what we set out to do."

I asked Kris, "What's the payoff at the end of the day. Has this kind of effort had a real effect on Kentucky? Is it worth all the effort or not?" He didn't hesitate for a second: "The payoff, at least for us, has been in seeing people begin to appreciate the value of ideas, begin to appreciate the value of relentless innovation, and appreciate the integration of those factors and how they interact to create an entrepreneurial environment and culture. In Kentucky we're seeing a real spurt in activity in terms of the start-up of new companies. We're also seeing a lot of very dynamic entrepreneurs beginning to take root. We see the school systems begin to look at it, understand the value of entrepreneurship not only in the education of kids, but also in terms of how they themselves operate. Of course, it hasn't happened overnight.

"One of the things that we worked hardest at, and we are really pleased with, is that the Kentucky Legislature, during its just-completed 2000 session, passed the first comprehensive Science and Technology package in the state's history. That package includes funds to help stimulate and invest in precompetitive research and development, both at universities and among private companies. I think that one of the big outcomes that we've seen was the passing of that bill, House Bill 572. That came out of, in large part, the *Kentucky Science and Technology Strategy* that KSTC developed and released in the fall of 1999. Governor Patton asked us to put together a science and technology strategy for the state, which is heavily based on the whole issue of creating an entrepreneurial economy. In fact, the legislation actually makes reference to the importance of creating an entrepreneurial economy right in the preamble. We were very proud of that because what that signifies, in addition to the specific measures that are in the bill, is a statement of public policy: 'It's in the state's interest to create an entrepreneurial economy'—and that was something we had been working on for some time. We're pleased and proud of the fact that creating an entrepreneurial economy has become, with the passage of this bill, a part of public policy in Kentucky."

15 What's Really Required to Create an Entrepreneurial Economy

We spent fifty-one years under Soviet communism. All the theories from Western economists and management experts confuse us. But when Larry Farrell describes it, even former communists can understand what it takes to actually create enterprise.

—TOMAS SILDMAE
MINISTER OF ECONOMY, REPUBLIC OF ESTONIA

I'm not tooting my own horn—well, maybe just a bit. But Minister Sildmae's comment was actually aimed at a very serious problem. The very young Tomas Sildmae, minister of economy for the newly independent Republic of Estonia, was using our simple definition of entrepreneurship to promote his economic development program. His dream was to foster a full-blown entrepreneurial economy in post-Soviet Estonia. But along the way, he was getting a lot of free, and confusing, advice from Western "experts." It seems that in the euphoria of the collapse of communism, New York and London bankers, Harvard and Cambridge economists, and legions of IMF bureaucrats were crawling all over Eastern Europe offering their "help" in the restructuring of the economies. Sildmae told me he appreciated the attention but the expert advice was mostly unusable: "Our problems are very, very basic—like getting old KGB agents out of the state-owned monopolies and encouraging young entrepreneurs to start new enterprises to compete with them. But the advice I'm getting is about global banking systems and economic forecasting models. I don't understand them and I can't use them."

No one is arguing that all challenges have simple solutions. But creating an entrepreneurial economy is one that does. For several years, we've been urging our government clients to "dumb down" their notions of what it takes to create entrepreneurs—and an entrepreneurial economy. Our message is simple: Forget all the aptitude and psychological testing nonsense, the seminars on how to write a business plan, and most assuredly, don't have people waste two years getting an MBA. What's really required is putting in place a few key fundamentals. Here they are—adapted to include the unique role that government should play.

THE THREE REQUIREMENTS: THE *NEW YORK TIMES* GETS IT

It's an odd feeling when something you've been preaching for years shows up as a revolutionary insight on the editorial pages of the *New York Times*. I didn't know whether to feel proud, vindicated, or ticked off. So I settled for putting it in this book as a form of blue-chip endorsement.

In early 1998, an op-ed piece by *Times* columnist Flora Lewis was headlined, "For Europe's Jobless, Self-Employment Might Work." Now this is the same *New York Times* that editorially has never seen a welfare program it didn't like. So when even the *Times* starts pushing entrepreneurship as the way to solve chronic unemployment, we have to believe we're on to something anyone could agree with. Lewis was writing about Europe, where the seemingly permanent unemployment rate hovers in the 10–20 percent range. She hits the nail on the head with the assertion that Europe's answer to unemployment has been generous benefits, followed by a lot of hoping and praying that someday more jobs will be created. She argues: "The new economic revolution reopens the question. Big factories and offices are laying off workers, but the possibilities for self-employment have been little explored. The assumption is that someone must hire you." Bravo!

Now here's where it gets interesting. The column goes on to suggest that there are three requirements to transform Europe's unemployed welfare recipients into self-employed entrepreneurs. The requirements are:

- Micro Credit: "The magic breakthrough tool is credit—microcredit—at commercial rates but without the commercial requirements of collateral or existing earnings."

- Advice on How to Do Business: "the provision of advice on how to do business, set prices, and so on."

- Reform the Regulatory Environment: "an important reform of the huge jumble of regulations, licenses, permits, and so on that countries impose on new small businesses."

There you have it—the *New York Times* version of "a bit of money, a bit of knowledge, and an entrepreneur-friendly culture." They sound familiar, don't they? Let's explore now what countries, states, and cities can do to make sure that the three requirements are not only met, but that they are *proactively* fostering a more entrepreneurial economy.

A BIT OF MONEY

We created a venture capital fund which is almost unheard of for a city.

—CHARLES MILLARD
FORMER PRESIDENT,
ECONOMIC DEVELOPMENT CORPORATION,
NEW YORK CITY

If your government leaders don't realize that funding entrepreneurship is a bargain compared to funding welfare, you might want to find out what planet they've been on for the past fifty years. Governments are embracing this new use of taxpayers' money for one very simple reason: They like the numbers. When they see that the average cost of starting a business is less than a year of welfare or a year at Harvard (or two years at their own state universities) or a year in prison, most government officials get very interested. You'll recall the numbers:

- Average start-up cost: $14,000
- A year on welfare: $17,500
- A year at Harvard: $25,000
- A year in prison: $30,000

So the first way to provide that "bit of money" the entrepreneurs need could be in the form of funding new solutions for some old social problems. Becoming self-employed entrepreneurs is the best hope for unemployed welfare recipients, downsized skilled workers, refugees and immigrants, and even some young criminals. Starting microcompanies is the best strategy for getting all these people off the public dole and enabling them to become positive contributors to the economy. Microcredits or microgrants to such people is an idea whose time has come in public policy circles. This financial assistance should probably be labeled a "long-term investment," given the enormous economic advantages of creating a business—even a very small one—compared to welfare and prison. Do the numbers and you'll agree. There really is no comparison in terms of job creation, tax payments generated, and the general prosperity of the neighborhood where the business is located.

For politicians, there's an added plus. This is an ideology-free idea—at least so far. The idea that it's better to help people start their own small business than give them food stamps forever is so compelling it has attracted political leaders from both the right and the left.

Second, more mainline entrepreneurial financing could and should be made available from the government. As all first-time entrepreneurs know, you don't have to be on welfare or a convicted felon to have problems getting start-up financing. That's why the U.S. Small Business Administration, established in 1953, is one of the most important economic tools of the American government today. It provides financial, technical, and management assistance to help Americans start, run, and grow their businesses. With a portfolio of business loans and loan guarantees worth more than $45 billion, the SBA is by far the nation's largest financial backer of small businesses. Last year, the SBA also offered management and technical assistance to more than one million small business owners. These are big, impressive numbers, and every country should have a well-funded SBA equivalent.

And as you'll see in the upcoming interview with Charles Millard on New York City's Silicon Alley, the SBA doesn't just *loan* money. The agency also *invests* it as venture capital. Millard initiated the concept of government-backed venture capital with the Discovery Fund in New York City, and helped create an economic miracle. If your country, state, or city is trying to develop a more entrepreneurial economy, but offers no help in start-up financing—loans, venture capital, whatever—you're fighting this battle with one arm tied behind your back.

And, finally, do the entrepreneurs in your area have access to the private venture capital industry? If not, your economic development team isn't doing its job. This is absolutely essential, and easy to do. Creating strong links to centers of venture capital should be a top priority for every economic development agency in the world. And your would-be entrepreneurs need to know how to attract venture capital and the kind of risk assessment all VC firms will put them through. For example, here are the four fundamental risks that John Doerr, the king of Silicon Valley venture capitalists, says he always looks at:

- People Risk: Will the founders stay or move on?
- Market Risk: Will the "dogs eat the dog food"?
- Technical Risk: Can the product be made?
- Financial Risk: Can capital be raised again, if needed?

In the larger scheme of things, why should government be fostering a more entrepreneurial economy? This was virtually unheard of when K. T. Li arrived on Taiwan in 1949 and started it all. But today, government leaders from Singapore to Northern Ireland to Kentucky to New York City are doing just that. Why the surging interest in using entrepreneurship as an economic development tool? What are these governments hoping to achieve? It's pretty simple. Creating entrepreneurs looks like the fastest, cheapest, and surest way to create a lot of new jobs, raise national prosperity, and ultimately win a fair share of the global, economic pie. As Nora Wang once told me, when she was still New York City's commissioner of employment: "If we can create one entrepreneur, he—or she—will create ten more jobs. The city will never get a better return on the dollar than that."

Speaking of returns, no example better illustrates the power of providing "a bit of money" to entrepreneurs than Silicon Valley. The venture capital industry started there thirty years ago. It consisted of a small group of individuals who were investing in companies that were destined to become household names, such as Intel, Apple, and Sun Microsystems. Since those early days, an amazing $15 billion of venture capital has been invested in some 2,700 start-up companies by more than 300 venture capital firms in and around Silicon Valley. There is no question, however, that this phenomenon was supported, if not created, by the great research universities in the area. Stanford, Berkeley, UC San Francisco (for biotech), Cal Tech, and the like, all provided the talent and breakthrough ideas the VC people were looking for. Which leads us to the next requirement—a bit of knowledge.

A Bit of Knowledge

We believe that a lot of the energy for creating these new companies is going to come from universities.

—Kris Kimel
President, Kentucky Science
and Technology Corporation

Are you producing the highest-skilled, most competitive workers in the world? Are your citizens, and especially your young people, receiving the very best in academic and technical education? Are you providing post-graduate research and education opportunities targeted to the high-growth markets of the twenty-first century?

Believe it or not, your answers to these questions will define your place in the world for the next fifty to one hundred years. This is not about who's going to be homecoming queen or which fraternity to join or who's bringing the beer for the big college football game this weekend. We're talking about the single most strategic thing you and your country can do right now to ensure that your grandchildren will live in a "healthy, wealthy, and wise" society. Our bias is that the best road to travel to reach that best-of-all-possible places, is one that makes plenty of room for a creative, competitive, and entrepreneurially driven economy.

There are two classes of knowledge essential to the creation of an entrepreneurial economy:

The first and, frankly, the most important thing is knowing how to create and make things the world needs. On this score, you can be sure that Kris Kimel is not talking about the business schools of the world when he says universities will have a huge impact on the creation of new companies. He's talking about the commercialization of breakthrough research and fresh ideas that will come out of all sorts of university laboratories and disciplines. He means the creation of new technologies and new products that will enhance and reshape the way we work and live.

This class of knowledge, in fact, has to lead countries and regions into their place in the Entrepreneurial Age. It can't be the other way around. This means (hopefully) no more National Industrial Plans that produced such colossal losers as steel mills in Saudi Arabia, airplane manufacturing in China, and computers in France. Creating businesses based on the interests and knowledge of a country's entrepreneurs has always been the best way to create national competitive advantage. This down-home method of establishing your *country strategy* surely flies in the face of the kind of careful analysis done by the "experts" (Harvard's Michael Porter and MIT's Lester Thurow come to mind), but let's look at the facts. Why is Finland number one in mobile phones or India so important in software or, to take a really offbeat example, why is Nashville, Tennessee, the number-one city in the world for writing and producing music? None of these success stories are due to sophisticated economic development studies by consultants or government planners. They were all, of course, based on the interests, skills, and knowledge of the people there. The second class of knowledge is knowing the basics of creating, growing, and maintaining the entrepreneurial companies that have to bring those new technologies and new products to the marketplaces of the world. In this class of knowledge, we've presented in this book what we believe are the time-tested fundamentals: having a powerful sense of mission, maintaining absolute focus on customers and products, practicing high-speed innovation, and fostering self-inspired managers and workers. Of course, there is a lot of other very useful business knowledge you can obtain, but neglecting these basics is a recipe for disaster. At the government level, we've seen a tremendous awakening of interest in the notion that government itself should be more entrepreneurial in the way it conducts its business—and that it could use entrepreneurial development as a major economic development tool. A sampling of governments around the world that have used our own entrepreneurship training is the best illustration I can give of how widespread this phenomenon has become.

- Asia: Malaysia/Singapore

- Europe: Estonia/Northern Ireland

- North America: Kentucky/New York City

- South America: Brazil/Uruguay

- Africa: South Africa

- United Nations: Secretariat for Enterprise Development

From advising government ministers and their staffs on developing an entrepreneurial economy at one end of the spectrum to training unemployed welfare recipients to become micro-entrepreneurs at the other, this certainly appears to be an idea that the world is ready to embrace. And what we've seen firsthand has to be just the tip of the iceberg.

I must offer one caveat to this proposition, however. It seems that once you get started down the "Let's develop some entrepreneurs" track, the possibilities are endless. A case in point: Dr. Clark Abt, the brilliant founder and chairman of Abt Associates, the largest social research think tank in the United States, with a staff of 1,100, has boundless enthusiasm for new ideas. I met Abt at the Economic Development Society's annual conference in Boston a couple of years ago. He became very excited about the possibilities for entrepreneurial development. He immediately proposed that we join forces to give entrepreneurship training to convicted drug dealers. In our next conversation, he wanted to make entrepreneurs out of unwed teenage mothers. Then it was school children in the ghettoes. And so on. Entrepreneurship is a great thing, but even I don't think it can solve every problem facing humankind!

Finally, what *are* your answers to the opening question? Do you have a country or region strategy to provide those "bits of knowledge" your entrepreneurs will need? However you answer, the following summary points should help you devise an entrepreneurial "knowledge strategy" for the twenty-first century.

The essential idea is that to be a successful entrepreneur, you must "get very good at something." We are talking about producing "experts," not graduates who can add a column of figures and write a coherent sentence. The education establishment, from vocational high schools to graduate universities, should be absolutely focused on enabling your people to make products and provide services that the rest of the world wants and will pay for.

Learning how to be a successful entrepreneur does not require a business school degree, period! In most cases it will just slow the process down. There's nothing wrong with having a few business schools around to educate managers, but that has nothing to do with creating entrepreneurs and entrepreneurial economies.

The competitive differences among countries, which are enormous, are being largely driven by shocking disparities in basic knowledge around the world. They range from a medieval 13 percent adult literacy rate in the central African country of Niger, to the United States where an amazing 81 percent of high school graduates are involved in some form of higher education. And the so-called "digital divide" is making things worse. While countries like the United States, Singapore, and Finland now have "two- and three-computer families," in war-torn Afghanistan only one of every four children will ever see the inside of a schoolroom. These disparities don't make for minor differences in a country's competitiveness. The acquisition of knowledge is the first line of battle in the global economic war. If you can't survive that battle, you've already lost the war.

It's one thing to create the best workers in the world. It's quite another to keep them in your own country or your own community. This phenomenon is called *brain drain*. According to The *Economist,* the top five countries for retention of highly educated people are the United States, the Netherlands, Chile (South America's bright star again!), Germany, and Japan. The bottom of the barrel: Russia, South Africa, India, Philippines, and Sweden—the only "rich" country in the bottom rankings. Of course, Sweden also has the highest rate of income taxes in the world. Talk about the hidden costs of overtaxing your most valuable asset—your educated people and your future entrepreneurs!

AN ENTREPRENEUR-FRIENDLY CULTURE

In the early years, believe it or not, it was government entre-
preneurship that built this country.

—KOH BOON HWEE
CHAIRMAN, SINGAPORE TELECOM

"Well, I'm the chairman of the board of Singapore Telecom—of course, we have a CEO and president running the company day to day. I'm also the executive chairman for Wuthelam Holdings, which is my full-time job. I'm on the board of some other companies such as Acer, the computer company from Taiwan, Excel which is a small technology company that just went public on the Singapore stock exchange, a medical group here called Raffles Holdings, and so on. I try to stay busy."

This is Koh Boon Hwee, manager, entrepreneur, overseer of government assets, and all-around wunderkind of Singapore. Koh got his MBA at Harvard and returned home to join Hewlett-Packard, perhaps the most respected multinational corporation (MNC) in Singapore. He worked his way up at HP, including spending two years at Hewlett-Packard headquarters in Palo Alto, California. Koh became Managing Director of HP Singapore at the young age of thirty-four. Six years later, and with nowhere else to go in the local HP operations, he was faced with leaving Singapore to move more or less permanently to the United States if he was going to continue his career with the company. He chose to stay in Singapore and took a huge entrepreneurial leap to become the CEO of a Chinese family-owned business, Wuthelam Holdings. While he was still at HP, the government asked him to be the chairman of the board of Singapore Telecom, the country's biggest company and a premier example of a Singapore company becoming a global player in the twenty-first century. On top of all this, he's a really nice person and an absolute delight to talk to, as I learned during a long interview in Singapore. Of all the people I've met in Singapore over the past twenty years, I don't think anyone has a better grasp of the economic landscape of this prosperous island nation. Koh knows it from all sides—the big MNCs like Hewlett-Packard, the entrepreneurial Chinese companies like Wuthelam Holdings, and the government's deep involvement in the economy through its holdings in large companies like Singapore Telecom. I think you will agree that he has a pretty good handle on what it takes to create an entrepreneur-friendly culture in Singapore.

The Role of the Multinational Corporation

I began the interview with Koh's background in mind: "I understand the thing you were most recognized for doing at Hewlett-Packard Singapore was to move from a third world kind of manufacturing facility to a full-blown business. And that HP was the first MNC in Singapore to do that. Is that right?" He answered: "Yes, and today the HP operations in Singapore have their own worldwide product line charters—for products such as keyboards, inkjet printers, and so on. Which means they are complete businesses, from research and development to product development, to manufacturing, to the marketing and sales of those products worldwide. Our original charter was to be a low-cost manufacturing center. So why did I embark on these things? I think my colleagues and I, at that time, did not believe that our level of intelligence was limited to just manufacturing. It was, in a sense, trying to prove that we were capable of more value-added work for the organization, which was important to us. After a time, I suppose like Maslow's hierarchy, there was a self-actualization that went beyond what we were doing and how much we were being paid by HP to do the job. A few other MNCs have done this also, but I believe HP was at the forefront. Today you've got good local product development programs at Motorola, Compaq, Apple, but I think they were probably a few years behind Hewlett-Packard.

"Anyway, my next move with Hewlett-Packard would have been back to our headquarters in the United States. That is a difficult decision. Unlike the first transfer, that would have been, in a sense, permanent because there would be no job back in Singapore at that level for me to return to. And by that time, Asia was really opening up. You could see the opening in China. I was on the board of Hewlett-Packard China to help them because the strongest manufacturing entity for HP in Asia at that time was clearly Singapore. China was opening up. You could see even countries like Malaysia and Thailand beginning to take off. Singapore itself was coming into its own in terms of doing product development and higher value-added stuff with a lot of new technology investments coming in. It was a very, very tough decision but I decided I was going to stay and participate in Asia's growth."

The Role of the Local Entrepreneurial Company

"I had always thought of myself as a professional manager so I initially considered offers from some other multinational electronics companies. That seemed like a very comfortable thing to do, given my background. Actually, it was my wife who made the critical comment one day as we were discussing this. It was sort of a flippant comment, but she said, 'Well that's sort of the easy way, but three years down the road you'll have the same problem.' That really set me thinking. And by coincidence a banker friend asked if I would consider working for a Chinese family company. At the time, my response to him was, 'Over my dead body!' My impression of those companies was that they were kind of chaotic, with lots of politics from family members, and no systems, etc. But he persuaded me at least to meet with the owners of the Wuthelam Group and I did. After some discussion and recognizing there weren't a lot of family members in the business, I decided to make a 180-degree change."

I stopped Koh at that point to ask what would seem to be a very important question for countries trying to move from poverty to wealth. I asked him, "Since you've had experience in both kinds of operations, what are the pluses and minuses of each for creating economic growth and prosperity as Singapore has done? Is one more important than the other? Does the economy need both? If you were constructing a country's economy, would you want all HPs, or would you want all Wuthelams, or would you want a combination?"

Koh Boon Hwee's frank reply: "My view on that is all countries need a combination of both. A balance. First of all, I should start off by saying that in my view not all multinationals are the same. In fact, if you look at it, there are at least two classes of multinationals. If you look at companies like Hewlett-Packard and Compaq, they come to Singapore and I firmly believe they have a genuine and long-term commitment. They continue to develop their people; as the country progresses, the level of their value-added activities increases; they move from manufacturing to product development to becoming marketing and distribution centers, and so on and so forth. This is a class of MNC that I think all countries should want to attract—because they have a deep commitment.

"But, to be frank, the commitment of the majority is a question mark. They are here for low labor costs. As those labor costs and wages increase, they move around the world chasing labor costs. They keep all of the technology, the value-added, the skill-enhancing kind of opportunities, in their home countries. Regrettably, I think the majority tend to be this way. And I think those are the ones that any country has to be wary of. They're not going to be around in a crunch. In a crunch, you have to have a ballast in the economy and that's got to be your own national companies.

"So why not *always* favor your own companies? The reason is because you have to be exposed to the outside world in terms of technology. These companies bring superior levels of technology, new ideas in how things are managed, and impose a level of competition that enhances the overall capabilities in the country over time. If you have a closed market, where entry or competition from the outside world is restricted, you will not be better off in the long run. The level of competition will be less intense, and that doesn't really spur your domestic companies to achieve what they really need to do to be competitive worldwide.

"It has to be balanced—but most countries really do need to pay a lot more attention to developing their domestic companies into, hopefully, world-class competitors. The reason I think that is important is with an increasingly open attitude around the world, the best people in any country are moved out of the country into the headquarters or foreign operations of the multinational companies. If the economy is overly dependent on MNCs, then over time the country suffers enormous brain drain. Your most talented people will be out of the country."

While Koh took a pause, I said: "You mentioned 'world class,' which brings up another important point, especially in Asia. The popular image of the Chinese is that they're very entrepreneurial—and they'll start a thousand small companies. But they may not grow large. You know the Chinese slogan: 'When you run out of relatives, close the business!' Will there be a Chinese IBM in the future or will the economies of Hong Kong, Taiwan, Singapore, and even the mainland, be driven mostly by small, family-owned businesses? In Asia, will the Japanese have all the big companies, while the Chinese create 10,000 small companies?"

Koh's response: "Great question, Larry. I think there's a tremendous propensity for that to happen. It is a very strong incentive for the Chinese to be your own boss. And there are many people who are much happier being their own boss of a small enterprise than being an employee in a large enterprise. Now, whether in the long run they will build an IBM, I don't know. I think the jury is still out. Obviously, they have been able to build some large enterprises, perhaps not the size of General Motors and IBM, but in many cases these enterprises have to make a difficult transition— from being family controlled and run by trusted relatives to so-called outside, professional management, as in my case at Wuthelam. This is simply because, if they want to continue to grow they *will*, as you say, run out of relatives.

"But if you look at the overwhelming trend toward a service economy, or an information-intensive economy, then I think, in the future, size and economies of scale and scope will not be so important. Look, for example, at the new industries, like the Internet or whatever. They don't take humongous capital to start up. Frankly, the principal assets are the human beings who walk in and out of the offices every day and the value of an idea is much more important than the value of fixed assets. Therefore, you can have an economy of small companies that can be successful. It is possible. Of course, our manufacturing industries aren't going to go away and in those, scale and scope are still going to be important."

At that point, I asked Koh the bottom-line question for Singapore, or any country trying to raise its national prosperity on the wings of the entrepreneurial spirit: "What should the role of the government be in fostering a high-growth, highly entrepreneurial economy? What, in fact, can the government do to mold an entrepreneur-friendly culture and, ultimately, create an entrepreneurial economy?"

THE ROLE OF THE GOVERNMENT

Here is Koh again, starting with a little background on "Singapore, Inc.": "The Singapore government has played a unique role in the development of our country. In the early years, believe it or not, it was government entrepreneurship that built this country. They took entrepreneurial risk with Singapore Airlines and Neptune Shipping Lines, and they initiated the shipyards that have become a very important industry in Singapore. Government was *the* entrepreneur in the mid-1960s when we became independent. At that point, the country was relatively poor and there just wasn't enough private-sector capital to embark on these kinds of projects. But it has always been the government policy that on the boards of these government enterprises, there would be a combination of government civil servants and also private-sector people. So in 1986, when I was still the managing director of Hewlett-Packard, the government asked me to become the chairman of the board of Singapore Telecom., which I did. Shortly after I came on the board, it was decided to privatize SingTel, so we turned it into a corporation and floated SingTel on the stock exchange of Singapore. The offering was oversubscribed. I should add, however, that the government still owns a very large share of the stock. So all these things have been coming and going, and I've been here watching SingTel go through these change processes."

Since this interview, the telecommunications market in Singapore has been completely deregulated. For the first time, international competitors such as British Telecom and AT&T will be entering the market. I happened to be giving a talk at Singapore Telecom on April 1, 2000, the very day the market was officially deregulated. I remember it clearly because my presentation was interrupted by the president of SingTel (not Koh, who is chairman) giving a pep talk over the intercom to the employees. He was urging them not to be afraid of deregulation, but rather to embrace it, since it was good for the country, the company, and the employees to have to compete at a world-class level.

I brought up to Koh the point that the Singapore government talks a lot these days about the need for entrepreneurs. The government seems very concerned that Singaporeans have become risk averse and complacent. I asked him, "What is your take on that current line by the government? Do you agree? And if you do what should the government do about it?" Koh's reply was very direct: "Well, I think the government's recognition that more entrepreneurship is needed for the continued development of the economy is a good thing. I firmly believe in that. If you look at the strength of the United States, for example, there was a period not long ago when everyone was throwing stones at the U.S. because it looked as though all of its companies were in trouble, they were all going to get defeated by Japan, and so on and so forth. I never believed that, not because I worked for Hewlett-Packard, but because I think the spirit of entrepreneurship and the willingness in the United States to dump old systems that don't work in favor of new ones that do, was very strong. It is both an economy that is creative in terms of new products and new ideas, as well as innovative, meaning the willingness to change what currently doesn't work for something that does. And I think those kind of skills are very important, especially for a country like Singapore, which is small in terms of its domestic market. Small countries can't use their domestic markets as levers. For economic development then, your relevance in this part of the world depends on whether you are more creative and more innovative. That means—whether in terms of products, or processes, or systems—you're always a step ahead. And I think that is where the entrepreneurs play the biggest role."

I asked Koh if he was saying that Singapore needed to do more in this area. "Absolutely yes," he answered. "There has to be greater willingness here to take risks. Society as a whole has to take a look at entrepreneurs and recognize that some will fail and that failure is not a stigma, that it is basically a lesson learned and you start again. As you know, its very normal in Silicon Valley for somebody to have an idea, get venture capital backing, and then fail. But if he comes up with another idea, it is usually possible to get financing again. Because the perception is: 'OK, it's not because he was dishonest. It was a genuine attempt but it didn't work. The guy has learned something from it. He deserves another chance.' Singapore needs to take on more of that kind of an attitude.

"The government is trying to do more to help the local enterprises to come up to speed, to regionalize their activities, and this requires some entrepreneurship, some level of risk taking. It also requires a willingness in Singaporeans to go live and work in other places whose environments are not like Singapore's. One of the jokes in Singapore is it's just too comfortable here! Singaporeans really don't want to go abroad and work. That has to change also."

"OK," I said. "But thinking about Singapore very specifically, if the manufacturing-type companies in Singapore price themselves out of the market, then what are the implications for Singapore? What kind of companies should be created here?" Koh answered, "My personal view is this: It's very clear that Singapore must make itself relevant in a service and information world. Because I do not perceive, with the exception of a couple of industries, that we can continue to maintain a significant edge over our neighbors for the next ten or twenty years in terms of a manufacturing location. That's why the HP way of developing MNCs as full businesses is so important. It's also why developing local Singapore companies into regional if not global MNCs is so important. A Singapore MNC would do its manufacturing elsewhere. Acer Computer, where I'm on the board, is a good example of a local Asian company that has become a multinational corporation with a brand name recognized the world over. This is the wave of the future I think for countries like Taiwan and Singapore, and all other similar countries."

After the Koh Boon Hwee interview, I was four-square back on the great K. T. Li's fourth principle: "Timing is more important than ideology." The remarkable thing about Singapore has always been that it is willing to buck the popular tide to secure the peaceful and prosperous future of its 3 million people. The Singapore government has been harangued for thirty years by the West, which says that it lays much too heavy a hand on the economy. Interestingly, over the same period, the economic results in Singapore have far exceeded those in the home economies of their critics. And today may be another time to go against the tide of "politically correct" economics. Singapore's government is fully embracing the entrepreneurial spirit and the need for a major effort across the country to create a more entrepreneurial economy. This, after thirty years of political and economic discipline, will call for significant changes to make Singapore an entrepreneur-friendly culture. Koh Been Hwee's wide-ranging comments show that Singapore's leadership not only is aware of the need, but is up to the entrepreneurial challenge.

But the exact approach may not please the more liberal economists and pundits across the globe. I think—no, I'm absolutely certain—that the government will be in the thick of this effort up to its eyeballs. In the latest blueprint for the economy, called "Singapore 21", "removing the barriers that inhibit local entrepreneurs" is a primary goal. And I can tell you for certain that Singapore is a hot market today for entrepreneurship training. We've worked with many of Singapore's most prominent companies on this: Singapore Airlines, the number-one company in revenue, at $4.7 billion; SingTel, the number-one company in market value, at $33 billion; Singapore Technologies; Sembawang Corporation; Television Corporation of Singapore, and others. All of them are racing—at the government's urging, I might add—to equip their managers with more entrepreneurial skills to compete in the global economy.

I wouldn't bet against Singapore, Inc.'s efforts to reinvent itself and create a highly entrepreneurial economy for the twenty-first century. If, as Koh Boon Hwee says, "It was government entrepreneurship that built this country," why not presume that the government can "rebuild" it. If timing is indeed everything, Singapore looks like it's very much on time!

ENTREPRENEUR-FRIENDLY COUNTRIES, STATES, AND CITIES

There is no God-given reason why the next Sam Walton or Bill Gates couldn't or shouldn't come from your town. But are there factors that seem to stack the deck in favor of some places over others? There sure seem to be. The entrepreneurial spirit is not exactly evenly distributed around the world. But, as should be clear by now, the reasons for that are almost always manmade. Remember Claus Schroeder's sorry story (in Part I—More Myths and Truths) from East Germany of how to turn a historically industrious society into a bunch of lazy, uninspired laggards, courtesy of Karl Marx. Manmade or not, if you're setting out to foster entrepreneurship in your country, state, or city, at least you need to know that differences do exist and, depending on where you call home, what you might be up against.

After all, there have to be reasons why, as a Kaufman Foundation study found, there are vast differences in entrepreneurial activity and inclination between countries. The range can be astonishing, even among the highly industrialized nations. At the high end, one in every twelve people in the United States is involved in a business start-up, while only one in every sixty-three people is similarly involved in Japan. The Kaufman study covers the G-7 countries. It measures the number of company start-ups per 100 population. The 1999 rankings of the G-7 countries are:

COUNTRY	START-UP RATE
USA	8.4
Canada	6.8
Germany	4.1
Italy	3.4
UK	3.3
France	1.8
Japan	1.6

This correlates very closely to another study tracking Entrepreneur Wannabes. This study was conducted by Warwick University in the UK and Dartmouth College in the United States. 25,000 people were interviewed in twenty-three countries. It shows the percentage of people, by country, that say they would prefer to be self-employed versus being an employee of an existing company. We've extracted figures from the same G-7 countries, and present the two studies, side by side. The rankings are very similar:

COUNTRY	START-UP RATE	COUNTRY	"WANNABES"
USA	8.4	USA	71 percent
Canada	6.8	Germany	64 percent
Germany	4.1	Italy	63 percent
Italy	3.4	Canada	58 percent
UK	3.3	UK	45 percent
France	1.8	France	42 percent
Japan	1.6	Japan	41 percent

The only surprises in the listings may be that Germany ranks a bit higher and the UK ranks a bit lower than their popular images. Bravo for the Germans, and whatever happened to the so-called Thatcher Revolution?

Even within the same country, there can also be huge differences. In the United States for example, the Small Business Survival Committee (SBSC) ranks all fifty states and the District of Columbia on a scale of entrepreneurship. The SBSC is a public policy advocacy group, whose listings are admittedly heavily weighted by public policy factors, such as taxes, crime rates, and labor laws. Their current listing ranks South Dakota at the very top and Washington, DC, dead last. Of course, the cultural differences between the Coyote State and the District, America's ground-zero of government bureaucracy, could fill several Ph.D. dissertations. If you're interested in packing up and moving to an entrepreneur-friendly state, the top fifteen states in the list are:

1. South Dakota
2. Wyoming
3. Nevada
4. New Hampshire
5. Texas
6. Washington
7. Florida
8. Alabama
9. Tennessee
10. Mississippi
11. Alaska
12. North Dakota
13. Colorado
14. Pennsylvania
15. Missouri

And finally, moving down to a microeconomic level, business magazines today love to rank the Best Cities for Business. Last year, *Inc.* magazine ranked American cities by the number of business start-ups per population. The top twenty-five are:

1. Las Vegas, NV
2. Boise, ID
3. Anchorage, AK
4. Ann Arbor, MI
5. Austin, TX
6. Boulder, CO
7. Houston, TX
8. Denver, CO
9. Dallas, TX
10. Fort Collins, CO
11. Colorado Springs, CO
12. Albuquerque, NM
13. Kalamazoo, MI
14. Fort Worth, TX
15. Provo, UT
16. Portland, OR
17. Salt Lake City, UT
18. Orlando, FL
19. San Francisco, CA
20. Salem, OR
21. Santa Rosa, CA
22. San Antonio, TX
23. Anaheim, CA
24. Seattle, WA
25. Eugene, OR

Do you notice anything odd about this list of America's most entrepreneurial cities? Twenty-two of the twenty-five are in the West and about two-thirds of the twenty-five are small- to medium-sized cities. Only four of these twenty-five entrepreneurial hot spots are also in the top twenty-five cities in population. Those four are: Houston (#8), Dallas (#12), Anaheim (#16), and Seattle (#22). Is there a message in here somewhere?

You're entitled to ask, what do all these surveys mean? Probably not too much. While fun and interesting to consider, the practical point is that there may be political, legal, and cultural (i.e., manmade) factors influencing the level of entrepreneurship in a country, a community, or even a family. If you find them negatively affecting your efforts to foster an entrepreneurial economy, you can try to change them, or find creative ways to circumvent them. You can be sure, however, that would-be entrepreneurs in your area don't really have to move to South Dakota or Las Vegas to start a company!

In the future, we're destined to see more government and public policy leaders like K. T. Li, the architect of Taiwan's economic miracle; Fernando Cardoso, the great finance minister (and now president) of Brazil; Koh Boon Hwee in Singapore; President Ragnar Grimsson of Iceland; Kris Kimel in Kentucky; and Charles Millard (a man you will meet in a few pages) from New York City's Silicon Alley. They may come from different parts of the world and different political camps, but they all recognize that the Entrepreneurial Age offers unparalleled challenges and opportunities. Creating prosperity at home and competitiveness abroad is the name of this game—and developing a more entrepreneurial nation, state, or city, may be the most important job any public leader will have in the twenty-first century!

From that list, the only person you haven't heard from yet is Charles Millard in New York City. And that's just fine, because we want to finish with a strong "closer" to really bring the entrepreneurial message home. Here, straight from the Big Apple, is the right man with the right message to do just that: the New Yorker with enough chutzpah to dare make Silicon Alley "hotter" than Silicon Valley!

CITIES: THE GODFATHER OF SILICON ALLEY

The first thing government should do is no harm.
—CHARLES MILLARD
FORMER PRESIDENT,
ECONOMIC DEVELOPMENT CORPORATION,
NEW YORK CITY

Having already interviewed several Silicon Valley entrepreneurs for this book, I became intrigued with the emergence of *Silicon Alley* in New York City. It's no secret that, for a couple of decades, New York wasn't even in the digital age race. That, of course, had been dominated by California's Silicon Valley, with little satellites popping up in Seattle (thanks to Bill Gates) Boston, Austin, and even Northern Virginia. Then I read in the *New*

York Times that seventeen new Silicon Alley Internet companies had gone public between March and June of 1999. This was actually a higher number of Internet IPOs than Silicon Valley had produced in the whole prior year! I decided to find out what was going on. During my search for the person most responsible for the creation of Silicon Alley, a reporter at the *New York Times* mentioned the name Charles Millard and then referred me to the editorial staff at the trade magazine, *Silicon Alley Reporter*. I asked the first person I talked to there, "Is it true that this fellow, Millard, knows something about Silicon Alley?" The immediate and very New York answer: "He knows everything. He's the Godfather of Silicon Alley."

I interviewed Charles Millard at the Harvard Club in New York City. He showed up with no tie, which the mid-afternoon, octogenarian nappers would see, if only they were awake, as a modern assault on the Club's centuries-old dress code. It was the first small, but refreshing, tipoff that I was about to meet a new breed of New York City mover and shaker. It's certainly true that Millard has been on a fast track: Phi Beta Kappa at Holy Cross College; Columbia Law School with honors; five years at Davis Polk and Wardwell, one of *the* blue chip, Wall Street law firms—and then things really got interesting. "I got married in the fall of 1990, by November my wife was pregnant, and in April of 1991 I left the law firm to run for the City Council [of New York City], basically asking the voters on the East Side of Manhattan to please give me a two-thirds pay cut! They did, so I was a city councilman, representing the upper East Side of Manhattan, about 140,000 people. I was elected in 1991. I was the first Republican elected from Manhattan to the City Council in twenty-five years. I was reelected in 1993. Then Mayor Giuliani appointed me to be president of the Economic Development Corporation (EDC) in late '95. I left there in May of 1999."

For almost four years, Charles Millard was Rudy Giuliani's point man for economic development. Giuliani came to office in January of 1994, so Millard's tenure covered most of the period that is already being called New York City's renaissance. It has clearly been a time of entrepreneurial and economic rebirth in the city. For one year after he left the EDC, he was a managing director at Prudential Securities, focusing on Internet companies. As of this writing Millard is shopping around for the next challenge, and seems hooked on remaining in the entrepreneurial arena: "By the time your book comes out, I'll be doing something different. I'm talking to incubators about running their offices in New York. I'm talking to venture capitalists. I'm talking to dot-com companies. I'm having a lot of very interesting discussions and we'll see what they result in."

So what *was* going on that catapulted New York City into the Internet world? How did this government do what governments almost never do—that is, to lead the way and set the stage for profound and long-lasting, cutting-edge economic development? It turns out that Millard, the "Godfather," does know everything about it. Here's the inside story: "At the Economic Development Corporation (EDC), there were many, many things that we did. I'll mention a few before I focus on Silicon Alley. I was responsible for the city's negotiations and the revitalization of 42nd Street, which everyone knows has been a fantastic success for the city. I also did all the negotiations on the tax incentive packages to keep large corporations in New York: Bear Stearns, Merrill-Lynch, McGraw-Hill, and many others. I also was the chairman of the Industrial Development Agency, which does get a little closer to your interest. The IDA issues triple tax-exempt bonds on behalf of small companies; that way their debt is tax exempt, which is obviously a tremendous benefit to them. Those bonds are used for all kinds of small companies around the city. I was involved in the negotiations on the Stock Exchange and the NASDAQ staying in New York, the stadium finance issues on the Yankees and the Mets, and so on."

I interrupted Millard to ask, "Now you've mentioned something *really* important. Tell us, are the New York Yankees really going to leave New York City?" His response: "Well, I've been gone for a year, and I don't know if there's any news, but I can't imagine . . ." Somewhat relieved I laughed and said, "Who *could* imagine? The New Jersey Yankees? Come on!"

Millard was quickly back on track with his story: "So, on to my role with Silicon Alley, and here's where we'll get into some interesting things that we did. We created a venture capital fund, which is almost unheard of for a city. We put $10 million into a fund called the New York City Discovery Fund. We leveraged that by raising additional money from other people who care about economic development: the New York Power Authority, Con Edison, Brooklyn Union Gas, and so on. We also went to the Small Business Administration and got them to put quite a bit of money in. They're a very, very interesting partner because they're impatient, but they're not hogs. In other words, if they give you $40 million, all they want is, let's say, an 8 percent return. They have to be paid *first,* before anybody else gets paid, but after that you basically get to—if you have a "ten bagger" and you pay them their 8 percent—you can leverage the rest. So it's very attractive. And I think it's smart for the SBA. The SBA is trying to be a venture capitalist. The SBA is trying to foster economic development in the best way that it can.

"Anyway, the venture capital fund was very successful. We hired a group called Prospect Street to run it. Prospect Street was a venture capitalist firm, so we weren't the actual decision makers. And I think this is one of the important things: People recognize that the guys in government are not actually venture capitalists. They don't really know how to do this and too often people in government think they do. They say, 'That's a great idea and we should do that.' There's no reason to think just because you got elected that you know how to negotiate a venture capital deal. And I think it was very insightful for the mayor to say: 'Yeah, we're not going to try to make these decisions ourselves. We'll have some veto power. We'll be able to control it in some ways. We'll set up some rules up front, like you have to invest in companies in New York or in companies moving to New York. But we're going to hire somebody else to run it like a private sector venture capital fund.'

"So the Discovery Fund was very interesting. I also created a Business Recruitment Division within EDC. New York City had never had a business recruitment team. Lots of other cities do, but not New York. I think it was out of arrogance really. You know, we thought that we didn't need to. So it was great when we started sending our team on the road. People said, 'Wow, that's so great that New York really wants my business, that's fantastic.' And that became our tag line: 'New York City—We Want Your Business.' It's not all that original, but so what? We ran some ads, and we had a team out on the road. We would mail ahead, and then send a team into a city. Maybe we'd be going to a conference, so we'd write, saying, 'We're going to be in town anyway. Would you like to meet while we're in town?' We'd send it to 250 companies, preselected because of their size or their industry or their growth rate, and then maybe ten of them would want to meet while our guys were there anyway for a conference. In the time that I was president of the EDC, we brought about forty new companies in the information technology world into New York City. So that was great. Now these things were simultaneous to the Silicon Alley development, so people wanted to come to New York when they learned how hot Silicon Alley was.

"We also created two venture capital shows. One of the biggest problems is that entrepreneurs need access to capital, but nobody wants to lend it to them. Nobody wants to take the risk. And in New York you didn't really have an infrastructure of venture capital five years ago. You just didn't. Not that there was nobody, but if they were here, they would go to California to look for technology companies to invest in. And so if you were a New York company and you went to a conference where you'd meet some venture capital people, you'd fly to California to meet the guy whose office was ten blocks away from your office in Manhattan. At a minimum, we thought we ought to be able to save everybody the airfare! The New York

City Venture Capital Conference is now in its fifth year, and it's become a very big deal. We also created, in conjunction with a publication called *Alley Cat News,* a Venture Capital Conference that *does* happen in California. It's called 'Alley to the Valley,' and we take New York companies out there to try to talk to California VCs. Obviously, we hope they'll get funding. We also want the California VCs generally to be aware of how hot New York is, so that even if they don't make those investments, they'll be more attentive to New York opportunities in the future. The Alley to the Valley conference is in its third year this year.

"We had to create, along with the Downtown Alliance, which is the downtown business improvement district, a program called 'Plug N Go.' Plug N Go provides small chunks of prewired, Internet-ready space, priced below the market. So if you're an entrepreneur, the idea of getting into an office in New York isn't insurmountable. If you have an Internet business, you can't take the seven days to three week it takes to get Verizon to wire your office or whatever else might be needed. So before you, as the landlord, can rent this as a Plug N Go location, its got to be prewired and you have agreed that you will charge a rent below the market rate. More important than even the price, you, as the entrepreneur, don't have to be creditworthy. And you don't have to take five or ten thousand square feet—you can take two or three thousand square feet. And you don't have to sign a five- or ten-year lease; you can sign a two-year lease. Why would you sign a five- or ten-year lease? You don't know where you're going to be in five or ten years when you're a start-up. So you just 'plug in and you go'! Over 200 Plug N Go leases were signed while I was at the EDC.

"There's one other important thing. I told you that we negotiated tax-incentive packages that traditionally have been with very large employers, like a McGraw-Hill or a Merrill-Lynch. Basically, when you get a tax-incentive package, you get it based on the sales tax. You only get the sales tax relief if you spend. If you have 10,000 employees, you're probably spending a lot. If you only have 100, you might not be spending so much so fast. So I found a way to create a new program focused on these fast-growing companies, that maybe have only have a hundred employees today. If you believe they're going to have 500 employees in four or five years, well, give them the incentives now to grow to 400 or 500 employees and make the whole deal tied to growth. You can cut the deal now and whenever they have to add new employees, they have an incentive to add them in New York. We did that with Double Click, Theglobe.Com, Star Media, and a number of others. The point is we took this old program and tweaked it so that it would apply better to Silicon Alley companies. And the mayor was fully behind these customized tax incentives."

As Millard paused and took a sip of coffee, I commented, "That's a lot of new activity, Charles. Was any of this kind of entrepreneurial economic development going on before Mayor Giuliani and you arrived on the scene? As I recall, there were always a lot of so-called community-based social programs in New York City, but not much in the way of start-up business development. Isn't that right?"

"Well, that's what I want to get to—the philosophy here. I just want to make sure we get it all out first. We discussed the Discovery Fund, the New York City Venture Capital Conference, Alley to the Valley, Plug N Go, the Recruitment Team, the small business tax packages—there may be a couple of other things—but I think those are the main activities regarding Silicon Alley. Anyway, for me it was all a great experience.

"Now, philosophically, which I think is part of what you're getting at, what *should* governments do? One of the most important things, I think, is that the mayor has stayed out of the way. You'll notice there are no regulations here—from any of the EDC activities. It's just like doctors. The first thing government should do is no harm. You really have to stop and think about that for a second. This goes beyond just entrepreneurs. Take the Internet, for example. Let's imagine some things the government *might* have done relating to the Internet over the last ten years. Knowing how government is, seeing how the Internet has evolved, let's take two things the government could easily have done.

"First, no advertising. A lot of government money and time went into the creation of the Internet. It would not be in any way out of the question to have imagined that in 1993 or '94, somebody in Washington might have stood up and said, 'Hey, this is a sacrosanct medium. We're not going to bastardize it with tawdry commerce. This is to be the electronic Encyclopedia Britannica, not just another electronic magazine or infotainment vehicle.' Now if that had happened, a lot of the things that you now have for free on the Internet, you wouldn't have for free. Think of all the things that are going through free. There's no way I'd pay for them all. I'd pay for some, but not all.

"Secondly, taxes! Imagine if all Internet commerce had been taxed by the federal government, up front. And you can imagine the argument, right? State taxes are different from state to state, and we don't want to favor any individual state. There's a tremendous loss in revenue to these states if they lose their taxes, so we're going to have the feds tax it. Of course, we won't tax it at the lowest sales tax rate, we'll tax it at the highest so nobody loses. So every state in the union will effectively end up with a 10 percent sales tax, and the feds will distribute it out to each state. Maybe it would be based on some pro-rata basis, or maybe, if your actual sales tax rate is 3 percent, you only get 3 percent but the feds get to keep the rest. So those two things could have happened. They really, legitimately, could have happened. And, thank goodness, they didn't.

"So before people start talking about 'things to do,' it's always really important to stop and ask, 'Is this the kind of thing that might be doing harm that I can't anticipate?' The City Council, to use a good example, created a second, smaller fund. It's $25 million. It's not leveraged. It's all city money, which I think was a mistake. Early on, that money was proposed by the City Council to be a *loan fund* for emerging industries—basically for Silicon Alley. Well, these entrepreneurs don't have the cash flow to pay the loans. So what you had was all these people saying, 'Hooray, the city wants to put more money aside for us.' Of course, putting money aside isn't what we should be doing anyhow. You know, investing it is different that putting it aside. The people on the City Council, I can tell you from experience, had no clue about the distinction between bonds and equity. I don't mean no one on the Council understood that, but the actual businesslike decision of what's an intelligent program was lost on them. So we had to go back and say: 'Look, if you're going to do this, it really should be equity because nobody will be able to pay the loans. And the great thing about the Discovery Fund is we've had a return. Do you want your grandiose new fund to be one with no return because people can't pay the debt and then you basically forgive the debt? Or do you want to make it equity so that if they do hit it, you get a return?' They went, 'Oh yeah. I guess that makes sense.'

"The second point is that you have to understand the needs of the businesses. And you have to listen to them because people in government, especially elected officials, don't really understand business. They really don't *like* business. I mean, they all say, 'Oh I like small business.' Well, even though the new jobs tend to be created by small businesses, an awful lot of jobs still exist in larger companies. Politicians, especially those left of center, and especially in New York, really don't believe in the profit motive. It's not something they value very highly. They view businesses as a necessary evil. Yes, they create jobs, thank goodness for that, but this whole profit thing to the average elected official in New York—they just don't care. They view profit primarily as something that's good because they can tax it. And they completely fail—your entrepreneurs will really agree with me on this, I think—they completely fail to understand that a young business is always at risk of going out of business. The people who you're writing for, if they're really early-stage entrepreneurs, understand this for sure. They're people who are mortgaging their house, are factoring their receivables because they've just got to get some cash flow, and are spending on their personal credit card because their business credit isn't even good enough to get a business credit card. But they love their business and they are getting somewhere, but it's a very tough hand-to-mouth existence. They could go out of business any day. And then, let's say you've had two good years, you could *still* go out of business. Politicians sort of seem to think that once you're in business, it's a static thing. That you always will be in business— and the only issue now is, How much do I tax you? And if you don't understand how a business works, you run into taxes that are just outrageous. And people don't grasp that, because they think, well, you're guaranteed a profit. You're a businessman, you make a profit, and so and so. They never think that this tax or this regulation might cause you to not make a profit."

As Millard was serving up this robust condemnation of politicians, I was thinking of some of the government officials I had met around the world who were as pro-entrepreneur and probusiness as Milliard himself. So I asked him, "Isn't the political landscape changing across the world and in the country? It certainly seems to be changing in New York City. Aren't we in fact on the right track now?" I think my description was a bit too optimistic for someone who had just spent four years battling all those "left of center" City Council members in New York. His response: "Changing, yes. But the New York City Council has fifty-one members, and if you took out the twelve, let's say, who are the most business friendly, the remaining thirty-nine would think that it's a privilege for you to do business in the City of New York and you should pay for it." As I laughed at what I instantly knew was going to be a great quote for the book, even Charles Millard chuckled a little at his own deft turn of phrase.

Back to the main point of the interview, I asked him, "The name Silicon Alley seems like such a great name, at least in the PR sense. Has it actually helped you?" Millard answered: "That's a good question. It really is. Actually there are a lot of things I should say. You know we sent our team on the road to bring people to New York. And we also sent some people on the road for focus groups for an advertising campaign. When our people first talked to others about Silicon Alley, they thought it was a typo! The people in California had no clue. They didn't know what it was. And the first year we did 'Alley to the Valley,' a lot of people came and said, 'New York, give me a break, you're nowhere! You're a pimple compared to what we have out here in Silicon Valley.'

"There were three points our skeptics were making: 'Where's your mayor in all this? Where are your academic institutions? And where are your IPOs?' That was the first year. The following year, in the spring of 1999, we'd just had something like fifteen Internet-related IPOs, more than

California had in the prior twelve months. I arranged to have an interview with Mayor Giuliani in the edition of *Alley Cat News* that ran the week of the conference. And we brought the Center for Assisted Technology from NYU with us to the conference. Thereby, hopefully, answering all three of those questions. After I related all that in my opening talk in the second-year conference, I sat down and Tim Draper of Draper-Fisher-Jurvetson, the California-based venture capitalist firm, followed me to the podium. I had called Tim about two and a half years earlier when he invested in Wit Capital, and said to him he should have an office in New York. And he said, 'Yeah I'm thinking about it.'

"Well, when I finished speaking that morning at the conference, and laid out what the city had done, responding to the criticisms of New York from the prior year, Tim said, 'Charles Millard is right. And in fact we're going to open an office in New York.' At that point, I said: Well, it's a two-day conference and it's only 9:20 A.M. of day one, but this has already been a success from my end because he's such a big name. The *New York Post* wrote about it, the California papers wrote that 'Draper says he's going to New York,' and so on. I don't mean it was front-page news, but in the right places, it was very, very important. It was someone important and influential validating what we had been working at for so long."

I thanked Millard for all the great information and insights, and asked him the type of closing question I try to ask everyone: "If the mayor or a team came to you from Phoenix, or Detroit, or Miami, or Timbuktu, and they said, 'Look, we want to get something like this going, so what do we do? What are the two or three most important things we absolutely must do to be successful?'" Millard took a deep breath and seemed to almost physically lean into this question, noting, "We've got to spend another minute on that.

"Just like the 'Do no harm' point, government can't really create this. Nobody at City Hall sat around and said, 'Let's get a bunch of young guys in black turtlenecks, give 'em some European cigarettes, make sure they have ponytails, stuff 'em in some lofts, get 'em some pizza boxes, and we'll call it Silicon Alley.' That's not what happened. First, I think you need to follow the market. When you see something bubbling in your environment, then you've got to go help it. But you can't be sitting there blowing the gas into the water so people will see the bubbles that you make—because that just isn't going to work. When you see something really, really begin to grow, that's when you need to water it. But if the government says, 'Let's set out to do this,' I don't think that ever works. I don't think the government can lead the market. The government has to help the market once it's moving.

"Also, in terms of what the government should do, you have to be cold at times. Small, failing businesses are always asking for government help. Philosophically, in a capitalist system, you have to have failure as a real option. You can't have government bailing out everybody whose business fails. Because it's that failure that makes the entrepreneur we were describing before work really hard, right? And if there's no fear of failure, he's not going to work that hard. Also, I don't want my tax dollars going to somebody who's already failed, right? So the second point is it's not government's role to make them successful, but to create an environment where they can succeed. If you see something growing, and you want to water it, that's fine. But the government can't be sitting there trying to plant a seed and say that it doesn't really know if that seed will grow in that soil.

"Any city should also look at ideas like Empowerment Zones or Enterprise Zones. But there are two very different concepts in Empowerment Zones. One is: Here's a hundred million dollars from the feds, a hundred million from the state, a hundred million from the city, to give or invest in this area. The other is: Here's x amount of tax credits or write-offs that we're going to give to people who make their own investments in this area. So if I give you money, I'm subsidizing hope. If I give you tax write-offs, you've got to have generated income and profits in order to get that benefit, so I'm subsidizing success. I'm giving you an incentive to succeed in that neighborhood, because that's the only place where you're going to get that tax incentive. But—and this is important—you don't have to apply to me for the tax benefit. So, do you want $300 million invested and administered by a combination of city, state, and federal governments, and all the politics that goes behind that—meaning you have to ask the politicians to get your piece of the action? Or do you want, if you've invested x amount of money, and you have x number of employees, in x area, to get the tax benefit—and you never have to talk to Charlie Millard, or Charlie Rangel (congressman from New York City) or anyone else. You just get it because it's in the tax code. And that's the way it ought to be."

I asked Millard for a quick summary of the three things he'd tell the people from Phoenix or Detroit or Miami. Here it is:

- "First, I would say the government can't try to figure out what industries are going to succeed. This was not an old-style industrial policy that New York City adopted. The city saw something growing and went all out to help it. That's number one.

- "Number two, whatever you do, you can't get suckered into helping losing propositions. People in government always want to be able to say *yes* to anybody who's asking. Sometimes the most caring thing to do is to say *no*.

- "And third, the best kind of programs are the ones, as I was saying on the Empowerment Zones, where you don't have to apply to a Charles Millard to get it. You don't have to apply to a congressman. It's a tax incentive that exists to encourage and support a certain kind of behavior. And once you set those rules, then nobody has to apply for it, and it doesn't get political. There's a big and important distinction between 'I'm applying for cash so I can go do something with it' and having a tax incentive, meaning 'I've *done* something that you asked me to do, now tax me less, please.'"

Silicon Alley, which bills itself as the Big Apple's high-tech district, actually covers a large area of Manhattan, from the Flatiron and Chelsea districts near Twenty-fifth Street, south through Greenwich Village and into the Financial District. From a handful of struggling companies in 1995, it is fast becoming a major force in the Internet world. Most of the companies are small, creative, and are media or financially oriented, which isn't surprising since they are sitting in the center of the media and financial worlds. Insiders say Silicon Alley companies will continue to concentrate on Web content, and leave the creating of Internet tools to Silicon Valley. As Jason Calacanis, the publisher of the *Silicon Alley Reporter,* says, "The Valley and the Alley aren't competitive; they're cooperative. But one day, the content will become much more important than the infrastructure that carries it." Long term, that could be a winning strategy. After all, what gets more attention today—the people who make television shows or the people who make the cameras and the microphones? That time could be nearer than we think. It took radio about forty years to reach 50 million homes; it's taken the Web just four to do the same. Already the demand for content is outstripping the demand for more tools.

Whatever the future may hold, one thing is clear from the story of Silicon Alley. Government has a big role to play in fostering entrepreneurship and economic development, and government agencies can be very successful at it—as Charles Millard's story makes abundantly clear. It does require, however, those same three fundamentals be in place:

- An entrepreneur-friendly culture, as in "Where's your mayor in all this?"

- A bit of money, as in "Where are your IPOs?"

- A bit of knowledge, as in "Where are your academic institutions?"

The best news in the Silicon Alley story is not in the specific actions Charles Millard took to respond to the skeptics—as innovative and impressive as those actions were—but rather that such success stories are actually possible. That economic development can really and truly be accomplished. That something so important and so valuable can be created in a short span of time. So take heart, everyone—an entrepreneurial economy *can* be created in your country or your state or your city. Trust me, if it can be done in the rough and tough political trenches of the Big Apple, your hometown should be a cinch!

CONCLUSION:
Getting Entrepreneurial!

DO SOMETHING GREAT!

The managers knew how to manage, but they couldn't do *anything.*

—STEVE JOBS, FOUNDER, APPLE COMPUTER,
NEXT INC., PIXAR

Doing something at the original Apple Computer meant making a better computer, not devising a better planning system or organization chart. But then Steve Jobs never attended a management seminar. And I doubt he spends much time now boning up on the latest theories from business schools and consultants. Of course he's been pretty busy creating three great companies over the past twenty years. And that's the point isn't it? It's the same point that needs to be made about a lot of development seminars, how-to books, and virtually all popular advice to aspiring entrepreneurs. Learning about and thinking about *being* entrepreneurial won't mean a thing unless you first learn to actually make or do something the world needs. We call it "doing something great."

The recent mania over *leadership training* provides a perfect analogy. If you watched all the leadership promotions and infomercials, you would have to wonder how we ever made it this far in the world without seminars, books, and audiotapes teaching us how to lead our fellow human beings. However, while the world is drowning in experts and advice on how to be a leader, the highest form of leadership still comes down to actually *doing something great*—pushing back frontiers and accomplishing big things. Truly great leadership isn't a management concept or a series of steps. It's creating and doing things that others will admire and want to be a part of. If a football coach took every seminar on leadership and read every how-to book, and never had a winning season, you can be sure we'd never hear him referred to as a great leader. Ditto with military people, many of whom over the years have been trumpeted as powerful leaders. If General Norman Schwartzkopf lost every battle in the Persian Gulf, he would never have commanded $50,000 a speech to lecture people on the principles of leadership. And, more to our point, the CEO who carefully follows the advice of every leadership guru around, but can't grow his company, isn't going to end up as a case study in corporate leadership at Harvard or the London Business School.

The real lesson to be learned is this: Concentrate on doing something great, and stop worrying about formulas and techniques. Focusing on techniques over actually doing something noteworthy is an old and bad habit propagated by business schools and corporate training departments. It's the same old story of form over substance. Successful entrepreneurs exemplify a refreshingly different approach. History clearly shows that the important and heroic achievements in business are almost always related to the creation and growth of new products and new companies—the work of the entrepreneur. And it's hardly the case, at the dawn of the twenty-first century, that we can't find something great to do. The world is full of great things to explore: There's cyberspace, inner space (biotech), outer space, and goodness knows what else. After all, this is the Entrepreneurial Age!

The evidence is clear: If you become great at making something useful or doing something important, as sure as night follows day, customers and shareholders and employees will scramble to get on board your rising star. You will actually be doing something the world needs. You'll be doing something great—and that's what really counts.

DOING IT JUST FOR THE MONEY—A RECIPE FOR DISASTER

> *People who just want to start a company because its a good way to become wealthy—well, they almost always fail.*
> —ED PENHOET
> COFOUNDER, CHIRON CORPORATION

Our second short, concluding thought is this: For God's sake, don't become an entrepreneur just because you think it's your best shot at getting rich!

To expand on that, here's Ed Penhoet (again), cofounder of Chiron and megastar of the biotech industry. Penhoet, the scientist-entrepreneur, has strong feelings about what really counts in starting and growing a new business. He talks passionately about what entrepreneurs have to bring to the table as opposed to what they expect to take away from it: "The critical aspect is to have built up a lot of 'capital' before you start one of these businesses. I talk to young students all the time and ask them what they'd like to do. The common answer: 'Well, someday I'd like to start a biotech company.' Well, why? 'Because it sounds like a real exciting thing to do.' But unless you have an edge on the field when you start, you can't just out of whole cloth say, 'Oh gee, biotech, or computers or whatever looks like a good industry. I think I'll start that kind of a company.' No, you have to have a competitive advantage going somehow.

"You see, you have never heard me say that I did any of this to make money. It wasn't a motivating factor for me. I can't say I don't enjoy the financial rewards that come with building a successful enterprise. That would be foolish. On the other hand, I know very few people who have been successful in any environment who simply went at it as a way of making money. It's almost a truism that people who are successful want to accomplish something; they may become wealthy as a result of what they have contributed to society, but not the other way around. People who just think, 'Oh gee, it says in the paper that Herb Boyer just made $100 million starting Genentech. Well, gee, maybe I'll start a biotechnology company too.' You know, that's almost a certain recipe for disaster.

"It's the same with MBAs. I've seen a string of very unhappy, young MBAs from very good places, who are very talented, who go and take CEO jobs in small companies and almost always flop. Because they're not trained to be entrepreneurs. They're trained to manage. They will function well in large organizations . . . but to be successful early on in a small company, well, the management of it is the least of your problems. You have to create value. That's the bottom line of these things. You will never be successful with just business manipulations in these kinds of enterprises. You succeed because you create some value. You feel a need in the marketplace, and unless you create that value, no amount of business razzle-dazzle or MBA training is going to overcome the fact that you have not created any fundamental value. This is a crucial issue. You don't have to be a scientist. If you're a businessperson, you align yourself with somebody who can contribute technically, an engineer or whatever, and together build one of these scientist-entrepreneur teams. People who just want to start a company because it's a good way to become wealthy—well, they almost always fail."

Or how about Ron Doggett, the entrepreneur who went "back to the future" with his famous Slim Jim brand? You will recall that Doggett started as a manager with giant General Mills, became a fabulously successful entrepreneur with GoodMark Foods, and exited by selling out to another giant, ConAgra. On this point, Doggett says, "If they're going after this to become rich, they're facing a very high failure probability. I think I'm probably like everyone else who considers themselves to be an entrepreneur. I never thought about getting rich or the 'richness' of it. I really never thought about it. I was always in it for the next achievement, the next accomplishment, the next growth goal."

And finally, for the "take no prisoners" version, listen to Ben Tregoe. You will remember him as the articulate cofounder of Kepner-Tregoe, the firm that has taught over 5 million people around the world how to make rational business decisions: "If somebody starts a business, they've got to be willing to be absolutely nuts about what they're doing, and be totally dedicated to it and work a hundred hours a week, or whatever it takes—and in my experience you just don't do that unless there's something more fundamental than just saying, well, we're going to make a few bucks at this thing."

We're not saying there's something wrong or immoral about getting rich, or even wanting to get rich. To the contrary, if you do the kind of things that the great entrepreneurs in this book have done, you *deserve* to get rich! Just don't get the cart before the horse. The evidence says that if getting rich is your driving force, it's tantamount to an entrepreneurial death wish. Don't take my word for it. You've just heard the same from Ed Penhoet, Ron Doggett, and Ben Tregoe. And you'll hear the same from ninety-nine of the next hundred entrepreneurs you meet. That's just about the average I've found after meeting several thousand of them over the past fifteen years.

STARTING OVER WITH THE BASICS

> *I decided to run the big company the same way I ran the small company.*
>
> —FRASER MORRISON
> CEO, MORRISON CONSTRUCTION

This final message comes from Scotland. It was one of the most often-quoted interviews in my first book and I think it's worth repeating here, albeit in summary form. As you will see, Fraser Morrison provides us with an extraordinary road map for reawakening the spirit of enterprise in any organization. Or, as we like to say, the power of getting entrepreneurial!

It's the story of Fraser Morrison in Edinburgh, Scotland. By the numbers, it's an amazing story of selling a profitable $3 million family enterprise and regaining it fifteen years later as a money-losing $300 million bureaucracy. To Morrison himself, the human side of the story is more important. He was saving his father's entrepreneurial business from the clutches of a giant, faceless conglomerate. Morrison fits nicely into a long line of legendary Scottish entrepreneurs going back to Andrew Carnegie. What makes him unique, however, is that he has seen it from all sides: from growing up working in the small family business, to a very long and tough fifteen years running the business under the most anti-entrepreneurial conditions imaginable, and then finally bringing it back to the entrepreneurial fold—with the added twist of having to stop the hemorrhaging losses quickly or lose it all forever. And in the process he has become a guiding light for showing what it takes to move your business from the death grip of an uncaring, bureaucratic world to the passion of a high-growth, entrepreneurial organization.

When I interviewed Fraser Morrison, it was clear this had been a gut-wrenching experience for him. In his own words, here's how it all started: "In 1948, my father started the business from a cold start with absolutely nothing. It was very small, what we called a jobbing contractor. He slowly built up the business, virtually on his own, within a very small radius of his hometown, which was a place called Tain, Scotland. I joined him right out of school. In that kind of situation you get the opportunity to get involved in everything that's going on. So I might have been setting roads or houses one day and go home that evening and help prepare the accounts. It was, very much, an all-hands-on-deck situation. Anyway, in 1974, we sold the family business to Mining Finance House, a large public conglomerate in London. We were still small, working only in Scotland, and turning over maybe £2 million. My father retired and I became the MD, reporting to people I didn't even know in London."

From these modest beginnings, Fraser Morrison traveled a long, miserable journey until he finally regained his family's business. Along the way, everything that could go wrong in a big conglomerate went wrong. The holding company changed hands four or five times. The construction group, which Morrison Construction was a small part of, began bleeding huge losses in Asia, the United States and even in the UK. Dozens of corporate managers came and went, each with their own agenda. Meanwhile, Morrison Construction was the only profitable piece of its group and was minding its own business in Scotland as best it could. But the losses from the construction group, now being run by finance people, were overwhelming the entire holding company. No one in London seemed to have the foggiest idea of how to fix it. Here's Morrison's description of the environment in which the giant conglomerate in London worked: "We were part of the big holding company, and we watched our parent group just write themselves off. You see it every day—companies that are having constant changes at the top or companies that are in an endless restructuring process. Again and again you see the focus of attention going away from the operation of the business. The senior people had lost touch with what was happening in the real business. They didn't understand what the people thought. They weren't particularly interested in what they were doing. I had always thought, even when you are in a financially difficult situation, if the day-to-day operations are working well, you'll get back to a strong position. But the more effort the headquarters people put into corporate politics and what was happening at the holding company, the worse the situation became down on the sites, and the weaker the overall situation became."

Finally the holding company became very disillusioned with the entire construction business and wanted to chuck it all. Morrison tried to buy back Morrison Construction but was flatly rejected. The holding company wasn't about to "sell the only good part and keep all the dogs." Instead, in a total misjudgment of Morrison's personal ambitions, they "promoted" him to run the entire Construction Group. He hesitantly agreed but asked for an option to buy the whole group if it were put on the block. Another rejection, this time because the Board was testing the market for a spinoff. Not surprisingly, there weren't a lot of buyers for a hugely unprofitable construction group. So finally Morrison was told he could buy "the bit in Scotland but only if he took the bad parts of the dog along with it." He decided to go for it as the only way to regain his company. He went deeply into debt, and to avoid financial collapse he would have to turn around the big losing operations practically overnight: "So we ended up buying back Morrison Construction. I had finally reached my long-held ambition to restore family control. But we also had to buy the parent company along with it. So I had a business with overall sales of about U.S.$300 million but losing very big. But we owned 100 percent and I thought I knew how to turn it around. Thankfully, my hunch was right. In our first year we increased sales and actually made a small profit! The next year, 1990, we pushed sales up a bit too and actually made a respectable $11 million profit—and have never looked back."

How exactly did Fraser Morrison change years of losses into profits in just twelve months? He simply transformed the total atmosphere in which the company worked. He started running the big business the same way he'd always run the small business—in a very entrepreneurial environment: "We made an awful lot of changes on day one. We retained only two directors and the rest, eight or ten, went. We structured the company so that it was operating on similar lines to the business that we had in Scotland. One of the great difficulties we found, when we added up all of the contract delays on the sites, was the sites were cumulatively eight years behind contract schedules. When you think of the overhead on our construction sites, they can be anything from £10,000 to £100,000 a month, and we were eight years behind schedule! So, I focused people's attention throughout the business on bringing those eight years' delay back to zero within twelve months. Everybody said it couldn't be done. Well, giving people impossible targets sometimes works. In fact, we got it back to plus thirty weeks on the twelfth month."

Morrison actually changed five key factors in the overall operating environment of the company. These translate into valuable general principles for reawakening any organization's entrepreneurial spirit:

➤ *Keep It Small*

"We split the business up into relatively small—I call them family-size—units. So a director will have a business between only £5 million and £20 million turnover. They have a team of between thirty and sixty staff plus the hourly paid employees. That way they can get to know all of their people quite well. It's worked very well for us. A small operation just works better. The people enjoy it more and take a huge amount of satisfaction from it. You can get the team spirit. which is very important in construction. The same with commitment. I think it's in the small companies that you tend to find it. As we grow, it's a priority to make sure that we create the structure to be able to continually feel like a small company."

➤ *Keep It Personal*

"I learned a lot of lessons from seeing them try to run our company because they always gave us the feeling that they knew what to do. We weren't important. We only just dug holes in the ground. It was a huge lesson to me on how to run a business because you have to let the people feel that they are the key element of the business. Hopefully, our structure now is such that people have got a strong personal interest in developing the business. A strong sense of feeling important and that they themselves have a strong entrepreneurial input to the business."

➤ *Keep It Honest*

"The main factor that contributed to our success is the enormous commitment that I and the people around me have. When we bought the business back, we sold about 18 percent of it immediately to the key managers. So we have all senior people who have a shareholding in the new company. I told all of them we want to run the business in a way that's in their best, long-term interests also. Business needs this kind of personal commitment and honesty at the top and I'm sure we have it today."

⯈ *Keep It Simple*

"As in life generally, you shouldn't try to make things complicated. You've got to try to make it simple. And, the simpler it is, the easier it is to understand by everyone. The single most important thing that I've learned throughout this process—and I haven't found a situation yet where it isn't appropriate—is that if you forget about the nuts and bolts of the business, you're lost."

⯈ *Start Over With the Basics*

"I'd been telling the parent company I knew what needed to be done to sort this business out for a long time, but they decided that they knew better, and weren't interested in our philosophy. They were running it as one big company. So when we got it, we split it up and refocused the attention of the people away from looking toward the group in London, back to the sites and the operations of the business. We put new directors in who we knew would put all their attention on the sites. We had to very quickly refocus everyone back to the basics of the business—toward the site, which in the construction business is the only place we make money."

WELCOME TO THE ENTREPRENEURIAL AGE: ONE LAST TIME

> *The inclination of my life has been to do things and make things which will give pleasure to people in new and amazing ways. By doing that I please and satisfy myself.*
> —WALT DISNEY
> FOUNDER, THE WALT DISNEY COMPANY

Fraser Morrison says it's time to get "back to the basics of the business." Which brings us full circle to where we began this book, with Walt Disney's eloquent description of those basics. Throughout the book we labeled them *Sense of Mission, Customer/Product Vision, High-speed Innovation,* and *Self-inspired Behavior.* Most people simply call it the *entrepreneurial spirit.*

I think there's no better way to finish this book than to repeat the short, final paragraph of the Introduction: "As you read and think about the great power of the entrepreneurial spirit—in creating success and prosperity for people, companies, and entire countries—I hope you will find *The Entrepreneurial Age* of great and practical value in your career and in your life."

I truly hope it has been, and will forever be, of great and practical value to you. And welcome, one last time, to the Entrepreneurial Age!

INDEX

Abt, Clark, 102, 275
Abt Associates, 275
agriculture, role in growth, 234–35, 263
Amazon.com, 171
Amdahl, 43
American Express, 133–34
Apple Computers, xxxii, 156
Aramco, xxiii–xxiv

Bangladesh, 240
Benz, Karl, 161–62
Boody, John, 31–34, 49–56
brain drain, nationalistic, 276
Branson, Richard, 103, 127–29, 181
Brazil
   economic future of, 237, 255–57
   entrepreneurs in, 3
   national sense of mission, *254*, 254–58
Breton, Thierry, 215–16, 222
Brombaugh, John, 51, 52, 53
Bruce, Nigel, xvii
budgets, in entrepreneurial organizations,
   221–23
Buffett, Warren, 3
Bull S.A., 215–16
bureaucrats
   bureaucracy bashing, 70, 185–86
   performance consequences of, 85–86,
      170, 203, 209
   syndrome, 37
   and the US Patent Office, 171–72
businesses
   best cities for, 286
   bigger is better myth, 305, 306
   life cycle of, 65, 238, *238*
   and MBAs, xx
business plans, 12, *14,* 14–16, 27, 29
business schools, and entrepreneurs, 101–2

business to business (B2B) online
   transaction industry, 38–42
business to consumer (B2C) online
   transaction industry, 42

Calandra, Franco, xiii
Canada, 239, 285
capital
   and high-speed innovation, 67, 175
   knowledge as, 59–60, 70–71
   from private sources, 272
   start-up, 4, 98–100
   for stimulating entrepreneurial growth,
      265, 271–73, 289–90, 293
   venture capital, 289–91
Cardoso, Fernando Henrique, 257
centralization, 173–74
chaos, role in discovery, 59, 65–66, 176–77
chief engineer system, 152
Chile, 239, 276
China, 4, 237, 280
Chino, Tetsuo, 184–85, 200–202
Chiron, xxxiv, 102, 164–65, 182–83
cities, entrepreneurship in, 286, 287–98
Collins, Francis, 60–61
Commerce One, 38–46
commitment, entrepreneurial, 81–83, 92, 142
comparative advantage and knowledge,
   60–61
competitive advantage
   in entrepreneurial culture, 141–42
   and values, 21–22, 144–45
competitive position
   and bureaucracy, 70
   as business value, 22, 23
   and market need, 16–21
   matrix, *20*
   on national level, 252–53, 274–75, 276

ConAgra, 104, 113, 115–17, 118n
corporate culture
    at ConAgra, 115–17
    corporate entrepreneurs and, 130,
        211–26
    corporate strategy and, 129, *129*
    at IBM, 138–41
    at Thomson Multimedia, 216–21
corporate entrepreneurs. *See also*
        entrepreneurial culture
    corporate culture and, 130, 211–26
    corporate strategy and, 129, *129*
    described, 121–23
    employees and, 123–25
    and EPS, 207–10
    ethical behavior of, 225, 305
    at Lincoln Electric, 227
    management and, 121, 122–23, 223–25
    training programs for, 223–25
    wealth and, 300–302
corporate strategy, *129*, 129–33. *See also*
        entrepreneurial strategy
creativity. *See also* high-speed innovation;
        inventions
    in business, 168, 169–70, 181
    role in entrepreneurial economies,
        274–76
crisis
    benefits of, 68, 170
    creation of, 181–82
Cruz, Ramon, 160
Crystal, Graef, ix
culture
    changing corporate, 217–26
    competitive, 138–40
    corporate, 114–18, 138–41
    corporate strategy and, 129, *129*, 130
    entrepreneur-friendly, 112–14, 216–21,
        277–84
    entrepreneurial, 140, 141–45, 264–65
    kanban, 152
customer-driven production system, 152
customer/product vision
    of craftsmen, 148–49
    customer input, 45–46
    at Dell Computer, 152–53
    described, 34, 56, 147, 156–57
    at Disney, 35–36, 36, 147, 154
    and functionalization, 148–51
    of Honda, 157
    of Jobs, 156
    of Kroc, 157

    of Lauder, 156–57
    loving the customer, 46–48, 158–61, 166
    loving the product, 48–49, 55–56,
        161–66
    at Taylor and Boody, 56
    at Toyota Motor, 151–52
customers
    courtesy towards, 47–48, 70, 155, 160–61
    and entrepreneurial strategy, 132,
        135–36, 155–56
    importance of, 17, 84
    input of, 45–46, 131, 173, 175
    keeping current customers, 48, 155, 161
    knowing your, 48, 136, 162
    and product knowledge, 47
    response to, 47, 159–60
    service towards, 138–39

Daewoo, 214–15
Daimler, Gottlieb, 161–63
decentralization, 218–19
deCODE Genetics, 57–67
Dell, Michael, 153
Dell Computer, 152–53
DHL, 179–81
Discovery Fund of New York City, 289–90,
        293
Disney, Walt, 35–36, 147, 154, 306
Doerr, John, 272
Doggett, Ron, 104–18, 301–2
downsizing, trend of, xxi
Draper, Tim, 295
Drucker, Peter, xix
Duell, Charles H., 170, 172
Dutch Disease, 258

e-commerce, public relations and, 73–74
economic development, 288–98
Economic Development Corporation
        (EDC), 288–98
Edison, Thomas, 68
EDS (Electronic Data Systems), 189,
        191–93
education, and global competitiveness, 276
Ellison, Larry, 41, 42
employees. *See also* corporate
        entrepreneurs
    and accountability, 114
    autonomy for, 82, 195
    behavior matrix, *80*, 80–81
    commitment from, 202, 305
    commitment to, 22, 114

as company owners, 205–6
compensation, 221–23
entrepreneurial culture and, 140,
  141–42, 144–45
and EPS, 207–10
as family, 90–91
front-line, 88
and functionalization, 148–51, 176
knowledge of, 69–70, 184–85
as mini-entrepreneurs, 92, 195, 199–202
performance of, 83–84, 139–40, 182,
  195–99
retention of, 89–90
reward/penalty systems and, 144–45,
  195, 196, 203–4
self-management, 123, 124–25
sensitivity training and, xxiii–xxiv
in service businesses, 76
shared destiny of, 82, 113, 195–96
stock options and, 113
employment, and entrepreneurial
  economies, 273
Empowerment Zones, 296
Enterprise Zones, 296
Entrepreneurial Age, described,
  xxxv–xxxvii
entrepreneurial basics. *See also*
  customer/product vision; high-speed
  innovation; self-inspired behavior;
  sense of mission
  described, xii, 306
entrepreneurial culture. *See also* corporate
  entrepreneurs; entrepreneurial
  economies
  competitive advantage, 141–42, 144–45
  compromise and, 143
  development of, 141–43, 216–27, 305–6
  employees and, 140, 142, 195–96
  in Iceland, 244–50
  in Kentucky, 261–67
  maintenance of, 143–45
  personal commitment in, 142
  simplicity in, 306
  in Singapore, 277–84
  at TMM, 216–21
entrepreneurial economies. *See also*
  entrepreneurial culture
  capital for, 265, 271–73, 289–90
  development of, 269–84
  knowledge required for, 265, 274–76
  in New York City, 287–98
  speed in, 266

Entrepreneurial Performance System
  (EPS), 207–10
entrepreneurial spirit, described, xii, 306
entrepreneurial strategy, 132, 135–36,
  155–56. *See also* corporate strategy
entrepreneurs. *See also* corporate
  entrepreneurs; entrepreneurial
  culture; entrepreneurial economies
  and business schools, 101–2
  characteristics of, 5–8, 37–38, 181
  commitment of, 81–83, 92
  and creativity, 248
  global, 4
  in Great Depression, 3
  in Industrial Age, 3
  performance consequences and, 202–10
  in Taiwan, 235–36
  and trade/vocational schools, 103
  training for, 276
  in United States, 4
  universities and, 101–3
  and values, 141–45
  wealth and, 300–302
EPS (Entrepreneurial Performance
  System), 207–10
Eriksson, Leif, 248–49
Estonia, xvi, 269
ethics, and corporate entrepreneurs, 225,
  305
experts, xx–xxi, xxiii

Fawcette, Jim, 100
Filo, David, 180–81
flextime programs, xxiv
Ford Motor Company, 41
Forte, Lord Charles, 143–44, 163–64
Foster, Jodi, 102
France, 211–16, 222–23, 285
free trade, 235–36
functionalization, organizational, 148–51,
  176
Furnham, Adrian, 101

Gantz, Kim, xiv–xv
Gates, Bill, 5, 103
GE (General Electric), 212–13
General Mills, 104–12
General Motors, 41–42, 158, 164–65
Germany, 276, 285
Giuliani, Rudy, xxii, xxvii, 288, 292, 295
global economy. *See also* growth
  competitive countries rankings, 239

education and, 276
as political issue, 237, 241–42
poor nations and, 240–42
role of creativity in, 248
GoodMark Foods, 104, 106–14
Gorbachev, Mikhail, xxii
governments
  and Empowerment/Enterprise Zones,
    296
  and entrepreneur-friendly culture
    development, 277–84, 285–87, 293–97
  entrepreneurial economies benefits to,
    273, 275–76
  and entrepreneurship funding, 265,
    271–73, 289–92, 293
  growth and, 234–35
  Internet and, 292–93
  and national self-inspired behavior, 253
  national sense of mission, 252, 253–61,
    254
  and nationwide competitive position,
    252–53, 274–75, 276
  and nationwide high-speed innovation,
    253
  and prosperity cycles, 236–42, *238*
  statewide entrepreneurship, 261–67
  and tax-incentive packages, 291, 297
Gratzon, Fred, 98, 100
Great Britain
  in competitive countries rankings, 239
  economic decline of, 237, 239
  entrepreneurial rebound of, 250n
  start-up rates, 285
Greenspan, Alan, xxv
Grimsson, Olafur Ragnar, 242–50
Grove, Andy, 102, 121–22, 123
growth. *See also* global economy
  and agriculture, 234–35, 263
  with customers and products, 165, *165*
  and free trade, 235–36
  government's role in, 234–35
  and inflation, 234
  and population control, 234, 238
  study of, 231–32

Hamper, Ben, 122
Hannebicque, Hervé, xv, 211–26
Harman, Jane, 232, 250n
Hewlett, Bill, 102
Hewlett-Packard, 277, 278
high-speed innovation. *See also* inventions
  and bureaucracy, 170, 172, 185–86

centralization and, 173–74
complacency and, 172
costs of, 67, 175
customer input and, 173, 175
and deCODE Genetics, 57–67
at DHL, 179–81
freedom and, 69–70, 178, 182–87
and HGI, 71–78
"lab in the woods" theory, 174–75
and management, 176–77, 186–87
by marketing departments, 175–76
on national level, 253
necessity of, 167–69
organizational efficiency and, 185
scientific management theory and,
  172–73
at Sony, 168–70
at 3M, 177–78
Hillblom, Larry, 179–81, 187n
Hoffman, Mark, 38–46
Honda, Soichiro, 157, 181, 184–85,
  199–202
Hong Kong, in competitive countries
  rankings, 239
Horn, Sabrina, 71–78
Horn Group, Inc. (HGI), 71–78
Hour Glass, The, xiii, 86–92
Hsieh, Chi, 259–61
Human Genome Project, 60–61

IBM, xxi, 17, 138–41, 173
Ibuka, Masaru, 169
Iceland
  in competitiveness countries ranking,
    244
  genetic study in, 58–59, 247
  individual entrepreneurship in, 244–50
India, 4, 276
Industrial Age, 3
inflation, in Taiwan, 234
information technology, 59–60, 70–71
innovation. *See* high-speed innovation
Intel, 121–22
Internet, government and, 292–93
intrapreneurship, 206–7
inventions. *See also* creativity; high-speed
  innovation
  necessity of, 67–69, 178, 179–82
Italy, start-up rates, 285

Japan
  brain drain in, 276

entrepreneurs in, 4
"rich get poor" syndrome in, 239–40
start-up rates, 285
Jim Pattison Group, 186–87
job descriptions, 154, *155*
Jobs, Steve, 103, 156, 181, 299
Johnson, John, 196–97
Johnson Publishing, 196–97
just-in-time production, 152, 153

kanban technique, 152
Kentucky, entrepreneurial economy
    development in, 261–67
Kentucky Science and Technology
    Corporation (KSTC), 261–67
Kepner-Tregoe, 302
Kimel, Kris, xiv, 261–67, 273
knowledge
    and comparative analysis, 60–61
    data relationship with, 60–61
    of employees, 69–70, 184–85
    for entrepreneurial economies, 274–76
    monetary value of, 59–60, 70–71
    of products, 47, 159
    role in entrepreneurial organizations, 265
    strategy, 276
Koh Boon Hwee, 277–84
Kroc, Ray, 103, 157
KSTC (Kentucky Science and Technology
    Corporation), 261–67
Kuznet trap, 258–59

"lab in the woods" theory, 149–51, 174–75
Lacalle, Luis Alberto, xvi–xvii
Lauder, Estée, 156–57
leadership, described, 299–300
Lever, William Hesketh, xxx, 193–94
Lewis, Flora, 270
Li, K. T., 232–36, 238, 260, 261, 283
life cycle of organizations, xxviii–xxx, 65,
    238, *238*
Lincoln Electric, xii, 123–25, 227
Long-Term Capital Management, xxv
loose-tight organizations, 219, 220
Lufthansa, 160–61
Luxembourg, 239

Mackenbach, Fred, xii, 123–25, 227
MacMillan, Ian, 100, 101
Malaysia, 239, 251–52
management
    bigger is better, xix–xx, xxi, 305, 306

and bureaucracy bashing, 70, 185–87
and chaos, 65–66, 176–77
compensation, 221–23
entrepreneurial, 121, 122–23, 223–25
and entrepreneur training, 102
high-speed innovation and, 176–77,
    186–87
origination of, xxiii
value-based, 224
marketing, and product improvement,
    175–76
markets
    and business plans, 16
    competitive position, 16–21, *20*
    needs of, 17–20
    for niche businesses, 18, 75–77
Matsushita, Konosuke, xxx, 130–32, 136
MBA (masters of business administration),
    xx, 8, 301
meetings, efficiency in, 186
Merton, Robert, xxv
Messer, Buel, 24–29, 93, 165
Mexico, 267n
Microsoft, 171
Millard, Charles, 271, 272, 287–98
mini-entrepreneurs, 92, 195, 199–202
mission statements, 21–22, 140. *See also*
    sense of mission
Moore, Gordon, 121
Morita, Akio, 49, 68, 98, 167–70, 172
Morrison, Fraser, 302–6
multinational corporations (MNC), 278, 279
Mustapa Mohamed, xvi, 251–52

Nallinger, Fritz, 161
nations, poor, 240–42
Netherlands, 239, 276
New York City
    Discovery Fund, 289–90, 293
    economic development of, 288–98
    venture capital programs, 289–91
New Zealand, 239
niche businesses, 18, 75–77
Nokia, 240
Norway, 239
Notman, Douglas, xiii–xiv

O'Brien, Robert, 186
Oracle, 41–42

Packard, David, 102
patents, 170–72

Pattison, Jimmy, 186–87
Penhoet, Edward, 102, 164, 182–83,
    300–301
PeopleSoft, 75, 78n
performance
    entrepreneurial, *80,* 80–81, 83–84, 92
    improvement in, 182
Perot, Ross, 164–65, 189, 191–93, 210n
Peters, Tom, 37
Philippine Airlines, 160
Philippines, 276
poor nations, 240–42
population control, 234, 238
Prasnicki, Kathy, 185
products
    bettering the competition, 163–64
    bureaucrat syndrome, 37
    and business plans, 16
    choosing, 16–21, 132, 136–37
    competitive position matrix, *20, 137*
    customer-driven systems, 152
    and customer/product vision, 35–36
    improvement of, 70, 136, 175–76
    knowledge of, 47, 159
    loving the product, 48–49, 55–56,
        161–66
    pride in, 49, 163
    quality of, 49, 84, 155
    salesman syndrome, 36–37
    scientist syndrome, 36
    of service businesses, 76
    and speed, 49, 164–65
prosperity cycles of countries, 236–42, *238*
public relations, e-commerce and, 73–74

RCA (Radio Corporation of America),
    211, 212–13, 214
research and development, xxvi, 177–78.
    See also high-speed innovation
"rich get poor" syndrome, 239–40
risk, 65, 114, 124
Rummler, Geary A., 210n
Russia, xxii, 276

salesman syndrome, 36–37
Sarnoff, David, 212
SBSC (Small Business Survival
    Committee), 285–86
SBU (Strategic Business Units), 218–19
Scholes, Myron, xxv
Schröder, Claus, 5–6
scientist syndrome, 36

self-inspired behavior
    commitment as, *80,* 80–83, 92, 192–96
    consequences of, 84–86, 202–7
    and corporate strategy, 130
    and EPS, 207–10
    intrapreneurship and, 206–7
    leadership as, 82–83, 84, 196, 198–99
    and mini-entrepreneur development,
        199–202
    on national level, 253
    performance and, *80,* 80–81, 83–84, 92
    and philanthropy, 92–93
    of Tay, 86–92
    and values, 141–45
self-management, 123, 124–25
sense of mission
    business plans and, *14,* 14–16
    business values as, 21–24, 27, 28, 29
    culture and, 12, 13
    described, 11–12, 128, 129, *129*
    employees and, 128–29
    and entrepreneurial culture creation,
        141–45
    of Messer, 24–29
    on national level, 252, 253–61, *254*
    strategy and, 12–13
sensitivity training, xxiii–xxiv
service businesses, products of, 76
Setubal, Olavo, 255–56
shared destiny, 82, 113, 195–96
Shima, Koji, 236, 239
Sigurdsson, Arni, 243, 250n
Sildmae, Tomas, xvi, 269
Silicon Alley, economic development of,
    288–98
Singapore, 239, 277–84
Singapore Telecom, 277, 281
Slim Jim snacks, 105, 106–7, 109
small businesses, xxvi
Small Business Survival Committee
    (SBSC), 285–86
Sony Corporation, xxxiii, 167–70
South Africa, xvii, 276
Soviet Union, collapse of, xxii
speed. *See also* high-speed innovation
    and centralization, 173–74
    as competitive advantage, 183
    and entrepreneurial economy
        development, 266
    performance and, 83–84
    products and, 49, 164–65

start-up
   and basics of entrepreneurship, 8–9,
      300–301
   and business values, 21–22, 29
   costs of, 4, 98–100, 293–94
   customer/product vision and, 34, 46, 48
   employees, 128–29
   government's role in, 287–94
   motivation for, 300–301
   product development for, 100–103
   rates per city, 286
   rates per country, 285
   rates per state, 286
   risk tolerance and, 64
   in Silicon Alley, 287–91, 293
Stefansson, Kari, 57–60, 70, 245
stocks, xxvi, 113
Storey, Robert, xiii
Strategic Business Units (SBU), 218–19
Sun Coast Resources, 185
Sweden, 276
Switzerland, 239
Sybase, 40, 43, 44

Taiwan
   in competitive countries rankings, 239
   economic history of, 232–36, 238–39
   national sense of mission, *254,* 258–61
   prosperity of, 237
   quality of life in, 260–61
tax-incentive packages, 291, 297
Tay, Jannie, xiii, 86–92, 93n
Taylor, Frederick, 173
Taylor, George, 51–56
Taylor and Boody Organbuilders, 31–34,
      49–56
Telegroup, 100
THF (Trusthouse Forte), 163–64
Thomson, Elihu, 212
Thomson Multimedia S.A. (TMM),
      211–26
Thorbjarnardóttir, Gurdrídur, 249
3M, xxx, 67–68, 130, 177–78
TMM (Thomson Multimedia S.A.),
      211–26
Toyoda, Eiji, xxxii, 151–52
Toyota, 151–52
trade schools, 103
Tregoe, Benjamin B.
   and business plans, 16
   corporate strategy of, 29n, 145n

on dedication to your business, 302
   and sense of mission, 11, 12–13
Trusthouse Forte (THF), 163–64

Uni-Charm, 239
Unilever, 193–94, 210n
United Kingdom. *See* Great Britain
United States
   brain drain in, 276
   in competitive countries rankings, 239
   entrepreneurs in, 4, 282
   prosperity of, 237, 240
   start-up rates, 285
US Patent Office, 170–71
US Small Business Administration (SBA),
      272, 289
universities, and entrepreneurs, 101–3
Uruguay, 240

values
   and behavior, 144
   behavior reflecting, 22
   competitive advantage and, 21–22,
      144–45
   criteria for, 22–23
   and entrepreneurial corporate culture,
      141–43
   keeping alive, 23–24
   and mission statements, 21–22, 27, 29
Venters, Craig, 60, 61
venture capital. *See* capital
Villegas, Bernie, xiv
vocational schools, 103

Walker, Sarah Breedlove, 79–80, 92–93,
      103
Wal-Mart, 158, 160, 204–5
Walt Disney Company, 35–36, *36,* 154
Walton, Sam, 103, 158, 160, 204
Wang, Jerry, 180–81
Wang, Nora Chang, xvi
Watson, Thomas J., Jr., 140
Watson, Thomas J., Sr., xxi, 17, 138–41,
      173
wealth, corporate entrepreneurs and,
      300–302
Wuthelam Group, 277, 279

Xerox, xxxii, 149–51, 174

Yahoo, 180–81

BOOKS FROM ALLWORTH PRESS

The Soul of the New Consumer: The Attitudes, Behaviors, and Preferences of E-Customers by Laurie Windham and Ken Orton (hardcover, 6 × 9, 320 pages, $24.95)

Emotional Branding: The New Paradigm for Connecting Brands to People by Marc Gobé (hardcover, 6¼ × 9¼, 352 pages, $24.95)

The Advertising Law Guide: A Friendly Guide for Everyone in Advertising by Lee Wilson (softcover, 6 × 9, 208 pages, $19.95)

The Copyright Guide: A Friendly Guide to Protecting and Profiting from Copyrights, Revised Edition by Lee Wilson (softcover, 6 × 9, 192 pages, $19.95)

The Trademark Guide: A Friendly Guide to Protecting and Profiting from Trademarks by Lee Wilson (softcover, 6 × 9, 192 pages $18.95)

The Patent Guide: A Friendly Guide to Protecting and Profiting from Patents by Carl W. Battle (softcover, 6 × 9, 224 pages, $18.95)

Dead Ahead: The Web Dilemma and the New Rules of Business by Laurie Windham and Jon Samsel (hardcover, 6¼ × 9¼, 256 pages, $24.95)

Money Secrets of the Rich and Famous by Michael Reynard (hardcover, 6¼ × 9¼, 256 pages, $24.95)

Old Money: The Mythology of Wealth in America, Expanded Edition by Nelson W. Aldrich, Jr. (softcover, 6 × 9, 340 pages, $16.95)

Your Living Trust and Estate Plan: How to Maximize Your Family's Assets and Protect Your Loved Ones by Harvey J. Platt (softcover, 6 × 9, 304 pages, $14.95)

The Retirement Handbook: How to Maximize Your Assets and Protect Your Quality of Life by Carl Battle (softcover, 6 × 9, 240 pages, $18.95)

Hers: The Wise Woman's Guide to Starting a Business on $2,000 or Less, Revised Edition by Carol Milano (softcover, 6 × 9, 192 pages, $16.95)

The Internet Research Guide, Revised Edition by Timothy K. Maloy (softcover, 6 × 9, 208 pages, $18.95)

Please write to request our free catalog. To order by credit card, call 1-800-491-2808 or send a check or money order to Allworth Press, 10 East 23rd Street, Suite 510, New York, NY 10010. Include $5 for shipping and handling for the first book ordered and $1 for each additional book. Ten dollars plus $1 for each additional book if ordering from Canada. New York State residents must add sales tax.

To see our complete catalog on the World Wide Web, or to order online, you can find us at *www.allworth.com*.